Shrines of the Slave Trade

Shrines of the Slave Trade

DIOLA RELIGION AND SOCIETY
IN PRECOLONIAL SENEGAMBIA

Robert M. Baum

NEW YORK · OXFORD

OXFORD UNIVERSITY PRESS

1999

Oxford University Press

Oxford   New York
Athens   Auckland   Bangkok   Bogotá   Buenos Aires   Calcutta
Cape Town   Chennai   Dar es Salaam   Delhi   Florence   Hong Kong   Istanbul
Karachi   Kuala Lumpur   Madrid   Melbourne   Mexico City   Mumbai
Nairobi   Paris   São Paulo   Singapore   Taipei   Tokyo   Toronto   Warsaw

and associated companies in
Berlin   Ibadan

Copyright © 1999 by Robert M. Baum

Published by Oxford University Press, Inc.
198 Madison Avenue, New York, New York 10016

Oxford is a registered trademark of Oxford University Press.

Library of Congress Cataloging-in-Publication Data
Baum, Robert Martin.
Shrines of the slave trade : Diola religion and society
in precolonial Senegambia / Robert M. Baum.
    p.   cm.
Includes bibliographical references and index.
ISBN 0-19-512392-1
1. Diola (African people)—Religion.   2. Slave-trade—Senegal—
Esulalu—History.   3. Esulalu (Senegal)—Religion.   I. Title.
BL2480.D54   1999
299'.6832—dc21   98-19659

9 8 7 6 5 4 3 2 1

Printed in the United States of America
on acid-free paper

To the people of Kadjinol
and to my grandparents:
Max and Rita Baum, Louis and Jessie Sachs

Acknowledgments

As I complete the final revisions of this book, I find myself thinking back to all the people who have helped me along the way. This book could not have been conceived of without the assistance and support of the people of Kadjinol, where I lived for nearly four years, and the people of Esulalu, the region in which I worked. I wish to thank my adoptive family, Alphonse Diedhiou, Elizabeth Sambou, Jean-Marie Diedhiou, Kumbumbatome Diedhiou, Virginie Diedhiou, Marie-Lazare Diedhiou, Natalia Diedhiou, the late Dionsal Diedhiou, the late Diongany Diedhiou, and the late Gnimai Diatta, for taking me into your home and into your hearts. You have extended to me a gift that I can never repay and only seek to return with equal affection. I am particularly grateful to those elders who went out of their way to give me detailed instruction in Diola history and religion and who included me in their daily activities. They include Siliungimagne Diatta, Sikakucele Diatta, Antoine Houmandrissah Diedhiou, Siopama Diedhiou, Indrissa Diedhiou, Adiabaloung Diedhiou, Kapooeh Diedhiou, Boolai Senghor, Antoine Djemelene Sambou, Anto Manga, Terence Galandiou Diouf Sambou, André Bankuul Senghor, Sihumucel Badji, Paponah Diatta, Kemehow Diedhiou, Hilaire Djibune, Sooti Diatta, Sawer Sambou, Pakum Bassin, and Agnak Baben. This list does not even begin to cover all the people who helped me in my research or by offering me assistance when I needed it.

I would especially like to thank my dissertation advisor, David Robinson. His skillful teaching helped me develop the analytical perspective necessary to transform vast quantities of data into a coherent study. Even after I had completed my dissertation, he has continued to be an advisor, friend, and constant source of moral support. Robert Harms also provided detailed criticism of my doctoral dissertation and has continued to offer advice and support. In the evolution of this work from a dissertation to a book, I have benefited enormously from the analytical insights of the late Marilyn Waldman, who through many discussions and readings of portions of this work, deepened my understanding of the subtle process of religious change in many different cultures. I have also benefited from the comments of Allen Wildman, John Rothney, Claire Robertson, Rosalind Hackett, Tom Lawson, Luther Martin, and Rosalind Shaw. Isaac Mowoe, the African Studies chair at Ohio State University, also provided support at an important time.

While conducting research on Diola religious and social history, I benefited from my association with the Institut Fondamental d'Afrique Noire. I am particularly grateful to Saliou Mbaye, the director of the National Archives of Senegal, and to Father Joseph Carrard and the late Father Noel Bernard, archivists for the Holy Ghost Fathers. Without their knowledge of their vast archives, my research would have been a much more difficult task.

I would also like to thank my parents and friends, who have suffered considerable neglect as I worked on this book. I would especially like to thank Bill Worger, Nancy Clark, and Pamela Baldwin.

I am grateful to the Thomas J. Watson Foundation for providing me with the initial funds to spend a year in Senegal to conduct field research before I began graduate school. I am grateful to the Social Science Research Council's Foreign Area Fellowship Program and the Fulbright-Hays Doctoral Dissertation Fellowship Program for enabling me to spend twenty months conducting archival and field research in France, Britain, and Senegal in preparation for the dissertation which was the foundation for this book. I am grateful to Ohio State University for funding a subsequent trip to Senegal. The American Council of Learned Societies and the Andrew W. Mellon Fellowship program at Bryn Mawr College provided me with financial support while I revised and expanded an African history dissertation into an interdisciplinary work in my home discipline and the history of religions. The W. E. B. Du Bois Institute for Afro-American Research at Harvard University has provided a stimulating environment in which to complete the final revisions.

Finally, I would like to thank my editors at Oxford University Press, Cynthia Read and Will Moore, my copyeditor Joy Matkowski, and Patti Neuman who prepared the maps.

A Note on Translation

Interviews were conducted primarily in Diola, though there was an occasional interview in French. All interviews I conducted I also translated. Some written source material can be found only in French or Portuguese. Where the citation is in French or Portuguese and no other translator is noted, then I did the translations.

A glossary of Diola terms is provided at the back of the book.

Contents

Maps

Shrines of the Slave Trade

Introduction

This work is a study of the religious and social history of a small cluster of Diola communities in southwestern Senegal, before the establishment of effective colonial rule by the French, British, and Portuguese. Prior to the colonial conquest, the Diola experienced a series of profound changes that affected nearly every aspect of community life. What are presently identified as Diola religious and social institutions developed during an era of political and economic upheaval that was fueled by the gradual penetration of transatlantic slave-trading networks and the growing importance of a world economic system. These pressures were aggravated by an uncertain environment, contact with diverse ethnic groups, and a variety of internal problems that developed in a cluster of independent townships at the northern limits of the Guinean forest. By focusing on the history of Diola traditional religion in the eighteenth and nineteenth century, before Muslims and Christians had become important influences in the region, I will be able to examine the ways in which an indigenous system of thought both shaped a community's responses to rapidly changing social conditions and was affected by that very act of interpretation.[1] Many of these changes are remembered in oral traditions and are analyzed by Diola oral historians who seek to understand the meaning of these experiences. Through the examination of Diola traditions, this study analyzes internal structures of innovation within a Diola religious system that enabled it to adapt to the social upheavals of the precolonial era.

Presently, the Diola number about 500,000.[2] Among them are the largest number of adherents of a traditional religion within the Senegambian region of West Africa (see map 1). They worked primarily as sedentary rice farmers and were usually described as a "stateless" peoples who governed themselves through village assemblies and had no specialized governmental officials. Although they have been in contact with Muslims and Christians since the fifteenth century, few Diola converted before the late nineteenth century. On the north shore of the Casamance River, where contact with Muslims was earliest and most violent, many Diola embraced Islam and, to a lesser extent, Christianity. However, membership in these

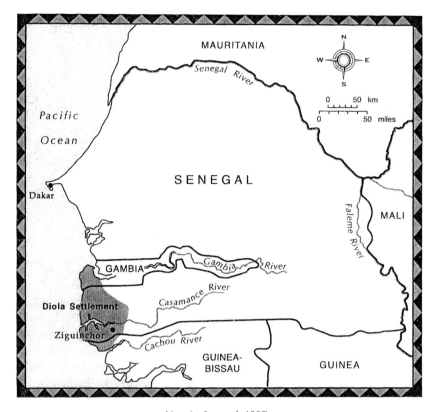

Map 1. Senegal, 1997

new communities began to grow significantly only after the firm establishment of colonial rule and the related expansion in the commercial peanut crop.[3] On the south shore, the vast majority of the population resisted the advance of Islam and Christianity until after World War II. Even though Christianity has recently made substantial inroads, Diola religion has remained dominant, in spite of extensive seasonal migration to the cities, the penetration of a cash economy, and the establishment of Catholic missions.[4]

The persistence of a vital traditional religion among the Diola communities south of the Casamance River makes them an important case study in African religious history. Given that the north shore Diola, the neighboring Mandinka, Serer, and other groups have embraced Christianity or Islam, what in south shore Diola historical experience and religious systems explains their continued ability to adapt to rapidly changing circumstances without conversion? It is true that the south escaped the devastation of the late-nineteenth-century Mandinka incursions and was integrated more slowly into the twentieth-century colonial economy, but these two factors are insufficient to explain the resilience of southern Diola traditions. To understand the southern Diola's ability to adapt to the challenges of the colonial era, we must look at precolonial structures for change, as I did during the course of my fieldwork.[5] While living in a south shore Diola community, I found evidence of a tradition of religious innovation traceable to at least the seventeenth century. This religious history has included the creation of new cults, the transformation of old ones, and a long tradition of direct communication by the Diola with a supreme being and a variety of lesser spirits. Furthermore, careful examination of these traditions revealed the existence of several different theoretical models in competition with one another within a Diola religious system. Together these materials provide clear evidence of the versatility of "traditional" societies and the ability of oral historians to reflect critically on the significance of such changes.

To analyze Diola religious history in depth, I confined my field research to a small and reasonably homogeneous area known as Esulalu (see map 2). Esulalu is an area of five townships on the south shore of the Casamance River, within the Department of Oussouye. Its people, also known as Esulalu, number approximately 15,000 and speak a common dialect of the Diola language. They share certain religious shrines and, in the precolonial era, they often united against external attack. During the nineteenth century, nine small *kudjala* (stranger) villages were established within Esulalu, populated primarily by immigrants from northern Senegal and Portuguese Guinea. In the 1920s, the French recognized Esulalu as a separate administrative unit or canton. In the 1950s, Catholic missionaries estab-

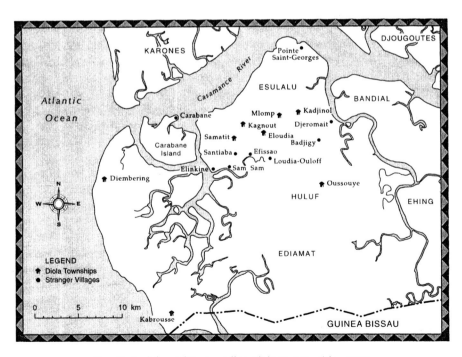

Map 2. Esulalu and Surrounding Diola Communities, 1997

lished the parish of Mlomp along the same boundaries. Since independence, the Senegalese government also recognized Esulalu as a *communauté rural*, the major unit of rural administration in contemporary Senegal.

Although I conducted archival and field research on the history of the Diola up to the 1990s, I have restricted this work to the period before 1880—that is, before the establishment of the French colonial administration and before a permanent Catholic mission presence. In 1880, the first Holy Ghost Fathers' mission in Diola territory was opened at Carabane, a French administrative center and strangers' village established on land belonging to the Esulalu township of Kagnout. This work focuses on the history of the religion of a politically autonomous Diola-Esulalu community, before Christianity and Islam began to attract followings among them. A subsequent study will examine the interaction between Diola religion, Christianity, and Islam during the colonial era.

This book is one of the few studies of the precolonial history of an African traditional religion. It begins with the earliest traditions of the various peoples who gradually developed a common culture known as Esulalu. It examines the influences of an indigenous people known as the Koonjaen, who already possessed an important tradition of "prophetic" revelation and important blacksmith cults, and of the people who conquered them in the late seventeenth century. This book also examines the problems of forging a common tradition from such disparate and antagonistic elements during the tumultuous era of the Atlantic slave trade. The methods by which the Diola-Esulalu became active participants in the slave trade, through reliance on religious authorities to regulate their commercial activities, is central to this entire study. The close involvement of religious leaders and their spirit shrines ultimately led to the proliferation of new cults and the redefinition of the nature of spirit shrines and their priests. Such changes extended far beyond those cults that were directly involved in the slave trade, generated a whole new group of spirit shrines that emphasized wealth over charisma as a source of ritual authority, and led to a lessening concern with the Diola supreme being, Emitai. Finally, the book concludes with the growing influence of the French and northern Senegalese strangers during the nineteenth century, before an effective colonial occupation of the region and before the establishment of permanent mission stations within Diola territories.

This analysis of Diola religious and social history is presented at two levels. One focuses on the specific instances of change in Diola religious thought and practice, social values, and institutions. Relying on a narrative structure that attempts to bring the reader into the Diola-Esulalu community, it attempts to illuminate the significance of these changes in terms of ordinary life experience.[6] To sustain this historical and phenomenological approach, I have tended to isolate, more thoroughly than in many narratives, a second level of analysis involving theoretical and comparative interventions, concentrating them in introductions and conclusions both to the book as a whole and within each chapter. Through the careful separation of these different modes of analysis, I intend to allow the reader to encounter Diola religious and social history in ways parallel to my own encounter, before I suggest the broader significance of such history in a comparative context.

In chapter 1, I examine some of the representations of African cultures that have affected the development of the study of the history of African religions. Then I turn to an analysis of the types of sources available for the study of Diola religious and social history, the use of oral traditions, and the field research techniques I used to gather such materials. In chapter 2 I describe the economic, social, and religious environment of contemporary Diola society to contextualize the oral traditions and participant observation that are at the core of this study. Then I shift into a series of chronologically arranged chapters that focus on the three historical periods covered by this study: the origins of Esulalu during the period before 1700, in chapter 3; the eighteenth century, in chapters 4 and 5; and the period from 1800 until 1880, in chapters 6 and 7. For the sake of clarity and in order to highlight different types of historical influences, I have separated primarily external forces (the growing influence of the Atlantic slave trade in the eighteenth century and the establishment of European settlements in the nineteenth century) from more internal forces (religious visionaries, intra-Diola warfare, and environmental disruptions), either through separate sections of the same chapter for the period before 1700 or in separate chapters for the more recent periods.

1

The Historical Study of
African Traditional Religions

Images of Africa and African Religions

Until recently, most studies of African religions have concentrated on various aspects of beliefs and practices while paying little attention to their historical development. When scholars have considered the history of religions in Africa, they have tended to focus on Islam and Christianity and to restrict their interest in African traditional religions to the processes of conversion to and syncretism with "world" religions. Current textbooks on African religions have focused on certain comparative themes in the study of religions and have assumed that the ethnic divisions related to these religions have endured for centuries. Historical chapters, if included at all, address the impact of colonization, Islam, and Christianity but overlook other types of religious change. For example, John Mbiti, the author of the most widely read textbook on African religions, addresses the issue of precolonial religious history in two paragraphs of his introduction, before asserting what he sees as a fundamental obstacle to such studies: "In the traditional set-up where the African concept of time is mainly two-dimensional, human life is relatively stable and almost static. A rhythm of life is the norm, and any radical change is either unknown, resented or so slow that it is hardly noticed." Such a representation of African religions both reflects and reinforces a basic assumption about "traditional" societies, that they have little sense of their own history. What changes have occurred are, from this perspective, merely fine-tunings to preserve a spiritual equilibrium, not major shifts in fundamental religious ideas. For Mbiti, significant religious changes begins in "the second half of the nineteenth century and swiftly gaining momentum towards the middle of the twentieth century" with the beginnings of colonization.[1] Other scholars, like the Diola specialist Jean Girard, assume that precolonial religious change is part of a predictable evolutionary progression from animism to monotheism: "Rather than a static cultural form, fetishist civilization is characterized by a fixed level of evolution on the path of modernization. Not all African societies are fetishist but all of them pass through this stage."[2]

Denying a history to African traditional religions or situating them on an evolutionary scale headed, however slowly, in our direction arises from assumptions that are deeply rooted in Western culture and its attitudes toward "traditional" societies. In *The Invention of Africa*, V. Y. Mudimbe has demonstrated the remarkable persistence of Western images of "otherness," which he traces back as far as the writings of Herodotus. Herodotus' description of an Africa populated by bestial beings, without history or religion, has been central to the representation of Africa as wholly "other."[3] This twofold exclusion separated them from peoples who prided themselves on their historical sense, the Greeks and Romans, and from religious communities, Jews and Christians, who believed in the progressive revelation of a god who acts in history. Furthermore, it established a set of dichotomies between Europeans, who saw themselves as the inheritors of a Western classical tradition, and the otherness of savages locked in an unchanging world in which superstition reigned. We can see this linkage in Hegel's *Philosophy of History*:

> Africa proper . . . the land of childhood, which lying beyond the day of self-conscious history, is enveloped in the dark mantle of night. . . .
>
> But even Herodotus called the Negroes sorcerers; now in sorcery we have not the idea of a God, of a moral faith. . . .
>
> At this point we leave Africa. . . . For it is no historical part of the world; it has no movement or development to exhibit. . . . What we properly understand by Africa is the unhistorical, undeveloped spirit, still involved n the conditions of mere nature and which had to be presented here only as on the threshold of the World's History.

Thus, for Hegel and many others who shared his views, the direct encounter between Europe and sub-Saharan Africa, beginning in the fifteenth century, was an encounter between world historical peoples and peoples without history.[4]

Central to the self-image of Western travelers, traders, missionaries, administrators, and scholars was a sense that Europeans' dominance of Africa resulted from their being in the vanguard of world history and at the pinnacle of a progressive revelation of ideas deeply rooted in their sacred traditions. Regardless of the disruption they brought to African societies through the transatlantic slave trade and subsequent colonization, they saw themselves as bringing Africa into history and into the light of religious faith. To reinforce this sense of otherness, Africa was labeled as pagan, animist, fetishist, polytheist, primitive, or oral. As Charles Long has noted, changing the terminology "will not suffice, for the cultural language of civilization that brought forth the structure of the primitive has not changed." All these labels proclaimed the absolute difference between European and African; the former possessed a dynamic culture and a long history, while the latter was frozen in primordial time.[5]

The growth of African history, in the 1950s and 1960s, played a substantial role in undermining the view that there have been few changes in African cultures sufficient enough to affect their ways of understanding their world. Jan

Vansina's pioneering use of oral traditions to uncover African historical perspectives marked what Mudimbe describes as a "radical transformation of anthropological narratives. A new type of discourse valorized the diachronic dimension as part of knowledge about African cultures and encouraged new representations of the 'native,' who previously was a mere object within African historicity."[6] As Africanist historians increasingly turned to oral traditions, they were able to begin a process of bringing African historical consciousness into the canon of discourses about African peoples and cultures.

Oddly enough, as this new African history was developing, little attention was paid to the history of African religions. Perhaps the early Africanist historians shared a common view of religion as resistant to change. Perhaps oral historians, like Freudian psychoanalysts, feared that religion was a dark tide that would overwhelm their new analytic school. Whatever the cause, the result of historians' lack of interest was the relegation of this field to anthropologists, who, for the most part, had not yet incorporated a diachronic dimension into their analyses of African cultures. Similarly, scholars in religious studies continued to use Africa and other "primitive" culture areas as testing grounds for theories about religion but did not incorporate them into global histories of religions because oral cultures lacked the written texts so central to the scholarly concept of the historical study of religion. For example, Mircea Eliade drew on examples from Australasian, American Indian, and African religions to illustrate various phenomena, but he narrowed his focus to the centers of Eurasian civilizations when he wrote about religious history. For him "other" religions form patterns but do not form history.[7] For most scholars, African traditional religions, to the extent that they were studied at all, were seen as relatively static entities that entered into history with their contact with Islam, Christianity, and world historical peoples.

By the 1970s, students of African religions began to develop more critical historical approaches to the study of African traditional religions. The collection of essays on African religious history assembled by Terence Ranger and I. Kimambo, as well as the work of Robin Horton, inaugurated a series of historical studies of African traditional religions.[8] These critical approaches have also contributed to an increasingly rich dialogue between Africanist historians and anthropologists with common interests in the multidisciplinary study of religions. This has been especially true of Africanist research in Central Africa, where studies of regional cults based on interdisciplinary fieldwork have placed specific religious institutions within their historical context and, in the process, have raised serious questions about the importance of ethnic boundaries in African cultural studies.[9]

However, this type of interdisciplinary work is far rarer in studies of West Africa, where the breadth and longevity of Islamic influences and the greater availability of written sources on Islam have tended to divert scholars from the historical study of African traditional religions. In one of the first comparative studies of West African religions, Geoffrey Parrinder attributed this lack of study to a paucity of evidence rather than an absence of historical development in West African religions.[10]

This present work is clearly influenced by these pioneering efforts but takes a more localized view of religious and social change in a cluster of Senegambian townships. In this way, the impact of these changes on ordinary life experience can be seen more clearly. For example, the history of specific religious cults are recalled through oral traditions associated not only with the lineages that control them but also with people who have elder status at competing cults. Each history sheds light on the relationships between various spirit shrines (*ukine*), families, and townships. Jack Goody has noted the importance of the introduction of new shrines that "brought in new ideas, new prohibitions, new taboos, and were never simply 'more of the same' . . . they often modified in significant ways the classificatory systems of the community into which they penetrated by introducing new evaluations of experience, sometimes having far-reaching effects on the political, moral, and cosmological order."[11] Similarly, visionary experiences and new trade access to iron are contextualized in terms of their effect on local religious and social institutions. In sharp contrast, however, this emphasis on the analysis of religious and social change in terms of ordinary life experience allows us to appreciate the significance of what Michel Foucault calls discontinuities in history, in terms of their impact not only on various domains of human knowledge but also on the conduct of daily life. Finally, as Fredrik Barth has urged social scientists to do, it allows us to examine the specific mechanisms for incremental change within a particular society.[12]

For many Diola, history provides a way to trace the origins of power back to the time of the first ancestors. Their relationship to a Diola past shapes the relative importance of various cults, rituals, lineages, and property rights. Diola visions of that history become powerful forces in their understanding and ordering of their world. By centering my analysis on Esulalu itself and by utilizing indigenous exegesis of oral traditions, the broader implications of changes in cult structures and ritual procedures, the emergence of new types of religious leaders, and the more widely diffused environmental, social, and economic forces that affected a Diola-Esulalu religious and social order can be more fully understood.

The Problem of Evidence

Much of the lingering reluctance to analyze African religions historically has shifted to the problem of evidence, both in terms of written sources and in terms of oral traditions. Scholars' reservations about inadequate sources for precolonial African religious history would certainly be well-founded if research was confined to the types of written documentation normally associated with historical inquiry. For studies of the Diola, relevant written sources include scholarly works on the Senegambia region and its peoples and primary sources provided by travelers, missionaries, and government officials.[13] Travelers' accounts, which date back to 1447, provide a limited amount of descriptive information concerning ritual practices and the physical appearance of altars and religious paraphernalia, as well as more detailed information about local economies and the political climate. However, the lack of major trading factories within Diola areas of settlement and a perception by Europeans that the Diola were not disposed to trade curtailed the length of travelers' visits and the detail of their accounts. The evidence provided by travelers is too fragmentary to provide anything more than a supplement to the richer material provided by oral traditions. Beginning in the midnineteenth century, however, the quality of written accounts improved. Travelers' accounts became more frequent and were supplemented by government and missionary reports.[14] As missionaries and administrators became established in the region, they could offer more detailed and insightful accounts of Diola life, but they continued to maintain their outsiders' perspectives.

Despite the diversity of written sources, even in the late nineteenth century, they alone are insufficient for a precolonial history of the Diola. Oral traditions provide a far broader view of Diola society and a deeper understanding of changes in their religious institutions. While conducting fieldwork, I combined participant observation in contemporary Esulalu with interviewing at three levels: oral traditions, personal recollections, and explanations of religious thought and ritual. Although these distinctions are familiar to African historians, they may be less well known to historians of religions. Oral traditions provide information about the past that is beyond the life experience of the informant. They have been handed down for at least one generation.[15] Personal recollections pertain to past events within the life experience of the observer, though they need not be firsthand accounts. Recollections collected in the 1970s, 1980s, and 1990s include materials on events since the first decade of the twentieth century. Informants' explanations of a Diola system of thought and rituals provide insights into the meanings of religious ideas and practices at the time of fieldwork. Each of these sources provides material that is valuable for the analysis of religious and social history. Together, they provide the core of the source material upon which this study is based.

While Africanists have utilized oral traditions for more than thirty years to broaden our knowledge of African history, most such studies have focused on societies with fixed oral traditions and on two areas of worldly activity, politics and economics.[16] Part of this reluctance to utilize oral traditions as a primary source for African religious history has arisen from certain assumptions about the limits of oral traditions as historical sources. For example, Jack Goody suggests that the absence of written texts that can be compared leads people in oral cultures to think "mythically" about their past and that a "true" historical consciousness develops only with the existence of written texts.[17] Furthermore, he suggests that the presentist perspectives of the reciters of oral traditions eliminates incongruities between contemporary needs and prior practices. In Goody's words: "what happens here is part and parcel of the tendency of oral cultures towards cultural homeostasis: those innumerable mutations of culture that emerge in the ordinary course of verbal interaction are either adopted by the interacting group or they get eliminated in the process of transmission from one generation to the next."[18] This would tend to eliminate evidence of significant shifts within a community's system of thought or even in ritual structures.

Jan Vansina, who has used a variety of techniques to study African religious history, also sees the tendency toward homeostasis as limiting the usefulness of oral traditions in the religious sphere:

Religious practice was so tied up with other institutions that it lacked sufficient autonomy and visibility to develop systematic traditions of its own. It
is diffused throughout society. Furthermore, change in the representations
and in the practice of ritual was so slow as often to be unconscious and hence
could not be remembered. Where change was not slow, the need to adhere
to the new consensus effectively prevented development of traditions that
would indicate what previous representations of ultimate reality might have
been. Oral traditions are therefore, sources that are not promising for intellectual history in general and religious history in particular except when
they touch on the ideology of kingship.[19]

Vansina argues that because political institutions overshadow religious institutions in Kuba oral traditions, most information about religious change has been
lost. Furthermore, he suggests that an ideological need for community consensus
would obscure any radical shifts in religious ideas or concepts.

  However, Vansina recognizes that societies with a less central tradition of kingship, such as the Shona and the Dogon, may very well have richer oral traditions
about religious history.[20] Similarly, in a society such as that of the Diola-Esulalu,
there is no central polity to overshadow traditions of religious change. Specialized political institutions do not become the cultural anchor of the society or the
symbol of its continuity over time. Royal reigns do not become the primary chronological guide to major events. Rather, adoption of new shrines and changes in
initiation rites are perceived to be the major events of history. Similarly, these
shrines and initiations become the focal points for the cultural continuity of Esulalu
society. The control of important shrines frequently provides an individual with
influence in society. In these communities, religious institutions serve as the primary mode of organizing social relations, as well as ritual life. Thus the founding
of a major shrine assumes as central a role as the founding of a new dynasty in an
equatorial African kingdom. Each spirit shrine has its own history, a founder, and
a historical situation in which the founder acted, as well as a changing role within
the community. In many cases, the adoptions of new spirit shrines reflect important changes in a community's concepts of power, ritual activity, and the role of
ritual specialists.

  Many anthropologists who have concentrated on the study of African systems
of thought have been critical of historians' use of oral traditions. Quite rightly,
they have said that oral histories must be analyzed in terms of indigenous cosmologies. By striking out what they deem to be "magical" elements, historians
have deprived the traditions of much of their explanatory value. As the anthropologist Wyatt MacGaffey contends, this separation of mythical and historical
elements cannot be justified: "To accept as historical even such portions of traditions as are real to the foreign eye is to submit unawares to the authority of indigenous cosmology as much as though one had also accepted the magical portions
as historically real. In fact, there is no boundary between the two, the myth is one
piece, and all of its pieces make sense from the same point of view."[21] For
MacGaffey, the historian must understand the historical categories from which a
tradition has developed and only then translate it into terms that are comprehen-

sible to Western readers. Historians of oral traditions have become increasingly aware of this problem. Thus Steven Feierman argues that "since oral traditions are not strictly historical texts, but living social documents . . . if we do not understand their social context and their social content, then we can not understand our sources."[22] The historian who uses oral traditions must seek to understand the oral narratives' relationship not only to the events described but also to the narrators and their audiences.

Nevertheless, some scholars who emphasize the mythic and cosmological qualities of oral traditions rely too heavily on synchronic models. For example, T. O. Beidelman claims that oral traditions serve primarily to "reveal certain social or cultural 'truths' quite outside the sphere of the historical."[23] In a recent monograph, he talks about the inseparability of Kaguru legend and history and the "unchanging cosmological verities that provide coherence to how Kaguru imagine their society. These do not alter and are structurally the same in nearly all clan legends, even though particular details may vary."[24] Yet there is no objective evidence for a static quality to Kaguru cosmology anymore than there is a constant concept of Kaguru ethnic identity. The "legends" that he chooses to analyze do address cosmological problems, but they also address the historical problem of forging a common ethnic identity out of the series of communities that sought refuge in Kaguru. Beidelman's conception of categories of thought or cultural truths that exist outside history betrays a lack of understanding of the historical process. Categories of thought shape the way people perceive and react to changes in their world, but in the process these modes of thought are themselves shaped and modified.

While it is true, as Beidelman suggests, that oral traditions serve the function of legitimation of a contemporary situation and are models for social behavior, these functions need not displace the historical content of such traditions. Careful scholars can identify value-laden elements within a historical account and recognize their didactic nature without detracting from other aspects that seek to illuminate the past. Furthermore, these value-laden elements themselves are important for the study of the history of ideas. They offer normative models for community behavior and aspirations.[25] These models are of particular importance to a historian of religion because changes in them are clear indications of changes in fundamental ideas about the world and society. Certain elements that might be identified as "mythic" might also be symbolic representations of long-term historical processes that are important to the community.[26]

Many scholars who focus on oral traditions primarily as myth overlook the many instances in which these materials contradict or ignore the basic ideological concerns of a community. There is no simple congruence between oral traditions and the contemporary needs of the community. Vansina suggests that those elements in oral traditions which appear to oppose the ideological needs of a community provide strong evidence of actual events and long-standing beliefs: "When, however, traits or anecdotes run counter to fashion, they should be seen as reliable. These data resisted the trend to idealization"[27] Like written texts, oral traditions must also be understood in terms of the self-interests both of their narrators and of the community whose collective memory kept the traditions alive.

Like written traditions, oral traditions change over time. The initial interpreters of events make certain choices about what is important to them in explaining their subject. This selectivity is essentially the same as the selective reportage of a written source. However, we usually have each written text in a tradition as it was set down, especially since the advent of printing. We receive an oral tradition after each recipient of it has heard the tradition, decided what was important, and passed this new rendition to the next generation. It would be analogous to a written document that had been edited several times over, after the original document was lost.[28] Fortunately, different oral historians edit their sources in different ways or meld them with other sources to which they have access to produce new traditions with a variety of viewpoints.[29] Certain material might be lost from one account but not from another. Some material might be lost altogether because the community finds it is no longer relevant to their concerns. This would be less true in cases of fixed traditions in which the exact duplication of a text is regarded as important for its proper narration.

During periods of rapid change in a community, oral traditions may contain conflicting materials that bear testimony to both the suddenness and the magnitude of events. Two or more accounts may coexist within a single oral tradition. Vansina refers to this as a *palimpsest tradition*, a term he adopted from the analysis of medieval parchment texts in which writings from different periods are found on a single piece of parchment. In describing a Kuba creation account, he noted it does "not reflect exactly and necessarily the world view held now, but still incorporates elements of different ages. For the readjustment of ultimate values and cultural identity is usually a slow process."[30] The areas of ambiguity, where certain elements do not seem to fit together, are, according to Vansina, clues to shifts in community attitudes about the world or in their interpretation of their history. There are several examples of these shifts in Diola traditions, often with major implications for the study of religious history. A sequencing of ideas may be determined by the degree of "fit" that it has with other religious concepts of the Diola that can be more accurately dated.[31]

Although the dean of Diola ethnographers, Louis Vincent Thomas, claims that the Diola "give little importance to events of the past," this is clearly not the case.[32] Despite their lack of professional historians, the Diola spend a substantial amount of time discussing their past. The origin and seniority of shrines are important for determining the influence of a given lineage or village. In Diola communities, being older generally means being more powerful. This point is well illustrated by one of the Diola defenses against Christian proselytization. While accepting that Jesus may be a child of God, many Diola insist that the *ukine* (spirit shrines) are God's first offspring. Thomas and subsequent commentators were misled into thinking that the Diola have little regard for history because history is so important to the present that it is concealed from outsiders and the uninitiated by an ideology of continuity over time and equality of social status. Given the transformative power associated with historical knowledge in Diola society, access to such materials was limited to those who demonstrated the maturity to use their knowledge responsibly.[33]

My initial interviews in Esulalu were governed by these ideological needs; shrines were said to have existed since the "time of the first ancestors." Slavery and other forms of social inequality were said to have never existed. Only after many months of interviews did I penetrate beyond what the Diola wish outsiders and young people to know of their past. In a culture in which elders can remember eight generations in genealogies, allowing that a particular shrine was created by an ancestor four generations ago situates it in a much more recent time than the "time of the first ancestors." Such an acknowledgment is significant because a shrine established as junior to another is seen as less powerful. In allowing that there was a time when such a shrine did not exist, it becomes clear that the community used alternative means of resolving problems. In many instances, contrary to the ideological need to stress continuity over time, traditions revealed that many shrines had founders or villages of origin outside of Esulalu, that they were created to meet specific problems or arose out of specific historical circumstances, and that their power waxed and waned in relation to the power of their priests and the changing needs of the community.

With the exception of songs and proverbs, Diola oral traditions are not formalized. Usually Diola elders narrate stories and engage in discussion about the past rather than perform a fixed tradition. Diola traditions would conform to what Vansina has described as "free traditions."[34] Knowledge of religious or historical traditions can be acquired in one of two ways: by learning it from elders of a previous generation or through the use of special powers. The first method is well known to students of oral tradition. Someone will say that a certain person sat at the feet of his uncle before he died. Knowledge is handed down from one generation to the next. In Esulalu, this type of oral tradition is analyzable in terms of chains of transmission, but most recitations are based on diverse sources.[35] The second type involves learning about Diola traditions from dreams and visions. In these cases, elders rarely refer to their source of information. The elder simply says, "I know" or "someone showed me," both of which imply extraordinary mental powers.

The way in which the informant had learned about the Diola past significantly affected the interviewing situation. In the first instance, I became a student learning lessons about the past in an educational process similar to that of my informant. Generally, these accounts contained a stronger narrative line and a stronger sense of chronology. With the exception of questions about sensitive subjects, such as social inequality or slavery in Esulalu, I was not challenged about the reason that I wanted to know about the past and what I was going to do with it. My explanation that I was writing about the customs of the past and how they had changed was accepted at face value. In the second type of interview, I was being trained how to think in the fashion of the elders. My questions were often parried by questions about why I wanted to know something or by claims that, if I thought about it enough, I would know the answer already. Throughout the interview, I was being tested to see whether I was ready to understand and accept the responsibility of acquiring new knowledge. In questions about specific shrines, I was often asked what I had seen and experienced during the rituals that I had attended in order to ascertain whether I was learning to "see" in a new way.[36] The second type of interview occurred invariably when I was in a small group or when I was alone with my teacher. They comprise a small portion of the total number of interviews but yielded valuable insights into the meaning of the material collected in all types of interviewing situations.

Personal recollections of the recent past were important in understanding the historical period between the time of my fieldwork in the 1970s, 1980s, and 1990s and the focus of this study, the precolonial period up to the late nineteenth century. They played a crucial role in the creation of a context for the oral traditions and the establishment of chronologies for such traditions. Like oral traditions, personal recollections must be analyzed carefully to be reliable sources of evidence. Because they touch directly on the lives of their narrators, they may be colored according to informants' interests in the events—materially, emotionally, politically, or morally. Still, the greater number of people who can provide descriptions of this recent past and the clearer sense of narrator self-interest allow these sources to be used effectively.

The third source—the explanation of religious ideas, rituals, and social custom—conforms to the basic approach of anthropological field research. Obviously, such explanations reflect contemporary perspectives, but with informants that I knew well, I could begin to question whether these interpretations had changed over time. In using this material, I evaluated the interpretations against my sense of the informant's knowledge, interests, and relationship to the material. I have relied heavily on Diola explanations of both the process of religious change and of their cultural practices. I share Anthony Giddens's view of the richness of indigenous exegesis:

> All human beings are knowledgeable agents. That is to say, all social actors know a great deal about the conditions of what they do in their day-to-day lives. Such knowledge is not wholly propositional in character, nor is it incidental to their activities. Knowledgeability embedded in practical consciousness exhibits an extraordinary complexity, a complexity that often remains completely unexplored in orthodox sociological approaches, especially those associated with objectivism. Actors are also ordinarily able discursively to describe what they do and their reasons for doing it. However, for the most part these faculties are geared to the flow of day-to-day conduct.[37]

The final source of information from field research grows out of participant observation. By living in a community and joining in religious, work, and social activities, the researcher acquires a wealth of information about the relationships among religious thought, historical consciousness, and daily life. A religion is something that is lived, as well as practiced. When I first began to ask questions about Diola religion, I received invitations to experience more than I received detailed explanations. A month after I first arrived in Esulalu, one elder told me, through an interpreter I still needed at that point, that although I had read about Diola religion, I needed to see it. He could not explain it to me; I had to experience it.[38] He then invited me on an almost daily basis to attend the rituals of the spirit shrines he controlled. This was his method of teaching. Another elder, in response to questions about his shrine, replied, "If you want to know the spirit shrine, get ten liters of palm wine, a chicken and rice, and go to the shrine."[39] To understand his shrine, I had to perform its ritual.

Participant observation also makes researchers informants. They become as situated in the society as other informants, with many of the same limitations and advantages. Participant observation allows researchers to acquire subjective experiences of their communities which inform their analysis of the material acquired in interviews. However, it also risks the danger, as Vansina suggests, of the researcher's becoming an influence in the ordering and presentation of reflections about the past and about religious life.[40]

In a provocative fieldwork memoir, Paul Rabinow has questioned the possibility of fully entering a community while studying it. "No matter how far 'participation' may push the anthropologist in the direction of Not-Otherness, the context is still dictated by 'observation' and externality."[41] While I agree with Rabinow that the researcher is always an observer first and a participant second, the longer one conducts fieldwork and the more fully one shares in community life, the closer those two aspects approach each other. Rabinow acknowledges that "participation changes the anthropologist and leads him to new observation, whereupon new observation changes how he participates"[42] This transformation, in many cases, leads to the researcher's increasing integration into the community. At that point Rabinow shares Vansina's concern that researchers influence their primary informants' perceptions of what they seek to explain. Rabinow describes his influence on a man named Ali:

> He was constantly being forced to reflect on his own activities and objectify them. Because he was a good informant, he seemed to enjoy this process and soon began to develop an art of presenting his world to me. The better he became at it, the more we shared together. But the more we engaged in such activity, the more he experienced aspects of his own life in new ways. Under my systematic questioning, Ali was taking realms of his own world and interpreting them for an outsider. This meant that he, too was spending more time in this liminal self-conscious world between cultures.[43]

I share Rabinow's concern that "systematic questioning" by outsiders moves informants into a liminal world of self-consciousness, but the field worker is not the only one who disturbs "usual patterns of experience." At least among the Diola, young people—some who have been to school and some who have not, some who are widely traveled in Senegambia and some who are not—are frequently asking questions of elders about their history and customs. Some of these people share very little of the life experience of their elders. The experience of Diola communities—and Moroccan ones—are considerably more diverse than we might imagine, and this act of explanation, perhaps more intense with a field worker, is repeated with some frequency in the lives of people who are seen as repositories of community knowledge. Indeed, the liminality of this experience of explanation can be minimized by seeking to learn in ways that are already utilized by the community. To do this, I became one of the students that certain elders took on, engaging in dialogues in which we discussed the areas of their expertise.

The historian who relies solely on oral traditions finds only fragments of the past. In the streamlining of traditions, continuities between past and present may not be described because they generate no controversy. The converse may be true as well: that memories of controversial subjects may be suppressed or restricted to esoteric traditions to which the researcher may not have access. The field researcher has access to a comprehensive understanding of religious and social history for only the period of the present and the very recent past. This more comprehensive view of the present may be used, cautiously, to project into the past a broader context for the fragments gleaned from oral traditions. Such projection is not limited to the study of nonliterate societies; it is often done implicitly in the historical analysis of literate societies.[44] Although such a method can overdraw the similarities between the past and present, the alternative is the failure to understand connections of data within incomplete visions of the past. The contemporary accounts obtained through participant observation and recent commentaries become the base line for charting the significance of changes in Diola religious and social history.

The Organization of Field Research

Having examined the problems of interpreting evidence gathered through field research, I now describe the methods I used to collect it. These techniques draw on anthropological research techniques and a healthy dose of common sense. My research design also had to overcome the special problems of the historian of religion. First, the absence of written theological statements made it difficult to study changes in religious thought through hermeneutic analysis, a method frequently used in the study of literate traditions. Second, an ideology of continuity since the time of the "first ancestors" had to be gradually breached. Third, the existence of esoteric knowledge meant that much of the detailed information regarding rituals, initiations, and shrine historians is forbidden for those who do not have a right to know about such things. This right can be gained through inheritance, by being chosen to become an elder at a particular shrine, or through initiation. Otherwise, such information could be dangerous to the listener. A person who reveals forbidden information is said to have "poisoned the ears" of his listener. Given the multiplicity of Diola spirit shrines, each with its own rules of access, it is considered dangerous for any one person to know all the shrines at this esoteric level. The temptation to abuse such powerful knowledge would be too great, not only for members of the community but also for the researcher.[45]

To minimize these obstacles, I limited the primary area of my field research to the Esulalu region. The microstudy had several advantages. First, it enhanced the possibility of maintaining adequate control over the quantity of data received while increasing the depth of access to such information. At least in Diola communities, the staggering profusion of spirit shrines makes it difficult for the researcher to understand the role of every shrine in a wider area. The types of shrines and the rules that govern them also vary considerably from group to group. Second, the microstudy enabled me to obtain greater access to informants and to develop strong personal bonds with members of each community in which I worked. Information, particularly of the more restricted type, may be gleaned only through extended personal contact with individuals. A researcher cannot walk up to per-

fect strangers and ask them to explain their religion. Even with the proper introductions, one could hardly expect, at first, to hear more than the public justification of religious practice, which stresses both its continuity since the time of the
ancestors and its harmonious functioning. Unfortunately, many researchers have
stopped there and then, like Thomas, inferred the absence of a concept of history
or of a concern with abstract principles.[46] Just because the researcher did not find
such materials, however, does not mean they are not there.

Localized fieldwork increased my access to the more restrictive shrines because
people knew me and what I was trying to accomplish. Participation in rituals did
more than allow me to observe religious activity; it provided a chance to get to
know the elders of the community. The small talk after palm wine libations provided an excellent occasion to pick up detailed explanations of the rituals and
the ideas they were designed to express. The shared experience of shrine rituals
also provided me with a tangible set of questions for initial interviews at people's
homes.

The limited scope of fieldwork also allowed me to have repeated interviews
with the same informant. During nearly four years in Esulalu, I interviewed some
informants as many as sixty times and also made additional visits without interviewing. The repetition of interviews permitted me to review material that had
been discussed before and to try a variety of approaches to a particular subject.
More important, it fostered a personal rapport between informant and researcher
that facilitated access to more restricted information and permitted me, in some
cases, to become one who "sat at the feet of" a particular elder. Finally, it allowed
me to understand a particular informant's mode of recounting historical and religious materials and thereby deepened their meaning.

To understand oral traditions concerning Esulalu religious and social history,
I had to learn the language in which that culture is expressed. Hoyt Alverson
stresses the importance of language in his study of the Tswana: "To deal with
Tswana experience, and in particular 'self-experience,' we must turn to the Tswana
speaking—using their language to communicate their beliefs. Their language is
our principal mode of access to the private, interior experiences that comprise
self-identity."[47] Without a thorough knowledge of the language of the community,
the researcher remains distant from the experience of his informants, even with
the best of interpreters. It is exceedingly difficult to translate abstract terms from
either a European language for questioning or an African language for the responses. Considerable material is lost because of inadequate translation. The context of the materials established by the language itself is lost altogether.

Lack of language skills affects more than one's ability to understand one's informants; it alters the social dynamics of the interview itself and the researcher's relationship to the host community. Any interpreter who could work for a researcher
would already have a distinct position within that society. A Catholic interpreter,
who was no longer an adherent of Diola religion, would have limited rights to hear
and hence to translate vital information. A young interpreter—and most interpreters are—might not have obtained the right to know such information. The use of
an interpreter also creates an artificial formality in the interview. Everything must

be repeated, and hence it is more difficult to pursue a question or a train of thought. It also impedes the use of small talk, which often quickly changes suddenly into some of the most important information. My first interview on reincarnation grew out of a discussion of the impact of World War I on Diola war veterans. Many of my interviews were extended conversations, meandering in and out of research-related topics and often lasting several hours. The relaxed discussion of everything from crops to water spirits and from wrestling to funerals allowed me to learn about Esulalu thought from the web of daily life. Evans-Pritchard noted the importance of general conversation to his research on the Nuer: "What I record I witnessed myself or is information given spontaneously during talk about other and more practical affairs or in comment on some event or experience. Such observations may, however, be more valuable in a study of religious thought than those derived from purposive inquiry."[48] Finally, speaking Diola made it far easier to develop the personal rapport necessary to my being accepted.

The two final aspects of my research design were related to living arrangements within Esulalu. By living with a family, I was provided with an unequaled way of learning about daily life and also with teachers of etiquette, guides to the community, and commentators on the material that I was receiving. My adoptive family clarified many things which were unclear and provided moral support for my work. Living with an Esulalu family created an environment where I could engage in community activities and where I could be observed by that community. This, in turn, significantly enhanced the acceptance of my work within Esulalu.

I also tried to minimize the differences between myself and my host community by adapting as much as possible to daily life in Esulalu. I lived at the material level of Esulalu families, choosing the village schoolteacher, roughly my peer in social status and age, as a model. Especially during the initial period of language training and orientation, I worked in the fields and forests and joined in the dances. My learning of a dance associated with the history of the rain shrine, Cayinte, and my subsequent public performance of it with other men opened my way into the community in terms of both community acceptance and access to the elders. The work and the dance themselves are rich sources of information about daily life and the influence of religion on it. In a society that does not have a specialized class of intellectuals, community wisdom is discussed in the idiom of daily life. Even if one literally hears the words, one may not grasp the meanings. It is necessary to understand the intricacies of daily life to understand the complexities of religious life.

I conducted research in Esulalu during seven periods, beginning in 1974 and ending in 1997. In September 1974, I began my first period of field research, residing with a family in the township of Kadjinol until August 1975. In May 1976, I returned to my host family in Kadjinol and remained until mid-August. I returned again in September 1977 and remained until February 1979. After completing my doctoral dissertation, I returned to Kadjinol in 1987, 1994, 1996, and 1997. Each time I lived with the same family, but each period of research was different. My recurrent visits were seen as a sign to the community of the seriousness of my desire to learn of "Diola customs from the past to the present."

During the first phase of field research, beginning in September 1974, I was brought to Kadjinol by a village schoolteacher and introduced to my host family. They had not received our letter explaining my plans to live with them. Needless to say, they were somewhat startled to find a stranger, equipped with five minutes worth of Diola, who wanted to live with them and study Diola history. I spent the first few days pointing at everything around the house, asking for its name, and memorizing it. Because the school term had not yet begun, there were plenty of young, French-speaking students still at Kadjinol. Several of them took me under their wing, helped me with Diola lessons, and introduced me to some of the elders of the community. During my first few months, I stayed largely in the township of Kadjinol, learning Diola, joining in work and rituals, and becoming part of the community. In many ways my first months in Kadjinol were more like those of an exchange student than a researcher. I joined in all the community activities to which I was invited and, because of inadequate language skills, relied primarily on participant observation rather than extended interviews.

This initial period, when I could not conduct substantial interviews without an interpreter, became an important period in which people in Esulalu could gradually get to know me. After about six weeks, I was formally adopted by my family and told to consider myself fully at home. Shortly thereafter, I received a Diola name and the first of many Diola nicknames. Outside the family, I was quickly accepted into the student group, young men in their twenties, and was included in many of their activities—dances, wrestling, social visits, and the like. However, by December, most of the older youths had left either for school or work in the major towns of Senegal.

Fortunately, by that time, my language skills had improved enough to conduct simple interviews with community elders. In January 1975, five months after I had arrived, there was a major initiation for a priest of the Cayinte shrine. The initiation was supposed to be open only to men who had completed the initiation rite of Calau, but I was allowed to attend. For six days we ate, sang, talked, and danced. During this time, the new priest learned the history of his shrine and his ritual responsibilities. On the seventh day, we performed the dances for all of Kadjinol. My participation in the sacred dances, the period of time with the elders, and my interest in community rituals opened my way into the community. It was during this rite that I received the nickname of "He who follows the priest-king (oeyi)" and became known to elders throughout Esulalu.

During the remaining eight months in Esulalu, my ability to conduct interviews gradually improved. I began to work more in the neighboring townships and to make the transition from exchange student to field researcher. During the latter half of that year, I began to conduct lengthy interviews on questions of history and religion. Usually I did not tape these interviews. I found that the tape recorder unnecessarily drew attention to my being a stranger. Furthermore, because elders regarded much of the information that I received as estoric in nature, much of this material could not be taped at all.

In 1976 I returned to Esulalu for a second visit of three months. My return brought home to many people that I was not simply interested in collecting data and then leaving Esulalu for good. I was seen as having an ongoing relationship with my family and the community of Kadjinol, an impression that was further reinforced by my third visit from 1977 to 1979, when I conducted my "formal" doctoral dissertation research. My return trips to Esulalu in 1987, 1994, 1996, and 1997 have allowed both me and Esulalu to witness changes in each other over a period that spans more than half of my life time.

2

Encountering Esulalu

An Introduction

The oral traditions that provide the core of evidence for this study of Diola history were gathered during seven periods of field research between 1974 and 1997. They represent the received traditions about the precolonial era as reflected upon by people who had recently become a part of an independent Senegal and who were enduring frequent droughts and an increasingly difficult integration into the world economy. They are reflections about Diola traditional religion before the implanting of other traditions, from the perspective of people in communities that have substantial Christian minorities. Furthermore, these traditions incorporate some of the long-term influences of Alinesitoué, a woman whose prophetic teachings continued to be important in Esulalu during the period of my fieldwork. Her teachings revitalized Diola religion during the crisis years of World War II. Her emphasis on the direct intervention of the supreme being in Diola affairs was used to reaffirm the integrity of the Diola community against the colonial order and against the growing influence of Christianity and Islam.[1]

Recognizing that oral traditions are "living social documents," I describe the environment in which they were narrated and received, as well as the more enduring climate in which they developed.[2] Thus, this chapter serves as a necessary prolegomenon to my reconstruction of precolonial Diola history. Not only does it provide a context for the analysis of new perspectives incorporated into collected oral traditions but it illuminates the social world experienced by an outsider as he sought to understand the meaning of the traditions that he was collecting. The primary focus of this chapter is the complex intertwining of economic, social, political, and religious aspects of Diola life during the period of my fieldwork; my intent is to establish the historical perspective that my informants and I came to share as we discussed the precolonial era.

While seeking to provide a more complete context for understanding the fragmentary evidence of the more distant past, this prolegomenon outlines some basic areas of continuity and discontinuity between postcolonial fieldwork and Esulalu's precolonial era. In doing so, I recognize, as Fernand Braudel suggests, that varying types of changes occur at different paces. Here I focus on what he calls the *longue durée*, structures of community life that change at a far slower rate than the types of innovations that receive greater attention in the narrative chapters that follow. However, I do not see the structures of the longue durée as constraining human histories, only as evolving at such a slow pace that changes within them become difficult to describe within a traditional narrative framework. Thus, my description of the continuities of the Diola social world becomes a heuristic device for contextualizing the microhistory that follows.[3]

In the first part of this chapter, I describe the organization of daily life with particular attention to the environment, the social and political structure of Esulalu communities, and the structure of economic life. In the second section, I turn to the analysis of Diola cosmology, ritual life, social values, and philosophy of history. These two sections are intimately related. Both a Diola system of thought and an elaborate system of spirit shrines structure and legitimate the operation of an Esulalu political economy. Simultaneously, environmental, social, and economic factors continue to influence both Diola thought and ritual practice. What begin as separate currents quickly flow into a common stream of Esulalu cultural practice.

I. The Organization of Daily Life

Like most predominantly agricultural peoples, the Diola organize their daily lives to efficiently exploit the ecological zone in which they live. They inhabit a well-watered coastal plain stretching from the Gambia River in the north to the São Domingo River in the south. Visitors to the region are struck by the profusion of vegetation: vast forests of silk cotton trees and oil palms, separated by rice paddies and tangled mangrove swamps. Bisected by the saltwater estuaries of the Casamance River, it is an area rich in fish and shellfish, which are the primary protein source in the Diola diet. The lower Casamance region stands in sharp contrast to the open savannah of northern Senegal or the upper Casamance. Despite the lushness of the vegetation and high average precipitation, drought is common, making agriculture an uncertain enterprise. Near the Gambia River, in the areas populated by the Diola of Kombo and Fogny, the forest competes with wooded savannah, and vast areas have been cleared for the cultivation of peanuts. South of the Casamance River, rainfall and forest areas increase; rice paddies become larger and peanut fields harder to find. This area, known as Kasa, includes Esulalu.

The people of Esulalu live along low-lying ridges overlooking alluvial valleys and marshes that they gradually converted into rice paddies. Beyond these areas is a slightly higher plateau which was, until recently, covered with dense forest. Beyond the plateau, to the south, are the settlements of Huluf, which maintain close ties with Esulalu.

Esulalu Township Organization

Esulalu's access to vast areas suitable for rice paddies and to rich fishing areas in the mangroves and estuaries allowed the region to support a large population. The labor-intensive nature of rice cultivation and the use of elaborate systems of irrigation and protective dikes, however, required the growth of social institutions capable of marshaling labor resources, resolving land disputes, and providing physical security for the farmers of the region. To address these problems, the people of Esulalu developed large settlements (*essouk, sissouk*), that I translate as townships.

Since the midnineteenth century, Esulalu has consisted of five townships, each located on a low ridge and nearly surrounded by rice paddies. From east to west, these townships are Kadjinol, Mlomp, Eloudia, Kagnout, and Samatit. Each possesses vast rice paddies, sometimes extending more than ten kilometers from the township center. Nine stranger villages, of recent immigrants to the region, are located on lands that formerly belonged to the Esulalu townships. Kadjinol and Mlomp, with populations of approximately 3,500 and 4,500, respectively, comprise about half of Esulalu's population. Kagnout has about 2,000 people, and Eloudia and Samatit are inhabited by about 500 people per township. The nine stranger villages range in size from 50 to 500 inhabitants.[4]

The Esulalu townships are not cohesive communities; each of them is composed of a series of independent quarters with their own interests and loyalties. In the precolonial era, each quarter did not feel obligated to come to the defense of neighboring quarters if they came under attack. There were numerous cases of armed conflict between quarters, not only in the precolonial period but also as recently as the 1970s.

Still, there was some sense of township unity. Two religious authorities, the office of oeyi or priest-king and the *boekine* (spirit shrine) of Hutendookai, actively promoted township unity.[5] Through the oeyi's performance of rituals designed to preserve the township's vitality by securing adequate rainfall, enhancing community fertility, and protecting it from external threats, he came to embody the spiritual unity of the township. Furthermore, his ability to stop interquarter disputes was crucial to the preservation of township institutions. The Hutendookai shrine, whose elders made decisions about the organization of township labor and regulated many disputes, also worked against township factionalism. Hutendookai's elders coordinated communal labor activity involving the maintenance of the fences, which protected the rice paddies from livestock, and dikes that protected them from salt water. Despite these institutions, however, the townships possessed only a fragile sense of unity.

An analysis of the relations between the six quarters of Kadjinol illustrates the complexity of township relations. Kadjinol consists of six quarters: Kandianka, Baimoon, Ebankine, Kagnao, Sergerh, and Kafone. Each quarter has certain shrines at which only people from the quarter can participate and which give spiritual sanction to their decisions. Each quarter has at some point been engaged in warfare against its neighbors. Together, Baimoon and Kandianka form a larger entity referred to as Hassouka.[6] It, too, has several spirit shrines restricted to its own community and certain ritual rules that differ from the other four quarters, collectively known as Kalybillah. Kalybillah also has its particular shrines and ritual rules. Thus, within Kadjinol, there are divisions between Baimoon and Kalybillah and between the six independent quarters. Furthermore, there are certain special links involving single subquarters of one quarter with other quarters. Thus the subquarter of Ecuhuh, within Kafone, has special links to Hassouka and is excluded from certain shrines of Kafone and Kalybillah.

The most cohesive social grouping was the extended family compound (*hank*), each containing as many as three generations of a single family. Within the hank, houses were constructed so closely together that they were literally within shouting distance. Some people claim that the density of settlement was a form of protection from the frequent raiding against Esulalu townships, but more effective social control by hank elders may have also been an important consideration.[7] Beyond the hank, the most effective level of community loyalty was the subquarter. Allegiance to the quarter was still significant, but within the township it diminished dramatically. It was the quarter that punished individuals or families who neglected community obligations or refused to abide by community decisions, even though these decisions were often made by townshipwide organizations such as Hutendookai. In a society that valued independence as much as the Diola, it was important that the task of forcing compliance with an unpopular decision be conducted by people who had a sense of belonging to the same moral community. Disputes within the subquarter could be more readily resolved because of the commitment of the inhabitants to settle a potentially divisive issue without recourse to violence.

Running deep in Esulalu society was a view of people beyond the quarter as outsiders who were not subject to the same degree of moral control. Until after World War I, children were not permitted to leave the quarter except in large groups or when accompanied by adults. Parents feared that their children would be seized and sold into slavery. Suspicions persist, but now it is more the actions of evil people—witches or experts in poison—whose activities are most feared. Until the 1920s, children grew up without knowing the majority of youth from neighboring quarters. Perhaps they encountered them at wrestling matches or at the homes of their maternal kin. Until they reached the age of physical maturity and were able to defend themselves, their community was the quarter. Many adults still do not make solitary social calls on people in neighboring quarters after dark, for fear that a quarrel could begin and they would be without the assistance of relatives.[8] Only within the quarter is one truly home.

The location of each quarter affected its economic development and its relationships with its neighbors. The quarters of Kafone and Sergerh in Kadjinol, Haer in Mlomp, and Bruhinban and Eyehow in Kagnout and the entire township of Eloudia are located close to the vast stretch of forest south of the rice paddies and away from the river (see map 2). As a result, they dominated access to the forest areas for palm wine tapping and for gathering other forest products. By contrast, the people of Kadjinol's quarters of Kagnao, Ebankine, Baimoon, and Kandianka; Kadjifolong in Mlomp; and Ebrouwaye in Kagnout have ready access to the river and estuaries that border Esulalu. These quarters controlled most fishing areas and the intermittent riverine trade. The township of Samatit and the Djicomole quarter of Mlomp are blessed with access to both the river and the forest, but they are exceptions. Otherwise, there was an economic complementarity within each township that was built on unequal access to certain economic resources. The trade of river products such as fish or salt for the palm wine and palm kernels of the forest reinforced the sense of allegiance to oeyi and Hutendookai with bonds of trade and economic self-interest.

The Centrality of Rice

In describing the ecology of Esulalu, it becomes clear that the forest, the estuaries and marshes, and the rice paddies were the primary areas of economic activity. Rice farming, however, shaped the way that all other economic activities were organized. Rice was the Diola staple; for a Diola not to have eaten rice at a meal was tantamount to not really eating.[9] It was more than a food, however; it was also used as a medium of exchange. One volume of unmilled rice could buy an equal volume of palm wine or half its volume in palm oil. Various measures of rice were used to buy pottery, fish, and even cattle. Stored in a full granary, it was a guarantee against famine. If the rains failed, farmers turned to their granaries to tide them over for the next year. If people were seized with illnesses by spirit shrines, they might have to provide rice for rituals or use it to purchase livestock and palm wine for ritual offerings. Rice, as represented by a full granary, protected a family against physical, economic, and spiritual hardship.

For most Diola, rice was also a vital part of cultural identity. Emitai, the supreme being in Diola cosmology, was thought to have given rice to their first ancestors and to have shown them how to farm it. Rice was seen as part of a covenant between Emitai and a people, a covenant based on the Diola's hard work in cultivating the crop and Emitai's responsibility to send them rain to nourish it. Francis Snyder collected a Diola-Bandial proverb that illustrated this task: "The Diola was created in order that he farm [rice]."[10] Rice was seen as having a life force within it, similar to the souls of people and animals.[11] Rice was a giver of life in that it nourished people and their domestic animals. Even the stalks provided essential fodder for Diola cattle during the dry season. The care of the paddies was a year-round task. Rice was not something that one could think of lightly or sell at will and expect to be blessed with a full granary and a prosperous family.

This linkage between the Diola and rice is as old as the Diola's presence in the Casamance. Archaeological evidence suggests that rice farmers have inhabited this region for more than two millennia. Excavations near Kagnout and Samatit indicate that Esulalu has been continuously inhabited by rice farmers for at least fifteen hundred years. How closely related these people were to the present-day Diola inhabitants remains uncertain, but there is clear evidence of continuity in land use and economic activities for an extremely long period.[12]

Not surprisingly, the Diola are considered the best wet rice cultivators in West Africa. Paul Pélissier, the leading student of Senegambian agriculture, testified to the care and ability of Diola farmers: "The Diola techniques of preparation and maintenance of the rice paddies, the most perfected of tropical Africa, have created permanent fields that for centuries have assured an uninterrupted production."[13] Diola rice farming techniques have won the respect of travelers to the region since the first European explorers in the fifteenth century.[14]

The Diola exploited several types of rice paddies, each with its own advantages for rice cultivation. The deepest paddies were reclaimed from the mangrove swamps in a painstaking process. Diola farmers cleared the mangrove trees, constructed dikes to protect the fields from the saltwater estuaries, and then waited for several years of rainfall to leach out most of the salt from the fields before they could actually plant them.[15] These paddies required rice varieties that could withstand saline soil and benefit from deep flooding. On higher ground, paddies were less saline but more vulnerable to drought. Small dams maintained water levels in all types of paddies. Finally, there were fields in the forest where upland rice was grown. It matured rapidly and needed less water than its wet rice cousin but provide smaller yields.[16]

Paddy land was individually owned but was often worked by brothers, together with their wives and children. Most rice paddies were passed down from a father to his sons, though a small number were inherited by daughters from their mothers. It has been suggested that Diola did not sell rice paddies and only rented them out, but this was not the case. In Esulalu, people sold rice paddies when they needed cattle for major rituals, for funerals, and, in the eighteenth and nineteenth centuries, to ransom relatives who had been captured by slave raiders before they were sold into slavery.[17]

Work in the rice paddies continued throughout the year. In February, after the harvest was completed, men returned to the rice paddies to plow under the weeds, returning valuable nutrients to the soil, and creating new furrows in the paddies to ensure proper drainage for the new crop. By April, women had prepared a fertilizer that was a mix of cow manure, compost, and ashes from the family hearth, which they would carry by head loads to the various rice paddies surrounding the township. This arduous task took several months to complete. During this period, men repaired dikes and extended them into new areas to convert additional land into paddies.[18]

With the first rains in June, men prepared rice nurseries and women selected and sowed the rice. Men also plowed the rice paddies, which was done without the assistance of animal traction; the scattered paddy holdings and the narrow footpaths that provide access to them made cattle-drawn plows impractical. There were also religious prohibitions on the use of cattle in plowing.[19] Work in the nurseries and rice paddies was done by family units; husband and wife worked together, each with his and her assigned tasks and with responsibility to supervise the children who assisted them. The harvest began in November and continued into early February. In Esulalu, women ordinarily harvested the rice, but when there was a shortage of women's labor, men assisted them.

Diola farmers performed these tasks by hand, with the assistance of some extremely well-adapted tools. The most important of these was the *cadyendo*, "a long-handled fulcrum shovel with an iron blade that is unique to the Diola and their immediate neighbors in Guinea-Bissau."[20] The basic cadyendo design was modified for different types of work. Smaller cadyendo were used for the waterlogged soils of the deep rice paddies and larger ones for the lighter soils of the rice nurseries. The metal cutting blade of the cadyendo was made by local black-smiths, the wooden portion of the shovel by local wood carvers, and the long wooden handle by almost anyone.

Olga Linares estimates that an Esulalu farmer could expect a rice harvest of 2,000 to 2,500 kilos of unmilled rice per hectare (1,500–2,100 kilos of milled rice). Given that an Esulalu man and woman could cultivate between one and a half and two hectares of paddy, they could anticipate a total harvest of between 3,000 and 5,000 kilos per year. Linares also estimated that an adult required approxi-mately 125 kilos of rice per year and a child about 75 kilos.[21] Thus, when the rains came, Diola farmers could expect a substantial surplus of rice. People in Esulalu distinguished between rice as a sustainer of life and rice as a source of economic power. Esulalu women controlled the rice used for food, which was stored in a separate part of the granary. Men controlled the rice reserve, which protected them against future crop failures and which could be used to purchase cattle and other goods. However, if the wife's portion was insufficient, the husband had to pro-vide for the family from his reserve.[22]

A good harvest depended on adequate rainfall and an adequate supply of labor. Although rainfall in Esulalu averaged 1,800 millimeters a year, actual rain-fall varied by as much as one-third.[23] Farmers compensated for erratic rainfall by using a variety of seed. Pélissier estimates that the Diola used about two hundred varieties of rice, each having its own requirements as to quantities of water, time of maturation, and soil types, while providing different yields. Women decided which varieties to plant, based on their knowledge of particular rice paddies and the amount of rainfall that had fallen during the planting season. Linares describes the way in which a woman uses "anywhere from five to fifteen varieties, which she constantly exchanges with other women, experimenting with new kinds, elimi-nating the less successful. . . . However, if halfway through the rainy season, it looks as if the rains will be insufficient, she may change tactics and transplant fast-growing varieties in the deeper fields."[24] The choice of seed helped combat the vagaries of a transitional climate zone while ensuring an adequate supply of rice in all but the severest drought.

The struggle to lessen the destructive impact of drought was also carried on through ritual. At various times of the year, rites were performed at men's, women's, and communitywide spirit shrines. Special rites known as *nyakul emit* (the funeral dance for Emitai) were performed when the rains failed. These ritu-als asked Emitai to have pity and send rain. The close association of the Diola name for a supreme being, Emitai ("of the sky"), with rain, *Emitai ehlahl* (liter-ally, "of the sky is falling"), demonstrated the connection between the supreme being and the gift of rain.

However, the continued supply of rain was ultimately dependent on more than rituals. Various traditions relate that Emitai gave the first ancestors (*situbai sihan*) what they refer to as "Diola" rice.[25] This rice carried a soul force given by Emitai to the Diola ancestors. It stood in spiritual relation to the Diola's ultimate origins and to the land shown them by Emitai. While European varieties of rice could be planted, some of the Diola varieties had to be grown to preserve the chain of power invested in the soul of Diola rice. Otherwise, the link to ancestors, who could intercede for their descendants, and to Emitai, who sends rain, would be broken. The fields would no longer receive rain. Prohibitions on such things as farming the rice paddies on the day of a funeral or during township rain rituals would provoke a similar break in the link of spiritual power and cause the crops to fail.[26]

Labor Relations

The nuclear family was the basic labor unit for rice agriculture in Diola communities. It was so important that divorce, normally a simple process, was not permitted during the planting and harvesting season. The labor-intensive quality of rice cultivation generated a need for labor that often exceeded what a family could supply. Because virtually everyone had access to land for cultivation, however, labor assistance had to be persuaded rather than coerced. Furthermore, the rights and responsibilities involved in such labor relations had to be carefully defined.[27] Labor relations were regulated by the elders of the town council shrine of Hutendookai. Shrine elders from each compound set wages for individual labor, enforced collective labor obligations, and provided a forum for complaints against employers who failed to meet their obligations.

There were three types of labor relations within Esulalu. The first was that of reciprocal aid, in which neighbors were recruited to work with the firm expectation that the favor would be returned. The second type of labor relation involved hiring individuals to help plant or harvest rice. Third, there was the hiring of work societies. The *embottai*, a society consisting of a group of friends, hired out to work for payments in money or livestock, with which they organized social activities. Other societies worked to procure the necessary palm wine, rice, and livestock for the celebrations of major initiations or to complete expensive rituals. Work teams and their employers negotiated remuneration, but Hutendookai ensured that the terms of the agreement were upheld.[28]

Other Economic Activities

Esulalu farmers grew other crops, but none of them approached the importance of rice. When not focused on rice cultivation, farmers worked on garden plots of manioc, yam, sweet potato, sorrel, and beans. In the nineteenth century, Mandinka and Wolof traders introduced sorghum, okra, bitter tomato, and peanuts. The peanut became an important crop for the paddy-short areas of the northern Diola and of Huluf, as well as the stranger villages within Esulalu.[29] Since World War II, some Esulalu farmers began to cultivate peanuts, individually or in work societies. The proceeds of the latter were used for collective projects such as support of the Catholic parish or a communitywide *awasena* ritual.

The second zone of economic exploitation was the forest or bush area. Within this zone, the oil palm was the most valuable resource. Its sap was used for palm wine, its kernels for palm oil, its branches for fences, and its trunk for building material. Harvesters sold palm wine for rice, fish, and, increasingly, for money. The forest zone was also the primary source of medicinal herbs, fruits, and, in scattered clearings, the types of grasses used in thatching roofs. Until recently, it was also a source of game, which provided an important protein supplement in the Esulalu diet. Until the 1960s, ownership of forest land was limited to rights to exploit certain trees. The land itself was not owned. In the past thirty years, some forest areas in Esulalu have been cleared for the planting of manioc, peanuts, and fruit orchards. Growing exploitation generated disputes over ownership rights in the forest zone. They, too, were resolved at the town council shrines of Hutendookai.[30]

The third ecological zone consisted of the mangrove swamps, the Casamance River, and its estuaries. The Diola's prime source of protein were the fish and shellfish that were taken from these waters. The oldest fishing techniques were bow and arrow, spear, and various types of fish traps. Rights to specific sites to erect reed fish traps, capable of snaring several bushels of fish each day, were individually owned and could be lent or sold. Serer strangers introduced net and rod fishing, which enabled Esulalu fishermen to exploit the deeper waters of the estuaries and the Casamance River.[31] Most fish and shellfish were sold for rice (though there is an increasing preference for money); some were dried for future use or for sale outside Esulalu.

Other economic activities were not limited to a particular ecological zone. They included livestock raising and various forms of artisan work. The Diola raised poultry, goats, pigs, cattle, and sheep. All of these animals could be bought and sold or given as payment for agricultural labor. Until recently, pigs, goats, sheep, and cattle were not killed except in connection with rituals or a work society. Both men and women could own most livestock, though only men owned cattle.

Diola cattle are of the tsetse fly–resistant *ndama* type, a variety that originated in the Futa Jallon. Despite some resistance to sleeping sickness, these cattle are highly susceptible to other diseases of the low-lying Esulalu area. Cattle were an important source of social prestige and a sign of wealth:

> For Diola peasants, cattle constitute the essential symbol of material success in combination with the rice granaries. We have seen that cattle make up a family inheritance. . . . one would have to be reduced to utter destitution to be totally without livestock. . . . wealth, social authority, family prestige are thus linked to the possession of a herd; each man has a permanent preoccupation to maintain and to increase that which he has charge of.[32]

Pélissier claimed that the Diola consider it a disgrace to sell cattle, even in dire circumstances. This was an overstatement. Given a decent-size herd, perhaps as few as five head of cattle, men would sell a steer for rice paddies. Such sales occurred only when people "without cattle" (a synonym for "poor") faced such an urgent need for cattle that they were willing to alienate vital paddy land in order to ransom relatives who had been seized in slave raids or to complete a major ritual.[33]

Despite the existence of a market for cattle, they were not valued primarily for their salability or as a food source. Milk was rarely consumed, and meat was normally available only as a result of ritual sacrifice. Cattle played an important role in the sacrifices that were required for people to assume priestly duties at major spirit shrines. Fathers killed cattle during the celebration of the circumcision ritual of *bukut*. These sacrifices in honor of a young man's initiation brought prestige to both father and son, while the magnitude of the offering helped to ensure the successful completion of this rite of passage. Major infractions of Esulalu customs could require the sacrifice of cattle to expunge the resultant pollution. During funeral rites, cattle were sacrificed to provide for wealth in the afterlife and to give added power to community prayers for the good fortune of the deceased. When cattle were sold, they were purchased by people who needed sacrificial cattle to fulfill ritual obligations. In exchange for a steer, the cattle seller received a substantial parcel of rice paddies. A man without cattle was not just poor; he was without the ability to protect himself spiritually against calamities and sudden twists of fate.

Until recently, Diola artisans had been able to supply most of Esulalu's needs for tools, clothes, and utensils. Although there is no record of Diola smelting their own iron, even the first European explorers described the Diola as working with it. Most of the iron was probably obtained from Futa Jallon or from European traders.[34] Diola blacksmiths forged the blades of the cadyendo, knives, machetes, tools, spears, and even muskets. Clients gave the blacksmiths twice as much iron as a given task would require. The blacksmith's pay was the surplus iron, which he could keep for his own use.

In Esulalu, only certain families could work with metal. Generally the blacksmiths went by the name of Diedhiou or Djabune.[35] To have the right to work as a blacksmith in Esulalu, one needed a combination of technical knowledge, which was only partially protected, and ritual knowledge, which was extremely closely guarded. The Diedhious had a series of ukine associated with their various lineages and with fire and the forge, each of which offered some protection against the dangers of working with fire. One of these dangers was leprosy, which resembled fire in the type of oozing sores that it inflicted on its victims. The ukine also enabled the Diedhious to have the strength to understand and manipulate fire at the forge. To work with metal without such protection would invite disaster, probably in the form of fire or leprosy, which could harm the offender and his entire family.

Within Esulalu, the overwhelming majority of blacksmith families live in the Kafone quarter of Kadjinol. There is one other compound of Diedhious in Kadjinol, two compounds at Mlomp, one compound at Eloudia, and two at Kagnout. All of them trace their family origins back to Kafone.[36] Since the eighteenth century, Kafone has controlled all of the blacksmith shrines in Esulalu and has kept the most powerful ones at Kafone. Kafone controlled the lucrative ironworking craft, which produced essential materials for agriculture and war, and it exerted influence in the region through its control of the senior blacksmith shrines.

Esulalu craftspeople made many other goods that were needed in daily life. Women made baskets used for the rice harvest, for rice threshing, and for other forms of work. Men made fishing baskets and rope. Still, certain essential goods were not made in Esulalu. The Huluf townships of Djivent and Edioungou were the main source of pottery for Esulalu. Potters sold their wares for the amount of rice that could fill one of their pots. In the precolonial era, most of Esulalu's cotton cloth came from the neighboring region of Bandial or from the Mandinka.[37] As trade with Europeans increased, they became important suppliers of cloth. Since World War II, most cloth has been manufactured in northern Senegal or imported from Europe.

For several hundred years, Esulalu has been actively involved in trade, not only within its townships but also with neighboring communities. Endowed with vast, well-watered rice paddies, Esulalu normally had a surplus of rice. Its extensive marshes and estuaries yielded considerable fish and shellfish. Its community of blacksmiths attracted people who wanted to purchase tools and weapons. Esulalu continues to purchase palm wine, cloth, pottery, certain food stuffs, and cattle from this regional trade network. Their most important trading partners have been the people of Huluf, who have a chronic shortage of rice paddies and poor access to fishing areas. Huluf continues to purchase Esulalu rice and fish by selling palm wine, palm oil, and pottery. Until recently, Bandial and Seleki sold cloth in exchange for Esulalu's smithing services and for herding some of Bandial's cattle. The people of Djougoutes and Kujamaatay sold livestock in exchange for rice from Esulalu. Finally, Mandinka traders visited the region, carrying with them cloth, cattle, and iron and purchasing Esulalu's primary export, rice.[38]

Despite the increasing importance of rural migration to the cities and the frequency of drought in the postindependence era, Esulalu continued to be able to provide most of the food that it required to sustain itself. This ability was sustained through a detailed knowledge of their particular agricultural environment, their continued use of well-adapted tools for rice farming, and an extraordinary amount of grueling physical labor. The close connection between the structures of ritual life and all Esulalu economic activities helps sustain this commitment to hard work and, especially, to the continued cultivation of rice. Providing meaning to this economic activity and a method of obtaining spiritual assistance in an uncertain agricultural environment was a Diola system of thought that sought to explain the complex relationship among people, the land, and a variety of spiritual beings. What Westerners often call "religion" was vitally involved in Diola economic life and community governance. The rituals the Diola performed sought to minimize the threat of famine, drought, and disorder and allowed them to engage in the often uncertain economic enterprises of a rural Diola community.

II. Diola Religion and Social Values

Before beginning any discussion of a Diola "religious" system, we need to examine the scholarly assumptions that sustain the use of the term *religion* to define a clearly demarcated object of study whose boundaries are seen as relatively constant cross-culturally and over time. In a provocative introduction to his *Imagining Religion: From Babylon to Jonestown* (1982), Jonathan Smith has argued that,

> while there is a staggering amount of data, of phenomena, of human experiences and expressions that might be characterized in one culture or another, by one criterion or another as religious—*there is no data for religion*. Reli-

gion is solely the creation of the scholar's study. It is created for the scholar's analytic purposes by his imaginative acts of comparison and generalization. Religion has no independent existence apart from the academy. For this reason, the student of religion, and most particularly the historian of religion, must be relentlessly self-conscious. Indeed, this self-consciousness constitutes his primary expertise, his foremost object of study.

Smith suggests that scholars, as they imagined "religion," created an object of study and then looked for what they imagined in the various societies that they studied. Smith demands that historians of religion critically examine their use of the term *religion*, recognize that it is a heuristic abstraction that can help us understand human experience, and become self-conscious about the criteria we use to determine what types of data we include in the category "religion."[39]

The Africanist historian Louis Brenner raised similar questions in reference to the use of the term *religion* in African studies. He argued that "most African languages did not include a word which could be convincingly and unequivocally translated as 'religion'" until Christianity, Islam, and foreign scholarship introduced or adapted words to represent that concept. "Nonetheless, most studies of African societies treat 'religion' as an institutionally and conceptually distinct category of analysis *as if* the author knew precisely what it was, not only for himself, but for the members of the societies under study as well. The result has been that consciously or not, external concepts have come to define 'religion' in Africa."[40] For Brenner and Smith, Western scholars have created an abstraction and reified it themselves, endowing it with specific characteristics and then imposing them on an object of study that they labeled *religion*.

Much of the process of generating this abstraction, "religion," involves setting its boundaries, deciding what is religious and what is secular, what is sacred and what is profane, as if such boundaries were intrinsic to "religious" experience. Winston King's article in *The Encyclopedia of Religion* illustrates this preoccupation with boundaries in religious studies: "The very attempt to define *religion*, to find some distinctive or possibly unique essence or set of qualities that distinguish the 'religious' from the remainder of human life, is primarily a Western concern. The attempt is a natural consequence of the Western speculative, intellectualistic, and scientific disposition."[41] This preoccupation with the boundaries of "religion" is not of primary concern to people outside the West, but, contra King, it is not a general characteristic of the Western "disposition." The idea of a bounded "religion" would make little sense to the Christian woman I heard testify in an Assembly of God church that the Holy Spirit had sent her an honest and able repairman to fix her washing machine.[42] Practitioners of "religion" are far less concerned with where the religious sphere begins or ends than they are with its ability to explain the world that they confront.

Smith does not, however, wish for an end to the academic study of "religion"; rather, he hopes that scholars will come to recognize their role in creating the category and begin to make explicit the types of criteria they used to determine what data should be included in the field.[43] To address Smith's mandate, I need to provide a brief history of my own approach to the history of religion among the Diola and how my conceptualization of the field of study was affected by Diola categories of experience. When I began my research on Diola religious and social history, I was primarily concerned with religion as a system of beliefs and rituals that sought to explain their world and to allow its practitioners to influence worldly events. When I asked people in Esulalu about religion, I had an idea of a bounded phenomenon, something that could be separated from daily life. I sought to understand the Diolas' mundane and spiritual theories of causality and the secular and religious motives for their behaviors. As a result, when I asked people about religion, I initially asked them what religion they were and to explain that religion to me. What I got in response were often misleading labels of particular religious traditions that implied tightly regulated boundaries between the three religious traditions found in Esulalu, scattered bits of data that I considered religion, and invitations to assist at various types of activities in community life.

As I gradually became more integrated into the Esulalu township of Kadjinol, my conceptualization of religion began to change. I found that there were religious dimensions to everything, from rice farming to wrestling matches. As my language skills improved, I became aware of four different Diola terms that could be associated with what Western scholars consider to be "religion." The broadest of them, *makanaye*, means "customs" (literally, "what we do"). It would include, but not be limited to, what Western scholars consider religion. A second term *boutine* (literally, "path") is presently used to indicate different "religions." Thus, there were the European (Christian) path, the Mandinka (Muslim) path, or a variety of other paths associated with particular ethnic groups. While we know that the term *boutine* was already being used in 1909, when Father Edouard Wintz compiled his *Dictionnaire de Dyola-Kasa*, we do not know if the term had religious implications before missionaries began to look for appropriate terms to use in translating Christian doctrine. Even if it was first used in a religious sense by missionaries, it now reflects a Diola approach to religious boundaries by associating Christianity and Islam with particular ethnic "paths." The third term, *kainoe*, is translated (to French) by Wintz as "foi" (faith) or "croyance" (belief), though I would translate it as "thought."[44] The fourth term, *awasena* is the word that is used for a follower of Diola religion, for one who performs rituals (*huasene* or *kuasene* [plural]).

What seems most important to Esulalu's awasena are concerns associated with customs, paths, thought, and the performance of ritual. The terms for customs and path are linked to "what we do" in our "path." People in Esulalu link customs and practices associated with their ancestors, even if they have changed over time, to the land in which they live and to their cultural identity. They contrast their customs with other people's customs (including other Diola groups in Bandial, Huluf, and elsewhere); they contrast their path, not only with those of Christians and Muslims, which are given ethnic labels, but also with neighboring ethnic groups. Perceptions of difference establishes boundaries for the awasena path, not to imply that other paths are wrong, since they were all made by the supreme being, Emitai, but to assert that the awasena path is the most appropriate one for the Diola. This Diola path can adopt practices from other communities but should not lose its rootedness in Diola customs, "what we do." Central to "what we do" is the performance of rituals that communicate the needs of the Esulalu community to various spiritual beings, to Emitai, and to the benevolent ancestors who assist their descendants in the place of the dead (*kahoeka*). However, the Diola way is more than a set of practices and customs; it is also a system of thought (kainoe) about the nature of the world and spiritual forces and about the purpose of human existence. The awasena path is one that is not only lived through action but also reflected upon. For the Diola, their path is a continually changing body of customs, rituals, practices, and thought that touches on all aspects of community life, that explains the world, and that provides means to influence events, a sense of linkage to one's community in the present, and an ontological connection to the "first ancestors" and the creation of the world by Emitai.

Reflecting Esulalu perspectives on what I had previously considered a bounded phenomenon, I began to ask about Diola makanaye, "what we do," when I sought to understand the role of what I considered religion in Diola life. The answers to my questions took me in many different directions in the study of Diola community life, from dances to rice farming. What I considered to be a "religious" dimension to human existence proved to be inseparable from other aspects of community life, not only for the Diola of Esulalu but also, outside the academy, in the Western experience of religion.

Emitai and the Supreme Being Debate

The concept of a supreme being has been a matter of considerable controversy in the study of African religions. Many commentators have placed what appears to be undue stress on a supreme being in an effort to present African religions as monotheistic precursors of Christianity, lacking only a sense of the future or a concept of a messiah.[45] Others have stressed the remoteness of a supreme being who created the world and then retreated from it. Into the cosmological vacuum rushed a host of lesser spirits who had power over the immediate concerns of humans. This image of a remote high god was central to Robin Horton's construction of a two-tiered "typical African cosmology," in which lesser spirits dominated the microcosm of community life and a supreme being dominated the macrocosm of "the world as a whole." While "the supreme being was defined as the ultimate controller and existential ground of the lesser spirits," its power was rarely invoked because, as he suggested, African "religious" life was focused on the first tier, of lesser spirits and on matters of local concern.[46]

Horton did not offer a static model, however; he argued that the expansion of social boundaries, brought on by economic and political changes, would produce a comparable change in the conceptualization of this basic cosmology. As people moved into broader spheres of social interaction, their focus would shift from the microcosmic level of lesser spirits to the macrocosmic level of a supreme being. While presenting this dynamic image of African religions, Horton insisted that Africa was a predominantly microcosmic world.

> The essence of the pre-modern situation is that most events affecting the life of the individual occur within the microcosm of the local community, and that this microcosm is to a considerable extent insulated from the mac-

rocosm of the wider world. Since most significant interaction occurs within the local community, moral rules tend to apply within the community rather than universally—i.e. within the microcosm rather than within the macrocosm. Given the association of lesser spirits with microcosm and supreme being with macrocosm, it follows from these facts that the former will be credited with direct responsibility for most events of human concern, will be the primary guardians of morality, and will be the objects of constant approach by human beings, whilst the latter will be credited with direct responsibility for relatively few events of human concern, will have no direct association with morality, and will seldom be approached by human beings.[47]

For Horton, it was the narrowness of their worldview that prevented most Africans from developing an elaborate concept of a supreme being and focused their attention on the network of lesser spirits. As a result, he argued, the supreme being was both remote and uninvolved in the moral concerns of microcosmic life; lesser spirits were the guardians of a local morality.

Studies of Diola concepts of the supreme being, Emitai, that relied primarily on the observation of ritual would support Horton's description of remote high gods, uninvolved in the activities of the microcosm or in issues of morality. Prayers made at the spirit shrines rarely invoked the name of Emitai; rather, they focused on carrying prayers to a particular spirit. Given a focus on Diola ritual life, Emitai appeared to be distant and uninvolved in matters of daily concern.[48]

Both David Sapir and Peter Mark reached similar conclusions. Sapir argues that Emitai had no role in determining human destiny: "In terms of traditional Diola belief, however *emit* remains a distant creative force, an unmoved mover that has nothing at all to do with the immediate, or even distant, fate of man, either during life or after death. It is with the *sinaati* [spirit shrines] that man must contend."[49] Mark also stressed Emitai's distance: "he was not directly concerned with the affairs of men. One did not approach him directly, either through prayer or sacrifice. Direct contact between men and spiritual forces was limited to the *sinaati*, which are occasionally described as intermediaries between man and God."[50] In a more recent work, Mark suggested that Christians and Muslims expanded the concept of Emitai within Diola religion through their equation of Emitai with Allah or with God. He dismissed any suggestion that Emitai was a moral force within Diola society: "The idea of a High God who keeps track of good and bad deeds is utterly foreign to the Diola."[51]

However, a very different view of Emitai emerges when informants are asked directly about the importance of a supreme being, the history of the various spirit shrines, and Diola concepts of life and death. It becomes clear that Emitai was active in the microcosm of Esulalu, both as a provider of the necessities of life and as a source of aid in times of troubles. The name of the supreme being, Emitai, was linked to the word *emit*, meaning both "sky" and "year," thus indicating a strong relationship between the supreme being and the sky and the order of the agricultural year. Furthermore, the term for rain, *Emitai ehlahl*, underscored Emitai's crucial role in the disbursement of that all-important resource. This linkage between rain, sky, and the supreme being is quite old. A dictionary compiled by the Compagnie Royale du Sénégal, around 1700, listed the word for "dieu" (god) as *hebitte* and the word for the sky as *himettai*. These are probably the same word, with a slight error in transcription.[52] In 1856 Emmanuel Bertrand-Bocandé also noted the close association of Emitai, rain, and fertility. "Their season has a name, it is the time of Emit, the time of the rains or the time of God (Emit in the Floup [Diola] language, signifies thunder, rain, God, power)."[53] Both the dictionary and the description of Emitai were recorded well before the opening of Christian missions within Diola areas and the Muslim invasions of the late nineteenth century.

Though people I encountered rarely talked about the creation of the world, Emitai was seen as its creator. There is a Diola proverb that illustrates this: "God made everything, even the little ants."[54] Emitai was seen as the source of human knowledge of cultivation, of fire and ironworking, and of healing. Emitai also established certain ways which these activities were to be carried out: a set of positive duties and a set of interdictions, ranging in intensity from merely bad manners to a heinous wrong or *gnigne*.[55] Emitai was described as all-knowing. When I asked whether Emitai hears the funeral prayer, one elder responded: "Well, what is Emitai? Emitai is the whole earth. It hears everything."[56] Nothing escaped the attention of Emitai. People were accountable to Emitai for their deeds and were obligated to live in accordance with duties received from It. However, "the burden that comes from Emitai is not heavy."[57]

Emitai communicated with humans through dreams and visions, selecting certain individuals to whom It revealed moral teachings, instructions about new spirit shrines, and advice about community problems. Such revelations were seen as inspiring the introduction of Bukut, the male circumcision ritual, and of Kasila, the rain shrine of Alinesitoué.[58] Oral traditions concerning the period before the colonial conquest in the late nineteenth century describe ten different men whom Emitai had selected, seven from Esulalu, whom It sent out to introduce various spirit shrines and teachings to Diola communities. Since the French occupation, however, more than forty prophets (literally, "those whom Emitai has sent"), most of whom are women, have emerged as religious leaders, using various means to teach Emitai's ways of retaining Diola traditions, procuring rain from Emitai, and resisting the fragmentation of religious communities by conversion to Islam or Christianity.[59]

Esulalu traditions contain many references to Diola who had revelations about the supreme being. The earliest account was of Atta-Essou, the founder of Eloudia, who was described as having had a series of visions from Emitai. His name means "of bird," which links his visionary role to that of birds, who are often seen as emissaries of the supreme being.[60] A man described as Atta-Essou's son, Aberman Manga, moved to Kadjinol and raised a large family before he, too, rose up to Emitai, leaving his descendants in charge of a spirit shrine that bears his name and that, until recently, was used for direct prayer to the supreme being.[61] In the eighteenth century, Kooliny Djabune, of Kadjinol, received the spirit shrine, Cabai, during a time when his soul was said to have gone up to Emitai.[62]

These traditions are also found in Huluf, the area immediately to the south of Esulalu. Djimilenekone Diatta, of the Huluf township of Kolobone, had visions of

Emitai during a period of famine. Based on his visions of Emitai, he introduced a spirit shrine that would assist people in obtaining a bountiful rice harvest. He told people to take mangrove branches, wild yams, papayas, and a small amount of rice. He would take these objects and perform a ritual, and then the small amount of rice would grow to fill a large pot. Mangrove trees, which grow in water, and papayas, with their moist fruit, are closely associated with the procurement of rain. When he died, it is said that birds carried him up to Emitai.[63]

Other accounts of men who were summoned by Emitai, leaving their bodies behind in the appearance of death, tended to assume a standardized form. At Kagnout-Bruhinban, a man with the family name of Sambou, whose first name was not mentioned because he died young, fell into a deep sleep, resembling death. Before he entered this sleep, he told his wife that Emitai "has summoned me." He told his wife " You should not cry. . . . You should not act as if I am dead." His soul was said to have gone up to Emitai. His wife did not follow his directions, however. Sambou had to tell Emitai: "Let me go quickly. My wife has summoned my death already." He returned to Kagnout to find that he had already been buried. He came back at night, a euphemism for the travel of spiritually powerful souls freed from their bodies, and told his wife that she had violated his instructions and caused his death. In another quarter of Kagnout, a man who was summoned to Emitai had a similar experience but was able to return before his funeral was completed. He lived, but the instructions that he was to have received were never completed.[64] These traditions shared a cliché which stressed the difficulties of communication with Emitai and the way that human concerns and social practices interfered with that communication. Nevertheless, there was a long-standing tradition of Emitai's attempts to reveal important teachings and new spirit shrines to the Diola. Clearly, Emitai was seen as an active force in the lives of the Diola and in the creation of the awasena path.

A second aspect of Emitai's attempt to communicate with the Diola was Its bestowing of certain powers on individuals. These powers included the ability to "see": to see spirits, witches, or far away events or to dream of events in the future, of spirits, or even of Emitai. "No one can teach you to 'see'. . . . Emitai shows you 'eyes' or It does not."[65] People with special mental powers could become messengers of Emitai or elders at important spirit shrines. Their powers were used to communicate with the spirits associated with shrines or with water spirits (ammahl), which might or might not be associated with shrines. Emitai's gift of special powers of "eyes" and "head" enabled people to receive visions, to have important dreams, and to see the spirits. They were important avenues for the renewal of the charismatic quality of the awasena path and for continued innovation in ritual practice.

Emitai provided a series of duties and obligations that accompanied the bestowal of these powers. Some individuals abused these powers in an attempt to gain wealth, power, or a large family. They were often said to be witches (kusaye).[66] Emitai was said to have created the witches, who took the lives of people when it was time for them to die, but some of them, seduced by the desire to consume the spiritual essences of human flesh, killed more than those designated by Emitai. Those who abused the power were punished by Emitai when they died. Those who received these special powers without abusing them, the *ahoonk*, worked for the good of the community and combated witches.[67] During those periods in human history when the power of witches dominated the world, Emitai chose to destroy it in the apocalypse of Adonai. The abuse of spiritual powers given by Emitai was a primary cause of evil in the world.[68]

Emitai punished human wrongdoing in this world and in the afterlife. In this world, as Thomas suggested: "It is a question of a basically religious sanction, that is to say willed by Ata-Emit [Emitai] and realized by the *ukin* (fetishes). Death, sickness, social failure, epidemics, excessive drought, are seen, for the individual and for the group, as certain indices of a known or unknown fault."[69] Emitai also passed judgment on the lives of the dead by deciding whether someone became an ancestor (*ahoeka*), a phantom (*ahoelra*), or a villager in a faraway land (*asandioume*). As an elder at Samatit suggested, "Ata-Emit will take you away. It will give you the word about what you have done" in your life and what your fate will be.[70]

From the preceding discussion, it becomes obvious that Emitai was actively involved in the Diola world, not only as a creative force but also as a continual bestower of life and rain, the establisher of moral obligations, and the ultimate judge of humanity's deeds. The Diola supreme being was neither remote nor inactive; rather, It provided the moral basis of the Diola world. While it was rare to pray directly to Emitai, most prayers addressed to the spirit shrines were relayed to Emitai. This hesitancy to address prayers to Emitai came from a sense of humility and a desire not to disturb It about the minor problems of daily life.[71]

In times of trouble, however, in times of drought, of serious illness, or community calamity, it was thought that Emitai would hear the community's prayers directly, without the mediation of spirit shrines. During droughts, Diola would perform a rite known as nyakul emit in which women conducted rituals at fertility shrines and requested that men do the same at their shrines. This rite was followed by a direct invocation of Emitai.[72] Thomas recorded one such prayer to Emitai: "'Ata-Emit, is it true that this year's rice is destined to wither in the rice paddies? *Ohe!* The other year's famine was bad—but this time the misfortune will be so large that we will not have the strength to speak. Give us water, give us life."[73] Emitai was addressed as the guardian of fertility, of good harvests, human fecundity, and abundant rain. Emitai assured the continuity of life from one generation to the next, as this prayer suggests:

Atan Batun, Our Father,
It is You, who has made us,
As you made our ancestors,
As you made the boekine
As you have made all that is,
We thank you.
Give us peace.
Give the rain that makes the rice paddies fertile.
Give us many children,
Who will come to honor you
And who will make us beautiful funerals.

Give us strength to farm.
Atan Batun, Our Father
You who made the boekine for us,
Make it so that they obey you.
As we obey you.
That our granaries will be full
That the bellies of our women will be fertile
That peace will reign among us
Atan Batun, you are our Father.
We thank you,
We supplicate you,
Because without you, we could no longer exist.[74]

Central to a Diola system of thought was the idea that Emitai created the spirit shrines and bestowed them with power. It was mentioned twice in the Diola-Dyiwat prayer just cited and appears in the histories of many shrines and in the explanation of the role of ukine as intermediaries between Emitai and humans. Many people in Esulalu claimed that "Emitai made the ukine."[75] Recently, people have suggested that Emitai created the ukine for the Diola, just as It created Christianity for the Europeans and Islam for the Mandinka.[76]

An examination of the histories of the ukine reveals that many of them were said to have been created by Emitai. As Thomas suggested: "The original fetish is, in most cases, revealed by God and given by him to man."[77] Emitai created the ukine in order to establish specific ways for individuals, families, or communities to seek assistance in the resolution of their problems. Thus, Kasila was used to address problems of drought, Ehugna for fertility, and Cabai for war. Each of these shrines was created during a time of crisis when people called on Emitai, who responded by creating a new spirit shrine and revealing it to someone It selected.

This brief examination of the role of Emitai in a Diola system of thought raises serious questions about Horton's, Sapir's, and Mark's representations of African or, more specifically, Diola conceptions of supreme beings. Emitai intervenes within the microcosm of township affairs when conditions warrant it. Furthermore, Its establishment of moral injunctions for individuals and Its central role in the judgment of the dead provides clear evidence of the close association of the supreme being with a Diola ethical system. Diola cosmology is monocentric; Emitai is an active but transcendent force, from whom all lesser spirits derive their power. Moreover, Emitai is directly involved with a prophetic tradition, going back to the foundation accounts of some Esulalu communities. Emitai is closely associated with many of the significant innovations within the awasena tradition, through Its revelation of new teachings, ritual practices, and spirit shrines.

The Ukine: Spirit and Spirit Shrines in Awasena Tradition

The most visible aspect of Diola religious practice was the many rituals performed at the spirit shrines in the townships or nearby sacred forests. Fundamental to the awasena path was the multiplicity of spirit shrines. Thomas listed more than a hundred different Diola shrines; my own inquiries yielded forty-eight types in a single quarter of Kadjinol.[78] Almost every economic activity of the community had a boekine associated with it, be it palm wine tapping, fishing, blacksmithing, or farming. Other shrines were important for healing, either as diagnostic shrines or for treating specific disorders. Others were concerned with the perennial problems of rain, crop fertility, and the fertility of women. There were several shrines associated with war, the well-being of the community, and township governance. Finally, there were ukine associated with the extended family and the lineage. For each type of problem there were several types of shrines. This multiplicity of shrines helped to ensure that one method could resolve the problem of the supplicant individual or group. It also encouraged broad access to religious authority; with so many ukine in a small community, chances were excellent that any given individual would become an elder or priest of at least one shrine. In such an egalitarian society, where individual prerogatives were carefully guarded, a majority of adults at one time or another exercised spiritual authority.

The shrines themselves, while on sanctified ground, did not contain the spirits associated with them. They contained ritual objects associated with the spirits that helped to summon them and that helped the worshipers to concentrate on the spirits that were being invoked. "The sanctuary and the altar are only the representatives of the *boekine*; it is to the spirit that Diola practice their cult, not to the sacred wood or to the sacrificial stone."[79] The most powerful ukine often appeared to be nothing more than a hole in the ground or a forked stick, whereas less important shrines might be more elaborate. In many cases, however, hidden inside the shrine was a series of medicines or symbols, designed to attract the spirit to the altar. They were buried secretly as the altar was being constructed and often contained soil from an older shrine.

Some ukine received a cult virtually on a daily basis because of the large number of individuals who sought their assistance. Others, especially the shrines associated with rain, received communitywide rituals at fixed times, with perhaps as much as a year separating ritual activities. Thomas noted six reasons for requesting a ritual: a request for something; a need for purification; what Thomas would call a "desire for vengeance," but I would describe as ritual accusations or mediation of disputes; a desire to be at peace or restore health; a need for rain; and a need to preserve oneself against all difficulties.[80] I would add a seventh reason, a periodic need to greet the ukine that were important to one's household or that had been of assistance in the past. The most frequented shrines, such as Kadjinol's Gilaite, Houle, and Ehugna, became foci of the social life of the community, as well as important ritual centers. In the daily participation in ritual life and the socializing afterward, the elders became a cohesive group. In less restricted ritual activities, young people were socialized into the ways of the elders. In the ordinary greeting of ukine, there was a fairly standard form in which the prayers were presented. Usually the supplicant would present ten liters of palm wine to the priest of the shrine and, in certain cases, an animal. A portion of the palm wine was poured into a piece of pottery or a wooden goblet associated with the shrine. Punctuated by libations of palm wine, the priest summoned the boekine and greeted it. Then an elder of the supplicant's compound would pray and the priest would repeat the prayer, once again punctuating it with libations of palm wine. The following is a prayer of greetings to a boekine.

> Palm wine of Sindé, the father of Koomaswai, the father of Djabune, he brought the palm wine for the rite. . . . Djabune brought the palm wine to salute you. Leave Djabune all that is good for his children, his brothers and his people. He should not have to ask this again. The family of Sindé will not repeat their request. Today he came to greet you. Greet him. From his sleeping place, for tomorrow, do all that you can. Today they came, he who was born of Sindé and Koomaswai. Today we are finished. Give to his children strong bodies; his wife who has children, give her a sweet body. Now Djabune's wife has children. Now Djabune has children. Leave all of his children in peace. Leave Djabune with only the good. My speech is over. My voice is finished. Djabune's palm wine from the family of Koomaswai, who fathered Djabune, who brought the palm wine. Leave his house in peace.[81]

Strong emphasis was placed on the family line: A supplicant at a men's shrine prays in the name of his father and his grandfather, who were better known to the boekine and who were closer to the time of the "first ancestors."

The libations of palm wine and sacrifices of animals were performed to attract the spirit to the shrine and to increase the power of the supplicant's prayers. The spirits and, in certain cases, the ancestors came and drank the palm wine and the blood of the animal. "If you have not given it [the boekine] something to eat, it will not come." The spirit preferred a rite that included animal sacrifice: "It is like with us when we make rice, but there is no fish. The rice is bad, plain white rice."[82] Both the palm wine and the blood were said to contain a soul. "Palm wine is like blood. If you cut into a tree, it comes out. Blood is like water, it gives life."[83] The soul of the palm wine and of the sacrificial animal nourished the spirit and released a power that strengthened the words of the ritual specialist. One of the major priests described how he could not see the spirit at the shrine, but after the ritual was completed, he could hear it. The spirit would talk to him.[84] Thomas analyzed the significance of the Diola ritual process: "At this moment, the soul of the priest, by intermediary of the word (kabag) alerts the fetish . . . , while the soul of the rice, the wine, or the blood spread on the altar nourish the boekine. This last thing provokes it at the level of thought (buhinum) and enriched by the vital force, enters into communication with God Himself."[85] Bound by the ingestion of the word, a spiritual link emerged between priest and spirit, who carried the word to Emitai. This was the ritual ideal; failure was frequent because of the inconsistency of the spirits and of humans. The communicants' partaking of the palm wine and the meat of the sacrifice bound each individual to the prayers. Any ill thought could undermine the spiritual power of the congregation and diminish the efficacy of the ritual.

While it was generally agreed that the ukine serve as intermediaries between humans and Emitai, Diola elders were not in agreement on the degree of independence that the various spirits possessed. Some argued that the spirits simply relayed the prayers of humans to Emitai and enforced Emitai's will in the world.[86] Others saw the ukine as exercising their own powers and deciding themselves whether to carry a particular prayer to Emitai, whether to refuse to do so, or whether to take action themselves. Only people with special powers to "see" the spirits could understand the behavior of a spirit shrine. Hupila family shrines were a particularly whimsical group of spirits; their mischievous and unpredictable characters were often commented upon. A prayer directed to a spirit shrine called Elenkine demonstrated the independent power of spirits and their ability to deny a priest's requests.

> Make it so that God will give water like I pray.
> All of the village has come behind me.
> In order that I be their intermediary between you and God.
> You are the fetish, I come before you to perform my libation.
> It is your task to go before God.
> This is all that I will say to you. It is for you to pardon me.
> Go to God, do not humiliate me before my people.[87]

At least in some cases, it was the choice of the spirit shrine whether to carry prayers to Emitai.

Part of the reason for the debate about the autonomy of ukine is that there were different types of spirits. Although knowledge of spirits was among the most closely guarded secrets of particular shrines and few individuals would admit to the power of "seeing" in the spiritual realm, one could distinguish four types of beings associated with the ukine. In the case of the shrines associated with community governance, like Hutendookai and Duhow, the spirits were seen as messengers, created by Emitai to sanctify and relay the decisions of the community, almost in a mechanical fashion. The powers or distinctive characters of these spirits were rarely discussed. The elders of Hutendookai sent their assistants, the *kumachala*, to enforce their decisions rather than relying on punishment by the spirit shrine itself.

In other cases, the spirit of the shrine could be communicated with and was considered visible to those who had "eyes" to see. In such cases, they were described in anthropomorphic terms as "children of Emitai. Emitai made them."[88] They were portrayed as human in form, either white or black, very hairy, and physically deformed. Like people these spirits grew old, married, had children, died, and were reincarnated (though always as spirits). These spirits could be either male or female. Like people, their moods could change without reason and they could be pleaded with or coaxed into answering one's prayers. However, as Kapooeh Diedhiou pointed out, "they must seize you. . . . if you perform a ritual, they will forgive. If you do not heed it, you will die."[89] Different spirits linked to the same shrine could display different temperaments. This was especially true of the family shrine of Hupila, where each extended family summoned a particular spirit, who then acted according to its own will.

Another type of being, the ammahl (literally, "of the water"), was less closely associated with the system of spirit shrines. Some ammahl, like other spirits, revealed themselves at such important shrines as Elenkine Sergerh, a town quarter shrine for the Kalybillah half of Kadjinol; Enac, a similar shrine for Samatit; and Calemboekine, the sacred forest shrine of the oeyi or priest-king. Shrines associated with ammahl were consulted about the wisdom of certain decisions, such as going to war. Their role as advisors was as important as their roles as intermediaries.[90] Other ammahl, however, chose not to have shrines created for them, but preferred to reveal themselves to individuals. Some ammahl provided new sources of knowledge about healing, war, farming, and other important and socially useful activities. Others offered individuals special knowledge for private gain—unusual skills to acquire wealth, to become a successful hunter, or to sustain a large family. However, these ammahl asked a price—perhaps the strength of the person's leg, leaving him lame; perhaps the life of one's child, which would be surrendered to the ammahl.[91] They could work through the community, at the spirit shrines, or in private appearances to gifted individuals. The ammahl could be a force for the public good or for personal advancement. They could also refuse to communicate with people altogether and act against those who sought them out.

The final group of beings associated with the ukine were the spirits of benevolent ancestors. They were summoned to the shrine of the dead, Kouhouloung, during all funeral rites and memorial rites and during the periodic greetings of the Kouhouloung shrine.[92] They also assisted at the rites of the family shrine, Hupila, and the various lineage-related shrines, such as Houlinway of the Diedhiou families and Housenghalene of the Senghor-Djikune families. These ancestors served as intermediaries between the place of the dead (*kahoeka*) and their living descendants. They were also sources of various types of information that they revealed through their appearance in dreams. They gave advice and warnings to their descendants among the living.

The role of the ukine was not limited to relaying messages between humans and the spiritual world. They seized wrongdoers with illnesses or hounded them in dreams. Such illnesses were seen as a sign of wrongdoing and a call for purification. "An illness, a death, a bad harvest, or whatever misfortune appears as a certain indicator of a fault that may not be intentionally committed, but of which he is definitely the author."[93] In cases of disputes between two people that were taken to a spirit shrine, the party in the wrong was the one who fell ill. Particular shrines and offenses often had their own disease or symptoms. Theft was punished with leprosy, a disease sent by the blacksmith shrine, Gilaite. Men's offenses against women were punished by a swelling of the stomach that resembled pregnancy, which was sent by the women's fertility shrine of Ehugna. Ukine also punished individuals for failing to provide promised sacrifices to the spirit shrines themselves.[94]

A person who was seized with an illness that resisted ordinary cures would seek out a priest of one of the divinatory shrines or someone who had the power to see beneath the surface of things. At the divinatory shrine of Bruinkaw, the spirit was said to speak, and the priest merely translated for the supplicant, thereby revealing the cause of the illness. In other cases, the priest or elders of the shrine would delay an answer until a dream provided them with a cause of the illness. Usually the priest identified the spirit that was involved, which lead to the victim's confession of misdeeds or the shrine elders' accusations of wrongdoing against the victim of the illness.[95] Once the causes and agents of the affliction were ascertained, a set of rituals were prescribed. Linares described the importance of confession and purification in these rites.

A *bakiin* traps a guilty person with symptoms general enough to require "divination" by an *awasenao* [ritual specialist] but specific enough to signal to the sick or otherwise misfortuned person which spirit may have trapped him and which *awasenao* to consult. By facilitating confession, expiation, and atonement by sacrificing an animal and contributing palm wine for communal feasting, the practitioner(s) is (are) in fact sponsoring a social act, a ritual of reintegration and reaffirmation of the solidarity of the residential group, through which an individual recovers his health and moral worth.[96]

In certain cases the ukine seized people whom they had selected to become elders of their particular cult. Hupila seized people whom it wanted to establish shrines by afflicting them with pains all over their bodies. Houlang seized people with fits of madness until they assumed responsibilities of ritual leadership. Bruinkaw also inflicted illnesses as a way of summoning people to ritual office. For many Diola, disease could be a sign of spiritual election; those who weathered an illness sent by a spirit shrine could cure through its power.[97]

The ukine became known in Esulalu in a variety of ways. The oldest were said to have been created at the time of the "first ancestors," in a time that was well beyond the longest of Esulalu genealogies. In the case of other spirit shrines, however, there were several modes of introduction. Some shrines were introduced by the Koonjaen, a people who inhabited parts of Esulalu before the arrival of the present inhabitants. Others were introduced by people who had special powers, who were said to have traveled up to Emitai or to have made contact with spirits in dreams or visions. Others were given to people who had special powers to see ammahl. Still others were borrowed from neighboring peoples in the Casamance or Guinea-Bissau region. While traveling outside Esulalu, people might encounter a cult that interested them. They would inquire about the spirit shrine, perform a series of rituals there, and then invite the elders of the shrine to come and establish a shrine in Esulalu. Another method of introducing shrines was for one township to give a shrine to another community. Elders of the shrine would come and establish it in the new community and instruct a group of local elders about its rituals, as a way of solidifying friendship between the two communities or as a reward for assistance in time of war.

Although the spirit shrines could be created in a variety of ways, the regularity of their cults depended on their ability to enter into the lives of the community. Shrines associated with healing had to be seen as able to cure illnesses. Shrines of the forge had to be able to protect blacksmiths. Otherwise, they risked the loss of supplicants or the abandonment of the shrine. The power of the ukine depended on the skill of the priests and elders, as well. A particularly wise or adept shrine elder might give a shrine a reputation for power that went far beyond what it had enjoyed under previous elders.[98] The ability of the spirit to appear to members of the community in dreams or visions, to instruct them, or to provide them with special knowledge was also important in the continuing ritual activity of a spirit shrine (boekine). A boekine that failed in its instrumental function and failed to penetrate the collective unconscious of the community was abandoned.[99] Within Esulalu, new ukine were introduced and older ones abandoned, thereby creating a dynamism to the awasena path that belied the claim of continuity with the time of the "first ancestors."

Concepts of the Human

In discussing Diola concepts of a supreme being and lesser spirits, it becomes clear that the central focus of Diola thought was on people and their relationship with Emitai and the spiritual intermediaries It created. Thomas claimed that Emitai's willingness to create intermediaries for humans was a sign that they were the only beings with the special capacity of thought (bruinom) that was capable of moral choice.[100] Within the Diola's anthropocentric view of the world, humans exercised a considerable degree of free will. While it was thought that everything was contingent on the will of Emitai, It was not viewed as operating on every detail of mundane existence. Emitai operated in terms of general laws, which did not extend to the minutiae of daily life. The spirit shrines, as watchdogs over human behavior, limited people's freedom of choice but did not control it. Through their knowledge of their duties as members of a community and members of families, people could manipulate the possibilities before them, at least to lessen the misfortune of bad fates. There is a Diola proverb, "Conjunctivitis is better than blindness," which means people can choose the lesser of two evils.[101] The ukine could be bargained with or flattered with lavish rituals. The Diola "knows that he depends on God and the genie; but the latter are not really harmful and it is always possible to act upon them through sacrifices that eventually will move them to pity. In fact, the fetisher always has the last word."[102] Humans could appeal to Emitai directly through urgent prayers, or through public rites of humiliation that underscored the supplicant's desperate straits. Emitai and various spirits limited human freedom, but there remained a considerable area where humans actively chose their paths. They were held accountable to Emitai at the time of death; decisions in life determined one's fate in the afterlife.

The vital principle is located within the soul (yahl), which is said to be located in the chest and flows through the body in the blood. One Kadjinol elder described it: "The soul houses the life of a person."[103] Another elder stressed its importance: "Without a soul, one could not think. Without a soul, one would not be alive."[104] Created by Emitai, the soul remained a mysterious force that was essential to the maintenance of life. It was also closely related to the mind and its capacity for rational thought. The soul was divisible into several parts, some of which could leave the body and move about, lodge in trees, or provide an intangible link to certain types of animals. The soul could leave the body during dreams; a person's experiences in such dreams were considered real but lived within a different plane of existence. They could be a source of spiritual knowledge, as the priest-king of Kadjinol suggested: "You go to sleep and dream. . . . What you see in your dreams will happen, then you know. It is said that you leave your body here and your soul goes."[105] Souls could also leave the body to harm their neighbors who had aroused their anger or jealousy. A severe illness or an emotional shock could force the soul out of the body. In such instances an awasena healer had to guide the soul back to the patient or the patient would die. At the time of death, the soul became unified and left the body. Only the soul passed into the afterlife.[106]

Many Diola thought that people and animals were spiritually linked through the existence of animal doubles, or *siwuum*. Every individual in Esulalu had a certain number of siwuum who shared parts of a common soul.[107] They could include a wide variety of animals: pythons, mambas, crocodiles, hippopotami, elephants, leopards, monkeys, antelopes, lizards, and sharks.[108] Siwuum were wild, animals of the bush or the sea, who were beyond the control of the community. They could be seen, but only people with special powers could distinguish them from ordinary animals. However, an animal that hung around a family compound and held its ground when approached was liable to be an animal double rather than an ordinary creature. Through some sort of mysterious bond, double and person felt each others' physical and emotional sensations: "The totem is born at the same time as the man, is sick like him, experiences the same joys, the same sorrows, and the death of one leads fatally to that of the other."[109] The double and the person shared a common soul and could not withstand the loss of the other.

The reasons for this mysterious link can be understood in terms of Diola biology and social obligations. The biological basis of the concept of animal doubles arose from the Diola idea of how life was created. The blood of the man, located in the semen, and the blood of the woman united to create a new life and a multiplicity of souls. Parts of the new souls, reflecting their diverse origins, entered into the bodies of animals, who returned to the homes from which the newly conceived person received blood and a portion of the soul. One double remained at the father's home with his agnatic kin, while others went to wherever the newborn had uterine kin. The system of doubles "replicates the original parental source of the individual."[110] One had doubles at one's birthplace and at those of one's mother, father's mother, and mother's mother. Animal doubles provided material bodies for the multiple sources of the individual. Socially, it provided a model for kinship relations. A separate creature that shared part of one's consciousness was under the protection of each of one's kinship groups. Neglect of a person's obligations to aid kinfolk could lead them to retaliate against him through the animal double.[111]

The siwuum system also bound individuals to their ritual obligations at the spirit shrines of their kinfolk. The obligation to attend the Housiquekou rites, when all the maternal kin came back to their uterine home and greeted the family spirits, received tangible reinforcement because the maternal kin lived with vulnerable animal doubles. Sufficient neglect could lead to serious consequences, even death. For example, Siopama Diedhiou described the dangers of neglecting one's obligations to greet the family's shrine associated with the blacksmith's lineage: "If you don't go to do the rites, they [the doubles] will all die. . . . If you don't do the rites, they won't let the doubles drink [water]. You will fall ill. They will instruct you to go to the rites."[112] A man's kin also performed rites to protect their kinfolk's doubles. In the rite of Kahit, an infant was brought to the shrine of the dead, Kouhouloung, Ekunga, Aberman, or another spirit shrine associated with particular lineages. During the ritual, the newborn's animal doubles were asked to stay within the area of the family shrines, in the shrine itself, or in a nearby spirit tree, inhabited both by ancestors and animal doubles.[113] This suggests the possibility that animal doubles were intermediaries between ancestors and their living descendants.

Visions of the Afterlife

Diola visions of the afterlife stressed the importance of human moral accountability and the judgment of Emitai. People's fate in the afterlife depended on their deeds in this life. When someone died, Kouhouloung reported to Emitai about the conduct of the deceased. The prayers, eulogies, and sacrifices performed at Kouhouloung during funeral rites were also carried to Emitai. Based on this information, Emitai decided between one of three possible fates. "Emitai will pay you. It will send you what you want. If you have done good, very good. . . . you cannot become a phantom [ahoelra]. If you violate things, then you are a phantom. If you did not violate things, then you become an *ahoeka*," an ancestor who lives near the family compound. The concept of ahoeka is quite old; it was listed in the seventeenth century dictionary compiled by associates of the Compagnie Royale du Sénégal.[114]

Evildoers were transformed into phantoms, who were condemned to wander in the bush alone and beyond the borders of the townships. Their fate was described in vivid terms. Phantoms were attacked by hyenas, who ate their arms and legs. Then hordes of mosquitoes descended upon them, but they were unable to swat them away. The arms and legs grew out again, and the process repeated itself, over and over again. After a certain amount of time, they died and were reborn (*ewe*) into this world. However, the misdeeds that caused their punishment in their former lives could not be repeated in the next. Occasionally, people were considered so evil that they were reincarnated as cattle.[115]

Those who led good lives became kahoeka, spirits of benevolent ancestors. While invisible, they lived in the townships and served as intermediaries between the living and the spiritual world by appearing to their descendants in dreams. The spirit shrine, Kouhouloung, was controlled by kahoeka, and they performed a crucial role in funeral rites. They helped their kin by warning them about witches, assisting at rituals, and informing them about future events or current duties.[116] For many Diola, the most blessed state one could achieve was that of ahoeka, an ancestor who served his or her kin among the living by helping them in the world of the spirit.

There was a third possible fate, that of being sent to Housandioume. Housandioume was a place that was far away to the south, a place where the dead lived much like they did when they were alive in Esulalu. This continued until they died again and were reborn. However, there were considerable differences in interpretation concerning who was sent there. According to Elizabeth Sambou, they were people "who die and then rise up again . . . the soul did not leave." Emitai decided who would rise from the dead and who would be exiled to Housandioume.

Those who were familiar with Christian doctrine equated it with purgatory, a place for those who committed misdeeds but who were not evil people. Some claimed that Housandioume was a place for those who died so prematurely that no moral judgment could be made about them. Unlike ancestors and phantoms, inhabitants of Housandioume maintained no connection with the village, either geographically or ritually, until they were reincarnated.[117]

The concept of reincarnation provided fluidity to Diola eschatology and a way of recirculating the life forces of the dead into the land of the living. At death, people became ancestors, phantoms, or asandioume, depending on Emitai's judgment of their moral worth. However, reincarnation rendered all these judgments impermanent. The evildoer was consigned to temporary damnation and then returned to the living. The righteous initially became ancestors and then were reincarnated as their own descendants. Many cited cases of small children who knew all the boundaries of the rice paddies or the esoteric knowledge of a particular boekine as evidence of reincarnation. Certain people claimed to remember their past lives.[118]

Ethics and Misconduct

Central to a Diola vision of the afterlife was Emitai's establishment of a series of moral injunctions which everyone was obligated to follow. To understand Emitai's judgment, it is important to examine a Diola system of ethics that was seen as coming from Emitai's instructions to the first ancestors. Fundamental to Diola concepts of morality was a sense that a series of calamities would result from a single prohibited act. For example, the theft of rice not only violated a deep-rooted Diola work ethic but also threatened the livelihoods of the entire farming community. Similarly, marriage to a distant cousin who lived in the same compound complicated the siwuum system and could split the compound into two factions if the marriage turned sour. Finally, one respected the restrictions on ritual knowledge, not only because an indiscretion could diminish the power of the shrines but also because it could place the hearer in danger.[119] Thomas saw a violation of an interdiction as creating problems at three levels: "it is contrary to nature, that is the equilibrium of forces making up reality. . . . it is a failure to recognize one's obligations to the spirits, that is rebellion and negation . . . it is a blow to the social order, that which risks to involve collective troubles that are more or less serious."[120]

The intent of the wrongdoer was also an important consideration. An involuntary act was less serious than one committed with the intent to violate the rules of the community. There were also degrees of seriousness to people's actions. That which was absolutely forbidden (gnigne) placed perpetrators in a state of pollution that could harm them and their families unless it was ritually removed. Such offenses included violating the rules of the ukine, menstrual avoidances, theft, and murder. Other offenses carried no pollution, only the disdain or mockery of the community. These acts were considered "bad" and included drunkenness, gluttony, miserliness, cruelty, and vanity. There were large areas of morally neutral acts, recommended behaviors, and, finally, positive obligations. The insane, the spiritually possessed, the senile, and small children were exempted from moral obligations to the extent that their conditions interfered with their judgment.[121]

Diola ethics also stressed the importance of community solidarity and egalitarianism. This was evident in their fear of anyone's gaining control over too many ukine or becoming too influential in township councils.[122] The necessity for cooperative work in herding animals, building dams, fencing the paddies, and roofing houses all reminded Diola of their interdependence. There is a proverb that illustrates this point: "With one straw one cannot cover a roof." Generosity was another value illustrated by proverbs: "A miser is buried in only one cloth."[123] This meant that a miser would not have people bringing gifts of death cloths for his or her burial. Only the immediate family would supply the deceased, and he or she would be buried with only one cloth. Another proverb, "If you give out tobacco one bit at a time, then your wife will leave you," also emphasized the obligation to be generous. Individuals were also obligated to help someone who needed rice; they could not reveal the name of the person who came to them, or they ran the risk of falling into a similar plight. Finally, Diola had to respect their elders by helping them in their work, deferring to their opinions, and by observing certain ritual avoidances.[124]

Although the practice has become less common, marriages were often arranged while children were quite young. As the children grew up, the boy and his family would pay occasional visits and bring gifts of palm wine. When the children were of marriageable age, as early as fifteen for a girl or eighteen for a boy, either one could break the engagement. Some parents forced their children to marry, but this seems to have been fairly rare. Within Esulalu, most marriages were monogamous, though occasionally a man took a second wife.[125] The blacksmith families with the surname Diedhiou and the Senghor-Djikune families were both exogamous. Other people with the same surname could intermarry, provided they were not closely related enough to have siwuum at the same compound.[126]

Diola families were patrilineal; all children received their father's name and remained within his family. Either husband or wife could decide on a divorce, though it could not occur during the planting or harvest season. Such a divorce would disrupt the family unit of production that was so important to Diola economic survival. While it was easy for a wife to divorce her husband, she could not take the children with her. Within the family, the husband was regarded as the senior partner, but the wife had a substantial degree of autonomy. She could offer her views freely, criticize, and even mock her husband's decisions. Fear of the women's shrine, Ehugna, and the ease of divorce pressured men to respect their wives and to refrain from abuse.

There was a second form of marriage, *boodji*, that was available to widowed and divorced women of childbearing age. Every three to ten years, a meeting was held in which all the unattached, previously married women of the township were required to choose a husband. Their choices could not refuse them. The elders of the community shrine of Hutendookai would fine any woman who refused to choose or any man who refused his selection. The new couple were obligated to live together for a trial period of several months. If they continued to live together after that time, they were considered married.[127]

Although the people of Esulalu strove to perform good acts in their daily lives, they often failed to live up to their obligations. In cases of serious misconduct, the violation of what is forbidden, they could cause a host of calamities for themselves and their families. The ukine seized people who violated Diola codes of behavior. A serious illness, termite infestations,or fire could be a sign of punishment by the spirit shrines or by Emitai. The disease could also strike relatives of the guilty person. Thus the son of a man who stole rice might be stricken with leprosy. When asked about the justice of punishing the innocent son, one elder replied that the son had eaten the rice, thereby sharing the fruits of his father's actions, and that the family shared responsibility and could be punished until the misdeed was righted. A murderer might cause his own death and that of his entire family.[128] There was a collective sense of guilt in the Diola ethical system. The family was bound by blood; it survived as a unit, and it shared the benefits and misfortunes caused by the conduct of its members.

In many cases of criminal activity, the community did not know the identity of the guilty party. In cases of theft, the wronged party could go to certain ukine and make an accusation against a specific suspect or simply ask that whoever stole from him be punished. Frequently, the guilty party, upon hearing of the ritual, would return the goods and attempt to rectify the crime by confession and ritual purification, rather than run the risk of leprosy.[129] The elders of Hutendookai could investigate accusations of theft and witchcraft, but they punished with the power of the community rather than the power of disease. Hutendookai imposed fines of livestock, rice, or money as punishment for refusing to participate in collective work obligations, villagewide rituals, or marketing decisions.

Until the colonial era, only the priest-king had authority over cases of murder. Once guilt was ascertained, the priest-king banished the murderer from the community, confiscated his or her rice paddies, and auctioned them off for cattle. Five of these cattle were sacrificed at the most important township shrines.[130] After the purification of the township was completed, the family of the murderer purified itself by sacrificing a bull at Calemboekine, the most important royal shrine and the shrine that watches over the main cemetery.

Moral wrongdoing left perpetrators and their families in an unclean state that had to be removed by rites of confession and purification. When someone committed offenses against men's shrines, against the dead, or against cattle, the perpetrator summoned the priests of the shrine Djimamo for a rite of confession. It might be that a woman accidentally saw a cemetery while visiting Dakar, or a man killed a cow that was invading his fields. All these offenses required an initial confession and, in most cases, a second rite involving animal sacrifice.[131] For serious offenses against the land, including usurpation of rice paddies, or revelations of restricted knowledge, many people went to Huluf, to the Elung shrine, for confession and ritual purification. At Samatit, people took such cases to the Enac shrine. Offenses involving witchcraft could be confessed at the shrine of the elders, Hoohaney, at Gilaite, or at the circumcision shrine, Bukut.[132]

A major women's shrine, Kahoosu or Djilem, was the site for confession of infractions against women. Men who acted improperly toward women or who violated menstrual avoidances (even inadvertently) purified themselves there. On the eve of circumcision, all uncircumcised boys performed the rite of Kahoosu so that they would be pure during their ordeal. Women who acted improperly, according to the responsibilities of women in Esulalu, or who failed to respect the ukine also confessed at Kahoosu. A person who traveled outside the Diola areas of the Casamance performed confessional rites at Kahoosu because of the possibility of having violated certain interdictions that were important to the Diola but not to other ethnic groups or the nonobservant populations of urban areas. In cases of minor infractions or of confession of only the possibility of committing an offense, the supplicant carried a container of rice to the shrine precincts. The supplicant audibly listed the violations he or she committed or could have committed. The destructive force linked to these actions passed into the rice before it was thrown away at the shrine. For more serious offenses, the supplicant also brought a chicken or a goat, which was left to roam the shrine precincts. Only the priestess and elders of the shrine could gather up the rice and animals and use them for food. To all others, they were contaminated with the misdeeds of those who had confessed.[133]

To many Diola, evil was a tangible force, capable of being passed out of a person and into an object, through the rite of confession. Confession purified by bringing into the light of the shrine the nefarious forces that worked internally. Ritual sacrifice allowed the life force, the soul of palm wine and animals, to cleanse the wrongdoers. At times, the entire community would come together to remove the force of evil within the township. On several occasions, the women's cult of Ehugna exorcised destructive forces from the Kafone quarter of Kadjinol. In 1978, such forces were seen as centering around a clearing where wrestling matches were held. It was said to be causing disease. One night, men and women gathered at the shrine associated with the maternity house, Houssana, and performed rituals to carry this destructive forced away to a stream that flowed into the Casamance River. By dawn, it had been carried far away from the Esulalu townships, and the communities were safe.[134]

Another source of life-destructive force was the power of witches (kusaye). It was said that Emitai gave them the gift of special powers to see beyond the material world, to travel at night without their bodies, and to transform themselves into animals. They were given these powers in order to eat the souls of people when their appointed time to die had come. As Sikakucele Diatta pointed out, "Emitai only does what is good. Emitai sends witches to bring those people It has already killed. . . . It says take that person."[135] However, in many cases, this power corrupted them and they became captives of their hunger for human flesh, a hunger that was satisfied by the souls of kusaye eating the souls of ordinary people. The priest-king of Kadjinol compared this corrupting process to giving birth to a child: "You have a child; perhaps it will be evil." Emitai punished those who abused the power It gave them.[136] Motivated by jealousy or greed, kusaye attacked their neighbors by carrying off the victims' souls, leaving them like husks of rice with no substance or strength to sustain life. The increasing corruption of the kusaye was cited as a reason that Emitai destroyed the world in the apocalypse of Adonai.[137]

Witchcraft accusations have a corrosive effect on community and family solidarity. Because witches act only at night and their work involves the souls of apparently sleeping people, a husband or wife may not know if the other is a witch. When the waves of accusations begin, often after several inexplicable deaths, spouses and neighbors can no longer depend on each other's support. Frequently the accusations arise out of personal vendettas or jealousies, rather than from dreams or visions. These accusations are often described as "politique," with the strong implication of dishonest and self-serving motives.[138]

Despite the suspicious quality of many of the accusations, the fear of kusaye was quite genuine. Many ukine were known for their ability to detect kusaye or to provide medicines to be worn or placed in the house to protect against witchcraft.[139] Certain people, known as ahoonk, were given the same powers as witches, but they refused to take the lives of others. Their ability to see and to travel at night allowed them to warn their relatives and neighbors of attacks and to battle against the witches directly.[140]

Life and Death in Esulalu

Many Diola conceived of life as a cyclical process that began at birth, continued through childhood and adulthood, and, at death, passed into an afterlife, which ended with reincarnation. This vision of life influenced Diola concepts of the relationships among people, lesser spirits, and Emitai and of community ethics and history. Life began when the blood of a male, located in his semen, mixed with the blood of a female within her uterus. During pregnancy the expectant mother continued her normal work routines and continued to have sexual relations, since semen was seen as a source of nourishment and strength for the developing fetus.[141] When she went into labor, however, she had to go immediately to the maternity house. Until recently, this was located in a forested area on the edge of the township. No man could enter the premises. A group of maternity elders and the elders of the women's fertility shrine of Ehugna helped the woman with her delivery. Any violations of Diola moral codes, particularly adultery, had to be confessed, or the woman ran the risk of a dangerous delivery. After giving birth, mothers remained in the maternity for six days. Before the establishment of the new maternities, senior women used this time to instruct a new mother in her responsibilities as a woman in Diola society and to initiate her into some of the special knowledge and rites that were reserved for childbearing women.[142] During this time an awasena father could not approach the maternity house or receive any news about the condition of mother or child. Childbirth was considered the exclusive domain of women. A man who witnessed a childbirth placed his life in jeopardy.[143]

Awasena parents presented their infant children to the various spirit shrines that were important to the family. They might request the protection of a major shrine, such as Gilaite or the Houle, so that a child would grow up safe from the menaces of disease and witches. In the rite of Kahit, an infant was presented to the shrine of the dead, Kouhouloung, so that the ancestors would know the child and so that the child's animal doubles would be protected. Offerings were made at the priest-king's shrine, Calemboekine, so that the spirit of the shrine, which symbolized the unity of the whole community, would know its new member and not act against it as a stranger.[144]

Diola children were educated through a combination of informal instruction and formal initiations. On a daily basis, parents and elders demonstrated the proper way of doing things and instructed their children about their responsibilities to the community. Young men spent much of the dry season in the forest, harvesting palm wine with their elders. Many stories about Diola customs and history were imparted during conversation over palm wine during the course of a day's work. Special children's shrines provided a place where young people were instructed in the way of ritual and the importance of the ukine. Until recently, every boy had his own family shrine of Hupila, a small shrine where he made offerings of the feathers or blood of animals that he killed. Girls had their own women's shrine of Ehugna. They gathered palm wine, performed the rites, and danced. Each quarter had its own priestess and group of "elders." There was also a shrine associated with wrestling, where boys sacrificed stolen chickens on the night before a wrestling match.[145]

Esulalu girls were initiated into the responsiblities of womanhoood in a series of events which, unlike the boys' mass initiation, were highly individualized. Just before the onset of puberty, a girl and her best friend would spend as long as a month sleeping over at one of their homes. They cooked festive foods and ate together. During this time, the women of the compound instructed the girls in matters relating to their imminent adolescence and the role of women in the community. A second and more intense period of education occurred in the maternity house when a mother gave birth to her first child. Only then could she become a full member of the community of women and the congregation of the adult Ehugna shrine.

The most important of the men's initiations remains the circumcision rite. It has undergone radical changes in the past three centuries and is discussed in chapter 4. Both the older form of male circumcision and the newer one gathered together a group of boys who had to pass through a physical ordeal, sacrifice a part of themselves, and demonstrate the essential male characteristics of courage and forbearance that were required of Diola men. During their seclusion, they were taught the responsibilities of manhood, respect for tradition and for the elders, and certain aspects of ritual knowledge.

A few years after the circumcision ritual, the young men were initiated for a second time, in the rite of Calau. It was held in the sacred forest of the Calemboekine shrine, where elders and young men spent six days together in ritual seclusion. There the initiates received detailed instructions about death and its significance, funeral rites, and ritual obligations, as well as their first information about the closely guarded mysteries of the priest-king. Having completed this initiation, men could assist at burials and attend the various royal shrines. Through initiation each man became "one who is of the ukine."[146]

A man was not considered fully an adult until he was married and had children.[147] Diola marriage rites focused on safeguarding the passage of the bride from one household to another and the transference of her reproductive powers to another lineage. These rites were conducted throughout the dry season that preceded the marriage itself. At the end of the rainy season, the future husband began the laborious task of acquiring several thousand liters of palm wine to present to the father of the bride. The bride's father used the palm wine to greet all the spirit shrines that were important to his family. In each case, prayers were offered for the fertility of the bride and the happiness of the couple. The most important rites occurred at the family shrine of Hupila, where a hog was sacrificed to inform the boekine that their daughter would be leaving the family and to enlist its assistance in enhancing her fertility. Failure to perform this rite could so antagonize Hupila that the bride's life, as well as her fertility, could be placed in jeopardy.[148] If the woman was marrying outside her township, her fiancé had to ritually greet his township's Calemboekine in order that it accept her, like the newborn, into her new community.

Diola attitudes toward death varied according to the age of the deceased and the way that the person died. When the deceased was an elder with children who had children of their own, then it was accepted as part of the natural order of events. The funeral dance, nyakul, became a celebration of the deceased's life, rather than the mourning of a tragic death. However, when an adult died without children or a child died, the death was considered tragic and outside of the natural order. Some force of evil, either committed by the deceased or against him, had to account for this aberration from the normal order. Without changing its basic steps or chants, the nyakul funeral dance was transformed into a powerful expression of sorrow and horror.

When there were untimely deaths, the casop, ritual interrogation of the corpse, became the central event of the funeral. The community had to find out what caused the death. Even the very old are interrogated, but there is a particular urgency in the interrogation at an untimely death. A senior relation asked the corpse, held aloft on a stretcher: "You have died. What has killed you?" The deceased responded by moving the stretcher up and down to indicate agreement or from side to side to indicate a negative response. The deceased was asked if a spirit shrine killed him. If the answer was yes, then the interrogators had to go through the list of ukine to find which one. Then they would ask, "Have you broken with the shrine?" If no, they would ask, "Was it so that you could rest?" If the latter was true, there was no problem. They told the deceased to go in peace. However, if the boekine killed the deceased because he or she neglected ritual obligations or violated its code of behavior, then the family of the deceased had to perform rituals to repair the wrong.[149] Witches could have also caused the death. In such cases, the witch had to be identified before it could do further harm.

Death was accepted as a part of the life journey of the soul. The soul passed into the afterlife, where it became an ancestor (ahoeka), asandioume, or a phantom (ahoelra) before being reincarnated, usually within his or her own lineage. Death was considered a necessary condition for the creation of life. It was said that long ago, the people of Samatit performed rituals at their shrine of Enac so that there would be no more death. For nine years, no one died, but no one was born either. Then, they lifted the prohibition on death. As Terence Sambou suggested, "Certain people were old. They did not have children to take care of them. They found that when one person died, another will have a child."[150] Death was recognized as an integral part of the cycle of life.

Philosophy of History

To many Diola, history, like life itself, was cyclical. Emitai's creation of the world was followed by a time of harmony, of powerful humans, and of few deaths. It was a period of close relationships between the first ancestors (situbai sihan) and Emitai. Gradually, as humans became more confident of their abilities and more distracted by the concerns of families and villages, the relationship with Emitai deteriorated. People became increasingly quarrelsome, greedy, and prone to witchcraft. Eventually, it got so bad that Emitai destroyed all life on earth and began the process again. This destruction of the world was called Adonai. As Djilehl Sambou suggested, "Emitai knows why It causes Adonai. . . . People had remained here for a very long time. It removed them and made new people." There have been many Adonai; there will be many more.[151] After the destruction of Adonai, the first new people had to live without the assistance of ancestors. They were dependent on Emitai for their knowledge of the world and of what was right and wrong. Emitai acted as a parent to the first people and gave them guidance in the conduct of their daily lives. Paponah Diatta described the first people to emerge after Adonai.

> They lived on the earth. . . . The man went to the woman's house. She struck him. The man went to see Emitai. He said the woman struck him. . . . Emitai said It did not know. . . . The man returned . . . wrestling . . . the man defeated the woman. This time the woman went to see Emitai and told It that the man had beaten her. It gave her pubic hair to cover her genitals. After It covered her, It gave her a cloth to wear. It told her that the next time the man comes for a quarrel, remove your cloth. He will sting you. He will marry you. [Both are expressions for intercourse.] The woman will bare her teeth and laugh. The man sees the genitals and he will be beaten. After a while she became pregnant. Man went to see Emitai and asked why the woman had a big stomach and big breasts. Emitai said to leave her alone. After a while the stomach matured. The woman disappeared. He did not see her. . . . He went to see Emitai. He said, "I have not seen her." Emitai said to leave her alone. After a while the woman emerged. She emerged with her child.[152]

Eventually she had other children, who began to populate the earth.

Central to this account are two themes, the relationships between man and woman and between people and Emitai. To many Diola, the relationship between man and woman is a source of continual quarrels. Man has a certain physical power, but woman has a sexual power that she can use to control men. Thus, Emitai established a balance between the strengths of men and women, beginning with the first couple. Finally, Emitai entrusted all matters related to birth to women and excluded men.

Emitai was actively involved in the lives of the first couple. It provided them with advice whenever they needed it. It was accessible and willing to teach the first ancestors. With the insights that Emitai imparted to them, they could gain sufficient understanding of the natural order to secure material prosperity and the ability to resolve their disputes in a just way. However, as people became more established, they neglected their obligations to Emitai. Once again, the world began its slow process of deterioration from the time of the first ancestors.

While Esulalu historians maintained a cyclical view of history, stretching from Adonai to Adonai, from one apocalypse to another, they divided their history since the last period of destruction into three categories. The earliest of these periods, the time of the first ancestors, was regarded as a time beyond the limits of the longest genealogies and a time of closer association between Emitai and Esulalu's ancestors. Traditions of this period emphasized the activities of founding ancestors and their spiritual powers. The second of these categories, the time of the ancestors, was linked to the present by chains of genealogies, shrine histories, and accounts of specific individuals, wars, and rituals. This period roughly corresponds to the late precolonial period, the eighteenth and nineteenth centuries.[153] Finally, there is the period of the recent past, lived through by the oldest members of the community, that roughly corresponds to the twentieth century.

Family, Spirit Shrines, and the Organization of Daily Life

Throughout the period of this study, the Diola-Esulalu farmed their rice paddies and conducted many other economic activities through what has often been called a family mode of production. Although most rice paddies were owned by men, husbands and wives jointly worked the fields with the assistance of their children. Although people in Esulalu carefully delineated male and female tasks in rice farming, the pressures of the agricultural year and periodic labor shortages often blurred the sexual division of labor. Husband and wife took charge of different portions of the harvest, and the wife assumed primary responsibility for subsistence needs of the family. Here again, however, necessity overrode the sexual division of the granary; when there were rice shortages, the husband's grain was also used to feed the family. The various spirit shrines associated with lineages and with the household, most notably Hupila, reflected this family mode of production and reinforced it through their emphasis on the family's collective relationship to the spiritual powers that were the primary source of fertility.

During most of the period covered by this study, the Diola-Esulalu sought to maintain political order, organize collective economic activities, and develop some degree of political cohesion without relying on what Westerners would consider political leaders or political institutions. During much of the eighteenth and nineteenth centuries, the spirit shrine of Hutendookai organized the use of labor resources in areas of townshipwide concern, ensured the validity of labor contracts, and established the prices (using unmilled rice as the basic measure of value) for both labor and trade goods. The priest-king (oeyi) served as the symbol of the spiritual unity of the community, both enabling him to seek the assistance of powerful ukine in enhancing the fertility of the community and empowering him to arbitrate disputes that threatened the fragile social fabric of the Esulalu township. Councils of elders deliberated at spirit shrines on a wide range of issues confronting the community and sanctified their decisions by pouring libations at various spirit shrines after their discussions had reached consensus. The multiplicity of spirit shrines and their often sizeable group of elders ensured that most married adults would eventually achieve a religious office and a role in community governance. Furthermore, an elaborate system of restrictions on the esoteric knowledge of key spirit shrines ensured that no individuals would gain such a degree of knowledge of the ukine that they would be tempted to abuse their power and seek to control the township.

This system of governance through spirit shrines and the elders who perform their rituals was not limited to the precolonial era. In both the colonial and postcolonial periods, shrine elders continued to exercise this role. French and Senegalese officials have complained about the lack of authority of government-appointed village chiefs and the tendency of the Diola to resolve most community disputes by themselves. In the 1990s, Hutendookai continues to regulate local prices and labor relations. Enac and Elung continue to arbitrate a majority of land disputes.

The spirit shrines also continue to be closely associated with other types of economic activities. Fishing, palm wine harvesting, blacksmithing, and farming all have ukine associated with them that offer protection for those who engage in such activities and establish rules that govern their actions. Recently, urban palm wine selling by women has come under the protection of the women's fertility shrine, Ehugna, suggesting that this close association of spirit shrines and the political economy of Diola communities remains important.

Any description of a Diola mode of production needs to look beyond the questions of who owned the productive resources of the community and who supplies the labor. Within that limited context, the Diola could be described as operating within a family mode of production. But as Linares demonstrated in her recent book, the ability of spirit shrines and shrine elders to control the authoritative and, indirectly, the allocative resources of Esulalu communities created a distinctive political economy that rested simultaneously on the family unit and the spirit shrines.[154] Families exercised control over land and labor, but the spirit shrines and an Esulalu system of thought governed the ways in which these resources were utilized. The continuing interaction of socioeconomic forces and an Esulalu system of thought, as mediated by the spirit shrines, is a central issue of this study.

This chapter examined Esulalu makanaye, "what we do"; the awasena path; and awasena thought as a dimension of human actions and concerns that cannot be isolated from other aspects of the complex web of community life. Where possible, I have indicated the degree of continuity or discontinuity between recent Esulalu practices or attitudes and the precolonial period. By doing so, I have provided a more complete context for the understanding of early Esulalu history than could be offered by an exclusive reliance on the fragmentary evidence of oral traditions or travelers' accounts. It also provides a sense of the extent and the limitations of the longue durée by allowing a continual comparison between the manifestation of basic structures of a given period of the past and the era from which the historian examines them. Indeed, this retrospective examination is implicitly one of the fundamental tasks that a historian performs.

3

The Origins of the Diola-Esulalu

Although the retrospective glance of the historian of the longue durée performs a vital role in illuminating the broad continuities of a Diola religious and social system, it has serious limitations in that it assumes a continuity in the ethnic boundaries of the group we know as Diola. Until recently, many researchers made similar assumptions that Africa's ethnic groupings of the twentieth century served as the primary social divisions for centuries before the European conquest. As Jan Vansina suggests, "many historians imagine that the cultural community, the 'tribe' is perennial . . . it does not alter throughout the ages. . . . It can easily be shown that tribes are born and die."[1] Many of the social divisions utilized by African communities themselves, as well as by scholars, are of recent vintage and describe social groups that became significant only in the colonial era. For example, the term "Diola" was given to a cluster of coastal communities of the lower Casamance by Wolof sailors who accompanied the French into the region in the nineteenth century. The French seized on the term in their eagerness to categorize the people whom they encountered as they colonized the region. The "Diola" did not utilize this label until they embraced a common ethnicity in the face of increasing integration into a multiethnic Senegal. Before colonization, they referred to themselves by their subgroup, such as Esulalu or Huluf, who spoke a common dialect of the Diola language. Even the category of "subgroup" is quite fluid and cannot be projected back into a primordial past.[2]

From an examination of oral traditions and travelers' accounts, it is clear that, as early as the sixteenth century, the ancestors of the Diola had formed several distinct subgroups that differed not only in dialect but also in political institutions and cult structures. As I began field work, I believed that Esulalu was one such relatively homogeneous group, an appropriate cultural unit in which to study religious and social history. As I was able to penetrate beyond the history of what the Diola wanted outsiders and the less informed in their own community to understand, this sense of homogeneity and an enduring Esulalu identity were also revealed to be limited. Esulalu ethnic identity was the result of a long process culminating in the eighteenth century, when two distinct groups, a community of "first inhabitants" called the Koonjaen and a newer group identified as Diola in recent oral traditions, forged a common tradition. Each community contributed important shrines, ritual practices, and ideas to what emerged as a distinctly Esulalu tradition. Moreover, the category Diola was created from the joining of several distinct groups, who migrated into the area from the south and east, before they conquered the Koonjaen. These long-standing divisions within an Esulalu identity remain important throughout the period of this study.

Similarly, "Diola religion" is not a primordial category. On the contrary, what we identify as Diola religion or the awasena path, like most religions, represents a tradition that drew on earlier forms of religious experience of the various groups who came to regard that tradition as authoritative. Some types of religious experience are associated with the Koonjaen and others with the Diola. Similarly, the histories of various spirit shrines reflect their diverse origins among the ancestors of the Diola and the Koonjaen and such neighboring peoples as the Manjaco. These shrines, often under different names, continue to be utilized among different peoples in the Upper Guinea region. As Richard Werbner has demonstrated for Central Africa and I have witnessed in regard to the Diola, many shrines command multiethnic allegiances.[3] The boundaries between various African religions are far more permeable than is often imagined.

Although archaeologists have shown that Esulalu has been inhabited by sedentary rice farmers for at least fifteen hundred years, evidence is too limited to determine the ethnic identity of these early inhabitants or the nature of their relationship to the Koonjaen or to the ancestors of the Diola.[4] Esulalu traditions concerning the Koonjaen do not cite a prior place of origins; rather, they are generally considered to be the region's earliest inhabitants. Called by various forms of the word Bainounk or Cassanga by European explorers, they were identified as occupying large areas of the Casamance at the beginning of the sixteenth century. By that time, the people who were identified in Esulalu oral traditions as Diola, whom the Portuguese called Floup or Felupe, had also settled in the area.[5]

By analyzing the history of each of the groups that came to be a part of Esulalu, this chapter examines the processes of initial interaction and partial incorporation that shaped the growth of a distinctive Esulalu cultural tradition. Beginning with the earliest known inhabitants of the region, I describe what is known of their economic activities, social structure, and religious life. Then I turn to a discussion of the migration of the ancestors of the Diola/Floup into the lower Casamance, their gradual domination of the region, and their eventual conquest of the indigenous inhabitants. It is from the process of incorporating the Koonjaen into the Diola townships and their gradual isolation from other Diola groups that an Esulalu ethnic identity was formed. Similarly, the awasena path was formed from separate traditions associated with the Koonjaen and Diola.

To avoid confusion between the modern use of the term "Diola" and its use in Esulalu traditions about their origins, I shall use the term "Floup" to describe the Diola newcomers who eventually conquered the Koonjaen. The term "Diola" or "Diola-Esulalu" will be reserved for the mixture of Koonjaen and Floup who together comprise the people of Esulalu. After tracing the diverse origins of Esulalu, I shift to the broader context of their interaction with Europeans and other newcomers, their growing participation in trade, and the influence of such activities in the development of Koonjaen, Floup, and Diola-Esulalu communities.

According to Esulalu periodizations of their oral traditions, the era when Floup and Koonjaen interacted with each other as separate and autonomous communities occurred before the time of the longest genealogies, placing it within the period of the "first ancestors." Only the final conquest of the Koonjaen, around 1700, is linked to Esulalu relative chronologies as a war in which the first ancestors of various lineages participated.[6] The infrequent and relatively brief accounts of European traders and some rather sparse oral traditions allow us to sketch only the broad outlines of the history of the Floup and Koonjaen as separate communities before 1700.

Koonjaen, Bainounk, and the Settlement of Esulalu

Before the arrival of the Floup, two areas of Esulalu were already occupied by communities that were eventually incorporated into the Esulalu townships. The first included two villages near the Casamance River: a settlement near the present location of Kagnout-Bruhinban and Elou Mlomp, which was located in the Hamak area north of the present-day township of Mlomp.[7] No prior places of residence are cited in traditions concerning these settlements, nor is an ethnic identity, Koonjaen or Floup, specified. The second cluster, located within the forest area south of the Casamance River settlements, included a series of villages inhabited by Koonjaen. Eloudia and Eloukasine were located in that portion of the forest that was closest to the coast, south of the present-day settlements of Mlomp and Kagnout. Further south, within the northern limits of Huluf, was the township of Hawtane (see map 3). These Koonjaen settlements are regarded as the oldest communities in the region. Furthermore, the people of these settlements are said to be the ancestors of a substantial portion of the present-day inhabitants of Esulalu.[8]

The people whom Esulalu traditions described as Koonjaen are part of the same ethnic group identified as Bainounk by early explorers of the Casamance region. The Bainounk dominated most of the lower Casamance during the sixteenth and seventeenth centuries but were gradually defeated and incorporated by Mandinka, Balanta, and Floup groups that were expanding into the region. When asked about the identity of the Koonjaen, Esulalu historians volunteered that they were Bainounk or Faroon. Furthermore, they suggested that people who are the same as the Koonjaen live in such Bainounk-dominated villages as Niamoun, Tobor, Djibelor, and Agnak.[9] Linguistic evidence also supports this linkage. Sapir's lexical count of West Atlantic languages shows strong similarities between Diola and Banhun (Bainounk), despite the fact that they are not members of the same subgroup of languages. These similarities are strongest with the Huluf dialect of Diola and, presumably, with the closely related Esulalu dialect, both of which are spoken in areas that absorbed the Koonjaen.[10] This would indicate greater contact between Huluf/Esulalu speakers and the Bainounk than with other Diola speakers. Because

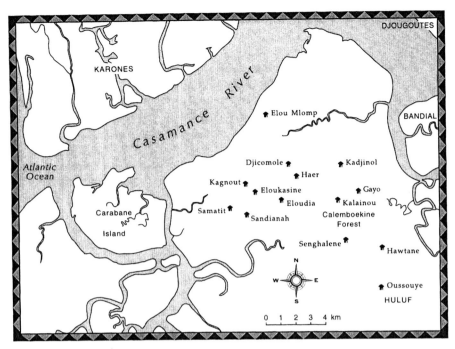

Map 3. Esulalu before 1700

no villages in the Huluf/Esulalu region are identified as Bainounk and several in other Diola areas are, there is a strong likelihood that the Koonjaen were the source of Bainounk linguistic influence.

Both the lack of studies of Bainounk history and the length of their presence in the Casamance make it difficult to determine the origins of this community.[11] We do know that by the beginning of the sixteenth century, the Cassangas, a Bainounk group, had established the powerful kingdom of the Casa Mansa in the eastern portion of the lower Casamance, extending to within thirty kilometers of Esulalu. According to Valentim Fernandes, writing in 1506, the Cassanga state governed an amalgam of Cassangas, other Bainounk, and Floup. The phenomenon of Floup and Bainounk living in the same polities was fairly common in the lower Casamance. Europeans often mistook one group for the other or described them as having a common origin.[12] Unlike other Bainounk, the Cassangas appear to have been strongly influenced by Mandinka political organization and, at various times, paid tribute to the Mandinka rulers of Gabou, in eastern Guinea-Bissau. The title of "Mansa" was clearly of Mandinka origin, as was the practice of having slaves who served as counselors to the ruler.

The wealth of the Cassanga kingdom came from its ability to control the interior trade between the Gambia and São Domingo Rivers, as well as its manufacture of cotton cloth. The importance of this craft was noted by Fernandes: "The inhabitants of this country are commercially all weavers and make cloths of many different styles and colors. And there the Christians go to trade their cloths of many different styles and colors." The Cassangas held trade fairs that attracted people from throughout the region: "It is the custom in this region to organize a fair every eight days [actually six] which, when it takes place the Tuesday of one week, the next week will be on a Monday. And thus, the day of the fair continues to retreat."[13] At these fairs, which could attract up to eight thousand people, the Portuguese sold iron, cloth, horses, beads, wine, and paper in order to purchase slaves, rice, ivory, and beeswax.[14] By 1500, the slave trade had acquired considerable importance to the Cassanga state: "their ready supply of slaves and exceptionally favourable treatment of the *lançados* made Cassanga territory a haven for the Portuguese. That the Cassanga king should have been in the habit of bestowing on his Cape Verde friends gifts of ten or a dozen slaves attests to amicable relations with the Portuguese, as well as his ability to produce this particular merchandise."[15]

In addition to their control of commerce, Cassanga kings performed ritual activities that were seen as vital to the prosperity of the state. They were seen as the spiritually powerful embodiments of the fertility of the people. The Bainounk initiated their kings by ritually bathing them in the Casamance River, thereby emphasizing their connection to life-giving water. Subjects brought black cattle, symbolic of dark rain clouds, to be sacrificed by the kings in the hope of receiving adequate rainfall for their crops. Kings presided over the important rain shrines in their domains; those who were unable to ensure the fertility of the soil and adequate rainfall were put to death.[16]

Travelers' accounts provide some descriptions of Bainounk ritual practices in the sixteenth century. De Almada described the Cassanga tradition of creating shrines at the base of large trees. Often these shrines appeared to be little more than a stake in the ground, covered with libations of palm wine and the blood of animal sacrifice. Both the location and design of such shrines were similar to more recent practice among the Diola. De Almada also described offerings of rice flour cakes, an offering the Diola associated with funerals and with fertility rituals.[17] Fernandes described the consecration of a shrine called *hatichira*:

> They consecrate this wood in this fashion: they take a forked stake that has to have been cut with a new hatchet, whose handle also has to be new. . . . Then they make a hole in the ground and they have a calabash of palm wine that contains three or four *canadas*. And also another of [palm] oil with the same quantity, and in a basket about a *quarta* of rice to be pounded. They bring a live dog there and then pour the wine, oil, and rice into the hole, and they kill the dog with the new hatchet; they cut off its head and let all the blood flow into the hole on the wine, oil and rice. Then they throw the hatchet in and fix the forked stick over it and cover it properly with earth, and on the forked stick that sticks up out of the hole, they hang some herbs from the bush and to perform this ceremony, one calls the most respected elders of the entire region, and then they cook the said dog with grand solemnity and eat it, and from then on they begin to worship this piece of wood.

The centrality of a new hatchet resembled a major Diola-Bandial and Ehing shrine called "the hatchet," which controlled important purification rites.[18] In the twentieth century, Diola sacrificed dogs at the family shrine of Hupila and the divination shrine of Bruinkaw. Eating the meat of the sacrifice bound all the participants to the words of prayer offered during the ritual.

Fernandes described the shrine as a place where people would take binding oaths. They would end their testimony with the words "may the *china* kill me while climbing down from a palm tree from harvesting palm wine" or other such imprecations. This practice also bore strong resemblance to Diola oath-taking rituals. The Bainounk term for spirit shrine, *china*, resembles the Diola-Esulalu term, *boekine*, and the Ediamat variation, *xinabu*.[19] This similarity may indicate that Floup or Bainounk had influenced the development of the category of lesser spirits in the neighboring community's religious system.

Both Fernandes and de Almada described other aspects of Bainounk ritual that parallel current Esulalu rites. Fernandes described a Bainounk method of protecting against theft: "If a black wants to leave something in his field without it being stolen, he takes a mass of palm fibers, makes a difficult knot and fixes it in the ground near the object that he leaves and no one will touch it."[20] This strongly resembles a Diola blacksmith's medicine called *houben*, which is still used to protect crops, fish traps, palm wine, and fruit trees against theft. Many Diola think that leprosy, a disease associated with the blacksmith shrine of Gilaite, will seize any person who steals. According to the Jesuit priest Manuel Alvares, the Bainounk had special chinas, where they performed ritual sacrifices to achieve victory in war.[21] De Almada described rituals in which Bainounk poured small offerings of palm wine on the ground, for their ancestors, before drinking it themselves. "In this kingdom, they never drunk wine whether in groups or alone, without offering a little to the dead, by throwing some on the ground and saying a few words of the kind used for a funeral oration."[22] This, too, resembles contemporary Diola offerings to the ancestors before consuming palm wine. Finally, de Almada described elaborate funeral rituals involving palm wine libations and lengthy eulogies.

> When any man dies, before he is buried, he is laid on the wooden supports which will be used for his tomb, which are covered with black cloth, and (this bier is placed) on the shoulders of blacks. Carrying the dead man, they go (round the village). They dance wildly, here and there, to the sound of numerous drums, ivory trumpets and conch shells, jumping about with such fury and force that it seems that they have devils in them. Other blacks called Jabacosses speak to the dead man, and put questions to him, so that he can tell them who killed him. And if the men who carry (the bier) on their backs and who dance here and there so furiously (happen to) meet an individual, and (immediately) quieten down, it is said that this individual is the person who killed the dead man. ... If those carrying the bier meet no one, then the Jabacosse who puts questions to the dead man says that he died from natural causes. But if they meet anyone, that person is (treated as) a murderer, and they arrest him for witchcraft, and sell him and all his relatives without sparing any.[23]

Again, we have close parallels between sixteenth-century Cassanga practices and Diola rituals described in the nineteenth and twentieth centuries. In both cases, the spiritual significance of any death had to be identified, and proper actions had to be taken to limit any spiritul repercussions.

Similarities between early Bainounk and contemporary Diola ritual practice are quite strong. The use of rice flour offerings, palm wine libations, and sacrifices of animals all parallel Diola ritual practice. Attitudes about the spiritual significance of death are strikingly similar. The use of specific shrines for the taking of oaths, the conduct of war, and protection against theft suggest similarities in ritual function, in ritual structure, and in the spiritual concerns of the two communities. Such common practices probably extended to the Floup contemporaries of the early Bainounk. These similarities of ritual purpose and methods encouraged borrowings from one religious system and incorporation into the other.

Closer to Esulalu and west of the Cassanga kingdom lived the Koonjaen, who were a Bainounk group that was less influenced by Mandinka culture or commercial activity. Living in the border region between Huluf and Esulalu, they were eventually incorporated into both Diola groups, whom they influenced by providing important artisan skills and religious traditions. Like the communities that followed them into the region, the Koonjaen concentrated their energies on the cultivation of rice. They had wet rice paddies in the low-lying areas just to the north and the south of the Calemboekine forest, and they cleared some forest areas for the planting of upland rice. One elder suggested that the Koonjaen taught the Floup new techniques of rice farming: "They [the Koonjaen] showed our ancestors how to farm rice. . . . They were more able to do it well."[24] The Koonjaen also kept cattle and other livestock. Hunting and fishing, however, provided their principal sources of protein. Koonjaen fishermen limited their activities to constructing fish traps along the estuaries and gathering shellfish in the shallows. The Koonjaen may have depended on the Floup newcomers for the construction of canoes and may also have purchased fish from them.[25]

Of the Koonjaen settlements in Esulalu, Eloudia is said to be the oldest and the most influential. It controlled a vast area, stretching from present-day Mlomp to the Huluf communities of Diaken.[26] There is some disagreement about whether the original township of Eloudia was settled by Koonjaen or by Floup. However, the fact that the descendants of the original inhabitants of Eloudia, the Gent compounds, control Djiguemah, a spirit shrine acknowledged as Koonjaen, provides strong evidence of Koonjaen origin. Most accounts of the founding of Eloudia do not cite a prior place of settlement. This stands in sharp contrast to the detailed migration accounts received from the townships settled by the Floup.[27]

According to Esulalu accounts, a man named Atta-Essou founded Eloudia. "They say Atta-Essou came from Emitai. Emitai gave him the ukine."[28] Atta-Essou is regarded as the first person in the land of Esulalu and the founder of the oldest village. He is seen as a man in close contact with Emitai, who received from the supreme being the necessary knowledge to be able to control many of the spirit shrines of the Koonjaen. From Emitai he received the shrine of Egol, associated with the Koonjaen priest-king, and revelations concerning Djoenenandé, an important royal shrine for Eloudia and Huluf.[29]

It is said that Atta-Essou did not die. In some accounts, he simply disappeared; in others, he flew into the sky and was received by Emitai. In the latter accounts, Atta-Essou made wings of fan palm fibers and, after taking leave of his many sons, flew up to Emitai.[30] The name Atta-Essou means "of bird" (birds are often seen as emissaries of Emitai) or of bird descent. It is important that he is said not to have died; the same is said of his descendants, the Diola priest-kings of Esulalu and Huluf. Like the priest-king, Atta-Essou is regarded as a symbol of fertility. Atta-Essou was created by Emitai, given land to settle by Emitai, and fathered thirty-nine sons by the grace of Emitai. Thus he received a creative power directly from the supreme being, received the land and its potential fertility, and received the fullest power of procreation. His spiritual power is said to continue to serve as a link between his descendants, the Gent compounds of Esulalu, and Emitai. Atta-Essou would appear to his descendants in their dreams to provide instruction about creating new shrines and moral guidance. Out of respect for his powers, his descendants created a shrine called Atta-Essou. Prayers were addressed to Atta-Essou, and palm wine was tossed in the air, a memorial to his ascent to Emitai.[31]

While the traditions concerning Atta-Essou describe the origins of Eloudia, the Gent lineage, and several important spirit shrines, they are also the oldest traditions of direct communications between Emitai and people. He is said to have originated with Emitai, rather than with a family, and to have returned to Emitai rather than to have died. He received knowledge of several important spirit shrines from Emitai, which he passed on to his sons. The emphasis on his birdlike characteristics underline his role as an intermediary between the Koonjaen and their supreme being. His celestial origins and immortality attest to his sacred "otherness" within Koonjaen traditions. Koonjaen traditions' emphasis on the supreme being appear to be the primary source of Diola concerns about Emitai. There is little evidence that the incoming Floup stressed the importance of the supreme being as a source of revelations.[32]

East of Eloudia, the ancestors of the Diedhious of Kalainou and Gayo established settlements. They were highly skilled metalworkers who obtained metal from trade, from the ilmenite sands at the mouth of the Casamance River, and, possibly, from smelting bog iron. Ilmenite, which contains titanium oxide in addition to iron, is described by the Esulalu as "white iron" (magne mahité). It was too malleable to make farm tools or weaponry but could be used for utensils or jewelry.[33] That the Koonjaen taught the Floup how to work with iron is doubtful, but the Koonjaen dominated the smithing craft even after the arrival of the Floup. This could have been because they controlled the bog iron deposits and most of the forest areas that supplied charcoal, because of superior technical skills, or because of certain spiritual powers that the Koonjaen smiths possessed.[34]

This spiritual power is said to have come from Emitai's revelation of the technique of the forge to the ancestors of the Diedhiou lineage. In many West African societies, the masters of the forge are feared because of their spiritual power.[35] To the Diola and, presumably, the Koonjaen, the smith was powerful because he had received the ability to manipulate fire. Fire is like blood, water, and palm wine. It contains a soul, the power of which can transform objects and spiritual forces that it touches or enters. Among their powers, the smiths control the disease of leprosy, the running sores of which resemble the festering wounds left by serious burns.

The Koonjaen smiths worshiped at a spirit shrine that both aided and protected them. This shrine, Silapoom (the hammer), is said to be the oldest shrine linked to the forge. Unlike the blacksmith shrines introduced in the nineteenth century, Gilaite and Duhagne, Silapoom is said to have originated in Esulalu, and its creation is attributed to the time of the first ancestors. It is acknowledged to be Koonjaen: "Our Silapoom is that of the Koonjaen." Silapoom served as a guild shrine; only master craftsmen could "finish" all the rituals to become elders and establish shrines in their homes. Completion of these rituals remains the only way a blacksmith can work at his craft away from his home township.[36] This shrine was brought to the Esulalu townships when Kalainou and Gayo settled in Kadjinol. In contrast with the newer blacksmith shrines, Silapoom's rites can be attended by women, who may partake of the palm wine and food that accompany the rites. The exclusion of women from Gilaite and Duhagne may well indicate a growing emphasis on sexual segregation in the ritual process and a decline in the status of women after the conquest of the Koonjaen.[37]

Eloukasine was a Koonjaen settlement located in the forest area between Kagnout and Eloudia. Little is known about this community, but it was conquered by the Floup of Kagnout and its inhabitants were scattered among the Esulalu and Huluf townships. Reciters of oral traditions cited three causes for the war that led to their removal: a dispute over oil palm tapping rights, the killing of Kagnout's stray pigs when they entered the forest, and Eloukasine's sexual misconduct. "Their [Kagnout's] wives, they [Eloukasine] deceived them. They seized them and married them [with the implication of 'by force']; this was why they [Kagnout] showed them."[38] Other than family shrines, there was no mention of Eloukasine bringing ukine with them to their new homes. At Eloudia and Samatit, however, they eventually became powerful enough to gain control over some of the royal shrines and to assume the position of oeyi. Whether they acquired these offices because of Koonjaen status, precedence in settlement of the area, or political intrigue remains unclear at this stage of research.

Hawtane was a large township located at the southern edge of the forest between Huluf and Esulalu. It covered the area from Edioungou west to Kahinda and north to include the Babindeck rice paddies. Some of Atta-Essou's descendants settled in Hawtane and maintained close links with Eloudia. Hawtane had its own priest-king and may well have utilized the Eloudia shrines of Egol and Djoenenandé.[39] As the Floup increased in numbers, they decided to remove the Hawtane township. Hawtane controlled valuable paddy and forest land and also raided them for captives. The Huluf townships defeated Hawtane in battle and forcibly resettled them in Huluf and Esulalu communities, where they became important holders of spirit shrines because of their long-standing ties to the land. The Hawtane descendants of Atta-Essou received control of royal spirit shrines and were recognized as shrine elders throughout the region.

The Koonjaen of these forest areas centered their ritual activities around a variety of spirit cults. They had a shrine of the dead comparable to the Diola shrine of Kouhouloung. They had a shrine to protect the well-being of the family that was comparable to Hupila. They had other shrines that are still in the forest area, though most of them are no longer used.[40] However, the shrine of Djiguemah, located near the Babindeck rice paddies north of the Huluf township of Kolobone, is still used. It is a family shrine dedicated to the protection of the Manga/Diatta lineage and the maintenance of its fertility. Men and women who were born in the Ekink quarter of Kolobone, regardless of where they reside, attend its annual rites.[41] A similar shrine, Kahlayoh, continues to receive ritual attention at Kadjinol. This shrine protects the family and ensures the fertility of the Gayo compounds in Esulalu. Only Gayo families and women who were born in a Gayo compound may attend.[42] As previously mentioned, the Koonjaen also had a blacksmith shrine called Silapoom. Whether they had other shrines associated with artisans or other economic activities remains unclear.

Based on limited information, it appears that the central spiritual concerns of the Koonjaen included protection of the family, the continuation of fertility, and the securing of a good afterlife. Prayer was accompanied by palm wine libations, offerings of rice flour, and animal sacrifice and was followed by the sharing of the sacrificial meal on the shrine premises. The community of supplicants was not separated by gender; while men controlled most cult offices, women could witness the rituals and partake of the consecrated food and palm wine consumed by the worshipers after the ritual. Furthermore, ritual activity extended beyond communication with lesser spirits to include communication with their supreme being.

The most important Koonjaen institution, in terms of its lasting influence, was the priest-king and the cluster of shrines associated with it. Atta-Essou is credited with having received the revelations that led to the creation of the shrine of Egol, one of the two basic shrines of the Esulalu priest-king.[43] Although Atta-Essou established Egol, he did not become a priest-king; one of his sons did. The Egol shrine was established in a sacred grove, Calemboekine, where men would gather to pray for rain, peace, and the general well-being of the community. As Atta-Essou's sons dispersed, they carried the Egol shrine with them to other Koonjaen communities, where they established new sacred forests. The fundamental difference between the Koonjaen Calemboekine and that of the Floup was that the Koonjaen's housed the shrine Egol and the Floup's housed a shrine called Coeyi.[44] Atta-Essou is also credited with having received revelations that led to the creation of a shrine called Djoenenandé, a rain and community shrine that became especially important to the Huluf priest-king at Oussouye.

These shrines associated with the Koonjaen priest-king, as well as several other ukine, were eventually adopted by the Floup as they incorporated the Koonjaen and began the process of developing a shared tradition. However, these borrowings do not indicate the degree of intellectual cross-fertilization that may have occurred. Many of the subtle differences in thought of this period have been hidden by the process of cultural integration and the gradual streamlining of oral traditions as they have been handed down. Such influences probably did accompany the incorporation of the Koonjaen shrines, but this occurred after the conquest and incorporation of the Koonjaen into an emerging Esulalu community.

The Floup Migrations

In sharp contrast to traditions about the Bainounk and Koonjaen, oral traditions about the Floup cite prior areas of settlement. There are two primary theories of the origins of the Floup. One set of traditions suggests that they came from the east, from the Mandinka-dominated area of Gabou, and that they are related to the Serer of northern Senegal. According to that interpretation, two sisters left Gabou by canoe and travelled down the Gambia River toward the sea. The canoe split apart, forcing the sisters to swim ashore. One of the sisters swam to the north bank of the river and became the mother of the Serer, while the other reached the south shore and became the mother of the Floup. This would explain the Gambia River boundary between Floup and Serer cultural areas. Thomas, while recognizing similarities between Floup and Serer, rejects this theory, noting that such traditions are rarely found among the Serer.[45]

The absence of strong linguistic or cultural links between Diola and Serer raises serious questions about a theory of their common origin. The Serer language is far closer to Fulbe or Wolof than it is to Diola. Most Serer came from Futa Toro in northern Senegal. As late as the seventeenth century, Father Labat described Futa Toro's Lake Retba as the "Lac des Serères." Wolof and Serer traditions suggest strong links between the Serer and the Wolof kingdom of Djollof. Although certain Serer groups, especially the Guellwar ruling clan of Sine and Saloum, came from Gabou, there are no accounts of a similar group entering the area inhabited by the Diola. Despite the lack of linguistic or cultural similarities, this tradition persists among certain Diola.[46] However, this may reflect the Diola's relative isolation within the ethnic politics of twentieth-century Senegal. The Serer and Diola dominate the Senegalese Catholic Church and are frequent political allies. The tradition of a common origin may reflect a Diola effort to reinforce this alliance, particularly since the Serer have dominated Senegalese politics during the last forty years, but there is little evidence to support it.

A second set of traditions, claiming that the Floup came from Guinea-Bissau, is far more plausible. It is supported by the strong linguistic, religious, and cultural similarities between the Floup and the coastal people of Guinea-Bissau. It is bolstered by the fact that most north shore Diola, at least in Djougoutes, trace their descent from the Diola of the south shore.[47] According to these traditions, the ancestors of the Diola came from the area south of the São Domingo River, an area presently occupied by the Manjaco. Perhaps under the pressure of a westward expansion of neighboring peoples, the Floup crossed the São Domingo and settled the region of Ediamat, along the present-day boundary between Senegal and Guinea-Bissau. An increasing population generated a need for more rice paddies, so the Floup expanded to the north, where they encountered the Bainounk-Koonjaen communities. Some of these people were incorporated into the Floup communities and were able to provide important assistance to the newcomers in adapting to their new homeland.[48]

The theory of a southern origin is supported by Diola attitudes toward the region to their immediate south. Many Diola think that one of the spiritual abodes of the afterlife, Housandioume, is located in Guinea-Bissau. The dead walk or travel by canoe south into Guinea-Bissau, reversing a journey made by their ancestors in settling the lower Casamance. Many of the Diola's most powerful spirit shrines originated either in Ediamat or in the Manjaco area south of the São Domingo.

The links between the Diola and their southern neighbors appear to be long and intimate.[49]

The Floup settled the Esulalu area in a series of population movements, sometimes involving lineages, sometimes involving entire villages. Although this northward movement of Floup into Esulalu occurred before the time of the longest remembered genealogies, the origins of specific townships, quarters, and lineages are recalled. For example, most of Samatit's population moved from Ediamat to Bouyouye, from which some people came and established Samatit. They claim that a major military defeat forced them from their homeland near the Bayotte village of Aramé. Neighboring villages coveted their large rice paddies. Bouyouye and Samatit share certain spirit shrines and a secret language used for ritual purposes. Both the cults and the language are said to have originated in Ediamat.[50]

Various Floup lineages can trace their migrations from Ediamat to Esulalu. Thus the Badji-Bassins of Kadjinol trace their movements from Efok in Ediamat, to Siganar in Huluf, to Kadjinol. The Diondiom Sambou lineage of Kadjinol traces itself back to Bandial and then back to Ediamat.[51] In many accounts, the shortage of rice paddies is cited as the major cause of migration. Usually an ancestor is described as discovering the Esulalu area while he was fishing or hunting. For example, Kagnout was settled by people from the Ediamat village of Kooloombung, who came there searching for fish and shellfish. As the Floup traveled north, they carried soil from the shrine precincts of their home villages so that they could reconstruct their shrines in their new communities and continue their ritual life. This soil, saturated with the palm wine and blood of past sacrifices, helped to attract the power of the shrine's spirit and the collective power of the shrine's prior congregations.[52] How different the Floup were from the older communities of Koonjaen or the village of Elou Mlomp remains unclear. The entry of the Floup into the region began a process of interaction between these groups that resulted in the incorporation of the older settlements and the growth of the Esulalu townships as a distinct Diola subgroup.

Shortly after the removal of Hawtane by the people of Huluf, Floup settlers established a new village called Senghalene on Hawtane's lands in the forest between Huluf and Esulalu.[53] Like the Koonjaen, the settlers of Senghalene had a priest-king, but he controlled a different form of Calemboekine than that of the Koonjaen. This Calemboekine had as its central shrine Coeyi, not Egol. It was the Senghalene form of Calemboekine that later became dominant in Kadjinol, Mlomp, and Samatit.

Senghalene, like the other Huluf townships, received its Coeyi from the township of Kerouhey in Ediamat. Ancestors of the Djisenghalene-Djikune lineage went to Kerouhey to receive the shrine from the senior priest-king of the region.[54] Accounts differ on the nature of this pilgrimage to Kerouhey. Sidionbaw Diatta suggests that it was a journey of the spirit, made in the night: "People of the strength of the night, went by their strength at night." Their souls went there while they appeared to be sleeping. These men had powers like those of witches, "but they did it for the boekine." On their return, they left the boekine at the Huluf township of Oussouye, but "a man from Kolobone, a certain man went and stole it. He brought it to Kolobone." Sidionbaw claims that it is theft that makes Huluf senior to Esulalu in matters affecting the priest-king and his shrines.[55] Central to his account are the role of spiritual powers in the acquisition of the boekine and the underhanded way that Huluf achieved a position of dominance over Esulalu.

Other accounts stress a more mundane form of pilgrimage. Both Antoine Diedhiou and Siliungimagne Diatta describe the pilgrims' travel by ordinary means, in small groups to avoid the appearance of a war party and to avoid being attacked by superior forces. They carried gifts of cattle and rice as offerings at Kerouhey's Coeyi and for the consecration of a new altar for their own Coeyi. Meetings were held at Senghalene to explain the nature of the new shrine and the institution of the priest-king.[56] Despite apparent contradictions, these accounts emphasize different aspects of the introduction of the office of the priest-king and its cluster of shrines. One account emphasizes the institutional process of giving a spirit shrine to a community and the initiation of that community in its ritual use; the other emphasizes the understanding of the spirit world necessary for the control and manipulation of such a powerful cult.

The Coeyi shrine did not originate in Ediamat. The people of Kerouhey received it from the Manjaco of Guinea-Bissau.[57] According to Jacques Lopi, the grandson of Manjaco immigrants who fled the Guinea-Bissau village of Basserel rather than take on the position of the priest-king, the Manjaco priest-king was actively involved in the procurement of rain and the fertility of the soil. "During the rainy season, he may not go outside." He performs rituals at his shrine to ensure adequate rain. At the time of the harvest, he performs new rituals but remains in seclusion. If he is seen in the rice paddies, all work must cease; otherwise, "all the rice will fall over." The Manjaco priest-king had to be obeyed. Women especially had to avoid him and could not greet him. Like the priest-kings of the Koonjaen and the Floup, Manjaco rulers regulated land disputes and controlled powerful rain shrines. Manjaco shrine elders, like their Floup and Koonjaen counterparts, initiated new rulers in a six-day ritual, in which the priest-king was secluded and died to his own name before reemerging with a new name and sacred office.[58]

By the late seventeeth century, the Floup migrations into Esulalu were virtually complete. Individuals and families would continue to come, seeking more abundant land or avoiding priestly obligations or punishments meted out to criminals, but the majority of the newcomers had already established the townships of Kadjinol, Djicomole (later to become the largest quarter of Mlomp), Kagnout, and Samatit.[59] These settlements were established to the north of the Koonjaen villages, along a series of ridges, with access to suitable paddy land between the townships and the Casamance River. As the townships grew, the settlers from the paddy-short regions to the south created a new scarcity of land within Esulalu. This shortage was aggravated by the frequent droughts of the middle to late seventeenth century, which restricted Floup farming with reliable yields to the deepest, well-watered rice paddies.[60]

The region's lack of drought-resistant rice paddies could be met in a variety of ways. Some people continued their migrations further north to the sparsely populated islands of Bliss-Karones and to Djougoutes. There they established townships that were similar to those being established in Esulalu.[61] People from Elou Mlomp joined this northward movement, contributing a large portion of the population of Mlomp of Djougoutes. They carried with them the type of priest-king institutions found in Elou Mlomp, as well as other spirit shrines. People who remained behind sought to expand the amount of paddy land by building dikes to hold back the salty estuary water. Both Esulalu and Huluf had another option, however—the occupation of the Koonjaen lands that separated them.

Increasing demographic pressure on the land available for rice cultivation generated tension between Floup and Koonjaen. According to Diola elders, "The Koonjaen did not like it that people came and settled on their lands."[62] Why the Koonjaen did not attack the Floup and drive them out before they were established remains unclear. One possible explanation is that the newcomers initially moved into the area with the support of a powerful state, a state which the Koonjaen were unwilling to antagonize.

The Floup Kingdom

During the period of the Floup migrations, the kingdom of the Mansa Floup controlled a large area between the Casamance and São Domingo rivers. Valentim Fernandes (1506) is the sole source of detailed descriptions of the Floup state, but his generally accurate descriptions of the Cassanga and other Guinean peoples lend credence to his report.[63] Like the Casa Mansa, the Mansa Floup was a strong ruler who controlled trade, levied taxes, and punished wrongdoers. His title, "Mansa," may be a sign of Mandinka influence, but it might also suggest Fernandes's greater familiarity with Mandinka political terminology. The Mansa ruled over a prosperous state, rich in rice and livestock and feared in war. War canoes, capable of holding fifty men, gave Floup warriors the mobility to attack isolated communities along the many estuaries of the Casamance River. The Mansa Floup taxed cattle and other livestock, palm wine, palm oil, and rice, but, in sharp contrast to the Cassangas, there is no mention of slaves being taxed or kept.[64]

Fernandes also claimed that the Mansa Floup inherited all the property of his subjects and then lent it back to the family of the deceased.

> If a man died in the land of this king, Mansa Falup, all that he had, the king inherited and also the farms of the deceased. And if some sons of the deceased remain, the king lends them things like cows and other things that he could use, but when he wants he can take them back. And if a man from his country . . . went and settled outside his realm, the king sends out a request for all the goods that remain and they give them to him immediatly without debate; they fear him so much.[65]

This suggests that the Mansa Floup had the authority to claim the goods of his subjects in other states and also that there was considerable trade. It indicates that all property was seen as a possession of the king. Jan Vansina claims that this idea of royal proprietary rights is extremely common: "The king is also the symbol of the kingdom . . . the king is the kingdom and as such all the land belongs to him in the sense that he has ultimate control over it. All the people belong to him. He can command their labour and the products of their labour. He is their supreme judge and retains the power of life and death. But this power is not unlimited."[66] It appears that the Mansa's claim to authority was at least buttressed by his role as the symbol of the unity of his people, a role that was retained by Diola priest-kings in the twentieth century.

Restrictions on the Mansa Floup's eating habits suggest that there was a sacred authority attached to the institution of kingship. "This king only eats in the evening because from morning to night he always has a calabash of palm wine close to him and after he speaks at most three times, he takes the calabash and drinks."[67] The priest-kings of Huluf and Esulalu were forbidden to eat in front of people who were not in their immediate families. This prohibition was justified on the grounds that it would be dangerous for an ordinary person to see an oeyi in the act of eating, but it was part of a broader effort to overlook the whole range of the oeyi's natural activities: eating, bathing, excreting, and dying. Such restrictions emphasized the sacred qualities of Floup and Diola kingship, while concealing the biological aspects of human existence.

Fernandes did not describe the geographical dimensions of the Floup state or the structure of government beyond the activities of the king himself. Esulalu oral traditions that I received contain no specific references to this Floup state. However, if it is true that the priest-kings of the south shore Diola evolved from the institution of kingship of the sixteenth-century Floup, an interpretation that I share with Thomas, then the area that is dependent on the senior oeyi at Kerouhey may well represent the boundaries of the Floup state.[68] It would at least include Esulalu, Huluf, and Ediamat of the present-day Diola subgroups. Both the oeyi of Oussouye, the senior priest-king of Huluf, and the oeyi of Kadjinol, make semiannual trips to Kerouhey to consult with royal officials there. Informants in Esulalu and Huluf claim that they received the shrines of the priest-king from Kerouhey or the nearby village of Yahl in Ediamat.

It appears that the priest-kings of Esulalu and Huluf were initially appointed by the Mansa Floup as his agents there. The Huluf priest-king at Oussouye served as the senior oeyi to both Esulalu and Huluf. This would explain the Esulalu accounts of Oussouye's theft of Eloudia's Coeyi and Djoenenandé shrines; it was not a theft of the shrines themselves but of the claim to spiritual seniority exercised by the sons of Atta-Essou. Members of the Senghalene-Djikune lineage of Senghalene, who eventually carried Coeyi to Kadjinol, and the Lambals of Oussouye went to Kerouhey and brought back the shrine Coeyi. They and their descendants served as priest-kings in Senghalene and Huluf.[69]

This theory that the Coeyi shrines were connected to the growth of the Floup state influences my interpretation of the Diola expansion into Esulalu. If Senghalene carried with it a shrine of the Mansa Floup when it settled in the area between Huluf and Esulalu, then it may have done so as part of an effort by the Mansa Floup to expand his domains. Perhaps the whole Floup migration was supported by the Mansa Floup, which would explain why the Koonjaen did not attack the Floup; they arrived with the support of too strong a state.

The Koonjaen Wars

As Floup settlers increased within the area we know as Esulalu, the Koonjaen did not seek a direct confrontation, which offered little promise of success. Instead, they chose to harass the new settlers when they entered the area that remained under Koonjaen control. Their methods become evident from the list of causes of the Koonjaen wars given by Esulalu historians. The Koonjaen were said to have stolen rice from Floup rice paddies, an act that is strongly condemned within Diola systems of morality. Esulalu elders also claimed that the Koonjaen raided them for cattle: "The Koonjaen, they did not like lots of work, but stealing cattle . . . a lot."[70] Cattle thievery, while a nuisance, was an accepted form of raiding and was commonly done by young men against unfriendly villages. Koonjaen attacks on people were regarded as more threatening. Children who entered the Koonjaen areas were seized as slaves. Adult men were killed. According to Antoine Diedhiou: "If you went toward Huluf, the Koonjaen would kill you."[71] The treatment of women generated the greatest anger: "Why did we show them? They worked in the forest and lived there. They did evil things [seize women] . . . to make them their wives. They did it [intercourse], did it, did it, a wife until the evening when they sent her home. This is why we showed them."[72] Although these descriptions clearly reflect a Floup perspective and omit any reference to similar acts by Floup against Koonjaen, they suggest that both groups engaged in bitter competition for paddy and grazing land, as well as for regional control. Such competition culminated in the Koonjaen wars.

While often described as a single war, the Koonjaen wars were a series of battles that stretched over several generations. It is only with the last of the wars, in about 1700, do we begin to get names of participants in the battles.[73] This war marks the transition from the period of the first ancestors to that of the ancestors. It was also the largest of the Koonjaen wars, including all the townships of Esulalu and Huluf. According to Sihumucel Badji, war leaders from Esulalu coordinated their attack with Huluf's leaders. "Kadjinol, Mlomp, and Huluf, they said they [the Koonjaen] will finish us off . . . we must get ourselves ready and fight them."[74] Esulalu and Huluf agreed to wait six days before attacking. The Huluf warriors went and offered palm wine libations at the spirit shrine Hoonig in order to obtain victory in war. Then they took up positions south of the Koonjaen villages. Esulalu's forces attacked the Koonjean from the north and pushed them back into an ambush by Huluf.[75]

Many Koonjaen were killed; others fled to Esulalu, where they sought asylum. Antoine Diedhiou describes the process as it occurred at Kadjinol. A Koonjaen "went to a house . . . for a drink of water. . . . It was forbidden to kill him, your house would come to an end." The host family, once it gave refugees a drink of water, was bound by rules of hospitality to protect them.[76] Badiat Sambou suggests that the Koonjaen sought asylum at the homes of their maternal kin in the Floup townships, thus indicating a substantial degree of intermarriage and acculturation between the two groups.[77] Male Koonjaen helped their patrons with the cattle, with farming, and in wars with Djougoutes. After a while, the patrons assisted them in finding wives and land, but they remained clients of inferior status. Koonjaen women provided less of a social problem. Once incorporated into their patron's compound, they helped out with farming and household duties, before marrying either within the patron's family or in other lineages. Their children assumed the status of their fathers. These processes of asylum seeking and incorporation were repeated in communities throughout Esulalu and Huluf. The Floup's relatively peaceful methods of incorporating their former enemies facilitated the process of selective adoption of Koonjaen religious ideas and ritual practices.

During the Koonjaen wars, Eloudia and Elou Mlomp managed to avoid being conquered by the townships. However Senghalene, itself a Floup settlement, was not so fortunate. Senghalene had established itself to the north of the collection of settlements around Oussouye. Like Hawtane before it, Senghalene refused to allow Huluf or Esulalu access to large areas of palm forest and rice paddies in the Calemboekine-Babindeck area. They also began to harass travelers between Esulalu and Huluf. By 1700, an alliance of Huluf and Esulalu townships defeated Senghalene in a surprise attack at a time when many of its men were away at work in the paddies or in the forest.[78] Some people from Senghalene fled to Kadjinol and Djicomole, but a substantial portion of the community was forcibly moved closer to Oussouye, to the present site of Senghalene. The Senghor and Djikune lineages of Kadjinol and Mlomp are descendants of Senghalene refugees.

Floup, Bainounk, and European in the Lower Casamance

Despite the focus on Esulalu and its origins, it is important to keep in mind that these events occurred while the expansion of neighboring peoples and Europeans brought dramatic changes to the economic and political life of the peoples of the lower Casamance. For this view of the "macrocosm" of multiethnic and international relations, both oral and written sources are extremely limited and permit only a general overview. The history of the lower Casamance region before 1700 was dominated by the expansion of the Mandinka westward toward the Atlantic Ocean and the expansion of the Floup and Balanta northward. These three peoples gradually conquered and incorporated large numbers of the indigenous Bainounk.[79] Beginning with the Portuguese arrival in the midfifteenth century, the region was marked by the growing influence of a world economy as European traders used various African middlemen to buy slaves, wax, and a variety of other products from the peoples of the lower Casamance.

By the early sixteenth century, several strong states, influenced both by Mandinka forms of political organization and the threat of a Mandinka conquest, developed in the eastern part of the lower Casamance. The Cassanga kingdom was probably the first of these states. By the end of the sixteenth century, several new Bainounk states had acquired their independence from the Cassangas: Jaboundes on the north shore and Iziguiche on the south shore. These kingdoms prospered because of their ability to control trade in cloth, beeswax, and slaves.[80] In the seventeenth century, Bainounk kingdoms with Floup minorities controlled substantial areas along the south shore of the Gambia. In these kingdoms, Fogny and Gereges, the Floup were described as reluctant subjects who were often raided by their ostensible rulers. Sieur de la Courbe described Gereges: "the Bagnons are civilized, but the Floups are mostly savages, and because they do not recognize him [the king] except by force, he frequently makes war against them and seizes slaves that he sells; he is always well supplied with arms and powder and has several men who know how to shoot."[81] These Bainounk-dominated kingdoms offered European traders a secure base from which to trade and a steady supply of wax, slaves, rice, and hides, which led to the establishment of small European trade factories in these states. From the sale of European goods, especially iron and firearms, these kingdoms dominated large areas of the Casamance.

By 1535, Portuguese traders, based in the Cape Verde Islands, had established several trading posts in the Bissau-Casamance region, including one along the southern border of the Floup state. The Portuguese traded iron, cloth, and beads for local rice, wax, and slaves. Some of the Portuguese traders settled in the area, married local women, and created small communities of Afro-Portuguese or lançados.[82] The largest volume of European trade in the lower Casamance appears to have been with the Casa Mansa. The Cassangas' large trade fairs attracted Bainounk, Mandinka, and European participants. The Floup state was a smaller trading center. Although we have no elaborate descriptions of trade fairs, Fernandes describes the Mansa Floup's taxation of livestock, palm products, and rice. The taxing of these goods and Fernandes's awareness of such practices suggest that they were important trade items. Furthermore, Pereira describes Portuguese traders as purchasing rice and meat on the southern fringe of the Floup domains.[83] Although both accounts stress the importance of slaves and slave traders at the court of the Casa Mansa, neither describes such a presence within the Floup area. The absence of a tax on slaves suggests that the slave trade was not important to the Floup.

By the late sixteenth century, important new areas of trade had opened up along the Gambia River. Europeans began to trade with the Combo-Mansa, a Mandinka ruler over a heavily Floup population. Floups supplied most of the beeswax and rice used in trade and were often seized as slaves for sale to the Europeans. The Bainounk states along the Casamance continued to supply wax and slaves, but trade routes had shifted away from the Casamance River to overland routes toward the Gambia or São Domingo Rivers. By 1600, Bainounk traders excluded the Portuguese and lançados from these new trade routes, preferring to confine them to trading posts along the rivers.[84]

Late-sixteenth-century accounts of the Floup areas do not mention a kingdom, only a deep hostility to any European presence and a fear of engaging in commercial relations with Europeans. The Cape Verdean, André Alvares de Almada, visited the Floup area, where Pereira had described a brisk commerce, only to find that the Floup would no longer trade: "They have absolutely no trading relations with us."[85] Olfert Dapper suggested that the slave trade had led the south shore Floup to refuse to trade. "The inhabitants of this coast are better made than those of Angola, & want no trade at all with the whites nor to enter into their vessels, that they do not have hostages, a right that whites under the pretext of trade & friendship have removed from their country."[86] This description, combined with accounts of Europeans who burned villages, suggests that south shore Floup voluntarily withdrew from direct trade with the Europeans because they could not trust them. Furthermore, they began to seize Portuguese ships that ran aground. According to de Almada:

> They used to kill all of our people whom they captured when ships were wrecked, without trying to sell them (for money) or exchange them (for goods). (However) these blacks and Buramos understand each other, and our people live in the land of the Buramos, so now by means of the Buramos, exchanges of those captured are arranged, and the Falupos no longer kill them. The Buramos go to buy the captives in the homeland of the Falupo blacks.[87]

De Almada provided the earliest description of Floup commerce in slaves, though he insisted that it was on a very small scale. He mentions that Floup traders sold some captives and livestock at periodic trade fairs along the southern borders of the Floup area. "Recently they began to trade with our people in the São Domingos River, at the entrance to a creek called Timisi. . . . Our people obtain from them slaves and cows." It is unclear whether "our people" refers to their Buramo agents or to Portuguese traders. He concludes by suggesting that if these "contacts were pursued, the Falupes might be tamed completely, and there would be great trade, since there are many cows in their land, and slaves would accumulate there."[88] The linkage between taming and trade suggests the kind of economic dependence that many historians of the slave trade came to recognize only in the last half of the twentieth century.

Esulalu informants insist that they traded only with African merchants; Europeans did not come until the nineteenth century. This would confirm de Almada's contention that the Floup in this area did not like to trade with Europeans and preferred to use African middlemen. Although people in Esulalu were aware of the presence of the Portuguese in neighboring areas, they described them as sending out blacks—*grumetes*, Bainounk, or Mandinka—to conduct trade. Others describe a black community based at Ziguinchor, the seventeenth-century center of Portuguese activities in the Casamance, that raided the coastal areas of Esulalu for slaves. The Ziguinchor raiders are referred to as "Aetingah" and "Ekabiliane," which are translated as *métis*. These Afro-Portuguese conducted raids but did not establish a regular trading presence in the Esulalu portion of the Floup region.[89]

The most important traders in Esulalu during this period were Mandinka, who were described as trading in the area before the Koonjaen wars. They would come to Esulalu in large dugout canoes, carrying with them cloth, iron, and cattle and seeking to purchase rice and slaves.[90] Many of the region's Mandinka traders were Muslim. André Donelha, a contemporary of de Almada, described the Mandinka as the best traders in Guinea,

> especially the *bixirins* [marabouts], who are the priests. These people, as much for the profit they draw as (because they desire) to spread the cursed sect of Mohammad among the uncivilized, make their way through all the hinterland of Guinea and to all the seaports. And hence at any port, from (those of) the Jalofos or of Rio São Domingos . . . one finds Mandinga *bixirins*. And what they bring to sell are fetishes in the form of ram's horns and amu-

lets and sheets of paper with writing on them, which they sell as (religious) relics, and while they are selling all this stuff they are spreading the sect of Mohammad in many districts.[91]

People throughout the region had contact with Muslims and were familiar with Muslim gris-gris and ritual practice. Although there were converts to Islam in the region, there is no record of attempts to convert the people of the Esulalu area itself during the sixteenth and seventeenth centuries.

In his pathbreaking study of Upper Guinea during the era of the Atlantic slave trade, Walter Rodney insisted that the Floup were not actively involved in the slave trade except as victims. He explains this by suggesting that there was no strong Floup state or ruling class: "The isolated exceptions only serve to reinforce this generalization, because it could scarcely have been simple coincidence that the Djolas and the Balantes, who produced the least slaves either by raiding or by preying on each other, were the very tribes with an amorphous state structure from which a well-defined ruling class was absent."[92] While this may be true of the Balanta, it does not describe the nonslaving, but highly centralized, Floup state.

Furthermore, by the end of the sixteenth century, the Floup began, on a very small scale, to raid for and sell slaves. They expanded during the seventeenth century, as was noted by the Cape Verdean trader, Francisco de Lemos Coelho: "These villages of the Falupos . . . are very productive of foodstuffs, especially rice, and they sell many blacks. The blacks are much given to warfare and piracy on the water, and they sometimes rob canoes belonging to whites at Cacheu, where they go each day in canoes loaded with foodstuffs, with blacks, and with dried fish, for sale to the population."[93] The volume of this early trade is extremely difficult to ascertain. Until the nineteenth century, no major trading posts were established in the Diola heartland. Both Cacheu and the European factories of the Gambia received goods from large areas of West Africa. Isolating statistics for the Floup slave trade would be extremely difficult, unless the origins of the slaves were listed. The tendency to overlook the Floup role in the slave trade was reinforced by the European reliance on Mandinka, Bainounk, and Buramos middlemen.

This expansion occurred when the Floup state, if for no other reason than the travelers' silence in its regard, appears to be in decline. No other state appears to have filled the political vacuum, which raises serious questions about Rodney's interpretation of the slave trade as a product of a mutually beneficial alliance between European and lançado traders and the indigenous ruling class. By the time of de Almada, the ruling classes of the Floup had collapsed, but a slave trade had emerged. Rather than an activity of a ruling class, the Floup slave trade was conducted by small groups of raiders who hoped to increase their cattle herds and landholdings.

In the seventeenth century, the Portuguese expanded their activities in the coastal area from the Gambia to the Casamance and São Domingo rivers. By 1640, Portuguese traders based at Cacheu were exporting significant quantities of wax, rice, cattle, and approximately three thousand slaves a year. Rodney suggests that this estimate by the Conselho Ultramarino overlooked slaves that were not registered with the government officials. Nonregistration was a common way of avoiding the tax on the export of slaves.[94] In 1676, the importance of this trade was recognized when a new slave-trading company was chartered, the Companhia de Cacheu e Rios de Guiné, for the express purpose of supplying slaves to Portuguese plantations in Brazil.[95] During the same period, Portuguese traders also established small factories at Ziguinchor and Bolor. The Ziguinchor post was a mere forty kilometers from Esulalu; Bolor was in the southern part of the Floup domains. These traders generated considerable tension among the Floup, especially after they burned some Floup villages in 1669. The Floup retaliated by destroying the Portuguese factory at Bolor.[96]

During this period, French, British, and Dutch traders successfully challenged Portuguese hegemony in the Senegambia-Guinea coast region. Jean Boulègue suggests that this new competition increased the ability of the African populace to manipulate prices and to make their participation in the growing transatlantic trade more lucrative. He cites a Dutch merchant who complained of the Africans' growing search for profits: "The blacks along the coast from Cape Verde to Cape Roxo [a Diola township] are spoiled by us, the English and especially the French, and are made really evil, such that we can not even take a hogshead of water or an armful of firewood without paying him double."[97] Although Portuguese law forbade them from selling firearms in the region, other European traders sold firearms to African traders, who valued them over other trade goods. The growing profitability of trade with Europeans may have been an important factor in Floup's decision to enter into the slave trade during the seventeenth century.

In the late seventeenth century, British and French merchants attempted to establish themselves in the region. In 1669, British officials in the Gambia attempted to enlist an Afro-Portuguese trader to explore the Floup area of Bliss-Karones "that up to the present has not been explored. . . . It is said that it will yield considerable trade; primarily in wax, skins, negroes, and ivory. The people are Floups."[98] Francisco Azevedo de Coelho declined the offer because of his loyalty to the Portuguese. Further south, along the Casamance itself, the Portuguese had established a sufficiently strong presence that they could close the river to other Europeans. Special exemptions were sold by the Captain Major of Cacheu at a substantial profit. Regional trade was profitable enough to limit access to it and to sell trade permits at a price sufficient to maintain the Portuguese garrison at Ziguinchor.[99]

The establishment of a more permanent European community within the region permitted greater social and religious interaction between Europeans and Africans. Portuguese traders often married local women, who became their commercial partners as well as their spouses. The Portuguese also embraced the practice of sealing commercial transactions with ritual sacrifice at local spirit shrines.[100] African grammatical patterns and vocabulary slowly transformed their language into a Portuguese creole. However, the Portuguese lançados continued to follow European styles of dress, wear saints' medals and crucifixes, and think of themselves as European and Catholic. A chronic shortage of priests prevented the lançados from receiving instruction in Christian doctrine or from receiving the sacraments. In the seventeenth century, the few priests in Portuguese Guinea rarely left Cacheu. European travelers in the area regularly complained about the lançados' lack of familiarity with their faith and their lack of ritual observances.[101]

Despite their lack of rigorous instruction, the Afro-Portuguese made some effort to spread their faith. The Afro-Portuguese trader, Azevedo de Coelho, claimed that the Floup "can already be made a good harvest for the Catholic religion." Father Labat claimed that the King of Gereges had become familiar enough with Christianity to request that missionaries be sent to his kingdom.[102] Labat also suggested that the "idolators" at Gereges were far easier to convert than the Muslims, thereby implying that local Europeans had some experience of both types of religious encounter. There may well have been some commerce in rosaries, crucifixes, and saints' medals for use as talismans.[103] At Cacheu, de Almada noted that the local Catholic church could assemble as many as eight hundred people during Lent, and there were large religious processions through the town during Holy Week. These attracted considerable interest from the local African population, possibly including some Floup.[104] Still, as Azevedo de Coelho noted,

> There is no record of any priest being sent expressly for the conversion of this pagan people, the Lord Bishops of this island—to which all the coast is suffragan—being content to send a vicar to the town of Cacheu, where the Captain-Major resides, to administer the sacrament to the inhabitants there. And when this benefit was extended further, it was only to send a cleric to administer the sacraments to the inhabitants of a specific settlement.[105]

Despite this lack of active proselytization, by the end of the seventeenth century, many Floup may have become familiar with some of the material objects and ritual practices associated with Catholicism.

The era when Floup and Koonjaen competed for hegemony over the Esulalu-Huluf area of the lower Casamance was also the period when European traders were becoming a powerful influence within regional affairs. The growth of a market for slaves and agricultural products aggravated regional instability and escalated the level of warfare. This commerce destabilized the Floup communities south of the Casamance, in the area governed by the Mansa Floup. It appears that the Floup state was unable to exercise control over increasing commercial activities or to maintain its authority in a region that was increasingly disrupted by slave raiding. Raiders from across the Casamance, in Djougoutes, came in canoes and kidnapped people working alone in the rice paddies. Small children were not allowed to leave their neighborhoods for fear that they would be seized. Men did not travel alone to the next township because of the danger of capture.

Raiding within areas occupied by the Floup was not controlled by any formal government; individuals or bands of men organized slave raids against neighboring townships or isolated travelers. Dense forests made ambushing a simple process, readily accomplished with bows and arrows or spears, which ordinary farmers could obtain. Neither the Mansa Floup nor local leaders could readily control a slave trade where it was so easy to become a participant.[106] Under the impetus of the slave trade, the Floup state lost its power to control commerce or maintain its authority. Increasingly, the township and village quarter became the only secure political entities and the primary moral communities.

There is no record that a new state emerged and gained control of the former Floup domains. Contrary to certain theories of state formation in Africa, the slave trade did not strengthen the Floup state.[107] I would suggest that it accelerated its decline. Religious authorities filled the void left by the collapse of the Floup state and established a rudimentary system of order. This change brought the spirit shrines and their priests into a more central role in Floup affairs and strengthened the religious aspect of the oeyi or priest-king. It is during this period, beginning in the seventeenth century, that the south shore Floup began a period of political organization described as stateless, relying on elders of the ukine for the preservation of order.

Within this context, the Koonjaen wars occurred. Perhaps the Floup state had been able to maintain the peace while Floup newcomers settled in Esulalu. By the time that the Mansa Floup's power was in decline, Esulalu's Floup had grown sufficiently strong to be able to withstand a Koonjaen military threat and to forcibly incorporate the Koonjaen into the new townships. Increasing pressure on the land caused by population growth and recurrent drought was a major factor in this escalating competition between Floup and Koonjaen. However, once the Koonjaen were conquered, their rapid incorporation into the Diola townships could provide some assistance against the political, economic, and environmental uncertainty that prevailed throughout the region. It is from this process of incorporation, beginning in the seventeenth century, but intensifying in the eighteenth, that a common Esulalu social and religious identity was forged. The gradual assimilation of Koonjaen and Floup traditions into a single community formed the basis of Esulalu cultural identity.

4

Koonjaen, Floup, and the Forging of a Diola-Esulalu Religious Tradition in the Eighteenth Century

The forging of an Esulalu religious tradition from the older traditions of Koonjaen and Floup began during a period of political, economic, and environmental uncertainty throughout the lower Casamance. This tradition began to take shape after the fall of the Floup state, when ritual elders and the cults they controlled became the major force for the maintenance of the social order. Indirect links to European traders operating in the Casamance region expanded the market for captives, rice, and beeswax while increasing the availability of such goods as iron, firearms, cloth, and cattle.[1] Contact with Europeans, through various African middlemen, also introduced new diseases. The greater mobility of people through various trade networks helped spread both new and old maladies with far greater speed. All of these changes had to be explained within an Esulalu system of thought and controlled through the development of appropriate ritual forms.

Central to the task of creating an Esulalu cultural tradition was the development of a system of thought that could appeal to both Floup and Koonjaen populations within the townships. The Floup majority itself was not unified; each lineage traced its origins back to a particular Huluf or Ediamat township. In many cases, lineage names reflected these diverse origins.[2] Settlers from each of these communities had their own shrines and a strong sense of loyalty to their group, a loyalty that was far stronger than their initial allegiance to the new townships. However, evidence of interlineage conflicts during the period before the Koonjaen wars appears to be beyond the memory of Esulalu historians.

By the late seventeenth century, the Esulalu townships had developed some degree of cooperation and social integration. Such sentiments were symbolized by the office of the oeyi, the priest-king, his series of shrines, and the elders who supervised them. Shrines associated with the well-being of individual quarters fostered a sense of quarter unity and provided a system of governance for the major subdivisions of the townships. Still, the lineage-based neighborhood remained the only true moral community, protected against most violent actions from within and able to command group solidarity in the face of outside challenges.[3] Although the threat of the Koonjaen encouraged the forging of interquarter bonds within the townships, they remained fragile.

Despite their close proximity to their fellow immigrants in Huluf, the people of Esulalu found it difficult to maintain regular contact with these communities. The frequency of Koonjaen raids discouraged travel through the thick forests separating Esulalu from Huluf and Ediamat. In relative isolation, the people of Esulalu looked to their own communities for leadership and new teachings about the awasena path. The lessening of commercial, social, and ritual ties with Huluf and Ediamat earned them the name Esulalu, a term that implied a distant or poorly known place.[4] With isolation came a growing preference for marriage within Esulalu, which tended to reinforce a growing linguistic and cultural distinctiveness. Rapidly changing political and economic conditions also influenced the development of distinctive Esulalu customs. With the conquest of the Koonjaen and their removal to the Esulalu townships, Koonjaen influences also began to contribute to an emerging Esulalu awasena tradition.

In this chapter, I focus on the problem of forging a unified and coherent awasena tradition capable of satisfying the needs of the various communities that had settled in Esulalu. The specific impact of Esulalu participation in an expanding network of trade is discussed in chapter 5. Enduring tensions between indigenous Koonjaen and invasive Floup and between Floup of different origins generated a series of challenges to a religious system that was integrally involved in the maintenance of community order. While such diversity was a source of tension and a not infrequent cause of warfare, it also provided a variety of approaches to the explanation and control, through religious means, of a rapidly changing world. I also examine the influence of environmental disruption, frequent and prolonged droughts, and plagues of insects and diseases that became common during the eighteenth century. The development of an Esulalu prophetic tradition, which stressed direct contact between people, Emitai, and a host of spiritual intermediaries, is also central to this discussion. Each of these forces generated new questions about the place of the individual in relation to family, community, and the spiritual world.

I contend that this emerging awasena system was able to interpret, explain, and channel these forces while developing an integrated Esulalu religious tradition. The relative youth of this tradition, its diverse origins, and its emphasis on individual initiative in all spheres of personal experience allowed the people of Esulalu to continue to endow rapidly changing circumstances with meaning and to continue to shape these forces of change within Esulalu society.[5]

Incorporating Koonjaen Traditions

With the ending of the Koonjaen wars in the early eighteenth century, most of the Koonjaen villages were incorporated within the townships. Koonjaen and Floup shared many ideas and concerns and had similar notions of how society should be organized. Both groups were farmers committed to the intensive care of their rice paddies and convinced of the spiritual bond linking soil, rice, water, humans, and Emitai. Their rituals reflected their concerns with this interdependence and sought, through acts of supplication and communion, to maximize the life-giving properties of their land and their communities. Both groups were accustomed to living in small, lineage-based communities, each of which jealously guarded its rights to land and political autonomy. For Koonjaen and Floup, the office of the priest-king provided the primary institution for community unity and legitimated some degree of political cooperation. Both peoples looked to their histories to determine rights to land and shrines and to rank the relative power of these shrines and their priests.

This common sense of the centrality of historical precedent provided the first major obstacle to the integration of Koonjaen and Floup. Each group looked at its past relations with the other and saw long stretches of warfare embittered by deaths, kidnappings, rapes, and raiding. Each community valued its own institution of the priest-king and its own cluster of royal shrines dedicated to community welfare and the procurement of rain. Both groups had their own networks of household and lineage shrines associated with fertility, healing, work, and governance. Furthermore, Koonjaen and Floup were divided by language and by custom, which each community wished to preserve. The incorporation of the conquered Koonjaen would prove to be a difficult task. Questions of Koonjaen social, economic, and ritual status had to be resolved, particularly because of Koonjaen links to the land as "owners of the soil." This task was complicated by the political and environmental uncertainty of the period.

Some links had been forged between Koonjaen and Floup even before the Koonjaen defeat. Commercial relations had provided a limited area for peaceful contact. Koonjaen traded iron and iron implements for Floup fish. The Koonjaen shared their adaptations of wet rice agriculture to the local environment, while the Floup shared their knowledge of carving dugout canoes and their techniques for catching fish.[6] However, there was a limit to the sharing of technical information. Koonjaen smithing techniques were not taught during this period. From these limited economic contacts, social relations began to develop. I have no indication of the extent of interethnic marriage, but it was not a rare occurrence.[7]

As the Koonjaen wars dragged on through much of the seventeenth century, some Koonjaen were incorporated into the townships. Individuals sought asylum with Floup families. Antoine Diedhiou described one such case in which a Koonjaen went to a house for a drink of water. Once having received the water, he could not be harmed. "It was absolutely forbidden [to kill him], your house would come to an end." The offering of water obligated the host family to provide asylum and hospitality. Male asylum seekers stayed with their "tutors" and helped with the cattle, with farming, and in wars with Djougoutes. Eventually, they were assisted in finding wives and were given some land. Still, they remained Koonjaen, clients of inferior status. Female Koonjaen were taken into Floup households, where they worked for their hosts until they married within the host's lineage, to other Koonjaen, or within the general community. Bridal gifts were presented to a woman's Floup host. Some refugees sought asylum with their maternal kin. They were incorporated as junior kin, dependent on their relations for protection and for access to land.[8]

In some cases, entire Koonjaen families were removed from the forest areas and brought to the townships. Unlike individual refugees, they came with household goods and with ritual objects associated with particular shrines. They needed less assistance than solitary refugees, had kin support, and, in certain cases, retained rights to paddy land and palm trees near their former homes. Koonjaen were given land within the townships, where they could build homes and plant gardens. Usually they were settled in quarters that were numerically weaker than their neighbors. Despite their greater self-reliance, these new settlers remained a subject people, taunted by the remark: "You are not anything. You are Koonjaen."[9]

Some people have suggested that the Koonjaen were incorporated into the community as slaves (amiekele). There appears to be little evidence of this. Unlike slaves, the majority of Koonjaen arrived in families and had strong ties to the land. They were houbook, people born on the land, and therefore of free status. Slaves were people without kin and without ties to the soil. Because of this distinction, slaves were buried in a separate strangers' cemetery and were subjected to humiliating rituals.[10] Koonjaen, despite their low status, were buried in the main cemetery. Although incorporated as subject people without political influence, the Koonjaen were seen as spiritually powerful. They were seen as the first inhabitants of the land given by Emitai to Atta-Essou. Their shrines for the fertility of land and women and for the procurement of rain derived their power from the special ties of the Koonjaen to the land.

Floup attitudes toward Koonjaen incorporation appear to have developed in three distinct stages. Initially, the conquered Koonjaen were seen as a political threat, a foreign ethnic group within the townships. They had powerful allies in Bainounk villages near Ziguinchor and across the Casamance River. Their use of a different language and their practice of a different religious path were central to their ethnic consciousness. Therefore, the townships attempted to suppress both of these aspects of Koonjaen identity. During the Koonjaen wars, many of the Koonjaen shrines were destroyed. Some shrines survived but could not be used because of Floup opposition. Many of the cults that did survive were practiced secretly, in the forest, away from the eyes of the leaders of Esulalu.[11]

The shrine that appeared most threatening was the Koonjean's Egol, located in the sacred forest of Calemboekine. This shrine, more than any other, represented the spiritual unity of the Koonjaen. It was said to have been given by Emitai to Atta-Essou, who passed it on to his sons, who became priest-kings. At its shrine, prayers were offered for rain, for the fertility of the soil, and for protection of each member of the Koonjean community. Publicly, the cult of Egol was abandoned when the Koonjaen were defeated. Kapooeh Diedhiou suggested that it was because: "If they seize you as a slave . . . you would not have the strength to perform its rites." However, rituals continued for a long time after the conquest. People would come and perform the rites, but the community at large did not know where the worshipers came from.[12] The Egol shrine enjoyed so much prestige that the Esulalu communities wanted to assume its power. When the Floup of Djicomole wished to establish their shrine of the priest-king (Coeyi), they took over the sacred forest of Eloudia's Koonjaen, which is to say, the sacred forest of Atta-Essou's Egol. This action by Djicomole served the dual purpose of weakening the indigenous cult and drawing the power of the Koonjaen shrine into the new cult presided over by a Floup priest-king.[13]

Several cults of Koonjaen origin survived the conquest and remained distinctly Koonjaen. Most of them were family shrines and were tolerated because the people of Esulalu had similar shrines and did not find them threatening. Kahlayoh, the lineage shrine of the Gayo Diedhious, still exists, and it serves to ensure the fertility and material and moral well-being of the family.[14] A second Koonjaen cult, Djiguemah, survives in the Huluf township of Kolobone. Members of the Gent lineage of Kolobone-Ekink and of one of the Gent lineages of Kadjinol attend the annual rites performed before the planting of rice. Both groups are said to be descendants of Atta-Essou.[15] During these nocturnal rituals, a pig is sacrificed, rice is prepared, and the sacrificial meat is eaten at the shrine site. Both men and women of the Gent lineage attend the annual event, but these rituals are closed to outsiders. The continued survival of such shrines indicates that family shrines were not seen as a political threat or regarded as potential competition with Floup shrines for ritual attention.

Despite the long period of hostilities between Koonjaen and Floup, there were strong pressures toward forging an effective union. One force working toward the rapid assimilation of the Koonjaen was the frequency of warfare with people from the north shore. People from Djougoutes and the coastal islands, who had mastered the use of large dugout canoes, would seize people from Esulalu while they worked in the rice paddies. This kidnapping often led to counterraids and occasionally into prolonged warfare.[16] The Esulalu townships needed peace within their communities and added manpower to protect themselves against the raiders of the north shore. Gradually, the Koonjaen appeared less threatening, and they were accepted in Esulalu war parties.[17]

Economic pressures also contributed to the incorporation of the Koonjaen. The most technically skilled and the largest number of blacksmiths in Esulalu were of Koonjaen descent. Most of them settled in the Kafone quarter of Kadjinol, where they became the primary ironworkers for the whole region. They introduced their boekine, Silapoom, which provided spiritual protection for craftsmen working with the forge and a shrine-based guild system for the protection of technical knowledge and the maintenance of trade rules. Like Djiguemah's, Silapoom's cult welcomed the participation of women, though only men could forge. This shrine was readily accepted in Esulalu, where Floup ironworkers welcomed the protection of Silapoom.[18]

Perhaps the most important factor in promoting a more complete incorporation of the Koonjaen was their status as "owners of the soil," the first and original inhabitants, whose ties to the land could be traced back to their first ancestors and to Emitai's assistance when they first settled the region. Diola historians acknowledge the influences of the Koonjaen. "The Koonjaen showed us many ukine."[19] While the Koonjaen had a shrine of the dead that was described as comparable to the Diola Kouhouloung, it is unclear whether this shrine was influenced by that of the Koonjaen. The Koonjaen also had a family shrine, comparable to the Diola Hupila, but I have collected no evidence to suggest that it influenced the various forms of the Diola Hupila.[20] Initially, the townships did not accept the Koonjaen shrines of Egol, Cayinte, or Djoenenandé. Their close association with the Koonjaen oeyi was a threat to the establishment of Floup political and religious hegemony.

As Esulalu confidence in the Koonjaen grew, they adopted a Koonjaen ritual of male initiation known as Kahat. This rite was closely associated with the Koonjaen shrine of the land, Ewang, and with Kahlayoh, the Gayo lineage shrine.[21] It remains unclear whether the Floup settlers in Esulalu had an older form of male circumcision. Had there not been a Floup form of male initiation, the Koonjaen rites of Kahat would have proven highly useful. They provided an occasion for the senior men to introduce younger men, approaching marriage, to a wealth of religious, social, and military knowledge while maintaining the authority of the elders. Kahat provided a means for a group of young men to establish strong bonds between them, forged through the shared suffering in circumcision as well as the communitas of the ritual seclusion.[22] It provided an opportunity to test the bravery and ability of young men to bear pain, an important virtue in a society in which all men were responsible for the defense of the community. Finally, there was the element of sacrifice. Kahat's sacrifice of a part of the male reproductive organ ensured its continued fertility and the fertility of the land. As B. K. Sagnia has suggested, "it is believed that the shedding of blood during the operation serves to bind the circumcised to the land and consequently to his ancestors. . . . Thus the circumcision blood is like making a covenant, or agreement between the circumcised, the land, the departed, the community and people among whom you are born."[23]

If the Esulalu already had a circumcision ritual at that time, I can suggest two factors that could have influenced their decision to accept Kahat: a preference for Kahat's ritual and a perceived greater efficacy of the Koonjaen rite. The Koonjaen's status as first inhabitants, whose ancestors were buried in its soil, and their special ties to the land supported the idea that their initiation rituals would be particularly efficacious. This idea of "owners of the soil" as a conduit of spiritual blessings led the Esulalu newcomers to embrace Kahat in an effort to ensure the fertility of the land and the community, as well as adequate rainfall to nourish them all.

During most of the eighteenth century, Esulalu practiced Kahat. Each township maintained a shrine of Ewang, whose priest controlled the process of male initiation. The most powerful of the Ewang shrines was located in the Huluf town of Kolobone and was controlled by the priest-king of Oussouye. Before a group of boys was initiated, rituals were performed at the Kolobone Ewang. To ensure the safety of the initiates, rituals were also performed at the township Ewang and at the Koonjaen shrine of Kahlayoh.[24] Boys were initiated in small groups, after puberty but before they married. After the actual operation, the initiates were secluded for one month, during which time they were taught about the awasena path and about Esulalu history, as well as etiquette, sexuality, and the responsibilities of manhood. Women could not enter the initiates' ritual enclosure (Houle), but they cooked rice and brought it to the edge of the retreat area. During this time, women were allowed to go about their ordinary business and work in the fields.[25] After having completed the rites, initiates were considered men and could prepare for marriage.

Despite Esulalu's acceptance of a limited number of Koonjaen shrines, the Koonjaen remained excluded from leadership roles in the townships. They were not named as elders at the most important decision-making shrines. Township and quarter meetings were open to them, but if they chose to address the assembly, their comments would be greeted by insults about their Koonjaen background.[26]

By the late eighteenth century, Esulalu took another major step toward the integration of the Koonjaen. They adopted the Koonjaen royal shrines and named the Koonjaen descendants of Atta-Essou as the priest-kings. This extraordinary development may be explained in several ways. It may have been brought on by environmental disaster, such as the locust plagues and the recurrent droughts of the 1780s.[27] The cause that is most commonly cited in oral traditions was that the Esulalu priest-kings kept dying. The owners of the royal shrines, the families that had gone to Kerouhey, to Oussouye, or to Kadjinol, to bring back Coeyi, had initially installed themselves as priest-kings. One of their descendants, the adjunct to the present oeyi of Mlomp, described the result: "It was bad. If you did someone [installed him] he would die. . . . We gave it to Gent. . . . If they seized one of Kolobone [his lineage], he would not have a year [of life]."[28]

Fear of the power of the royal shrines when not properly integrated within the spiritual order of the land led the Floup elders of Coeyi to surrender their offices as priest-kings. At Kadjinol and Djicomole, they passed their shrines to the Koonjaen descendants of Atta-Essou, the Gent lineage, because of its long-standing ties to the land. The Esulalu owners of the shrine felt that they did not have this spiritual bond.[29] The deaths of Esulalu's oeyis could well have indicated Emitai's displeasure with the newcomers as priest-kings. The plagues of locusts and the withholding of rain, a gift of Emitai (*emitai ehlahl* means "rainfall"), were probably seen as further signs of Emitai's displeasure. The Gent lineage was chosen because they were the descendants of the creators of the indigenous royal shrines, those established by Atta-Essou with the blessing of Emitai. Simultaneously, they allowed Gent to install their royal shrine of Egol in the sacred forest in close proximity to the Floup shrine of Coeyi.[30] Both shrines were seen as crucial to the maintenance of community fertility and the procurement of adequate rainfall.

While Koonjaen and Floup shrines were brought together in a single sacred forest, strict controls were placed on the independence of the new priest-kings. The Floup owners of the shrine retained the right to select each new oeyi from among the eligible Koonjaen families. They also controlled the initiation of the new priest-king and supervised his activities. They made sure that the oeyi followed the multitude of rules that governed the conduct of his daily affairs. The rigorous restrictions on the priest-king's activities, including prohibitions on crossing streams, carrying weapons, or engaging in wars may well have originated during this period.[31] At this time the oeyi was excluded from participation in the township council shrine of Hutendookai.

The oeyi offered sacrifices for the fertility of the land and of women, and he prayed for rain. However, he was not supposed to involve himself in political disputes. While granting the Gent lineages control of their most powerful shrines and allowing the community as a whole to benefit from the power of the Koonjaen shrines, township elders would not allow the priest-king to exercise political authority. At the shrines, the priest-kings ruled. Within the townships, shrine elders, primarily of Floup descent, controlled community affairs. While the limitations on the mobility and political influence of the priest-king were said to ensure the purity of this powerful office, they were also designed to prevent the concentration of too much power in the hands of any individual.[32] By sacrificing his former name, his former pattern of economic activity, and his rights to engage in local disputes, the oeyi obtained a new power and became the symbol of the spiritual unity of the community. As a Koonjaen priest, under the control of Diola elders, he became a symbol of Koonjaen status within Esulalu. He was king and client, pure and savage, Diola and Koonjaen.

With the elevation of the Gent lineage to the position of oeyi, the Koonjaen entered fully into the life of the townships. The history of Atta-Essou became a part of Esulalu traditions, alongside the histories of Esulalu migrations from Ediamat and the histories of Floup shrines. Accompanying these traditions of Atta-Essou, came the Koonjaen tradition of Emitai's revelations to people in order to create new shrines and communicate Emitai's expectations for the community. Within Diola traditions, narratives of Koonjaen origin, rather than Floup, provide the earliest accounts of the supreme being summoning individuals to receive instruction.[33]

In this developing tradition of Emitai's revelation to people in Esulalu, Aberman Manga represents a transitional figure. Born in a Koonjaen lineage at Eloudia, he moved to the Esulalu township of Kadjinol. Said to be the son of Atta-Essou, though the term could also refer to a direct descendant, he received visions that are strikingly similar to Atta-Essou's, but on behalf of the entire township. Like Atta-Essou, Aberman had many children. When a severe drought caused a famine and he was unable to feed his family, he prayed to Emitai and said: "There is no water. Emitai has not rained." After he prayed, "Emitai provided a large rain, which is why we would pray at the boekine."[34] Like Atta-Essou he was said not to have died; rather, he fashioned a pair of fan palm fiber wings and rose up to the heavens. Pieces of his wings, however, fell back to earth, where they were gathered up and placed at the shrine that bears his name, Aberman. At this shrine, men of a Gent lineage of Kadjinol-Ebankine, his direct descendants, performed rituals in which they invoked Emitai and asked for Its assistance in obtaining rain for the people of Esulalu.[35]

Although Esulalu culture became a synthesis of Koonjaen and Floup, Diola elders insisted on distinctions. The term "Koonjaen" remained a grave insult, and few people would admit to Koonjaen descent.[36] Among the powerful elders of the shrines, ritual distinctions between Coeyi and Egol and between the owners of the office and the priest-king who took it on remained central. In traditions circulated within the community as a whole, both shrines became Diola, while the Koonjaen were regarded as a barbarous and conquered people.

Despite the unification of two traditions of priest-kings and the integration of the Koonjaen into the townships, a limited ethnic boundary persisted in Esulalu community life. While such a boundary may appear to be an anachronism, Fredrik Barth suggests that it reveals important insights into the nature of Esulalu society. The maintenance of the distinction between Koonjaen and Diola supported a shared concept that the wide diffusion of spiritual and political authority was necessary for the maintenance of a relatively egalitarian community.[37] A continuing belief in the "savagery" of the Koonjaen provided a way to limit the power of those who were acknowledged as spiritually powerful. The priest-king's "savage" ancestry would undermine any attempt by him to dominate the community. Even a priest-king, the embodiment of the spiritual unity of the townships, in other spheres, "was not anything"; he was Koonjaen.

Spirit Shrines, the Townships, and the Problem of Warfare

The incorporation of the Koonjaen into the Floup settlements was not the only task confronting the inhabitants of Esulalu. There were sharp divisions between different factions within the townships. Floup who traced their migration back to different villages in Huluf and Ediamat and who controlled different types of spirit shrines competed for influence. Aggravating such divisions were frequent disputes over rice paddy and forest land and over livestock. Perceived violations of women also provoked disputes. Occasionally, these disputes would escalate into battles, pitting quarters of the same township or several Esulalu townships against each other. As a Diola proverb suggests: "It is for children, women, and the land that the Diola fights."[38] The frequency of such battles (Kadjinol's quarters of Kafone and Sergerh fought at least three) make them difficult to date but is eloquent testimony to the weakness of townshipwide institutions and the insecurity of daily life. In describing this period, Diola historians talked about the tensions generated by the fear of communal conflict. Men went to sleep with a sword or machete within easy reach. Elders avoided socializing in other quarters because minor disputes could turn into bloody confrontations. Children from different quarters would only meet through kinship networks or through township wrestling matches.[39] Esulalu architecture reflected the turbulence of daily life. As early as the seventeenth century, houses were being built like fortresses of clay, surrounded by walls and with only one entrance.[40]

At the beginning of the eighteenth century, only the authority of the priest-king and his townshipwide shrines provided a symbolic and institutional structure for the creation of township unity. The priest-king's shrine of Coeyi safeguarded the lives of the entire township. Wives from outside the township and children born within the community had ritual offerings of palm wine and rice made on their behalf at the Coeyi shrine. By doing so, they would receive the spiritual protection of the shrine. The oeyi and his group of elders discussed township problems and struggled to maintain the peace. Sinyendikaw Diedhiou described the priest-king's role in preventing interquarter conflict. Upon learning of a battle, "the oeyi would come and summon the elders [involved in the war]. They would be fined seven cattle."[41] Other Diola historians described war leaders plotting battles in secret, lest the priest-king learn of their plans and prevent them. Once the priest-king arrived at the scene and waved his ritual broom, all fighting had to stop. Anyone who continued fighting invited not only his own death but also the deaths of his entire family.[42] Although this description may represent an idealized vision of the ability of the priest-king to stop wars within Esulalu, it does illustrate the fundamental opposition of the priest-king to warfare that would endanger Esulalu's unity.

Despite the authority of the priest-king, interquarter hostility was a persistent problem. Most ritual life and decision making occurred within individual township quarters. While respecting the office of the oeyi, each quarter turned to its own shrines for protection in war and to reach community decisions. At these shrines, decisions were made to engage in war, plans were developed, and the aid of the ukine was requested. Participation was limited to the inhabitants of the area protected by the shrine, perhaps a quarter, a series of quarters, or only a single neighborhood within a quarter. The restrictions on participation at these shrines indicate the types of alliances, the boundaries of a moral community, that existed at the time of their creation. For Kadjinol's shrine of Elenkine-Sergerh, men from Ebankine, Kagnao, Sergerh, and most of Kafone could participate, but not that portion of Kafone called Ecuhuh, which was a part of the Hassouka quarter at the time of Elenkine-Sergerh's creation. Rites at the Kafone quarter shrine, Dehouhow, included Ecuhuh, indicating that it was created after the Hassouka-Kafone War.[43]

Many of the quarter shrines traced their origins back to powerful individuals who claimed that they could see into the spiritual world. They claimed to see ammahl, spirits that wandered the world and who were often associated with water.[44] Ammahl can choose to reveal themselves to certain individuals, though only people with special powers can see them. In many cases, those who received the initial revelations were women. Thus for Elenkine-Sergerh, Boolai Senghor described how "a woman went to find grass. She saw it [the ammahl] but not everyone could see it." It told the woman to tell Sergerh that they should do a ritual there to Elenkine-Sergerh. According to Kapooeh Diedhiou, the ammahl of Elenkine-Sergerh resembles a large serpent and is called *ediumpo*. It is said to intervene with Emitai on behalf of Kalybillah, to procure rain. A woman also revealed the Kandianka quarter's shrine of Elucil. She was a slave seized from Djougoutes and later released. The priests of Elucil (also known as Kanalia) and Elenkine-Sergerh are male, as are those permitted to attend their rituals. This pattern of women who introduce what become male shrines seems particularly important in reference to quarter shrines.[45]

When the ammahl revealed itself, it would provide instructions about the establishment of a cult and an offer to aid the worshipers in matters of community concern. In such consultations, the spiritual powers of the priests and elders of the shrine were of critical importance. According to Boolai Senghor, when the quarter shrines were consulted about community needs, they would "summon those with head [special powers]. They will say what is there. . . . When they had finished listening, people would ask them what they think. If they think, we are in the wrong then there will be no war." At Samatit, the ammahl associated with the Enac shrine was also consulted by summoning elders with the powers of the "head." At both Elenkine-Sergerh and Enac, the ammahl were said to guide these elders in their decisions. Once Kadjinol-Sergerh made war when it was said to be in the wrong. The ammahl of Elenkine-Sergerh deserted the shrine and went to another township; Sergerh lost the battle. Even the way sacrificial animals were selected emphasized the working of spiritual forces. Stray cattle and goats, "without owners," were led by the ammahl to the elders of the shrine and sacrificed at Elenkine-Sergerh.[46]

While quarter shrines provided a place for war-related discussions and attempts to gain spiritual assistance, the turmoil of war itself helped to produce new leaders, who created new cults. The most important of these leaders was Kooliny Djabune, a man who claimed to have had visions of Emitai during an interquarter war at Kadjinol. Although it is difficult to pinpoint the date of this war, it probably occurred in the late eighteenth century,[47] when Hassouka was the most populous and most powerful section of Kadjinol. Its opponent, Kafone, was smaller and included a far larger number of former Koonjaen, especially blacksmiths of the various Diedhiou lineages. The war began after Hassouka's men attacked and raped some women of Kafone as they went to get water from a spring in the rice paddies.[48]

In the midst of this crisis, Kooliny Djabune fell into a sleep that resembled death. Before he went into his sleep, he told his wife and son that he was going to see Emitai and that they should not do anything to his body that he was leaving behind. According to Sinyendikaw Diedhiou, Kooliny "went to Emitai. . . . he had a strength. He slept. . . . His strength went [to Emitai]. Someone who saw you would say you had died. Siopama Diedhiou described Kooliny's sleep. "You die. You cannot do anything . . . for six, seven, eight days."[49] Kooliny's soul was said to have gone to Emitai while his body remained behind in a deep sleep, resembling death. Kooliny's soul described Hassouka's rape of the Kafone women. According to Antoine Diedhiou, "Emitai wept. . . . It is forbidden to marry [a euphemism for sexual intercourse] in a meeting place."[50] His soul was away for so long that his wife feared that he had died. She wanted to tell her brother so that they could begin funeral rites. To protect his life, Kooliny had to hurry back to the living before his instruction was complete. However, he had learned enough to expect Emitai's aid. Nothing happened.

He returned to Emitai in a dream and described the fears of the community. Emitai gave him a pipe. It told Kooliny that the next day he should look for a spear in his backyard. If he found it, Kafone could go to war. Kooliny found the spear and summoned his quarter of Kafone to perform a ritual at the new shrine, Cabai, "the spear." Then they prepared for war. When Hassouka arrived at the field of battle, Kooliny lit his pipe and a cloud of smoke covered the area. The men of Hassouka could not see their opponents, but the men of Kafone could see Hassouka. Kafone forced Hassouka to retreat, where they were attacked by men from the Haer quarter of what was to become Mlomp. In appreciation of their aid, Kafone gave Haer a Cabai shrine and a portion of forest land and vowed never to fight a war against Haer.[51]

While Esulalu accounts of the creation of the world and its destruction refer to Emitai's revelations to the first people and Koonjaen traditions describe Atta-Essou's visions, Kooliny's teachings provide another example of the incorporation of Koonjaen traditions of divine revelation into an emerging Esulalu tradition. Kooliny Djabune fell into a deep sleep, lasting several days, during which time his soul encountered the supreme being. There were two such visions. This account stands in sharp contrast to the description of Atta-Essou's ongoing visions of Emitai. Kooliny's visions appear to have ceased after the creation of Cabai.[52] There appear to be no broader teachings, only the suggestion that Emitai would aid those in dire need, in the pursuit of a just cause. From this account, it becomes clear that in eighteenth-century Esulalu Diola thought that Emitai would intervene in local affairs when calamity threatened, but only on the side of the righteous. However, contacts with Emitai were difficult, attainable only by people who possessed spiritual powers (houkaw). The messages from Emitai were often incomplete, requiring additional visits when possible or resulting in fragmentary teachings when additional visions were not possible.

The Cabai shrine became the major war shrine for the Esulalu townships. Sacrifices were offered before battle. The spirit associated with Cabai would enable those it aided to hide in the forest and to defeat their opponents. Within its precincts, plans for battle were developed as well. Kafone's shrine, created by Kooliny, was the oldest in Esulalu and the only one that was given directly by Emitai.[53] Kafone gave Cabai shrines to its allies in war. Elders of the shrine would carry consecrated earth and ritual objects to another quarter, perform the necessary rituals, and instruct a local priest. Thus Haer received its Cabai for its assistance in the war with Hassouka. Hassouka received one for its aid in defeating a township in Huluf.[54] The new shrines bound the recipients to the community that had given them the shrine. Djatti Sambou, the priest of Haer's Cabai, described the crisis that would be generated by a war between Kafone and Haer. "If there is a war with Kafone, Cabai will be destroyed because the Cabais are the same." The spirit associated with a single type of Cabai could not fight on both sides of a battle.[55] Thus, the spread of the Cabai shrine system lessened the possibility of warfare between various Esulalu communities. Although some Cabai shrines did not trace their origins back to Kooliny's, most Esulalu quarters eventually established a shrine.

As a result of the Hassouka-Kafone war, a portion of Hassouka, the subquarter known as Ecuhuh, became part of Kafone. Because of its origins, it was excluded from participation in the rites of Elenkine-Sergerh. However, the people of Ecuhuh brought other shrines to Kafone. While some of these, such as the subquarter shrine of Hougondone, were restricted to the men of Ecuhuh, others were of townshipwide importance. The most significant of these was the confessional shrine of Djimamo. At this shrine, people would confess those wrongs they had committed for which they could be punished by the ukine associated with the priest-king. Because of its incorporation of Ecuhuh, Kafone obtained a large number of new shrines, which helped shift Kadjinol's ritual balance of power from Hassouka to Kafone.[56]

Quarter shrines and Cabai provided Diola warriors with a sense of a collective relationship with the spiritual powers that protected their community. Rituals at these shrines not only provided them with a sense that forces in the spiritual world were honoring their requests for assistance but also offered a place where men sharing a common mission and common anxieties could commune with each other in the seclusion of a shrine precinct. The meat of the shrine sacrifice the warriors ate was also said to provide them with additional strength.

In addition to the collective rituals at the quarter shrines and at Cabai, individual warriors would seek personal protection through ritual action. Before battle, many warriors would have rituals performed at a shrine called Katapf. This shrine was said to protect those who sought its assistance from being wounded by knives, machetes, or other types of metal blades.[57] Some warriors had rituals performed at lineage shrines to make protective objects that they could wear in battle. Sometimes earth from a shrine altar is placed in a goat or antelope's horn and then sealed, thereby invoking the power of a particular boekine wherever it is carried.

Others sought various forms of protection that did not involve the spirit shrines. Esulalu warriors sought to conserve their martial powers by eating meat and by avoiding sexual relations. For many Diola, to lose semen is to lose a life-enhancing power associated with the blood; to lose it just before battle is to make oneself vulnerable to attack. Some warriors sought out special medicines (*bouboon*) that would protect them in battle. Individuals who were said to have spiritual gifts prepared these medicines from a variety of roots and herbs, leather, and metal. Some warriors wore various objects that were thought to bestow certain qualities on those who wore them. Warriors wore mirrors to repel bullets and arrows and wore roots from trees that were noted for their strength and endurance. It remains unclear whether eighteenth-century Esulalu fighting men sought the assistance of Mandinka marabouts who traded in the area in preparing Muslim talismans that offered similar forms of protection.[58]

A less common but more celebrated form of assistance was provided to warriors who had spiritual gifts associated with the power of the head (houkaw). These individuals, who were said to be able to see into the spiritual world, tapped the power of certain ammahl who chose to help them. Such warriors were said to be able to transform themselves into animals and fly away when overpowered or sneak up on an enemy and spy on their adversaries. Several elders described ancestors who could transform themselves into domestic animals, who could then approach an enemy's home and overhear family discussions of impending battles. At Samatit, Emitai was said to have provided such powerful men with arrows that could be shot in such a way that they followed their victims. If a victim turned a corner, the arrow would follow. These martial powers were similar to those used by witches but were used for the benefit of the community.[59]

Despite the celebration of the spiritual powers of warriors, the people of Esulalu, in the eighteenth century, had a certain ambivalence about war. The most important community leaders, including the priest-king and his adjunct, could not participate in it. People who returned from warfare and had either taken a life or handled a corpse had to perform the purification rite of Hougonayes before they could worship at any of the ukine or enter their homes.[60] Warfare that was waged when a community was in the wrong would result in disaster. Such people could not rely on the assistance of the quarter shrines, the ammahl, or Emitai. Heavy casualties and the weakening of their shrines would result from ignoring the advice of shrine elders or the spirits that endowed the shrines with power.

Spiritual assistance was available in the event of a "just war." When Kooliny Djabune sought the assistance of Emitai to keep Hassouka's men from raping

Kafone's women, Emitai was said to weep with outrage and then provided Kooliny with the Cabai shrine and the power to vanquish the wrongdoers. Individuals were said to be given special powers to aid them in war when they were in the right. Presumably both sides would seek the assistance of shrines and the supreme being, but Emitai and the ukine would ally themselves only with the righteous.

Governance through the Spirit Shrines

Despite Esulalu's acceptance of a concept of just war, many people were troubled by the persistence of local warfare. This discomfort was indicated through initial interviews that I conducted with people who sought to conceal the existence of interquarter and intertownship wars and who claimed that it was absolutely forbidden (gnigne). It was also evident from their insistence that the priest-king was excluded from making war plans, that he would stop any battle that he discovered in progress, and that he would levy fines in cattle against those involved. Such warfare undermined the stability of Esulalu society. It transformed blood relations and kin through marriage into adversaries. It sapped the energy of the community to farm, hunt, and, especially, to maintain dams and fences that were essential to rice cultivation. Such warfare also threatened the ability of the Esulalu townships to protect themselves against Diola raiders from Djougoutes, Bliss-Karones, and Huluf and against Afro-Portuguese raiders from Ziguinchor.[61]

Again, Esulalu turned to awasena shrines to strengthen community bonds. In the early eighteenth century, Kadjinol installed a new town council shrine called Hutendookai. Senior men from Kadjinol learned about it from the neighboring township of Seleki, with whom it had various commercial ties.[62] Elders from Seleki installed the shrine at Kadjinol, where it served as a forum for the discussion of community problems. It eventually spread to the other Esulalu townships. Meetings were held on Huyaye, the sixth and final day of the Diola week, a day of rest for the rice paddies and a day when many rituals were performed. At the time of its introduction, the priest-king appointed senior men from each compound as representatives to Hutendookai.[63]

At Hutendookai, problems concerning the whole township were discussed. Work on the dams that regulated water levels in the rice paddies and on the fences that protected the paddies from roaming livestock were coordinated through Hutendookai. Shrine elders also adopted regulations governing the hiring of individuals and collective labor. During most of the eighteenth century, these sessions were presided over by the priest-king. His spiritual prestige and the power of the Hutendookai shrine reinforced the power of the town council's decisions. A group of younger men, called Kumachala, served as the enforcement arm of the Hutendookai.[64] Selected from each compound, they inspected fences and dams, seized stray livestock in the rice paddies, and, together with shrine elders, enforced unpopular decisions in their compounds. These decisions, while consecrated with palm wine libations at the shrine, were enforced by the Kumachala, who would seize wrongdoers' livestock and even raid their granaries. Unlike many spirit shrines, Hutendookai did not seize wrongdoers with illness.

Hutendookai also served as a tribunal, hearing cases of land disputes and accusations of theft and witchcraft. Decisions were made by consensus rather than by a majority vote. Convicted thieves would be fined livestock, usually pigs or goats.[65] In the most serious form of witchcraft accusations, when people were accused of eating human flesh, they would lose all their rice paddies to Hutendookai. People in the community bought these paddies with cattle, which would then be sacrificed at the shrine.[66] Hutendookai, a shrine that originated in a neighboring community, was incorporated by the Esulalu townships, gained a central place in the regulation of economic life and disputes, and became an important institution in the identification of various forms of antisocial behavior.

In the late eighteenth century, the institution of the priest-king underwent a series of changes that reinforced the oeyi's symbolic role as a spiritual emissary for the township as a whole. As previously mentioned, the transfer of the office of oeyi to the Gent lineage and the incorporation of Egol in the priest-king's cluster of shrines responded to a need to tap Koonjaen spiritual power as the earliest inhabitants of the region. While the removal of the priest-king from direct intervention in political disputes served to exclude Koonjaen from exercising political power, it also lessened the possibility that the priest-king would be identified with any particular quarter or faction in township disputes. His exclusion from an active role in cultivating rice not only served to prevent his violation of the interdictions surrounding his office but also removed him from having a personal stake in land disputes.[67] These restrictions freed the priest-king to offer prayers for the well-being of the entire community and all its various factions. They also strengthened the impartiality of the priest-king in the mediation of disputes that threatened township unity. By restricting the involvement of the oeyi in economic and political life, the institution of the priest-king became a symbol of the spiritual unity of the community. Removed from other interests, the oeyi could provide strong moral leadership for the township. Thus, one elder could describe him as above the rivalries that threatened community life: "The priest-king is a shepherd. This is a spirit shrine of shepherding."[68]

While removing the priest-king from community disputes, Esulalu elders sought to extend his role in the ritual life of the quarter. A new shrine, Cayinte, was introduced from Huluf and established in every quarter. Cayinte's ritual focused on the procurement of rain, something that was particularly important during the frequent droughts of the late eighteenth century. The priest-king, his adjunct, and the council of elders of the priest-kingship controlled the selection of the Cayinte priests and the elaborate initiation rites that they went through before assuming their offices. Initiation of new priests lasted seven days and was accompanied by lavish sacrifices of livestock. The priest-king and his associates seized the new priest from his home and placed him in seclusion for a week of rigorous instruction. On the seventh day, he emerged from his retreat and assumed his office. These priests were regarded as representatives of the oeyi in the township quarters and subquarters. Kadjinol's six quarters had twelve Cayinte shrines and priests. The introduction of a system of rain shrines coordinated through the institution of the priest-kingship reinforced the role of the oeyi in quarter ritual life. The network of Cayinte priests provided another institution to strengthen an often fragile sense of township unity. Its rituals, attended by elders from several quarters, provided an important meeting ground for community leaders.[69]

During this period, a new shrine of the elders, Hoohaney, was created to provide a forum for community elders throughout the townships to discuss problems in a less public place than at Hutendookai. Included among the elders of Hoohaney were those men who controlled the shrines of the priest-king, the priests of the major shrines, and some of the wealthier members of the community. Descendants of the Koonjaen were specifically excluded.[70] The elders of Hoohaney assisted at the initiation of the priest-king and controlled the young men's initiation into the rites of the dead, Calau. It also provided a discreet forum where community leaders could discuss the moral climate of the community and such problems as witchcraft and other forms of social deviance. The shrine itself was usually described as a society (embottai) in which ritual served to "seal" the decision of the elders, but the spirits associated with the shrine were said to seize people who worked against them or who refused to "take on" the responsibilities of the shrine when summoned to do so by its elders.[71]

The Hoohaney shrine is unique to Esulalu and dates back to the late eighteenth century.[72] The first Hoohaney shrine was established in the Suzannah subquarter of Kadjinol-Hassouka. Despite its goal of providing a forum for all of Kadjinol, divisions between different quarters plagued Hoohaney from the beginning. Elders from Kalybillah sat on one side of the shrine and elders from Hassouka, who officiated, sat on the other. There was apparently little mixing between the two halves of Kadjinol. Shortly after its creation, a man from Kalybillah refused to pay a fine imposed by the officiating priest. Men from Kalybillah supported him, and they established a new Hoohaney in the Kagnao quarter. This split resulted from the tensions surrounding the Hassouka-Kafone war. The first priest of this new Hoohaney was Penjaw Djabune.[73] Shortly after the creation of the Kagnao Hoohaney, Penjaw became involved in a dispute with the elders of Kafone. Though the elders of Kafone paid one fine levied against them, as the dispute dragged on, they refused to pay any additional fines. Kafone established its own Hoohaney. Similarly, the Kandianka quarter established its own Hoohaney after war broke out between Kandianka and the Baimoon section of Hassouka. From Kadjinol, Hoohaney spread to other Esulalu townships, but it ceased to be regarded as a source of spiritual unity.[74]

To provide a more effective means of preserving township unity, the people of Esulalu introduced two new shrines from their neighbors in Huluf and Bandial. They also created a new shrine, Hoohaney, which provided a means for wealthy elders to discuss issues of broad community concern. Finally, Esulalu elders removed the priest-king from the economic activities of the community so that he could become fully a representation of the unity of the entire township. These efforts were only partially successful. While the oeyi became associated with the entire township and Cayinte brought important rituals into every neighborhood, interquarter warfare persisted, eroding the authority of both Hoohaney and Hutendookai. Still, they provided new fora for addressing issues of community concerns.

Male Initiation: From Kahat to Bukut

In the waning years of the eighteenth century, men fom Kadjinol's quarter of Sergerh introduced a new form of male circumcision called Bukut, which was held approximately every twenty years. Rather than a prelude to marriage, like the Koonjaen's Kahat, this form of initiation was used to mark generations, each of which was given the name of its initiation ritual. Men who were initiated together developed intense loyalties to each other and acted like an age grade within the greater community.[75]

The origins of this new type of initiation has been variously attributed to the Mandinka and the Manjaco. It entered Esulalu after members of the Djisenghalene-Djikune lineage of Kadjinol-Sergerh visited Djirikanao (Kamobeul), a Diola community to the east of Esulalu, where they learned of the new type of initiation. Where the people of Djirikanao learned of it remains unclear, though the priest of the royal shrine of Enampore claims that the priest-king (avi) received the new form of male circumcision from a Mandinka traveler, who taught him how to install the shrine and perform its initiation. While there may some Mandinka influence in Diola Bukut, Mandinka circumcision rituals, like Kahat, are held just before or after puberty, not to mark generations, as in Bukut.[76] Despite the lack of a specific place of origin, several elders of Bukut insisted that it was introduced by a woman. "A woman showed them everything. She gave it to the men. Emitai gave it to her." Emitai was said to have revealed this to the woman in a dream.[77] Others suggested a more mundane method by which this unnamed woman learned about Bukut. For several days in succession, as she carried fertilizer to the rice paddies, this woman heard the sounds of animated singing and dancing coming from across the Kadjinol Bolon, from the area around Bandial. She could not resist it and began to dance. That evening she returned to Kadjinol-Sergerh to tell her husband about it. He accompanied her to Bandial and decided to ask Bukut's elders to teach them this new form of initiation.[78]

Despite the tradition that a woman introduced Kadjinol to Bukut, women are carefully excluded from its rituals. Women are not allowed to approach the sacred forest of circumcision (Sihinna) or the ritual enclosures (Houle), where the initiates remain in seclusion. In Kahat, women had been allowed to bring food to the initiates and could see them from a distance. In Bukut, all food is prepared by initiated men, and it is thought that a woman who sees any of the Bukut rituals would die. Some women, desperate to see if their children had survived the operation, were said to transform themselves into vultures. However, when they returned, they would be afflicted with a distended stomach, which would eventually burst.[79] Despite the severity of the sanctions against women who tried to see the initiates, women were said to know all about Bukut. Boolai Senghor claimed: "Women know more about it [than men], but they will not speak. . . . Perhaps they would cry. Perhaps they would laugh. So we said it was absolutely forbidden (gnigne)."[80] It is interesting that the origin of an important prohibition on women's participation in male initiation is male self-consciousness in front of women, rather than the fears often associated with "taboos."

Jean Girard has argued that the change in circumcision from Kahat to Bukut strengthened the male aspects of circumcision, with its emphasis on secrecy and the exclusion of women. "The Bukut accentuates the masculine cleavage relative to the female world, and surrounds initiation in mystery and fear and reaffirms to the female community a male personality that had become vacillating because of changing circumstances."[81] While Girard attributes this incorrectly to the destabilizing impact of French and Mandinka hegemony in the early twentieth century, he is correct in suggesting a changing relationship between the sexes. Women were far more systematically excluded from Bukut than from Kahat, though their role in creating Bukut hardly suggests the cleavages that Girard claims. The exclusion of women, rather than a need to strengthen a masculinity embarrassed by colonial domination, represented a growing conviction among Diola awasena (that had been less true among the Koonjaen) that male and female spiritual power should be kept separate. Diola reliance on women as creators of shrines demonstrated the acceptance of female spiritual power, but they conceived of it as having a different nature—that male and female should be carefully separated to maximize the power of each. Thus the exclusion of women from even marginal participation in male initiation coincides with their exclusion from assisting at the sacrificial meals of Hoohaney. While excluded from Bukut, women had created it, they knew what happened there, and they accepted the new circumcision form as more powerful than Kahat.

Accompanying this change in male initiation was a growing sense of reticence between the sexes in discussing sexually explicit subjects. Cotton cloth purchased from Mandinka traders or weavers at Seleki increased the availability of clothing and helped to extend notions of sexual modesty from a covering of the genitals to, for women, a covering of the area from the waist to the knee.[82] As part of their initiation, young men learned sexually explicit songs, many of which they would be embarrassed to sing within earshot of women. Men were unsure of the women's response to male initiation. They did not know if women would cry or laugh at their efforts. With this new form of initiation, they could instruct the next generation of men as they saw fit, leaving the initiation of women to female elders at the maternity huts in the townships.[83]

Informants offer four major reasons why the Bukut form of initiation was adopted and Kahat abandoned. First, in Bukut, the initiates were kept in a sacred forest for two to three months, during which time they would be more effectively taught about their responsibilities as men, as warriors, and as elders of the community. In Kahat, they were not secluded for as long or separated as completely from women. Second, the elaborate preliminary rituals of Bukut, the festivities held on the day of the boys' initiation, and the elaborate sacrifices necessary to become an elder of Bukut created a greater opportunity for feasting. Large numbers of cattle and pigs were sacrificed at Bukut, whereas the sacrifices at Kahat had been far more modest.[84] Third, there was a preference for the surgical technique performed in Bukut. Fourth, Kahat was seen as a Koonjaen form of male initiation. Given the growing spiritual authority of the Koonjaen minority, Kadjinol's elders may have welcomed a different form of male initiation that lessened the Koonjaen role.[85]

Elders of Bukut have stressed the importance of the longer period of ritual seclusion for the initiates as a time for teaching the initiates about manhood, warfare, and their role in the awasena community, which was particularly important
because Bukut was instituted during a period of social instability. Certainly, a
longer period of seclusion would be useful in offering systematic ritual instruction. However, Kahat's initiation was limited to boys on the verge of marriage. In
Bukut a whole generation of boys, all those who had been weaned since the last
Bukut (they could range in age from three to thirty) would be circumcised together.
The younger boys would be incapable of absorbing much information they received, though once initiated they gained the right to such knowledge, and it could
be retaught as the boys matured.

From Kadjinol, Bukut spread to the other Esulalu townships, but it was not immediately adopted. The adoption of Bukut encountered significant opposition
throughout the region. Men held meetings to discuss the relative merits of the two
forms of circumcision. As Kapooeh Diedhiou suggests, some people objected to the
abandonment of "our customs." His son, Tibor, suggested that their ancestors left
Kadjinol-Sergerh for the neighboring quarter of Ebankine because most of Sergerh
opted for Bukut.[86] Resistance was concentrated among certain families of Koonjaen
descent who controlled the various Ewang shrines associated with Kahat. In addition to their loss of ritual authority, Kahat's elders were concerned about the possible removal of a fertility ritual, undergone by all the young men of the community, from the protection of the shrines most intimately connected with the land,
the various Koonjaen shrines associated with circumcision and the priest king.[87]
They may well have feared that the high mortality that resulted from introducing a
"foreign" Coeyi shrine and priest-king would be extended into the ritual initiation
of a whole generation of young men who were circumcised at a "stranger's shrine."

Eventually a compromise was achieved. Certain families would still be initiated at Kahat. At Kadjinol, only one family still has its sons initiated in the Kahat
form, which is performed at Oussouye. Members of this family, a Gent lineage at
Kadjinol who are related to the royal lineage at Oussouye, continue to seek the
blessing of the Ewang shrine of Oussouye and the Kahlayoh shrine at Kadjinol
before the remainder of Kadjinol's young men are initiated at Bukut. Elders of the
Kahat-associated shrine of Ebila (the knife) continued to perform the actual circumcision.[88] These remnants of Kahat initiation provide crucial links between
Kahat and Bukut and between the "owners of the soil" and the new rites of the
Diola majority. The initiates of Bukut still secure the spiritual protection of those
shrines most fully integrated into the spiritual hierarchy of the region.

Awasena Healing

Central to the awasena path in the eighteenth century was the problem of healing. In many cases, the people of Esulalu regarded illness as a sign of a moral in-
fraction or spiritual summons. A person who was seized with an illness that resisted ordinary cures would seek out a priest of one of the divinatory shrines to
assess the spiritual cause of the illness. At Bruinkaw, the major divinatory shrine

in Esulalu, the boekine was said to speak, and the priest translated for the supplicant, thereby revealing the cause of the illness. In other cases, at Eboon, Ekisumaye,
and Houlang, as well as, in some instances, at Bruinkaw, the priest would learn
of the cause of the illness through dreams or by interviewing the patient about
possible misdeeds. Shrine priests would often take a bundle of rice provided by
the supplicant and put it under their pillows to aid in dreaming about the
supplicant's predicament. While they slept, the spirit associated with the shrine
would travel in the night to ascertain the cause of the illness, which would be
communicated to the shrine priest while she or he slept.[89]

Once the cause of the affliction was determined, palm wine libations and animal sacrifice at the shrine whose rules had been violated would often be prescribed.
The afflicted would also have to confess the specific nature of the wrongs committed as a part of the healing process. These four shrines are generally considered to be among the oldest in Esulalu. Their origins are said to be beyond the
times of the first ancestors.[90] They were probably used throughout the eighteenth
century. Each was a shrine of affliction; their priests were selected from those who
had survived illnesses associated with the shrine. Surviving the illness required
that you take on the shrine, a process involving elaborate sacrifices. However, only
some of those who became elders could discern illnesses; that power was seen as
a gift of Emitai.[91]

In eighteenth-century Esulalu, a developing religious tradition was integrally involved in the struggles to procure the necessities of life, the establishment of a
stable society, and the protection of community health. Shrines became closely
associated with many phases of economic activity, community governance, and
healing. As new problems arose, the Esulalu turned to the awasena path to find
new ways to overcome these difficulties. Esulalu demonstrated an openness to
innovation within its own traditions and a readiness to borrow from the conquered
Koonjaen and neighboring Diola groups. Recognizing a spiritual power in the
longevity of the Koonjaen presence in the region, they readily accepted various
shrines but insisted that the shrines and their priests be stripped of their political
power. To structure the transition from boyhood to adulthood, they embraced the
Koonjaen initiation rites. To protect blacksmiths, Esulalu welcomed the guild
shrine of Silapoom. In a time of crisis when their own priest-kings kept dying and
when drought threatened community existence, they turned their shrines of the
priest-king over to the Koonjaen descendants of Atta-Essou. They accepted the
shrines of the Koonjaen priest-king and allowed them to share the sacred forest.
Finally, they combined Koonjaen and Floup traditions about the origin of the
priest-kingship.

Esulalu's changing attitudes toward the religious traditions of the conquered
raises serious questions about theories of African traditional thought that suggest
a lack of innovation or a sacred rigidity. In an essay regarded as a classic in the
study of African belief systems, Robin Horton has argued that the fundamental
difference between African traditional thought and Western science is the absence
of a "developed awareness of alternatives to the established body of theoretical

tenets" in the former. He identifies African systems of thought as closed and Western science as open and describes each of them: "the 'closed'—characterized by lack of awareness of alternatives, sacredness of beliefs, and anxiety about threats to them; and the 'open' characterized by awareness of alternatives, diminished sacredness of beliefs and diminished anxiety about threats to them."[92] Clearly, eighteenth-century Esulalu does not fit within Horton's vision of a traditional system.

The awasena of Esulalu were surrounded by other communities with different systems of thought and different shrines. The people of Esulalu adopted some new shrines while rejecting others. They accepted only some of the ritual rules associated with the new cults while rejecting others. More significantly, they altered their vision of their place in the regional spiritual order involving land, shrines, humans, and Emitai. Initially, the Floup newcomers established their own shrines and attempted to destroy or suppress the shrines of the indigenous inhabitants. As they became aware of the power of some of these shrines, particularly in areas where they were weak, they accepted certain Koonjaen cults.

As their own shrines associated with the fertility of the land and women and the procurement of rain encountered the disasters of drought, locust plagues, and the mortality of their own priest-kings, they began to question whether these shrines could root themselves in the spiritual soil of Esulalu. Descendants of the Floup rejected their own view of Koonjaen savagery and subservience and entrusted some of their shrines to the spiritually powerful descendants of the Koonjaen. They welcomed the Koonjaen priest-king shrines into their sacred forests and trusted their youth to initiation through first a Koonjaen ritual and then a newer form blessed by the older Koonjaen shrines. Finally, they embraced a Koonjaen tradition of Emitai's revelations to Atta-Essou and his descendants and made them their own. Koonjaen visions of the relationships among people and Emitai and the land and the spiritual order became an integral part of awasena tradition. A single system of spiritual tenets became a dual one, thereby internalizing a creative tension that became a significant source of innovation in a developing Esulalu tradition.

The role of Emitai in Esulalu accounts of spirit shrines also raises serious questions about Horton's description of a basic African cosmology in which lesser spirits control the microcosm and the supreme being is left with a relatively unimportant macrocosmic realm. Horton describes an African supreme being who "will be credited with direct responsiblity for relatively few events of human concern, will have no direct associations with morality, and will seldom be approached by human beings."[93] Esulalu's vision of a supreme being does not conform to Horton's "basic cosmology." Emitai's role in the creation of spirit shrines and Its ability to enter into the microcosmic world of Esulalu's internal affairs are demonstrated most vividly by the tradition concerning the visions of Kooliny Djabune and the creation of Cabai. In this instance, a bitter dispute between two quarters of the same township generated a situation in which a man believes his soul travels to the supreme being, receives instruction in a new cult, and returns to his community to install the shrine. Emitai is described as weeping at the outrages committed by one quarter against another and then intervenes to aid the weaker and morally wronged community. Contrary to Horton's suggestion of a distant and morally neutral supreme being, Emitai intervenes in local affairs to restore a moral balance to Esulalu. This instance is not isolated; central to awawena thought is the idea that Emitai created ukine as intermediaries between Itself and people. Many informants claim that "Emitai made the spirit shrines."[94]

Esulalu explanations of these changes also challenge certain models of African oral history that suggest an incapacity by recounters of the traditions to explain major changes by mundane causes. Joseph Miller has argued that "nonliterate thinkers" see the world as "stable and unchanging" and that:

> Events perceived as constituting an upset in the status quo, as a matter of logical necessity, can have no mundane explanation, and so oral historians must resort to "other worldly" causes to account for them. This philosophical proposition leads oral historians, who are as concerned with change as their literate counterparts, to posit magical agencies to explain what they see as historical change. Magic necessarily predominates in historical narrative precisely because these tales exist to explain the (mystical) changes that brought the world from its beginnings to the state of the historian's present.[95]

Miller is correct in asserting the importance of what he describes as "magical," and I would describe as "sacred" concepts of causality in African visions of their histories, but in many instances Diola historians have no difficulty offering what Westerners would consider mundane explanations for major changes. In the case of the transition from Kahat to Bukut rites of circumcision, there are no miracles or magical manifestations. Diola historians offered four reasons for the abandonment of Kahat: a longer period of ritual seclusion for the initiates, greater opportunities for feasting in the community, differences in surgical technique, and the lessening of Koonjaen influence. None of these qualifies as "magical." Rather, they represent the reflection of Diola thinkers about the comparative worth of two forms of initiation.

The innovative tradition within Esulalu traditions was not limited to borrowing from Koonjaen or other Diola traditions. It also drew on the religious experience of individual men and women. Such an emphasis on individual experience and initiative also challenges scholarly images of traditional societies that emphasize group continuity over individuality and innovation. Within an emerging Esulalu tradition, certain individuals were said to possess special mental powers that allowed them to see in the spiritual world. Based on their experiences, they created many of the quarter shrines and other ukine within Esulalu. Others had dreams in which they were visited by spirits or by Emitai. Finally, there is the tradition of Kooliny Djabune, whose soul was said to have left his body and visited Emitai. Emitai summoned a teacher of a new ritual and created the shrine of Cabai. Thus, Emitai was the primary guardian of the moral order and a source of aid in a time of troubles.

From the earliest period when an Esulalu tradition began to differentiate itself from those of Huluf and Ediamat, it had to offer an effective explanation for the rapidly changing temporal order. The existence of the alternative traditions of the

Koonjaen and of other Diola offered additional approaches to awasena problems. Similarly, the emphasis on personal experience and the importance of dreams and visions provided an important source of innovation within an emerging Esulalu tradition. New teachings, new shrines, and a continuing awareness of charismatic renewal reinforce the ability of the tradition to adapt to an unstable world. The broad diffusion of shrines throughout the townships linked most people in the community to particular shrines and allowed them to feel personally involved in the direction of community life. Finally, the concept of a supreme being who intervened in the lives of the people of Esulalu reinforced a sense of an ultimate moral order, despite the uncertainties of daily life.

5

Slaves, Trade, and Religious Change in Eighteenth-Century Esulalu

As the people of Esulalu faced the difficult task of integrating Floup and Koonjaen communities and creating a common Diola tradition, they also confronted the disruptive influence of a growing European commercial presence in the region. As early as the midseventeenth century, European willingness to sell such strategic items as muskets, gunpowder, and iron created clear military and economic advantages for those societies willing to engage in trade. An expanding market for slaves and the increasing availability of iron and muskets escalated both the level and frequency of violence throughout the Casamance. Despite the Diolas' initial reluctance to trade directly with Europeans, it became increasingly difficult to avoid participation in this Atlantic trade system. By the early eighteenth century, Diola communities utilized various African middlemen to become actively involved in the sale of rice, slaves, and beeswax in exchange for cattle or for European trade goods.

This chapter examines the impact of this commerce, particularly in slaves, on Diola society and the awasena tradition. It focuses on four issues: the structure of Diola participation in the slave trade, the involvement of the spirit shrines in its regulation, the impact of such involvement on the spirit shrines, and the changes in Esulalu religious life that grew directly out of increased trade. By placing the slave trade in the context of religious history, it becomes possible to focus on the spiritual challenges posed by Diola participation in the slave trade, the ways in which this participation was legitimated and regulated by religious authorities, and the ways in which an awasena system of thought shaped Esulalu participation in the slave trade.

Until the eighteenth century, European commercial interests in the Casamance focused on the Cassanga kingdom and the Bainounk states of the middle Casa—mance. By 1650, the Portuguese had established a major trading center at Cacheu, along the São Domingo River, and two smaller posts at Ziguinchor and Bolor. The Ziguinchor post was a mere forty kilometers east of Esulalu; Bolor was in the

Ediamat areas forty kilometers to the south. In the late seventeenth century, French, British, and Dutch traders brought an end to the Portuguese monopoly over regional trade. Jean Boulègue suggests that this new competition increased the ability of the local populace to manipulate prices to their advantage and to make the growing trade more lucrative.[1] Unlike the Portuguese, the new traders could sell firearms, which were in great demand throughout the region. Their primary trading posts were to the north of the Casamance, near the mouth of the Gambia River, where exports of slaves reached seven thousand per annum by the late seventeenth century.[2]

Written accounts of this period suggest that the impact of the European presence was to encourage slave raiding by the more centralized states against the Diola townships. There is no doubt that Diola captives were among the slaves who were sold by the Cassangas, Mandinka, and Bainounk to the Portuguese.[3] Afro-Portuguese, referred to as Aetingah or Ekabliane in local oral traditions, conducted slave raids against Esulalu farmers working in the rice paddies. Arriving by canoe, the Aetingah could seize their captives and make a rapid escape. As early as 1605, Diola slaves were being transported across the Atlantic to such places as Brazil, Colombia, Hispaniola, Mexico, Peru, and Venezuela.[4]

While it is clear that Diola were victims of the slave trade, most commentators have assumed that slave raiding was organized by aristocratic warrior groups operating in highly stratified societies, rather than relatively egalitarian, acephalous societies like the Diola. Thus, Claude Meillassoux describes the essential social groups necessary for the development of a slave system: "Slavery involves two social classes, depending on the form of acquisition; the aristocratic class which captured for its own use and the merchant class which bought slaves from the aristocrats."[5] Simarily, in his study of the Casamance–Upper Guinea region, Walter Rodney argued that the Diola's lack of centralized state structures and the absence of a powerful ruling or priestly class prevented significant Diola participation in the slave trade: "it could scarcely have been simple coincidence that the Djolas and the Balantes, who produced the least slaves, either by raiding or by preying upon each other, were the very tribes with an amorphous state structure from which a well-defined ruling class was absent."[6]

Despite Rodney's claims of minimal participation, a careful examination of travelers' accounts and oral traditions reveal that the Floup raided for and sold slaves. Floup slavers preferred to use African middlemen rather than trade directly with Europeans because there had been several incidents when Floup traders were themselves sold into slavery. As early as the late sixteenth century, Floup sold captives to the Buramos (Manjaco, Mancagne, or Papel), who then sold them to the Portuguese.[7] Esulalu elders insist that their ancestors traded only with African merchants; Europeans did not come until the nineteenth century. While aware of the presence of the Portuguese at Ziguinchor and Cacheu, they described them as sending out blacks—grumetes, Bainounk, or Mandinka—to conduct trade. The Esulalu description is supported by Sieur de la Courbe, who visited the region in the late seventeenth century: "There are Portuguese who send out black assistants to the villages in order to purchase whatever they can find."[8] It is also confirmed by a British traveler in the late eighteenth century:

The merchants of Bissao procure this number of slaves [two thousand per year to Brazil] by means of a class of natives called grumetes, who have generally been brought up from infancy in their houses, and who are in general an honest, industrious, and faithful class. They navigate all their small craft, whether canoes, or decked schooners and sloops; and carry on, for all their principals, all the commerce of the country. The merchant, who seldom quits his own habitation, sends them with goods to the value of a certain number of slaves, whether to Zinghicor, Cacheo, Geba, or any other place; where they make their purchases, and then return to their employers. . . . Most of these slaves are procured from the Mandingoes at Geba; some from the Cacheo and Casamanza rivers.[9]

The Mandinka were said to be the most important of these traders and were active in the area before the removal of the Koonjaen. They would come to Esulalu in large dugout canoes: "They carried clothes here to sell. People bought with rice. The Mandinka sold the rice at Ziguinchor."[10] Some of these Mandinka traders may have been Muslim, but there is no record of any attempts to convert the Esulalu to Islam in the eighteenth century.

The slave trade became an important force in south shore Diola societies at a time when no major state could control trade. By the end of the sixteenth century, the kingdom of the Mansa Floup had collapsed. Political authority was limited to the township level, where it was embodied in the office of oeyi or priest-king. However, this unity was severely tested by interquarter wars. There were no government officials, such as the *alkati* of northern Senegambia, to enforce trade regulations and no warrior class to forge alliances with external slave-trading groups. Thus any form of Diola slave trading would have to develop in different ways than the warrior–trading class models suggested by Rodney and Meillassoux.[11]

Raiding and Trading: Captives and Slaves

The earliest accounts of slave seizures in Esulalu refer to the Koonjaen's kidnapping of Floup, mostly children, from the Floup settlements. In the seventeenth century, captives were sold to the Bainounks, who would sell them to the Portuguese at Ziguinchor or Cacheu.[12] Despite the willingness of the Koonjaen to sell them, there are no accounts of Floup seizures and sale of Koonjaen, even during the Koonjaen wars. Although some informants have suggested that Koonjaen refugees were incorporated into the townships as slaves (amiekele), there is little evidence to support this. Unlike slaves, the majority of Koonjaen arrived in families. Furthermore, they came with a certain spiritual prestige as "owners of the soil," the first inhabitants of the region.[13] The absence of Koonjaen enslavement by the Floup indicates the limited importance of slavery in Esulalu before the eighteenth century.[14]

Esulalu participation in the slave trade appears to have developed from cattle raiding and from the frequent warfare between townships during the eighteenth century. In an effort to demonstrate their martial prowess and augment their wealth prior to marriage, young men would sneak into a compound at night and seize cattle. If caught, they were held prisoner until ransomed for cattle.[15] Intermittent warfare grew out of increasing competition for rice paddies, oil palms, fishing zones, and hunting grounds between the townships. Both prisoners of war and captured cattle thieves could be ransomed by their relatives, but unransomed captives could be sold as slaves to traders who visited Esulalu. The pressure of frequent raiding by the better-armed Afro-Portuguese, Bainounk, and north shore Diola led to Esulalu's escalation of raiding activities, so that the Esulalu began to conduct raids specifically to procure captives. The Afro-Portuguese trader, Francisco de Azevedo Coelho, described the Sacaletes, a northern Diola group who raided Esulalu.

> On the north shore live a group of people called Sacaletes. They live without a king, except that he who is most able is the most king. They are great pirates and keep peace with no one. Their life consists of riding the sea in their canoes and no one navigates without arms as precaution against these people. They sell those they capture and do not excuse even a white, though they would do no other evil than to require his ransom.[16]

Raiders from the north shore were particularly noted for their ability to hide their canoes in the salt marshes, near isolated rice paddies, where they would ambush Esulalu farmers. Because of their ready access to the Gambia trade factories, the Sacaletes could obtain firearms, gunpowder, and iron, all of which gave them an advantage in warfare against the south shore Diola. As John Thornton has noted, European military technology was becoming increasingly important in West African warfare by the late seventeenth century.[17] The Esulalu townships may have joined in the slave trade to obtain that era's strategic weapons.

Warfare in Esulalu was categorized according to the number of combatants and their township affiliations. Diola distinguished between battles that involved substantial numbers of warriors on both sides and raids by smaller groups who seized captives or cattle on the outskirts of an enemy township. They also distinguished between wars within Esulalu and wars with neighboring Diola or non-Diola groups. For most of the eighteenth century, raids for captives were conducted only against non-Esulalu groups. Taking captives from Kadjinol was "forbidden [gnigne], even Mlomp, even of Samatit. . . . Kagnout, all of them, it was forbidden."[18]

Esulalu conducted most of its raids against the two Diola groups that raided them, Djougoutes and Huluf. In the raids against Djougoutes, a small group of men from the same quarter would take large dugout canoes across the Casamance, seize people working in the fields or forest areas, and put them in the canoes for the return to Esulalu. Against Huluf, most of the slave raiding was done by land. The rainy season was the primary time for raiding; people spent long hours working in rice paddies that were often far from their homes. "If they found you in the rice paddies, they seized you."[19] The rainy season's lush vegetation also provided excellent cover for preparing ambushes. Raiders' loss of time from farming could be compensated for by hiring work teams to work their fields. As some elders described it: "Some people did not want to work [in the rice paddies]. [They wanted to] War only."[20]

Individual martial prowess and skill in organizing raiding parties were more important to the success of such operations than large numbers or the latest weaponry. Ambushes had to be done quickly and without attracting attention to make a successful escape with the captives. As one elder described it, this required a special type of power: "If you have the strength . . . you will go . . . to seize slaves." Such strength was often associated with specific spirit shrines, gifts from ammahl, or the individual warrior's power of the "head."[21] Raiding parties were organized by skilled warriors, who called on friends and relatives to join them. Except in the case of captives seized in intertownship wars, little control of raiding was exercised by the township as a whole.

The technical instruments of warfare were readily available to any aspiring raider. Bows and arrows and spears, which were often used in hunting, were the preferred weapons. The loud firing of muskets would draw too much attention to the raiders for them to make good their escape. Jack Goody has described the bow and arrow as "essentially a democratic weapon; everyman knows how to construct one; the materials are readily available, the techniques uncomplicated, the middle easy to replace."[22] Every Esulalu man had them. Canoes were used for fishing and trade and were widely distributed in the townships as well. The horse, which was of such importance to the military power of the Sudanic kingdoms, was of little use in the tsetse fly–ridden swamps and forests of the lower Casamance. The means of participation in raiding were readily available to any man in Esulalu. It would have been difficult for a warrior class or state institution to control such a "means of production" when its primary instruments were tools of everyday life.

Captives were not immediately sold as slaves. Their families were given the opportunity to ransom them for cattle. Due to lack of cattle, an unwillingness to ransom by kin, or the captive's lack of kin, some prisoners were not ransomed. Only after sufficient time had elapsed, during which a ransom could be performed, was the status of prisoner transformed into that of a slave. Eighteenth-century Esulalu practice closely follows the model proposed by Miers and Kopytoff, that slaves were essentially people stripped of kin. The absence of kin support for their ransom transformed prisoners of war or captives from raiding into slaves.[23]

Raiders from Esulalu sold unransomed captives to fellow Diola in Ediamat, Diembering, and Djougoutes in exchange for cattle. They also sold captives to Afro-Portuguese and Mandinka traders. Afro-Portuguese slave traders provided more than cattle. Elders from Samatit claimed: "If you sold to these people perhaps they would give you a musket, perhaps gunpowder, perhaps ejasse [something connected with muskets]."[24] Mandinka traders purchased slaves with cattle or cloth and then sold them to the Portuguese or to such inland states as Gabou. Prices for an individual slave ranged from five to ten head of cattle.[25] When it was necessary to take captives to market, a raider might commission someone from his township to transport and sell his slaves. Usually a slave trader had a series of contacts in towns along his route who would provide him with shelter and protection. A trader with commissioned slaves would receive a cow for his trouble. However, if he allowed a slave to escape, he had to compensate the raider with the number of cattle he would normally have received.[26]

While Robertson and Klein's book on women in African slavery has demonstrated that, in most of Africa, women were the primary victims of the slave trade and that they commanded higher prices than male slaves, this does not appear to be the case in Esulalu. Although it is impossible to quantify any aspect of the Diola slave trade, given their reluctance to trade directly with Europeans, the differential in ransoms between a male's seven cattle and a woman's six may reflect a greater demand for male slaves. This exception, however, may support Robertson and Klein's basic contention that Africans preferred women slaves, in part because women did most of the farming. Diola men performed a substantial portion of the agricultural labor, including the heavy plowing and dike preparation essential to Diola rice agriculture. Furthermore, Esulalu's close proximity to European coastal trade entrepôts, where male slaves were preferred over women, may have influenced local prices. Finally, the origin of Esulalu's captive trade in the ransoming of cattle thieves and prisoners of war may have contributed to this unusual emphasis on male captives.[27]

Regulating the Slave Trade

Such a dangerous and potentially disruptive occupation, even when it was not controlled by an aristocratic class, developed rules to govern seizures, ransoms, and sales. In the absence of state control, the people of Esulalu turned to their spirit shrines, whose prestige and power were seen as an effective means to control this growing economic activity. This approach was not unusual in Esulalu. Ukine regulated such diverse activities as palm wine tapping and the hiring of labor. A number of shrines provided sanctions for the rules governing rice cultivation. There was adequate precedent to involve a spirit shrine in the regulation of raiding and ransoming.[28] For such a complex enterprise, a variety of shrines were involved; some enforcing a series of rules, while others offered spiritual protection for various aspects of the trade.

Esulalu's shrines played a radically different role than such shrines as the Igbo's Aro Chukwu. Aro Chukwu's power as an oracle of the supreme being was used to punish wrongdoers or losing parties in disputes by selling them into slavery. More important, traders associated with the oracle used the shrine's prestige to ensure their safe passage throughout southeastern Nigeria as they purchased slaves.[29] It also differed from the lower Congo region's Lemba cult, which joined together in a ritual community individuals engaged in similar economic activities, slave trading, and who suffered from one of various illnesses associated with the Lemba shrine.[30] The Diola did not develop an idea of a spirit comparable to the Yoruba Aje cult, which, under the influence of increasingly important and well integrated trade networks, transformed a goddess of beauty and moral rectitude into a goddess of wealth, symbolized by the cowry shell currency that was common in the region.[31] Although Diola engaged in trade, trade specialists and markets did not become central to Diola economic life in the way that it did in southern Nigeria or in the Congo. In contrast, Esulalu shrines enforced the rules of the trade at the local level and offered protection to raiders. However, these shrines were based in particular townships or associated with particular families. Diola shrines seized no slaves themselves and did not ensure safe travel for Diola traders in long-distance trade.

The most important rules about raiding defined the acceptable boundaries between people who could be victimized and those who could not. Normally, only non-Esulalu, people who were not part of the essouk (a common land), could be seized as captives.[32] The shared system of spirit shrines involved with the protection of communities and the conduct of war made such raiding disruptive. Marriage ties within Esulalu's five townships also discouraged raiding. Furthermore, it threatened the more vital economic activities involving the exploitation of paddies, marshes, and forest areas shared by the townships. Exceptions to this rule were made when parents sold some of their children to pay off major debts.[33]

Sanctions against seizures within Esulalu were associated with the office of the priest-king, which symbolized the spiritual unity of the township and which was situated within a clear hierarchy in relation to other priest-kings among the southern Diola. The oeyi's Calemboekine, associated with the dead and the living community as a whole, protected the township from harm. It would punish any overzealous raiders with disease, disaster, or even death if they seized captives from within their own community.[34]

Seizures within Esulalu were also punished by spirit shrines associated with the victim's lineage or the household shrine of Hupila. Thus, in the eighteenth century, the seizure of a captive from a blacksmith lineage would have resulted in a punishment inflicted on the raider, his property, or his kin. This punishment would have been inflicted by lineage shrines such as Hoolinway or Kahlayoh or the blacksmith guild shrine of Silapoom.[35] These sanctions were said to be imposed through the actions of spirits linked to these shrines. Such spirits could wait years before they seized their victims. While this did not rule out direct actions by victims or their kin, spiritual punishments were seen as more certain and more devastating.

Special relations between lineages also placed limits on the seizure of captives. One lineage might have special ties with another, which required that family members would go out of their way to avoid conflict with the other group. This extended beyond Esulalu and was a useful way of developing commercial contacts. It prevented members of one lineage from seizing captives from the other (though it did not prevent them from fighting in war). Nuhli Bassin described an incident that illustrates this bond. One of his ancestors seized a woman from Djougoutes when she was going to a well to draw water. Upon learning that her surname was Djisenghalene-Djikune, he released her to people from another township, who returned her to her village. Bassins are not allowed to harm members of that lineage or be harmed by them.[36] Violations would be punished by lineage shrines.

It was strictly forbidden for raiders to kill captives who did not resist their seizure. "If you seize someone, you cannot kill him." Such a death was seen as murder. Spirit shrines associated with war, such as Cabai, Katapf, and the quarter shrines might seize the killer within his own community. Such an act would also bring punishment by shrines associated with the well-being of the deceased's community.[37]

Once a captive was bound and transported back to Esulalu, strict rules that governed ransom or sale of the captive took effect. Captives were taken to their captors' homes, where their legs were placed in wooden fetters (hudjenk), in close proximity to the family shrine of Hupila.[38] They were provided with adequate food and water, and their safety was the responsibility of their captors. Other than being fettered, they were not to be harmed in any way. "It is forbidden to beat him [the captive]. If one beats him, perhaps he will die. If he dies, your house will be destroyed. Everyone will die off."[39] Such an act was described as gnigne and would lead to a punishment by Hupila.

When captives were discovered to be missing, their relatives would send out a group to inquire if they had been seized as captives. This process was called Kagalen, "the inquiry." They carried a red rooster with them. This emblem of the Kagalen ensured their safe passage while they sought their relative. Once the captive was located, the relatives would inquire about the size of the ransom, which was usually paid in cattle. A standard ransom of six cattle for a woman and seven cattle for a man was closely linked to the mourning period of six days for a woman and seven days for a man. Because a captive's relatives were ransoming back a life, they had to pay cattle equivalent to the mourning period.[40] Once the negotiations were completed, a rooster was sacrificed at the captor's Hupila. The inquiry party gave thanks to the captor's family shrine for extending its protection to the captive. Then the inquiry party returned home, gathered the necessary cattle, and returned to ransom their relative. Once the inquiry had been made, the captive could not be sold elsewhere. "It could not be done. It would bring ruin to the compound."[41] Hupila would punish them.

The sale of captives was permitted only if no inquiry was made by the captive's kin. Some say that the holding party waited only a few days; others suggest as long as a year. While awaiting ransom, captives were used as farm labor, but few of them were kept permanently. When no inquiry was made, the captive became a slave and could be sold to other Diola, the Mandinka, or the Afro-Portuguese. "If you do not see a rooster, well then you get him to Diembering [the most active slave trading Diola community]." Shorn of kin who would ransom them, captives became strangers who could be sold without spiritual sanction.[42]

Violations of the rules that governed the ransom and sale of captives were said to be punished by Hupila. Hupila could attack the wrongdoer by sending termites or fire to destroy his rice granary, cattle to eat his rice in the paddies, or disease to kill his livestock. It could also seize the wrongdoer or his kin with disease, leading even to death. One of these diseases, called hupila, was said to make one's legs feel like a stick of wood. When one awoke in the morning, it made one feel like all one's limbs were bound in rope. It was difficult to move. The disease associated with Hupila resembled the binding up of a captive.[43]

The involvement of the family shrine of Hupila in regulating the ransom or sale of captives was quite different from the involvement of the occupational shrines of the forge, fishing, or palm wine tapping. The latters' central focus was on the economic activity itself, and they were created to carry the spiritual concerns of those involved in such activities to Emitai and to receive guidance and protection in these activities. Hupila's link to the raiding, ransoming, and sale of people was of a different nature. Its central task was protecting the material well-being of the household and protecting the fertility of its women. Hupila's responsibility for the rules of raiding was an extension into a new area, building on its role of safeguarding the household. But why did Esulalu choose Hupila for this new role in community life?

There are three possible explanations for the extension of Hupila into the affairs of captives. The first focuses on the origins of the link. One of the major sources of captives, in addition to raiding, was the seizure of cattle thieves. If they were caught, the young men who would sneak into compounds to seize cattle were placed in wooden fetters until they could be ransomed for cattle. Because cattle were held collectively by the men of an extended family, this wealth was watched over by Hupila. Because the thief had been working against the protective responsibilities of Hupila and was caught through the aid of Hupila, he was fettered near the shrine. Gradually, the linkages became more complex, and the fetters themselves were linked to Hupila.[44]

The second explanation focuses on the collective nature of the responsibilities and benefits of a ransom or sale. Once a captive had taken a drink of water or eaten food, the captor's family took on the responsibility for the well-being of the captive. They had to see to it that their prisoner was maintained in good health. Abuse of the captive would bring disaster to the household. It was the responsibility of the household's Hupila that such a disaster never took place. Should a captive die while awaiting ransom, through no fault of her or his keepers, sacrifices would have to be made at the captor's shrines of Hupila and Kouhouloung. For ritual purposes, the captive would become temporarily a part of the captor's family. Shorn of one's kin, there was no alternative ritual for a proper burial, though he or she would be buried in a separate cemetery reserved for strangers.[45]

Just as there was collective responsibility for the well-being of the captive, there was a collective benefit from a successful ransom or sale. When asked why the captives were linked to Hupila, Moolaye Bassin replied, "If you have something of value, you will summon your brother." In a similar vein, Siopama Diedhiou said that it was because "only the house will take it [the ransom]."[46] The cattle paid became the property of the family. As they shared in the wealth, they shared in any responsibility for the welfare of the captive.

A third explanation, which was not offered directly by any Esulalu interpreters of the phenomenon, centers around the exchange of cattle, seven for a man and six for a woman. In most of Kadjinol, as well as most of Esulalu, this number corresponds to the period of intense mourning, which ends with ritual sacrifice and prayers at Hupila and Kouhouloung.[47] By linking ransoms and sales of captives to Hupila and the mourning period, people seem to be saying that these economic transactions are exchanging lives, that they must be considered as equivalent to death. The number of cattle assumes a symbolic quality, equaling the days of mourning. Hupila watches over the exchange of lives, just as it safeguards the lives and reproduction of the Esulalu household. Hupila not only guards the well-being of its supplicants but also guides them in the spiritually dangerous task of exchanging lives.[48]

Once the ransom or sale process was completed, two shrines received part of the proceeds. Katapf, a shrine linked to war through its ability to protect against wounds from knives and machetes, required a ritual of thanks that consisted of an offering of a chicken, rice, and palm wine. Katapf's protection was considered vital in the often dangerous process of seizing captives. Should the sacrifice be omitted, Katapf would seize the negligent party or someone in his family.[49] In the Kalybillah half of Kadjinol, there was a further obligation, to offer a calf to the priest-king of Kalybillah to fulfill one's obligation to the Djumpoc shrine of Elenkine Sergerh. This shrine protected Kalybillah and was particularly important for war. At Samatit, one steer had to be offered to the township shrine, Enac.[50]

From Shrines of the Family to Shrines of the Slave Trade

The close involvement of Esulalu shrines in the sale of captives had a profound effect on the shrines themselves, particularly Hupila, where an entirely new form of the shrine was introduced with new rules governing its priesthood and its accessibility. To understand this process, it is necessary to examine what people called the "old" Hupila, which was brought to Esulalu when the townships were founded. This Hupila, like its successors, was seen as a powerful ally in the protection of a family's well-being, wealth, and fertility. The old Hupila had a relatively simple altar made of clay with a libation cup in the middle and a pig's jawbone on either side. This was a shrine of affliction; one undertook the sacrifices and religious initiation when one was seized with a disease associated with Hupila. To recover, the afflicted made a series of sacrifices in which they "took on" the priesthood of the shrine. One could not refuse such a summons. "If you did not do it, the kahoeka (the benovelent ancestors) would kill you."[51] A shrine was established in the afflicted's backyard, and after suitable instruction and sufficient sacrifices, he became a priest of Hupila. He could offer prayers for his extended family and help initiate others into the priesthood. Sacrifices were relatively simple: two pigs, a goat, a dog, and chickens. No cattle were sacrificed, and there was a limit on the number of pigs sacrificed. Initially, it had no wooden fetters associated with it, and it had nothing to do with slavery. This shrine was consistently held to be one of the very oldest in Esulalu.[52]

As a closer relationship between the slave trade and the Hupila shrine developed, Esulalu traders gained a greater familiarity with the townships where they sold their captives. They were particularly impressed by the close connection between the slave trade and the Hupilas of Ediamat, Diembering, and Niomoun, major slave-trading Diola communities. In each of these areas, the wooden slave fetters, hudjenk, were an integral part of the shrine itself. The blood of animal sacrifice and the palm wine libations were poured over the consecrated fetters of the shrine and over the altar. Further inquiries revealed that to become a priest of the shrine, one had to have captured a slave and one had to sacrifice far larger quantities of animals, including a steer. To active slave traders who were acquiring substantial numbers of livestock, these new forms of Hupila provided a more efficacious protection of the captive and the slave trader. They also provided a socially acceptable way for traders to display their newfound wealth, while avoiding the appearance of hoarding it or of practicing witchcraft.[53]

The most widespread form of the newer Hupila was introduced from Ediamat by Diola from Bouyouye and Samatit. Judging from its wide diffusion in Esulalu, as well as its close association with the seizure of captives, it appears to be the first of the new forms, probably being established in Samatit by 1750.[54] Members of the Badiat lineage of Samatit brought the shrine from Bouyouye, a township which shared a common origin with Samatit. As an elder suggests, "Samatit, they are the senior ones" for Hupila. From Samatit, members of a Kafone blacksmith lineage brought it to Kadjinol. Finally, it spread to Mlomp, Kagnout, and Eloudia.[55] In each case, the family that introduced it was also active in the seizure of captives.

This Ediamat form of Hupila fulfilled many of the same functions as the older one. It protected the family from harm, ensured its fertility, and protected its wealth. The placement of wooden fetters on the shrine added another function, the protection of captives and those involved in their seizure. Access to this shrine was quite different from the old Hupila. In the older shrine, one became a priest after successfully weathering an illness associated with the cult. In the new one, priests were still seized through illness, but new qualifications were added. To become a priest of Hupila Hudjenk, one had to have seized a captive. "If you seize a slave/captive, you will have a Hupila. Anyone who has Hupila," you know his ancestors seized slaves or captives.[56] In fact, each Hupila was named after the slave who was seized initially. "His name will remain." Songs were sung at the shrine about the slave who was captured.[57]

This new form of Hupila did not completely replace the old. In the late nineteenth century, certain elders finished two Hupilas, the newer Hupila Hudjenk and the older form without fetters and without familiar names (casell). Opposition to the installation of the new shrine may have delayed the abandonment of the old. This opposition appeared to have been the strongest in the various communities that became Mlomp.[58] In addition to loyalty to an older cult, opposition focused on the way that the new Hupila required the seizure of a captive to become eligible for its priesthood and lavish sacrifices to perform its rituals.

These were profound changes in what was the most basic cult of Esulalu. In the older Hupila, selection of the priesthood was a spiritual process. The spirits associated with Hupila would seize their desired priest with an illness, whose origin would be detected by a priest or priestess of the divinatory shrine, Bruinkaw. The illness itself was seen as a sign of spiritual election.[59] Affordable sacrifices of a few pigs, some chickens, and a dog enabled the afflicted to begin the ritual instruction to perform all of the family shrines' rituals and to initiate others into the cult. With Hupila Hudjenk, the illness became a sign of Hupila's command to establish a shrine, but it did not enable one to become a priest. Families that did not engage in raiding established small shrines without the wooden fetters. The shrines were installed by those who had become priests who had also seized, ransomed, or sold captives. When such a family needed a ritual performed, they could not do it themselves. They had to summon the trader priests to perform such rituals as giving thanks for a good harvest. Slave raiders became the essential intermediaries between families and the spirits who protected them.

Even in death, the distinction between those who seized captives and those who did not was maintained. Only those who had seized captives could have cattle sacrificed at their funerals. These cattle had the fetters of Hupila attached to their legs. "When you had seized a slave, then you had arrived. If you had not seized a slave, they could not seize cattle [at your funeral]. . . . Now, even for a woman they can seize cattle. . . . You know the world is not the same as in the past. In the past, they did what was true."[60]

The introduction of Hupila Hudjenk was closely associated with the increasing wealth of those who raided or sold captives. When asked why a new form of Hupila was adopted, informants frequently cited a desire to display their new wealth in a socially acceptable way. "The rich men" wanted to show "that you are a big man, that is why they did it this way."[61] This can be demonstrated by the sharp increase in the material demands made on an aspiring priest of Hupila Hudjenk. Hudjenk required sacrifices of twenty to forty pigs, a duck, a goat, large numbers of chickens, and one head of cattle. Cattle were still scarce in the mideighteenth century, and few people could afford to sacrifice them. In addition, the initiate had to supply enough rice and palm wine to feed a large crowd for six days of festivities. On each day, celebrants performed the nyakul, a funeral dance that honors the ancestors. The taking on of Hupila became a large spectacle, in which the new priest showed his status as an *ousanome*, a sharer of wealth, who used his abundant reserves for the good of the community.[62] Linking good works for the general populace with slave raiding also helped to generate support for this increasingly important activity.

Once these elaborate rites were performed, the new Hupila was considered to be so powerful that its altar could not be attached to the walls of the home. It needed its own house, detached from other dwellings but still within the compound walls. The releasing of the soul force of all the sacrificial animals endowed this shrine with a greater power than the old Hupila. The inclusion of the wooden fetter, Hudjenk, ensured that some of this power would protect the ransom and sale of captives. This new form of Hupila reflected additional demands on the shrine— demands for the effective protection of a new form of wealth. It also reflected a new ethic that celebrated the wealth of the raider, ransomer, and seller of captives. As the wealth generated by the raider economy increased, the raiders transformed more old shrines and created new ones that would ensure that their economic power was reflected in their religious influence.

Resistance to Hupila Hudjenk seems to have been overcome because of Esulalu's widespread participation in the seizure of captives. Most genealogies list ancestors who seized captives and ransomed or sold them. Virtually every extended family in Kadjinol and many that I visited in the other townships have this form of Hupila, complete with wooden fetters. The ease of entry into the captive trade made such widespread participation possible. Any man could pick up his bow and arrows or other weapons and join a raiding party. Any man could aspire to have a Hupila Hudjenk.

A second form of Hupila was introduced during the last decades of the eighteenth century.[63] This new form of Hupila, named after the towns of Diembering and Niomoun, was also closely linked to raiding but was much more closely linked to the slave trade than Hupila Hudjenk. Both Diembering and Niomoun were market centers, where, in sharp contrast to Esulalu, traders sold slaves directly to Europeans.[64] As part of the installation of this form of Hupila, the sacrifice of a slave was required. Hounakaw Diatta of Mlomp, who is a priest of this shrine, described the special and difficult part of taking on this shrine: "They would seize people ... slaves" and attach them in wooden fetters at the Hupila shrine. At Diembering, they killed the slave, whereas at Mlomp they only beat them. Kapooeh Diedhiou claims that they refrained from killing them because it was "forbidden (gnigne) since our ancestors." He suggest that, rather than kill a slave, they included human remains in the consecrated soil brought from Diembering and placed in the altar of Hupila HouDiemberingai.[65] Although suggestions of human sacrifice made in another locale must be taken with a grain of salt, the frequency of the assertion by people who participated in the cult lends it credence.

The link to human sacrifice, through consecrated soil or actual sacrifice, is cited as the primary reason that there was such strong opposition to this shrine in Esulalu. Its influence was limited to the communities of Djicomole, Djibetene, and Kadjifolong, which eventually became part of Mlomp, and the township of Kagnout.[66] This link to human sacrifice is also regarded as the cause of the failure of cult followers' families to grow. The children of the cultists died from illnesses inflicted by various spirit shrines because their parents had violated the rules of protection and hospitality required even for a slave. Thus, Kapooeh Diedhiou claims that to kill a slave: "If you do it, all of your family will die."[67]

Like Hupila Hudjenk, Hupila HouDiemberingai was closely linked to the slave trade. The man credited with introducing the shrine to Esulalu had the nickname (casell) of Hunome Boukhan, "seller of people," and is generally described as being extremely wealthy. When asked why people would establish this type of Hupila, people replied: "They who had lots of wealth, they went because they were very rich."[68]

The sacrifice of a slave would greatly enhance the spiritual power released through the sacrifice of massive numbers of pigs, chickens, a cow, duck, goat, and dog. It was seen as a still more efficacious way of safeguarding family wealth and slave-trading activities. However, its reliance on human sacrifice or human remains impeded its growth and brought other spiritual powers against them, attacking participants' abilities to have children. With Hupila HouDiemberingai, not only did it cease to be primarily a shrine of affliction but it transgressed Esulalu ideas about the polluting nature of the act of murder.[69]

New Defenses and a New Hupila

The increasing frequency of raids for captives, during the second half of the eighteenth century, encouraged the people of Esulalu to take a series of measures to heighten the security of their communities. Men went to work in the rice paddies and forests armed with muskets, bows and arrows, and spears. Frequent raids against people working in rice paddies encouraged both women and men to work in groups, either as families or in single-sex work teams.[70] It may have also provided an added incentive for the development of the labor society (embottai), a social club that hired out its labor in exchange for livestock that were killed on festive occasions. Furthermore, the areas surrounding the townships were not cleared. Paths were intentionally left as winding and narrow as possible to make it more difficult for raiders to flee. Armed groups of men from each quarter of the townships guarded the forest or estuary areas to prevent raiders from seizing cattle or people. Houses were built to serve as fortresses in addition to lodging; they had only one door to the outside, which could be bolted shut. There were no windows on outside walls. Their backyards were walled with adobe and covered with fan palm leaves and thatch, both to protect them from rains and to ensure that no one could climb over them quietly.[71] Finally, people limited their travels beyond the townships during the day and beyond the quarter at night. As Nuhli Bassin describes it: "In former days, if you went even a little away, you were seized and sold."[72] Only Mandinka traders who were buying slaves and rice in exchange for cattle, cloth, and other goods enjoyed freedom of travel. "In the past, you would not see anyone going anywhere, only the Mandinka. You sit, you farm, you eat, only."[73]

Better defenses and greater caution exercised by the people of Esulalu and other Diola areas made the task of raiding more difficult precisely when the European demand for slaves was growing. Although I have not collected any materials on changing prices for slaves in Esulalu, Philip Curtin has shown that in the area immediately to the north of the Casamance, an area that was firmly linked to Diola slave traders through Mandinka middlemen, prices and demand peaked in the late eighteenth century.[74] With a growing demand for slaves and the continued success of more centralized raiding systems, some Esulalu raiders looked for new ways to procure slaves. In many African societies, judicial authorities or rulers could impose punishments of selling someone into slavery for a variety of offenses, ranging from adultery to murder. As the demand for slaves increased, so did the number of crimes punishable by enslavement. Such an alternative was not readily available in Esulalu.[75] Judicial decisions were made through consensus at certain shrines in which all lineages were represented. There was little chance that lineage members would allow their kin to be sold into slavery for crimes committed against another group. One exception was the crime of murder. Murderers were exiled from Esulalu and could become easy prey for slave traders in other communities, but there is no evidence that Esulalu traders sold murderers or other criminals at this time.

One method of slaving that minimized the risk of armed combat with other townships and the long delay in waiting for a ransom was the seizure and sale of local children. As easy as this form of slaving might be from a logistical point of view, it posed serious social and religious problems. Although the sale of unransomed prisoners of war, cattle thieves, or victims of raids from beyond Esulalu was socially acceptable, the seizure of captives from within Esulalu was not.[76] Such seizures would strike at the social stability of the townships, make work in

the rice paddies and forests more difficult, and threaten an intricate web of marriage and ritual ties. Seizures of children threatened the ability of Esulalu to sustain itself.

At a moral level, the seizure of local children violated an absolute ban on the
taking of people from a common land or essouk. Such strictures were enforced by
the priest-king's shrine of Calemboekine, which was responsible for the lives of
all members of the township and which had links to the other Calemboekine of
the region. It also would bring punishment by the victim's Hupila and any lineage shrines that might protect the victim's matrilineage or patrilineage. Such
punishments could come in the form of diseases, ranging from leprosy to Hupila's
rope disease. Punishment was seen as certain; there were only questions of time
and whether the shrine would seize the perpetrator or some of his close kin.

A slave-trading system based on kidnapping children from the community had
to overcome community resistance and the certainty of punishment. For such an
illicit form of slave trading, secrecy was essential; for such a polluting activity,
some form of spiritual protection was also required. A new shrine, Hupila Hugop
(Hupila of the rice granary) was instrumental in solving both problems. Hupila
Hugop, like the other forms of Hupila, was associated with the protection of the
family that had taken on the shrine. Even more than the other forms of Hupila, it
served to protect the families of slave raiders from capture or from spiritual danger brought on by their activities. It had a small altar, complete with wooden fetters. Unlike the other Hupila, located in full view of visitors, Hupila Hugop was
hidden inside the rice granary, a two-room area that was an integral part of every
Esulalu home. Both the existence of this shrine and its rituals were kept secret;
only other families that possessed the shrine could attend its rituals.[77] Like Hudjenk
and HouDiemberingai, Hupila Hugop was introduced from major slave-trading
areas outside Esulalu. Kadjinol's originated in Diembering and may have been
passed on to Niomoun before it was established within Esulalu. The shrine was
also adopted in part of Djougoutes and the islands of Bliss-Karones, both areas of
extensive slave raiding.[78]

The secrecy surrounding Hupila Hugop made it particularly suitable for illicit
forms of slave trading, most notably kidnapping children. Captives seized in socially acceptable ways—that is, people seized from outside Esulalu—could be held
in public view. Captives seized in violation of these norms had to be hidden away.
They were fettered in an inner chamber of the rice granary, out of sight, beside
the shrine of Hupila Hugop. The shrine provided a place for the storage of illicit
slaves, where plans could be developed for future raids and sales of slaves. Because of its violation of community norms, Hupila Hugop became known as a
"boekine of theft" or an "evil boekine" (boekine boulapoute).[79]

The association of kidnapping children and Hupila Hugop is firmly established
in Esulalu oral traditions. After discussing the shrine, Siopama Diedhiou described
the kidnapping process: "One would seize someone to take away . . . a small child
who is not able to go. Keep it in the house." People would search for the child,
but no one could search a man's granary. Djibalene of Kafone, who was a priest of
Hupila Hugop in the early nineteenth century, seized so many people that he was
nicknamed Adiouke Boukhan, Seizer of People. He used to tell children, "Come

to my house, I have some bananas." Then he would seize them, put some cloth in their mouths so they could not scream, and hide them in the granary until he could safely take them away for sale. In each case, children were hidden in the granary until being taken away for sale. One steer, a part of the sale price, was sacrificed at Hupila Hugop, in thanks for its aid in this endeavor.[80]

One might wonder how such a socially explosive activity could be carried out and why a community would not move decisively to eliminate it. First, it would be difficult to prove whether a child was seized by neighbors or by raiders from outside Esulalu. With captives hidden safely away from public scrutiny, only witnesses could lead to the captive. When a kidnapping was discovered, the child was freed, and the slaver might be severely beaten or even killed.[81] Second, the elders of the shrines who could move most effectively against slave raiding were often slave traders themselves, who had used their wealth to acquire ritual offices. Third, it appears that the seizures were a way of settling grudges, particularly against unpopular people in the community. One could deprive a parent of any security in old age by seizing his children and selling them into slavery. Father Joffroy described a north shore Diola institution of unspecified vintage called *punkus aye*, which involved the seizure of a man's children in order to ruin his house. Thomas suggests that this practice was done by other Diola, as well as by the neighboring Bainounk.[82]

It is virtually impossible to come up with an estimate of the number of children seized from within Esulalu. However, sufficient numbers disappeared to make parents worry about their children. Children who were too small to work were locked in the house, often under the supervision of someone who was too old to work. They were instructed not to unbar the door until they were sure that their parents were outside. Children were not allowed to wander about the quarter until they were strong enough to draw too much attention to any attempt to kidnap them.[83] Another measure of the extent of this practice is to see how widespread the shrine became. Although it exists in Diembering, Bliss-Karones, and Djougoutes, I have no accurate measure of its frequency. However, in Kadjinol's quarter of Kafone there were at least four; in Sergerh and Kagnao, two each; and at Ebankine, three. Comparable numbers are suggested for Mlomp.[84] They are considerably less common than ordinary Hupilas, but it had a far more specialized function. While each of these shrines was created after the illicit seizure of a slave, one cannot be sure of how often the practice was repeated.

A second major function of Hupila Hugop was to protect people who kidnapped children and sold them into slavery. Seizing children as slaves within Esulalu was believed to be punished with death. In reference to raiding for children, Kubaytow Diatta claimed: "If you seize slaves, you will die. Everyone in your family will die." Hupila Hugop was supposed to be able to protect its supplicants against seizure by other shrines. "If you did not have it [Hupila Hugop] you would be more afraid." Other ukine could not punish you for kidnapping their children. However, failure to sacrifice a portion of the sale price would lead Hupila Hugop to seize you with disease or to destroy your rice or livestock.[85]

The protection offered by Hupila Hugop was only temporary. In Esulalu, expiation of serious sin must be accompanied by public confession of wrongdoing, public sacrifice, and rituals of purification. With Hupila Hugop, not only were the sacrifices considered unequal to the taking of a life through kidnapping but also the rituals were performed in secret within the very group that organized to seize children.[86] One had to repeat the sacrifice at Hupila Hugop whenever an illness or calamity was diagnosed by the divinatory shrine of Bruinkaw as coming from Hupila Hugop. The necessity of repeating the sacrifices of propitiation continues to the present day. Most of the shrines are still active, despite the fact that their role in the slave trade has long since ceased. Now its primary function seems to be warding off punishment. In 1978, Boolai Senghor, a man who did not take on his family's Hupila Hugop, warned his sons that they would have to do it. "If one does not do it, Hupila Hugop, everything in the household will be destroyed. You will lose all your cattle, everything."[87]

This form of slave trading was not accepted by the Esulalu townships. Shrines associated with the priest-king, the various lineages, and the family all protected against kidnappings within Esulalu. In response to the spiritual dangers of such an action, slave traders in Esulalu brought in a secret shrine designed to protect them. It was regarded as only temporarily successful, and it did not gain them social acceptance. Informants in Esulalu often describe the traffickers in children as witches. Like witches, they drain the life blood of the community, its children, and they operate in secret. While witches lust for meat, the kidnappers of children lust for wealth. A witch will kill your children; a kidnapper will sell them.[88]

Spirit Shrines and the Slave-Trading Elite

Profits from the ransom and sale of captives heightened differences in wealth between families in Esulalu. Before the growth of the slave trade, wealth was determined by the size and location of one's rice paddies, one's skills as a farmer and herder, and a little bit of luck to withstand nature's adversities. Commerce in captives introduced a new and more rapid way to acquire wealth. A successful raider could acquire large numbers of cattle through ransoms. Through the sale of slaves, he could acquire livestock, guns, iron, and cloth. With access to guns and gunpowder, he could extend his hunting and raiding activities. Increasing supplies of iron would increase rice production by improving the supply of such farm tools as the cadyendo.[89] Cloth was important not only for making clothes but also for wrapping the dead before burial. One could gain social prestige by giving a cloth for a friend's or relative's burial.

The most important asset gained through this commerce in captives was cattle. In addition to the social prestige of having a large herd, cattle fulfilled an important religious and economic role. Cattle were needed for ritual sacrifice to honor the dead, to become a priest of certain shrines, or to atone for a grievous sin. Cattle also served vital economic functions. They could be used to ransom a relative who had been seized. Cattle were the only commodity accepted for the purchase of rice paddies. Paddies were only sold in times of crisis and with great reluctance. Only the pressures of needing cattle for funerals, atonement, or ransom would convince a man to sell his rice paddies.[90] Those who held cattle could supply the need, thereby expanding their landholdings. Raiders' cattle reserves made them a highly influential group, able to assume ritual responsibility, honor the dead, protect their relatives, and expand their lands. The cattleless poor and those who did not engage in raiding found it difficult to resist their influence.

This influence extended beyond raider control of the new forms of Hupila. In the late eighteenth century, they extended their control over the new form of circumcision, Bukut, and the town council shrine of Hutendookai, and they helped to create an influential elders' shrine called Hoohaney. In each case, wealth, rather than spiritual knowledge or charismatic powers, was emphasized in the selection of shrine elders.

The change in male circumcision from Kahat to Bukut had many causes, which were discussed in the previous chapter. One of these causes related closely to this tendency to emphasize wealth in ritual. Informants suggested that the reason Esulalu abandoned Kahat was because one could not sacrifice cattle, either during the initiation or in the process of becoming an elder. One could sacrifice only pigs and chickens and not too many of them. At Kahat, "you could not have a good festival."[91] At the initiation of Bukut, you could kill cattle to honor or strengthen your son or nephew. There was much feasting over several days. To be chosen for membership in the group of elders that control the circumcision shrine, one had to "finish Bukut," which involved a series of rituals, the sacrifice of many pigs, and large quantities of palm wine and rice. One had to demonstrate one's status as an ousanome, a sharer of wealth. There was no question of spiritual election or a special illness. Once again, the newfound wealth of the captive trade could be put to socially acceptable uses.

The township council shrine, Hutendookai, was also affected by the growing influence of the wealthy. When Hutendookai was first introduced from the Seleki area in the early eighteenth century, the senior men of each lineage were representatives at the shrine. Such appointments were made by the priest-king.[92] By the late eighteenth century, representatives to Hutendookai were being selected on the basis of wealth. "The weathy of the past . . . if you have [a lot], then you will go to Hutendookai." This practice was justified on the basis that the rich would be listened to in a meeting,[93] which suggests a rapid decline in the intensity of Esulalu suspicions of the rich. As the wealthy took over Hutendookai, they used fines to enforce the shrine's edicts. Those who refused to pay fines risked losing rice paddies, which would be sold out for cattle. Once again, the newly wealthy would be the primary beneficiaries.

The shrine of the elders, Hoohaney, created in the late eighteenth century to control the activities of the priest-king, was structured in such a way that wealth became a critical factor for participation in its rituals. The elders of Hoohaney controlled the initiation of new priest-kings and the initiation of young men into the rites of the dead, and they represented the most respected men from each lineage in the townships. Although shrine elders were not a legislative body, their deliberations were instrumental in developing community attitudes on moral issues, ritual responsibilities, and on religious concepts.[94]

Selection for membership in the elders of Hoohaney was done by the other elders, who wished to ensure that all lineages were represented. They favored the wealthy because only men with substantial holdings of livestock could hope to complete the four stages of initiation. Once selected, a new elder would perform the rite of Kikillo. He sacrificed one pig and offered libations of palm wine at the shrine. By doing so, he accepted his obligation to enter the shrine's council of elders. Yet he was not a full member. He had to perform the rite of Kanoken, "to enter," which required the sacrifice of three more pigs and provision of palm wine and rice for the adepts of Hoohaney. At this stage, he would receive certain limited information about the shrine and would be allowed to assist at some of the rituals. Two large pigs, palm wine, and rice were required to enter Eleng, the next stage of responsibility at Hoohaney. This step qualified the adept to be called a Lingona, an elder of the shrine with full access to its esoteric knowledge.[95] To those who had not achieved this level or who had not been chosen as shrine elders, such knowledge was vigorously guarded. To reveal such knowledge to those who had no right to hear it would "poison their ears" and could even bring death to the hearer.[96]

"Breaking the Country": The Legacy of the Slave Trade

It might be belaboring the obvious to point out that there were no formalized state structures that regulated Esulalu participation in the slave trade. Diola concerns about the problems of centralized polities and a reliance on a complex system of spirit shrines (ukine) to regulate most aspects of social and economic life shaped their responses to the increasingly important Atlantic trade system. Beginning at the modest level of ransoming and selling prisoners of war and raiders of cattle, the slave trade eventually became a source of significant wealth. Then both spiritual and human authorities became involved in the form of spirit shrines and their shrine elders. Together, elders and the ukine with which they were associated shaped Diola responses to the Atlantic trade system and sought to limit its influence within the Esulalu townships.

Despite efforts to shape and contain these influences, Diola involvement in the ransom or sale of captives had a profound impact on Esulalu society and the awasena path. Cattle and trade goods introduced into the community from the proceeds of captive transactions contributed to widening social differentiation within the townships. Large holdings of cattle allowed raiders to expand their rice paddy holdings and to exercise greater influence within ritual life. Simultaneously, those who were not involved in raiding found what security they had sharply diminishing, both at an economic level and at a spiritual one. Subject to raids from outside Esulalu, they needed cattle to pay for ransoms. For the acquisition of priestly office, to atone for serious sins, and to honor the dead, poorer Esulalu had to sell their rice paddies to procure cattle. These cattle quickly passed out of their hands as sacrifices or ransom, leaving them with fewer paddies to feed their families. Remaining suspicions that the wealthy were witches, bargainers with ammahl spirits, or antisocial individuals contributed to rising tensions within the townships.[97] The fragility of the traders' wealth, however, provided some easing of these divisions. Wealth in cattle was highly perishable in the tsetse fly—ridden and swampy Casamance. Herds could be rapidly depleted by disease, theft, or ransom and ritual needs. A wealthy man could soon find himself without cattle.[98]

In religious life, Esulalu's participation in the sale and ransom of captives also had profound effects. Through the creation of new Hupilas, traders and ransomers of captives placed themselves in a position as intermediaries between individuals and the spirit shrines that protected their families. Ordinary people had to rely on this new elite for their basic family rituals. Surviving the afflictions of Hupila no longer ensured the survivors of entry into its priesthood. The wealthy also gained a place among the group of elders who controlled male circumcision. In Hutendookai, the town council shrine, the wealthy elite replaced the most senior men as representatives. It was believed that their words would carry more weight.

With the emergence of the Hoohaney shrine cluster came the development of new type of spirit shrine, one limited exclusively to the wealthy. Those men who could not afford its extensive initiatory sacrifices were excluded from attendence at its rituals and from participation in its deliberations. Like the titled men among the Igbo and the Kalabari of southeastern Nigeria, Hoohaney's elders spoke with added authority at village or township assemblies. At both Hutendookai and Bukut, the less privileged could still participate in rituals, partake of the meat of the sacrifice and the palm wine libations, and engage in shrine deliberations, even while being excluded from leadership roles. At Hoohaney, they could not. Many important decisions about community welfare and religious life were made in deliberations at the Hoohaney shrine, deliberations from which the vast majority of Esulalu adults were excluded.

In a Yoruba context, Bernard Belasco has suggested that the slave trade encouraged "the emergence of deities restricted to a particular social stratum, and of cults which ritualize the person's socioeconomic self-consciousness." He saw this as "emblematic of the process in which individuals are torn loose of kin bonds and are propelled deeper into the pursuit of wealth, outside of customary labor arrangements and traditional controls over the product, its materials, or the instruments of production."[99] While overstating the degree of rupture with "traditional controls" and kinship bonds among the Yoruba, Belasco does point out the serious challenges posed by the Atlantic trade system to ideas of religious and social authority. Within Esulalu, the wealth generated by the slave trade began a process of class formation in which the slave-trading elite gained greater access to rice paddies and livestock and was able to invest in the ritual offices that provided access to community leadership and helped to legitimate its growing economic power.[100] Still, by channeling a portion of the slave traders' wealth into a complex system of competing spirit shrines, some of which were not primarily accessible by wealth, Esulalu was able to limit their influence and preserve a structure of diffuse power through senior members of lineages and groups of elders at a wide variety of spirit shrines. Further limitations on the slave-trading elite grew out of the close association of excessive wealth and witchcraft accusations. The newly wealthy had to be careful how they displayed their wealth or how they wielded power, lest they be accused of using nefarious means to achieve their preeminence. While Esulalu's structure of spirit shrines expanded to incorporate the slave-trading elite, they did not exempt the new elite from long-standing forms of social control.

In channeling this new source of power into the shrine system, Diola elders did far more than permit the entrenchment of a new elite in ritual offices. They began to redefine the very concept of a priest or elder. In many of the older shrines, priests and elders were chosen from the successful survivors of certain diseases, from visions of spiritual power surrounding a particular person, or from the special knowledge that an individual displayed. Such an individual took on the shrine and communicated with the powers associated with it. Such priests were said to be able to "see" into the spiritual world and to negotiate with the emissaries of Emitai. As wealth became an increasingly important criterion for selecting priests and elders, such powers were considered less important. A priest of Hupila Hudjenk might have seized a slave, sacrificed animals, and received all the necessary ritual instruction, but no one could teach him to see into a spiritual world.[101] With increasing frequency, priests of these shrines became mere "technicians of the sacred," masters of ritual technique without charismatic authority. The office of a priest became a symbol of status. The people who really knew the shrine and its spiritual powers, people who were said to have houkaw ("head"), might be seated far down the row of logs around a shrine. People still dreamed and had visions, but their influence was diminished. By the end of the eighteenth century, the authority of wealth rather than charisma proved to be the most heeded guide.

In a series of articles on religious conversion, Robin Horton has suggested that trade and other activities that tend to break down the localism of African village life would strengthen the concept of a supreme being in African religion. He argues that lesser spirits are associated with local activities within the "microcosm" of the villages, while the supreme being governs the "macrocosm" of the wider world.[102] Such a shift did not occur in Esulalu. In Esulalu, the increasing insecurity that accompanied raiding turned people's spiritual concerns inward, toward protecting their families from attack and spiritual danger.

Even the slave traders, who had the strongest taste of macrocosmic experience, turned inward to protect their families and to invest their wealth in socially acceptable ways, through elaborate rituals that gave them priestly office. They concentrated their religious activity on those shrines that did not stress charismatic experience, experience that had included visions of Emitai. By concentrating on the more institutional aspects of religious experience, they turned away from Emitai toward Its emissaries, the spirits ukine. While trade strengthened Esulalu's links to the macrocosm, it also reinforced the influence of lesser spirits. Esulalu's supreme being, long active in the microcosm of township religion, found that with less attention to charismatic experience, there was less emphasis on Emitai's role in the creation of the ukine.

This new commerce forced people to think about the nature of captivity and slavery. People in Esulalu had little trouble in accepting the idea of detaining cattle thieves and prisoners of war until they were ransomed. Recognizing the captives' humanity, the Esulalu extended certain rights of hospitality and protection to them. If captives died, funeral rites would be performed at their captor's shrines of

Kouhouloung and Hupila. To symbolize that relation, the captive was fettered at the shrine of Hupila. To sell people who were not claimed by relatives was seen as a necessary and profitable way of disposing of unneeded strangers. Such sales were seen as a legitimate form of commerce—a legitimate slave trade.

This was not the case when slave traders kidnapped children from the townships. This activity had to be done in secret, and captives were hidden in granaries until they could be carried away for sale. Hupila Hugop was created to protect such slavers from spiritual punishment for their illicit slave trade. Still, Hupila Hugop provided only temporary protection because there was no public confession, atonement, reparation, or purification for what was seen in Esulalu as a grievous sin.

In looking back on this period of raiding, ransoming, and sale of captives and of an increasing emphasis on economic criteria for access to ritual office, the present priest-king of Kadjinol has said: "Men did not think well. They thought only of cattle. They committed sins against the spirit shrines and the spirit shrines destroyed the country. They brought in diseases that wiped out families; diseases that not even shots could cure."[103]

6

Strangers within Their Borders

Esulalu Religion in the Era of
French Expansion, 1800–1880

During the first eighty years of the nineteenth century, the French expanded their activities in the Casamance from sporadic trading expeditions to permanent settlements, while gaining formal recognition of French sovereignty over the Diola townships. During this period, however, they did not attempt to establish the type of formal control expressed in taxation, forced labor, and land cessions typical of their activities in northern Senegal or seek to regulate the internal affairs of the Diola townships. Rather than French administrators, African Muslim and Luso-African traders were the primary representatives of French expansion. These groups established a series of small villages throughout the region, including Esulalu.

The people of Esulalu continued to govern themselves through the various spirit shrines and councils of elders that they had developed. During this period, there was no spiritual crisis of conquest, no sense of a world that had changed beyond their capacity to influence events. The awasena path continued to interact with the incoming traditions of Christianity and Islam on an equal footing, while commanding the full support of the people of Esulalu. Still, these new religions brought with them new ideas and ritual practices and enjoyed the prestige of being associated with powerful European or Muslim communities. In the nineteenth century, Esulalu became increasingly aware of the nature of these traditions, both as a source of religious innovation and as a challenge to their own traditions. However, the newcomers also confronted a new religion, that of the Diola, which influenced their own practices and often became a source of spiritual comfort in a new land.

There was dramatic change, however, in the nature of the source material during this period. For the first time, European traders and administrators were living in predominantly Diola communities and writing about them. Beginning in the 1840s, we have detailed descriptions of Diola religious and social life from sources that were fixed during the period they describe. They do focus, however, on pluralistic communities, trading entrepôts, with a Diola majority and significant minorities of Europeans and other African groups, settled in new communities that were becoming centers of trade. A central factor in Esulalu's religious history during this period was the process of cross-cultural contact. Such contacts, before the colonial conquest, developed at a time when Diola communities interacted with European, Afro-European, and African Muslim newcomers, as fully independent communities.

Initially in this chapter, I discuss the growth of the European presence in the lower Casamance until 1850, its influence within Esulalu, and the interaction between Diola and newcomers ("strangers" in Diola terminology) within the European-affiliated communities that were established during this period. I include an analysis of Diola religious life, as described by Europeans in the centers of regional trade. Then I examine the changing objectives of French policy in the period from 1850 until 1880, their impact within Esulalu, and the cross-cultural contact developing in the "stranger" villages established during this latter period. Both sections focus on the influence of powerful political, commercial, and religious groups, whose gradual penetration of the Diola region allowed a process of mutual influence and accommodation, rather than a direct assault on the foundations of Diola community and spiritual life. A subsequent chapter examines those changes that were not directly associated with the increasing presence of strangers within Esulalu's borders.

France and the Lower Casamance

Before the nineteenth century, the European presence in the Casamance had been limited to a few trading communities on the periphery of the Diola areas of settlement. From commercial centers at Gorée, Cacheu, Ziguinchor, and the Gambia, Mandinka, Bainounk, Manjaco, and Afro-Portuguese traders brought European trade goods to the Diola. They purchased Diola rice, beeswax, and slaves. Until the nineteenth century, European influences were felt most intensely through the increased demand for slaves and the expanding availability of iron and other European trade goods. European cultural influences were limited by the sporadic nature of direct contacts with the Diola. During this period, neither European nor African traders attempted to exert direct control over Diola townships.[1]

In the late eighteenth century, the French became interested in establishing a permanent trading presence in the Casamance region. In 1778, the governor of Senegal visited the Casamance and negotiated trading rights at the north shore Diola community of Itou. He described the enormous potential that he saw among the Diola: "the village of Itou [is] where the French have acquired exclusive docking privileges to the exclusion of all other nations. The rice trade is quite abundant as is that of slaves, elephant teeth (tusks), and wax and will become very advantageous if we establish a more secure possession."[2] Although Le Brasseur's assessment of the Casamance's potential was echoed by other French visitors, little action could be taken before the conclusion of the Napoleonic wars.[3]

In 1826, Governor Roger of Senegal visited the Casamance to assess its economic potential. He was impressed by Diola farmers, who produced an abundance of rice in fields protected by an elaborate system of dikes. His report emphasized the richness of the region's agriculture, its importance in relation to the growing British control of the Gambia, and its importance to the slave trade. He saw that a major commercial presence in the Casamance would allow the French to abandon their poorly situated post at Albreda.[4] The British also were aware of the Casamance's potential as a slave-trading route:

> Not withstanding this restriction, however, a very considerable Slave Trade is carried on by the French factors of Albreda throughout the whole length of the river Gambia: For, although the authorities at Bathurst do not permit any vessel with slaves on board to pass that settlement, yet they are carried in canoes to the left bank of the river, and thence conveyed by land to Cacho or Casamens, whence they are shipped for the West Indies.[5]

In 1828, French officials negotiated the rights to establish a commercial post at Brin, ten kilometers downriver from the Portuguese settlement at Ziguinchor. Concerned about the possibility of British incursions, they also negotiated a treaty with the village of Itou, which controlled the northern entrance to the Casamance and which had close ties to the Esulalu township of Kadjinol. In both cases, treaties were signed only after village leaders had consulted with local assemblies.[6] Itou's treaty guaranteed their freedom of religion: "Article 8: His majesty promises to have anyone severely punished who proceeds to insult Couloubousse [the priest king] or his subjects or attempts to abuse their religion or customs of the country."[7] Given the absence of such a provision from many treaties of a similar type in the Senegambia region and Itou's long-standing trade relations with the French and Portuguese, one may assume that Itou was wary of any interference in community life that could grow out of ties with Europeans. It also indicated that the French, at this stage, were more interested in establishing a commercial presence and excluding other Europeans than in interfering in Diola affairs.

In the same year that French officials negotiated treaties at Brin and Itou, a small group of Afro-French traders from Gorée, led by Pierre Baudin, established themselves at Carabane, an island that belonged to Kagnout (see map 4). From there, the Gorée traders could penetrate the various channels near the mouth of the Casamance and trade for rice, beeswax, hides, and slaves. These goods were sold to French merchants at Gorée.[8]

No official French mission returned to Casamance until 1836. Finding the leader of Itou unwilling to allow the construction of a fort, Lieutenant Malavois decided to negotiate with Kagnout for the cession of Carabane, where Baudin had settled. The people of Kagnout, led by the priest-king Guindal, welcomed the French and agreed to rent half the island for thirty-nine iron bars a year. Kagnout insisted on retaining its rights to harvest palm wine on the island and on retaining control over a portion of the island called Djibamuh, where a major shrine is located. Raiders from Djougoutes and Diembering had made the area too dangerous for farming, so Kagnout's elders welcomed an alliance with French traders who could protect them.[9]

Carabane's swampy and unhealthy location prevented it from becoming France's primary base of operations in the Casamance region, but it was retained

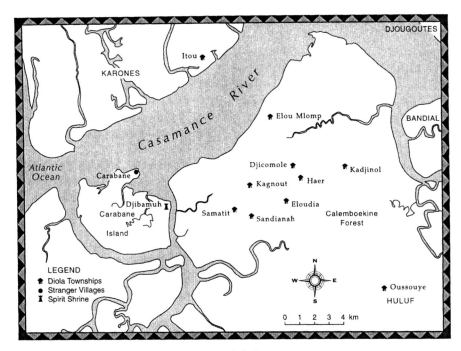

Map 4. Esulalu in 1828

to control the mouth of the river and to tap Diola agricultural production: "They make sufficient harvests to permit them, in many circumstances, to come to the aid of other groups on the coast, where there is famine; although they already have a large quantity of land cultivated, there is a still larger part that does not produce and remains uncleared."[10] By 1840, the French appeared to have secured a position as the leading European power in the Casamance, though neither the Portuguese nor the British would recognize their claims.

Luso-African Ziguinchor and the Peoples of the Lower Casamance

While the French were expanding their presence in the Casamance, Portuguese influence was in sharp decline. Their garrison at Ziguinchor consisted of a small detachment, stationed in a fort made of sun-baked clay and branches. Local officials went years without pay. In 1808, Silvester Golberry had described Portuguese trade from Ziguinchor as "a very advantageous trade in slaves, elephant's teeth, native wax, raw hides, aromatic seeds, and dying woods," but it was sharply reduced by 1840.[11] Weakened by political instability at home and revolts in their colony, the Portuguese could do little more than make formal protests against French encroachments on what they regarded as a part of Portuguese Guiné.[12]

In 1850, Ziguinchor contained about a thousand households and included Luso-Africans, Bainounk, and small groups of Diola, Manjaco, and Balanta. There was also a considerable slave population, which farmed rice, collected palm wine, and traded in outlying communities.[13] Luso-Africans and some Bainounk used Portuguese Crioulo as their primary language and wore European-style clothes. They identified with the metropole by embracing Christianity and wearing crucifixes. It is clear from Hyacinthe Hecquard's description of Ziguinchor that the label of Christian was an important component of their definition of community and in the maintenance of ethnic boundaries: "All the inhabitants call themselves Christians even though they do not fulfill any obligations of their religion; they called the neighboring peoples, pagans."[14]

Roman Catholic Christianity was an important part of the identification of the people of Ziguinchor with Lusitanian culture, but the depth of their knowledge and commitment to their religion was unclear. The people of Ziguinchor were often left for years without benefit of clergy. The church hierarchy, based on the Cape Verde Islands, paid little attention to the pastoral needs of the Casamance. The frequent absence of any clergy at Ziguinchor left little time for religious instruction among local Catholics and no time for proselytization in neighboring African communities. In 1864, when Father Lacombe visited Ziguinchor, church services were conducted by a Luso-African priest in his own home, on an ordinary table covered with a ragged cloth. The church had burnt down thirteen years before.[15]

Outside observers tended to focus on the Luso-Africans' lack of religious instruction, their use of African religious elements, and their veneration of sacred objects. The All Souls' Day celebration, common to Luso-African communities, was often cited as an example of African ancestor veneration polluting a Catholic ritual, as well as an occasion for great bouts of drinking and lascivious behavior. In an important essay, George Brooks shows that the stress on making offerings to the dead on All Souls' Day, as well as their festive behavior, was not unique to Luso-African communities but was shared by their rural contemporaries in Portugal.[16] Rather than a Luso-African borrowing from African religions, All Souls' supplication of the dead represented an area of vital overlap between African religious concerns and the concerns of Portugal's rural Christians. Because it was important to the Portuguese who entered the region, Casamance Christians learned about All Souls' Day; because it addressed a concern of local religious communities, it also became an important holiday for Luso-Africans.[17]

While Luso-Africans baptized their children and attended mass when clergy were available, they also sought the religious assistance of their neighbors:

> Muslim Mandinka and Portuguese, and Luso-African Christians alike evinced great respect—often times expressing fear and awe—for the spiritual powers of coastal riverine groups, and frequently had recourse to their religious specialists for a variety of purposes: for establishing social relations; for ratifying commercial agreements; for mediation with local spirits; and for medical and spiritual healing.[18]

In the absence of clergy or when marrying African women, local rituals were often utilized. Afro-Portuguese also sought out African spiritual healers, African amulets, and Muslim gris-gris, containing various types of medicines that were said to have curative or protective power.[19]

Perhaps in exchange for their use of African rituals and medications, Luso-Africans provided neighboring Africans with saints' medals and crucifixes, which were said to perform similar protective and curative functions among Christians. These became items of trade, not only in Ziguinchor but also in Diola and Bainounk villages visited by traders. Hecquard described Ziguinchor's sacred commerce:

> They [the inhabitants of Ziguinchor] have a great veneration for images, the medals and the Christs, to which they associate a wide power to protect them from all accidents. This belief is widespread among the Floups [Diola] and the Bainounk, the Portuguese traders having made of these images, medals and cruxifixes, an object of commerce, and trade them for slaves that they keep or exchange again for livestock. Little time has passed since this type of traffic has stopped, not because it was immoral, but because the products were no longer sought after by the natives, since a Floup who had dearly purchased a copper Christ which he had carried among his gris-gris, was nevertheless killed by a gunshot.[20]

This trade in images, medals, and crucifixes provided the major source of Christian influence among the Diola during the early nineteenth century. From such contacts, they acquired a modest familiarity with Christian symbols, saints, and Jesus. It is unlikely that there was any sustained religious instruction of Diola catechumens by Portuguese priests during this period. Through commercial contacts, Diola learned of certain instrumental aspects of Christianity, the importance of religious objects in warding off evil, a facet of Christianity that was shared by rural Portuguese and Luso-Africans. Apparently, they also learned the limits of such protection.

Diola, French, and Northern Senegalese at Carabane

Like Ziguinchor, Carabane was a diverse community, composed of Afro-French, Wolof, Serer, Manjaco, and Diola, as well as a slave population of various origins. An 1842 census indicates that approximately one fifth of the population were slaves who cultivated rice and worked as sailors on the boats that plied the estuaries of the lower Casamance. Most slaves had French or Muslim Senegambian names, suggesting that they had been brought from Gorée rather than purchased locally.[21] The relative ease with which Diola captives could escape from Carabane discouraged their use. Diola were the largest free community at Carabane and supported themselves by farming and fishing. Afro-French and Wolof traders from Gorée controlled local commerce by purchasing rice, salt, and wax from the Diola townships, which they resold to European merchants in the region.[22] The export of slaves was also an important part of French commerce at Carabane throughout the nineteenth century: "The slaves were bought by the French at Sedhiou and Carabane with official approval at least until 1848 when pressures from the British in Gambia forced a halt. Slaves were sent to Gorée or North Senegal where the French incorporated them into their military forces, or apprenticed them to tradesmen. . . . Until 1902 Carabane served as a market center for slave trading."[23]

In 1849, Emmanuel Bertrand-Bocandé was appointed as the new resident at Carabane. He had spent twelve years trading in the Casamance and had learned Mandinka and Portuguese Crioulo.[24] During his eight years as resident, he attempted to make Carabane the primary trade center for the entire Casamance. He built a wharf, had the village surveyed, and encouraged additional traders to settle at Carabane. He built up a personal trade network and established small trading posts in several other locations, which he supplied from Carabane. He also established several small industries for processing local raw materials and a ship repair shop that increased Carabane's importance in regional trade. In 1850, Hecquard described Carabane's growing influence in the Diola townships: "The traders travel to the Floup [Diola] and Bainounk villages, where they remain until they have traded their merchandise."[25] Most of these itinerant traders were Euro-Africans or Muslims from northern Senegal.

Despite the presence of French and Euro-African traders at Carabane, there was no regular clerical presence until 1880. Carabane's small Christian community could rely on only occasional visits from priests stationed in northern Senegal. After Father Aragon's visit in 1848, the Holy Ghost Fathers requested permission to establish a mission at Carabane. While Bertrand-Bocandé supported the proposal, colonial officials feared that missionary work would provoke Diola opposition to French activities in the area and that they would have to incur considerable expense to protect mission workers. In 1851, the request for a Carabane mission was denied.[26]

Religious Pluralism at Carabane

Despite the diversity of Carabane's population, its religious life was dominated by the Diola. Lured by opportunities to sell crops, fish, salt, and other goods, as well as the chance to hire out their labor, substantial numbers of Diola settled at Carabane. Some of these people were runaway slaves or people convicted of crimes within their townships.[27] Individual Diola came with a knowledge of awasena tradition, though probably without having achieved ritual office.

With the assistance of elders from their home communities, Diola immigrants established five spirit shrines at Carabane, two primarily for men and three for women.[28] There were two different types of women's shrines, both called Ehugna. They addressed problems associated with the fertility of women and the land, the procurement of rain, as well as a broad array of women's issues. They were also involved in the healing of children and in protection against witches. According to Dyaye Babu Faye, Carabane's main Ehugna came from the north shore Diola township of Niomoun. It was a major shrine, where bulls could be sacrificed. Such sacrifices were part of the extended process of "finishing," or becoming a priest of the shrine. Its rituals were attended by awasena, Christian, and Muslim women. A smaller Ehugna shrine was brought from Kagnout, but only pigs could be sacrificed there. The other women's shrines were called Kasick and Badian Kasall. One of the men's shrines, called Djikamhoukaw, was located outside the village. Only initiated elders could attend this powerful shrine. The male circumcision shrine of Bukut was also established at Carabane and was used to initiate men from all three religious communities at Carabane.[29]

Carabane was the first predominantly Diola community where European observers settled and witnessed community life on a prolonged basis. Such observers' descriptions of the close association between Diola concepts of a supreme being and the procurement of rainfall are of particular importance. In 1856, Carabane's resident, Bertrand-Bocandé, described this linkage: "The rains bestow upon the land its fertility: their time has a name; it is the time of 'Emit,' the time of the rains, or the time of God. Emit in the Floup language signifies thunder, rain, God, and power."[30] Rain is the natural phenomenon that bestows life. Emitai is the spiritual being that bestows life. The two forces are intimately linked, not just by a shared name. Rain is seen as an emanation of Emitai Itself. In 1850, Hecquard described the most important of Diola rain rituals, the performance of which he witnessed at Carabane during a drought.

> For some time the rains had ceased, the rice yellowed under foot, everyone was worried about the harvest. The women assembled, took branches in their hands, then divided into two groups who met dancing, they ran all over the island, singing and praying for their good spirit to send them some rain. Their chanting continued for two whole days; but the weather did not change. From prayer they then switched to threats; the fetishes were knocked over and dragged into the fields amidst cries and threats that did not cease until there was rain; which led to the renewal of the fetishes with the customary respect. This ceremony, which lasts until the change in the weather, always has infallible results, they assure me that they would not have rain except for the fear they inspired among their fetishes.

In 1878, Father Gabriel Sène described a similar ritual at Carabane, during a period of drought: "When the rains are late the entire village gathers around the sacred tree carrying many rich presents. Wearing the strangest costumes, festooned with climbing plants from head to foot, the entire crowd advances, dancing to the sounds of tamtams and the most savage shouts, each of them grasping a mangrove branch."[31] As previously noted, mangrove branches are associated with water. The weaving of climbing plants onto ritual costumes is linked to the fertility of the earth. Except for the conclusion that the purpose of the rite was to frighten the spirit shrines, this description closely conforms to descriptions that I collected describing a rite called nyakul emit, "the funeral dance for Emitai." Paponah Diatta described the ceremony at Mlomp: "Women will rise up, they will do the nyakul funeral dance, they will cry, they will dance the *ignebe* [a dance associated with Ehugna]. They visit the ukine. . . . They dance for Emitai and return." That night Emitai sends one of the women *pite* (special mental powers), which are important for the successful completion of the ritual. Econdo Sambou claims that some women would wear only a small cloth around their loins to show Emitai that they had nothing and that they desperately needed rain. Mungo Sambou echoes that sense of desperation by calling the ritual a "crying for Emitai."[32] In the nyakul emit, all the shrines received sacrifices. Women moved from shrine to shrine, exhausting all spiritual remedies available to them. Then, in a final act, they beseeched Emitai directly through prayer and dance and asked It to provide them with rain.

Droughts were not the only calamity that confronted the people of Carabane; death was all too common. European observers had ample opportunities to describe Diola funeral rites and attitudes about death. A Holy Ghost priest, Father Lacombe, provided a detailed account of a Diola funeral that he observed at Carabane in 1864.

> During my stay one of the most curious and bizarre ceremonies attracted
> my attention. . . . It was a funeral ceremony. During the preceding night I
> heard funeral chants; . . . The next day, I saw planted in the middle of the
> road, some stakes, in the form of a square. Someone stretched some black
> cloths around it in such a way that it could provide shelter from the harsh-
> ness of the sun. . . . I saw the deceased arriving, carried by his age mates.
> They put him in a chair with his back against a stake to which they attached
> him securely. . . . They had clothed him in festival clothes; his feet and hands
> were weighted with silver and copper bracelets. . . . The mother of the de-
> ceased, a woman of sixty, with a shaved head, covered with ashes and sand,
> with her torn cloth around her thighs, would come constantly to interro-
> gate her son and demand of him the cause of his death. Then, receiving no
> response, she screamed loudly, stretched her hands on her son and went
> and rolled in the sand, as a sign of mourning and affliction. She entered the
> house and returned and presented it to him and asked what he lacked that
> he should leave his family and his community. . . . Throughout the day some
> forty women assembled for their tears and their funeral chants. They would
> leave the place where the deceased was, distance themselves up to ten
> meters, then retrace their steps, chanting and crying at the same time, and
> those assisting, seated on the ground would reply in the same tone.[33]

Lacombe described the funeral of a young married man whose premature death was difficult to comprehend. He left a wife and family and did not outlive his mother. His mother's interrogation reflected a Diola idea that some people do not like life and seek a premature return to the world of the dead. Lacombe's description could be of a Diola funeral in the 1990s, except that Lacombe did not observe any men dancing the nyakul, funeral dance.

After the performance of the chants and the women's mourning dance, the body was prepared for burial, at which time an essential task was performed.

> The remains of a canoe, attached to four stakes, lengthwise and widthwise,
> served as a coffin. The entirety was elevated by six cows' skulls with intact
> horns. . . . At a certain time, starting with a number of gun shots, six men
> take this type of bier and place the deceased upon it. . . . The widow . . . takes
> a calabash used by him [probably filled with palm wine which she pours
> over the cattle skulls]. Several times, in a loud voice, she asks her dear spouse
> to reveal the cause of his death. Several times, they carried the coffin near
> her and several times she pushed it back, continuing her questioning. Fi-
> nally, when her husband responded that it was a witch who had eaten his
> soul, she broke the calabash against the cattle horns attached to the coffin
> and pointed with her finger the route to the cemetery. The six men who
> carried the deceased left at full speed.[34]

A crucial part of a Diola funeral is the establishment of the cause of death. Pour-ing palm wine over the coffin horns while interrogating the corpse is the Diola equivalent of an autopsy. The deceased is asked if he or she had died because of an offense against a spirit shrine. If the coffin, carried by the six men, dipped downward, it meant an affirmative answer; if it moved to the side, it was a negative one. If the answer was affirmative, then the precise spirit shrine involved had to be identified, so that the proper propitiatory rituals could be performed. If the answer was negative, then questions were asked about witchcraft. An affirmative answer would be followed by questions about the identity of the witch, who was usually related to the victim by kinship or marriage. If the answer was again negative, then the deceased was asked if his death was due to the will of Emitai, a death not caused by human failing and without dangerous repercussions. Once the deceased had revealed this information, he was hurried off to the cemetery so that his soul could fully leave his body and start its journey to whatever path in the afterlife it might follow.

Father Lacombe witnessed the funeral of a young man who was said to have been killed by witches, "who had eaten his soul." This concept of witchcraft is common not only among the Diola but also among most Senegambian peoples. Carabane's various African communities had a common idea of witches who could travel in the night, attack their victims, and eat their souls. After such attacks, victims would lose their will to live and gradually wither away and die. After the burial, a group of witches were said to remove the body and take it to the forest, where they held a nocturnal feast of human flesh.[35]

Bertrand-Bocandé witnessed a witch-finding procedure conducted by a Muslim leader or marabout:

> The inhabitants of Carabane, whomever they are, are extremely superstitious. They believe that several deaths in succession here . . . were not all by natural causes, but were produced by witches who, like vampires, come invisibly to suck the blood of people and to enter into their bodies to devour them, or rather to eat their souls, even though they see that the bodies of the dead remain intact. . . . What is deplorable is that they identify several individuals, almost publicly, as having the habit of devoting themselves to these feasts of human flesh and one of them, who was a slave, had at one time submitted to torture at Carabane, so that he would confess to having eaten the wife and child of his master.[36]

The procedure used to identify this slave as a witch was initiated by Jean Baudin, the former French resident at Carabane and a Christian. He asked Bertrand-Bocandé for permission to hold a meeting at which a Muslim marabout would search out witches within a predominantly Diola community. The marabout performed various rituals, then killed some chickens, and examined their entrails. By reading the entrails, he claimed that he was able to identify the witches: "He said that the witches were not at all from the Diola who came from the region to live at Carabane, but that he would have to search among the freed slaves. He identified two men and two women; one of these men, was an honest worker, with a perfectly tranquil temperament, and who always has his consent when it was a question of reestablishing order."[37]

Bertrand-Bocandé's description reveals a second method of exposing witches, the use of maraboutage, the divinatory skills of a Muslim leader. It appears that the marabout's claims to be able to detect witches were accepted by the Afro-French, Diola, and other African groups at Carabane. From Lacombe's description, it appears that they also accepted the Diola method of interrogating the deceased. It is unclear whether any of the four spirit shrines at Carabane was used to protect against or to identify witches, though both Ehugna and Bukut were used for those ends within Esulalu.

These descriptions also reveal that there was considerable social tension surrounding the position of slaves and former slaves and that this tension was expressed through witchcraft accusations. Beginning in 1848, French Senegalese officials began to actively discourage the slave trade. In that same year, Jean Baudin was removed from his position as resident because of his attempt to retrieve runaway slaves from a British ship. At Carabane, domestic slavery was tolerated but no longer supported by the French authorities, which engendered considerable anxiety among Carabane's slave owners. The witchcraft accusation process described by Bertrand-Bocandé reflected this fear. It centered on the alleged killing of a master's wife and child by one of his slaves. The accusation process was initiated by the family that had dominated Carabane until three years before. The marabout who conducted the investigation quickly dismissed the possibility of witchcraft among the free population and told the community to concentrate their search among "freed slaves," a liminal group whose legal freedom had not yet relieved them of work obligations toward their masters. Although there may well have been considerable anxiety over the frequency of deaths at Carabane, these accusations also reflected new tensions surrounding the unresolved status of freed slaves, people who were no longer legally in bondage but who had not yet begun to exercise their freedom.

Bertrand-Bocandé's attitude toward the marabout also reveals a considerable mistrust of Islamic leaders, an attitude that was common among French officials in nineteenth-century Senegal. Bertrand-Bocandé wrote a letter to Felix Baudin, designed to curtail the influence of marabouts at Carabane and to rebuke the Baudin family for inviting the marabout's activities.

> I had asked you verbally to come see me in order to discuss the procedures that it is important to take to prevent blacks from I don't know where, who call themselves marabouts or diviners; who create discord in the country by leading the inhabitants of Carabane to kill one another, under the pretext of vengeance for an imaginary crime, like the one who arrived yesterday. . . . All of this odious intrigue was done with the goal of acquiring some merchandise. It seems that this is the only work to which these men will devote themselves.[38]

Bertrand-Bocandé did not confine himself to letter writing. Accompanied by several French soldiers, he confronted the marabout, seized the goods that the marabout had received for his witch-finding activities, and gave them to the victims of his accusations. Then he "seized all of the marabout's gris-gris which I burned the next day to the astonishment of our inhabitants who expected a miracle: they protested that these gris-gris would not catch fire at all and fled, believing that thunder would crush all the spectators at this sacrilege."[39] Whether this action led to a general mistrust of marabouts at Carabane or was limited to a disavowal of this particular marabout's skills is not stated. However, it does reveal that, by 1852, a mixed population at Carabane was receptive to the claims that marabouts could seek out witches and create various medicines that could protect people from evil and misfortune.

Despite the presence of Europeans and non-Diola Senegambians, Carabane did not become a major source of Christian or Muslim influence within Esulalu for most of the nineteenth century. The absence of a permanent missionary presence until 1880 made it difficult for Europeans or Euro-Africans at Carabane to participate in Christian ritual, much less attempt to convert the Diola of Carabane and Esulalu. Carabane's marabouts appear to have concentrated their efforts on the making of gris-gris and the detection of witches, activities that were of vital concern to the vast majority of Carabane's inhabitants, regardless of religious affiliation. There is no evidence that the marabouts directly challenged the authority of Diola priests at Carabane or tried to convert substantial numbers of Diola. While the marabouts' activities stimulated a growing awareness by Carabane's Diola of the more instrumental aspects of Senegambian Islam, these activities were seen as a source of supplemental power in a multiethnic environment rather than as a challenge to the fundamental ideas of the awasena path.

Nevertheless, Carabane provided a very different environment than the Esulalu townships. For many Diola, Carabane was their first experience of a pluralistic community. Although Diola religion commanded the allegiance of most Diola and received ritual attention from many non-Diola, some people removed themselves from its authority. This was equally true of some of the Christians and Muslims of Carabane, who also sought to live beyond the moral dictates of their religions, which disturbed leaders of all three communities. Father Lacombe lamented the woeful moral climate of Carabane: "You are familiar with this locale and the moral misery that reigns there is also not unknown to you. It is like a rendez-vous of all that is the most evil in the European coastal centers: St. Louis, Gorée, Gambia, Cacheu. This moral degradation is encouraged by the abuse of alcoholic beverages and by the example set by our traders."[40]

Despite the stresses of Carabane's plural society, it appears, on closer inspection, that a Diola moral order, influenced by outsiders, continued to guide the vast majority of Carabane's people. This order, however, was guided by a smaller number of ritual specialists and spirit shrines than one would find in the Esulalu townships. It focused on four communitywide shrines concerned with the socialization of men (Bukut) and women (Ehugna) and the ensuring of the fertility of the people and the land. Its ritual rules appeared to be less stringent than in the Esulalu townships because men could drink palm wine at the women's shrines of Carabane. There also appears to have been an absence of lineage shrines because many of the Carabane Diola retained close ties to their home townships and lineages. Despite the simplification of the ritual order, major ceremonies such as nyakul emit and Bukut commanded the participation of the majority of Carabane's inhabitants. Carabane remained a predominantly Diola ritual community.

Gambian and Diola at Elinkine

In the 1840s, Gambian traders established a similar multiethnic community at Elinkine. They were a diverse group, including Wolof, Serer, Manjaco, and Aku (descendants of freed slaves from Sierra Leone). One of these traders, Wari Diow, decided that they should establish a permanent settlement near the Esulalu townships where they were trading.[41] Samatit provided the newcomers with a small strip of land at the junction of several coastal estuaries. The Gambians were not given any rice paddies, both to preserve Samatit's own paddies and to keep the Gambians dependent on them for grain. According to Dyaye Babu Faye, the only reason that Samatit allowed them to settle was their fear of slave raiding by the Djougoutes township of Thionk Essil. People would be seized while working in the rice paddies near Elinkine. Samatit's leaders hoped that the Bathurst traders would use their guns to protect them from the men of Thionk Essil: "They kept away the strangers [from Thionk Essil]."[42]

Although Elinkine was settled by Gambians, British officials declined to appoint a local resident or provide support for them. Still, the Gambians sought to extend British influence in the region. At Samatit they met with the Diatta family, gave them a paper naming a member of that family as village chief, and presented them with a British flag.[43] These traders were primarily interested in purchasing rice and peanuts, for which they exchanged such items as the heavy indigo cloths that the Diola use for important rituals. In 1853, Bertrand-Bocandé complained of the growing influence of these Gambian traders:

> These Diolas . . . have been led to raise the price of rice and it seems that they and the English struggle in their desire to see who sells rice more expensively and on the other hand who exchanges merchandise the most cheaply. I can say that this competition has become a real madness; the Diola from the largest villages have tried to organize the others to form a league to compel those who come to them to purchase rice to give away rather than sell their merchandise.[44]

The Gambians were willing to pay higher prices for Diola rice and were able to sell highly valued English rifles and ammunition. Such competition encouraged Diola to seek out the highest bidder for their goods. Bertrand-Bocandé, who was an active trader as well as resident, was clearly concerned about the ease with which the Diola adapted to the increasing competition for their produce. He was also worried about Gambians, who were negotiating on behalf of the English for trade concessions at Samatit, Kadjinol, and Thionk Essil. Aware of Britain's lack of interest in Elinkine, Bertrand-Bocandé negotiated a treaty with Samatit and formally annexed the settlement in 1851. Nevertheless, the people of Elinkine maintained their close ties to the Gambia.[45] They also developed closer ties to the Diola communities that surrounded them.

There is an alternative account of the founding of Elinkine, in which a Diola woman from Itou or Niomoun asked the elders of Samatit for land. Because intermarriage with Diola women was common among traders, she may well have been the wife of one of the founders of Elinkine. Whether she founded Elinkine or not, this woman, nicknamed Ayou Ahan (grandmother), played an active role in the growth of the village. Given the close ties beteen Itou and Esulalu, she may well have aided the Gambians' trading activities through her extensive regional contacts.[46] Ayou Ahan brought with her a shrine of Ehugna (Ehugna-Esoobaw) from Carabane and established it at Elinkine. As priestess of this shrine, Ayou Ahan was considered extremely powerful, "a powerful priest-king."[47]

Because a majority of the men at Elinkine were non-Diola and either Christian or Muslim, it was Diola women who provided the initial introduction of Diola religion and language into the community. Freed or runaway Diola slaves, particularly from Diembering, as well as free Diola who were ostracized for criminal acts or social offenses, also settled at Elinkine, thereby contributing to the diversity of ethnic groups and religions. Eventually, Elinkine had its own Bukut and Cabai and the family shrine of Hupila and Kouhouloung. It also had the Cayinte rain shrine, which was linked to the priest-king of Samatit.[48] Diola elders provided the village's primary spiritual leadership. No missionaries worked at Elinkine until after 1880, when the Carabane mission opened. Although marabouts may have visited Elinkine, it did not become an Islamic center.

Diola settlers at Carabane and Elinkine carried with them their own ritual forms and continued to adhere to their own religious concepts. They accepted the skills of Muslim marabouts in searching out witches and in making gris-gris. Similarly, they accepted the claims of Christians in Ziguinchor and Carabane that crucifixes and saints' medals offered protective power. Despite such contacts, there was little interest in converting to these new traditions. Christianity and Islam offered supplemental powers for the Diola to utilize in combating witchcraft, disease, and misfortune, but Diola religious ideas themselves were not challenged by the new religions. On the contrary, in the new settlements with their shortage of Christian and Muslim leaders, Diola established a number of shrines and welcomed the strangers to assist at their rituals, thereby increasing their own influence at Carabane and Elinkine.

French Sovereignty and the Esulalu Townships

During the period from 1850 until 1880, the French intensified their activities in the region with the objective of excluding other European powers from the Casamance and obtaining Diola recognition of French sovereignty. By allowing the French annexation of Elinkine in 1851, the British demonstrated their lack of interest in the region. However, the Portuguese tried to revive their influence through a diplomatic offensive in the area immediately around Ziguinchor; they secured treaties with various African communities but stopped about twenty-five kilometers east of Esulalu.[49] Diola recognition of French sovereignty was achieved through a series of treaties, negotiated between 1850 and 1865, which established the rights of the colonial government to mediate intertownship disputes and disputes between Diola and non-Diola. At times these treaties were accompanied by a show of force, but the most vigorous resistance to the French came only when they sought to impose the more formal institutions of colonial rule. During this period there were no systematic attempts to spread Christianity within Esulalu, though French Protestants and Catholics did establish missions at Sedhiou in the middle Casamance region.[50]

The first Esulalu community to feel the effects of France's new regional objectives was Kagnout, which owned the island of Carabane. As Carabane grew, the people of Kagnout felt pressure from the French to cede Djibamuh, a small portion of the island that included a sacred forest with a shrine of the same name that was said to be one of the most powerful at Kagnout.[51] In 1850, cattle raiders from Kagnout stole three head of cattle from Bertrand-Bocandé. Bertrand-Bocandé demanded compensation:

> They offered me an indemnity worth less than half the value of the cattle. I refused. Since they had resold the cattle and told me to go and find them where they were sold; I responded that I wanted the same satisfaction that they require of themselves, when one has stolen: Following the customs of the Floup country, the rice paddies of the thieves are sold to indemnify the person who was robbed.[52]

The punishment described by Bertrand-Bocandé, selling a thief's rice paddies, was usually imposed by the elders of Hutendookai, the town council shrine. However, it was not imposed on raiders against other townships. Negotiations over Kagnout's payment of an indemnity broke down in an atmosphere of increasing hostility. According to Bertrand-Bocandé, Kagnout considered the possibility of attacking Carabane: "All of Kagnout was assembled . . . and deliberated, while drinking a large quantity of palm wine, to learn whether they should attack us or not; I do not know yet the response of the fetishes that they consulted, but I organized a national guard commanded by the leading inhabitants."[53] At least one of the spirit shrines consulted was Cabai, a shrine associated with the conduct of war, whose assent was considered essential to their success in battle and on whose premises military plans were often made. The palm wine was said to have a soul, whose power was used to summon the spirits to the shrine, give force to their prayers, and bind the community to its decisions. Whether Kagnout decided to attack Carabane is unclear.

Later that year, Bertrand-Bocandé asked for reinforcements and enlisted the assistance of the Gambians at Elinkine and the Diola of Samatit and Mlomp, who were involved in disputes over rice paddies with Kagnout. The firm response of the French led to renewed negotiations. Kagnout offered Bertrand-Bocandé thirty-one bushels of rice: "They assured me at the same time that they wished to live in peace with us and were ready to perform the religious ceremony that, following local custom should ratify all treaties." The payment was accepted but held to be incomplete.[54]

In 1851, French ships bombarded Kagnout. Then, French soldiers led away 120 cattle and killed many additional livestock, before setting the township on fire. The bombardment, which shattered silk cotton trees, is vividly remembered in Kagnout. It served as a stern example to other Diola communities.[55] The leaders of Kagnout were obliged to sign a treaty surrendering their rights to rent from Carabane and transferring ownership of the island, including the sacred forest of

Djibamuh, to the French. Four elders of Kagnout signed the treaty: Badicomea, the priest-king; Awa and Foumben, both described as chiefs; and Atabougaye, described as the owner of Djibamuh and presumably the priest of its shrine. French sovereignty and the right of French officials to mediate intertownship disputes were recognized.[56] Following the treaty signing, ritual libations were offered to an unspecified spirit shrine at Elinkine and then, at a later date, at a shrine at Kagnout. Bertrand-Bocandé attended both rituals: "They gave drink to what they call the bakine, but it was not accompanied by all the customary prayers to hold those who violate the treaties and it is the custom to go perform the same ceremony at their home. I will have it done in full detail, because if fear stops public crimes, superstition can prevent crimes that they think remain secret."[57] It appears that the Diola invoked the spirit shrines to give power to the treaties that they undertook. Bertrand-Bocandé does not reveal whether his soldiers and the citizens of Carabane, whose ideas of witches he criticized, would feel bound to respect the citizens of Kagnout for the same reasons.

As a result of the Kagnout war, the French created the office of village chief to serve as an intermediary between the colonial authorities and the Diola. Though his name does not appear on the 1851 treaty, a man named Simendow Sambou was the first chief at Kagnout.[58] In each of Kagnout's accounts, Simendow was alone fishing or gathering shellfish when the French came upon him and asked him to show them the route through the mangrove swamps to Kagnout. Despite his fear or perhaps because of it, Simendow led them to his township. As a reward for his services, he received a red shirt and cap and a pair of baggy pants (chaya). They appointed him as township chief and told him that the French would return in a few days. When they did, Simendow went to the premises of his Hupila shrine, dressed himself in the clothes he had received, and then appeared before the French. They greeted him as a friend and announced to the township that he was their chief. It is apparent from these accounts that the French imposed a chief rather than allowing the township to elect one. Their choice was a wealthy man, a leader who was able to finish a Hupila Hudjenk with all its elaborate sacrifices, from a family which controls several shrines associated with the priest-king. Simendow was clearly a man who was influential in his community.[59]

Kagnout was the only Esulalu township that was attacked by French forces. Its destruction discouraged other communities from directly challenging French initiatives. On the same day in 1851 that Kagnout signed its treaty, Samatit also signed a treaty with the French. The treaty was signed with "the goal of strengthening the friendship that has existed for a long time between the French and the inhabitants of Samatit" and established French rights over the Gambian settlement at Elinkine.[60]

Initially Kadjinol, like Samatit, had friendly relations with the French. In 1854, a community leader called Heêk by the French and Haieheck by the Diola, invited Bertrand-Bocandé to Kadjinol to discuss the establishment of a trading post along the Kadjinol estuary at a place called Djeromait. Bertrand-Bocandé accepted the invitation only when he learned that a Gambian trader had established himself at the site.[61] In 1860, Haieheck signed a treaty with the French ceding a small piece of land at Djeromait. Haieheck was described as the principal chief of

Kadjinol. It appears that Kadjinol signed the treaty to secure French protection against raiders from Djougoutes and Karones. In this case, a recognized community leader served as the first chief. His position was based on his wealth and his control of a large number of the most important spirit shrines, including Hoohaney, Cabai, and a group of blacksmith shrines.[62]

Perhaps it was Haieheck's influence at Kadjinol or his role in an attack by several of Kadjinol's quarters against the quarter called Sergerh that prevented Haieheck from remaining as village chief. In colonial records, a man named Simembo Sambou of Sergerh was described as Kadjinol's first chief. He summoned the French to protect his quarter against an attack by the Kafone and Kagnao quarters. The French resident came, stopped the fighting, and presented Simembo with a French flag. Simembo was also noted for his wealth and influence. "The case of the nomination of Simembo Sambou as village chief was favored by his great riches, his physical strength, and the respect which he received from his village. He directed one of the major fetishes [Hoohaney]."[63] Hoohaney was a shrine of the elders associated with the initiation of men into the funeral societies. Only wealthy men could afford the initiation rites into the group of elders of the shrine. However, Simembo's influence was not as great as that of Haieheck, who also was an elder of Hoohaney but who controlled several other major shrines and had introduced several new ones.

The benefits of French protection and trade were not sufficient to stem a growing suspicion of French ambitions at Kadjinol and Djeromait. In the 1860s, Kadjinol refused to cultivate cotton and peanuts as required by French officials. Furthermore, they refused to allow the traders at Djeromait to do so. The commandant at Sedhiou complained about their increasing distrust: "The Yola [Diola] only will begin cultivation [of peanuts] with difficulty, and will allow the establishment of strangers among him with even greater difficulty; he fears that he will be chased from his country and believes that we would like to remove him . . . their idea, their certitude in their country [is] that our only goal is to make ourselves masters of their country."[64] Although the French were initially welcomed by Kadjinol to protect them from raiders and to trade, that welcome changed to suspicion when French officials sought to introduce new crops, expand the trade settlement at Djeromait, and compel them to sell cattle to the French. From that point on, the Diola of Kadjinol were seen as "difficult."

The township of Mlomp, which had only recently united, had a similar pattern of relations with French authorities. Despite some quarrels with Djicomole, the largest quarter of Mlomp and the conqueror of the older community of Elou Mlomp, the French were welcomed there.[65] Bertrand-Bocandé was interested in establishing a trade factory at Pointe Saint-Georges, a peninsula extending into the Casamance River, which was owned by Mlomp.

> Of all the sites on the lower part of the river, there is one which is most favorably located, the possession of which has been always the most desired by traders of all the nations that trade along the Casamance. It is . . . Pointe St. Georges . . . part of the lands of Djicomole or Mlomp. The inhabitants of this village, who farm there persecuted by diverse tribes or pirates who are their neighbors . . . have abandoned it and retreated into the interior.

Bertrand-Bocandé sought to acquire the territory in a rather unorthodox fashion. "I will try to obtain the land first in my name, to then offer it to France, proposing only for compensating me for what this acquisition cost me to create an agricultural establishment if my work and commercial interests conform to this type of exploitation."[66] Eager to prevent raids by Djougoutes and Karones, Mlomp welcomed the establishment of a trading post, while reserving their rights to fish and harvest palm wine there. In 1860, France formally annexed Pointe Saint-Georges and signed a treaty with Mlomp to confirm this acquisition.[67]

During the period of treaty making with the various Diola communities of the lower Casamance, French objectives remained limited to the extension of their sovereignty and the encouragement of trade. Although their efforts to encourage peanut and cotton production stirred up some resistance in Esulalu, generally these communities were left to govern themselves. During the period before 1880, there was no sense of French occupation, only a sense of more frequent French intrusions: attempts to persuade or compel the sale of cattle to Carabane, interventions to stop intra-Diola wars, and sporadic attempts to collect a tax in rice.[68]

One announced goal of French expansion in the Casamance, the abolition of the slave trade, would have had far-reaching consequences, had it been consistently enforced. While French intervention in intra-Diola wars did reduce the number of captives, Diola continued to keep slaves and sell them. Mandinka and Wolof traders purchased captives from the Diola and sold them as slaves in Mandinka-dominated areas of the interior of Futa Jalon. In 1860, Bertrand-Bocandé announced that he was prohibiting the sale of slaves from the Casamance to the Gambia.[69] However, five years before, Bertrand-Bocandé himself had been accused of keeping slaves. French officials found that "these captives were no longer his property, but those of a woman who lives with him at Carabane," Dominga Lopez, a Luso-African he met at Ziguinchor. French authorities permitted the export of slaves, sometimes referred to as volunteers or indentured workers (engagé à temps), until the 1860s. Slaves were also redeemed for service in the Senegalese army. Carabane was one center of this last stage of the Atlantic slave trade.[70]

The "Stranger" Village of Pointe Saint-Georges

Growing French influence encouraged the activities of local traders who were working on behalf of the commercial houses based at Carabane. These firms employed Luso-African, Wolof, and Mandinka traders who would buy Diola produce while selling them iron, rifles, gunpowder, cloth, brandy, and other goods.[71] As commercial activity increased, they sought to establish permanent settlements closer to their trading areas and with some room to farm and to establish households. This led to the creation of several small villages on lands given them by the Esulalu townships. These villages are referred to by Esulalu as "stranger" (Kudjala) villages because outsiders settled on land that was given them by those who were born there. Elinkine, whose founding has already been discussed, was the first of these villages. Beginning in the 1850s, it was followed by Pointe Saint-

Georges (or Punta), Djeromait, Loudia-Ouloff, Efissao, Santiaba, and Sam Sam (see map 5).[72] All but the first of these were founded by Muslim traders.

The village of Pointe Saint-Georges was established by Bertrand-Bocandé and his mistress, Dominga Lopez, in the mid-1850s. Bertrand-Bocandé regarded Punta as an ideal site for a trading post, with ready access to the major population centers of the Diola and with adequate land for some agricultural activity.[73] Given the French resident's obligation to spend much of his time at Carabane, Dominga Lopez became the chief of Pointe Saint-Georges, a leadership role that she retained at least until 1886. According to Captain Brosselard-Faidherbe, she lived in a two-story European-style house with a large porch, where she received visitors. Current residents of Punta often describe the beginnings of their community as a time when "women commanded" the village and its land.[74] Though founded by French and Luso-African traders, Pointe Saint-Georges attracted some Diola settlers, mostly from Djougoutes, as well as a few Manjaco, Wolof, and Mandinka.[75]

Under Lopez's leadership, Punta became a prosperous community whose traders purchased goods throughout the lower Casamance. However, it was highly vulnerable to attacks from Djougoutes, Karones, and Esulalu. In 1857, Thionk Essil, the largest Djougoutes township, attacked Punta, killed four people, and carried off seventeen women and children, including Dominga Lopez and her son, Emmanuel Bocandé. The captives were taken to Thionk Essil to be ransomed or sold. A French trader ransomed all the captives, including his wife, and then recommended to the acting resident that the French attack Thionk Essil.[76]

The people of Pointe Saint-Georges identified with European culture and the Christian religion. Like most Casamance Christians before the opening of the Carabane mission in 1880, the people of Punta had only the rarest of opportunities to receive the sacraments or religious instruction by priests. In 1881, Father Kieffer visited the community and was dismayed by the state of the Christians there:

> At Pointe St. Georges, there is a small population, mostly Portuguese with some Diolas. It is baptized but not instructed. All of the religion of these poor people consists of wearing around the neck either a crucifix or a large medal of Saint Anthony. This suffices for them then to be, they say, in the religion of the good Lord.
>
> The children, after having been baptized, grow up in religious ignorance. It finishes by no longer recognizing anything other than their *razza* or prayer for the dead. On November 2, they spend the entire night in orgies and chants of "Our Father" and "Hail Mary" in Portuguese.[77]

One finds the same note of disdain for Luso-African Christianity that Brooks described among Portuguese clerics visiting Bissau and Bolama. Pointe Saint-Georges's Christianity stressed the relationship between the living and the dead (ancestors/saints), and the living and the community. Their emphasis on Saint Anthony of Padua stemmed from his importance as the patron saint of Lisbon and his association with healing.[78]

Though founded by French and Luso-African traders, Pointe Saint-Georges attracted some Diola settlers, mostly from Djougoutes, who introduced a small number of spirit shrines. The villagers' emphasis on the Luso-African *razza* ritual

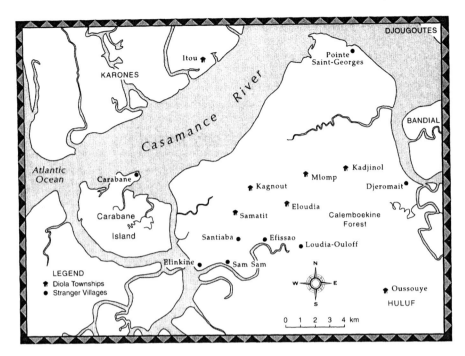

Map 5. Esulalu in 1880

on All Souls' Day, together with their lack of long-term ties to the community, discouraged the growth of spirit shrines associated with the lineage, household (Hupila), or the dead (Kouhouloung). The spirit shrines at Pointe Saint-Georges tended to be communitywide and gave unusual prominence to women. Probably the oldest shrine was the women's fertility shrine of Ehugna. Punta also practiced the male circumcision rite associated with Bukut, for which they joined together with the village of Djeromait.[79] Bukut was the only shrine that was exclusively for men. Depah was a "shrine of the entire community," which both men and women attended. It had been brought from the Djougoutes community of Elena. Rituals were performed there whenever there was a need and always just before the rainy season. At that time rice cakes were made and offered at the shrine while prayers for rain were recited. Hutoompaye was also a shrine for men and women and concerned itself with communitywide problems. For serious problems, rituals were performed at both Depah and Hutoompaye.[80]

While Pointe Saint-Georges was initially dominated by a Luso-African community, Diola rituals and ideas became an important part of village religious experience. Shrines were introduced to fulfill needs that were not met by the limited contacts with Christian clergy and their limited knowledge of Christian beliefs. Diola shrines were not accepted where their power was associated with problems that the Luso-African Christian rituals addressed satisfactorily. Thus, Diola shrines of the dead and the hearth did not displace the All Souls' celebration, the razza. Pointe Saint-Georges also became an important source of Christian influences within Esulalu and other Diola regions, familiarizing the Diola with basic Christian teachings and symbolism and establishing a pattern of peaceful interaction of the two religious systems prior to the advent of Christian missions.

The Muslim "Stranger" Villages

Like Pointe Saint-Georges, the stranger village of Djeromait was founded on the initiative of the French at Carabane. However, it was founded by Muslim Serer, Wolof, and Mandinka traders. Kadjinol allowed them to settle there because it was situated on a primary raiding route against Kadjinol's farmers as they worked in the rice paddies. They hoped that the traders' presence would scare off the raiders from Djougoutes and at least provide them with a well-armed ally. Djeromait was not given land to farm but was lent a limited number of rice paddies by friends at Kadjinol.[81]

The first chief of Djeromait, Mangoy Djiba, was not only a prosperous trader but also a marabout. While he may have tried to spread the teachings of Islam to Kadjinol, there was little interest in conversion, which would have required a rejection of the awasena path. However, the people of Kadjinol expressed considerable interest in Mangoy's gris-gris, charms filled with words from the Qur'an placed in goats' horns or small leather purses, which could provide protection against injury or misfortune. Mangoy was said to have gris-gris that protected him from bullets and knives. The making of such gris-gris was the source of considerable income, and their power inspired fear among Kadjinol's Diola.[82]

In the 1870s, a second group of strangers settled at Djeromait, a group of Manjaco, Papel, and Ediamat Diola from the south.[83] These settlers had some familiarity with Luso-African Christianity but also brought several of their own spirit shrines with them. One of these was Casine, "the horn," a shrine of Manjaco origin that served a similar function as Hupila among the Diola. It was located in the home and had a series of stuffed horns on its shrine. Its priests were seized with an illness that drove them temporarily insane. Both men and women could be seized by this shrine. A second Manjaco shrine, Khameme, was brought by Pasena Lopi when he settled at Djeromait. It, too, was a shrine for both men and women. Prayer can be offered at this shrine for a variety of community and individual problems. Women purify themselves of certain types of wrongdoing at the Khameme shrine. Khameme was located in a small hut and consisted of a series of small horns stuck in the ground, open on top to receive palm wine libations.[84] A Manjaco form of the women's fertility shrine of Ehugna was also established at Djeromait. The Diola circumcision shrine of Bukut was established nearby, at the former site of Kadjinol's circumcision forest, Kapy. Khameme, Ehugna, and Bukut attracted Muslim participation along with non-Muslims, though the former abstained from drinking the palm wine that accompanied the rituals.[85] Such religious cooperation between Muslim, Manjaco, and Diola may have been facilitated by the frequency of intermarriage between the three communities, the persistence of women's cults like Ehugna within a Muslim environment, and a shared concern about the importance of male circumcision and initiation, as represented by Bukut.[86]

The stranger village of Loudia-Ouloff was founded by Wolof traders from the Djollof area of northern Senegal. A group of men, including Aliou Diop, Moussa Seck, and Abdoulaye Suare, asked Eloudia for a small piece of land. Fear of cattle raiders from Huluf, and a suspicion that the traders might just seize the land contributed to the decision to allow the strangers to settle there. Both Aliou Diop and Moussa Seck married Diola women and were lent some farm land by their wives' relations. The community also supported itself through trade and through the sale of muskets that they manufactured.[87]

Loudia-Ouloff was founded by Muslims, but, unlike Elinkine and Djeromait, it did not allow the establishment of Diola spirit shrines within the community. Both Aliou Diop and Moussa Seck were marabouts and possessed a small library of Arabic manuscripts. They were members of the Tijanniyya order and maintained close ties with other Tijani leaders in the region. The settlers at Loudia-Ouloff made little effort to convert their neighbors. While there were few male converts, Diola wives of Loudia-Ouloff's Muslims usually did embrace Islam. Diola visitors also sought out the marabouts to make gris-gris and medicines to protect them.[88]

Despite the systematic exclusion of Diola cults from Loudia-Ouloff, there were certain ritual practices and concerns that were shared by this community and the Esulalu townships. Like the Esulalu, the people of Loudia-Ouloff established a special forest for the circumcision of their youth. Men from the village insisted that there were no spirit shrines located there, only gris-gris to protect the boys during their ordeal. As in Bukut, women were strictly excluded from the forest, and the boys were kept in seclusion for several months. During this time, they learned many of the responsibilities of manhood that might be overlooked in a qu'ranic education. The non-Diola origin of their circumcision ritual is supported by the fact that circumcision rituals there were not done according to the ritually prescribed order of Diola Bukuts. However, they shared the Diola idea that a woman who entered the circumcision forest during initiation would die.[89] Whether that idea, the special powers attributed to blacksmiths at Loudia-Ouloff, or other concepts that seem to mirror those of Esulalu are of Diola origin remains unclear. However, their extensive intermarriage with Diola women could have become an effective if subtle source of Diola influences.

Efissao was founded by a group of Muslims from Loudia-Ouloff who wished to live closer to their millet and peanut fields. By 1868, they had gone to the elders of Kagnout's quarter of Eyehow and asked for land. Like the Muslims of Loudia-Ouloff, they frequently married Diola women, but they did not incorporate Diola shrines into their religious life. Their male circumcision rites did not involve a lengthy ritual seclusion like that of their neighbors; the initiates slept in their own homes.[90]

The stranger village of Sam Sam was founded by Tukulor Muslims who had fought with Abdou N'diaye in wars in Portuguese Guinea. Samatit agreed to give them some land to avoid conflict with the warrior group and to enlist their aid against Djougoutes raiders. Initially, the people of Samatit were afraid of Sam Sam. The Tukulor of Sam Sam kept a considerable number of slaves and were well armed. The willingness of Sam Sam traders to sell cattle, guns, and knives to them eased Diola suspicions; friendships and even intermarriage developed. Like

Loudia-Ouloff, Sam Sam was dominated by the Tijanniyya order. Traditions persist that Al Hadji Umar Tal visited Sam Sam on his way to Diembering to visit a spirit. He is said to have created a spring at Sam Sam that never runs dry. While the tradition is probably untrue, it demonstrates the veneration that the people of Sam Sam maintain for Senegambia's most distinguished Tijani religious leader.[91]

Although the Muslim communities within Esulalu's stranger villages have not been adequately studied, it appears that they can be divided into two groups, those affiliated with the Tijanniyya *tariqa* and those that were not. Both groups frequently married Diola women and increasingly used the Diola language. However, they differed substantially in their attitudes toward Diola religion. In those communities with largely unaffiliated Muslim communities—Carabane, Elinkine, and Djeromait—Muslims accepted the creation of Diola spirit shrines and often participated in Diola rituals. Isolated from substantial Muslim communities, they allowed themselves to incorporate certain Diola ritual forms and ideas that helped them to explain and control their lives in a far more heavily forested environment, with different types of crops to plant and diseases to fight. In all these communities, Muslim women participated in rites associated with women's fertility shrines. Muslim men joined their Diola neighbors in initiating their sons through Bukut and frequently accepted the protective rituals of cults associated with fishing.

In the Tijanniyya-dominated communities of Loudia-Ouloff, Efissao, and Sam Sam, Muslims overcame their isolation from more established Muslim communities and did not permit the introduction of Diola cults in their villages. The Tijani strangers felt a part of a vast movement of reform in West African Islam and looked to the examples of Al Hadji Umar Tal and Ma Ba Diakhou as examples of leaders who resisted the common West African practice of tolerating indigenous cults.[92]

While Muslims in Esulalu differed sharply in their attitudes toward Diola religion, Esulalu Diola generally showed little interest in Islam as an alternative path. They were suspicious of the Muslim strangers in their midst. Islam's rejection of palm wine and, at least among the Tijani, of the spirit shrines themselves did not encourage Diola conversion. Generally Muslims were given land to settle along major raiding routes used by hostile neighbors. It was hoped that Muslim traders could supply them with guns, advance warning, and military aid in the event of an attack.

However, they were also aware of the attacks by Muslim leaders like Fodé Kabba and Fodé Silla against north shore Diola who were unsympathetic to Islam.[93] They were also aware of the cooperation that existed between French and Muslim traders because of their common interest in commerce and the more prolonged familiarity of northern Senegalese with French colonial customs. Muslim traders were often used as interpreters and intermediaries between French and Diola. Such relations could be readily manipulated to the disadvantage of the Diola.[94] The literacy of the marabouts and their ability to use the power of the word in gris-gris also frightened many people in Esulalu. This fear of Muslims was noted by the French resident at Carabane, F. Jalibert: "The natives fear these men; they do not dare expel them because they regard them as kind of henchmen of the devil, as all powerful, capable of dominating our [the French] will, of having us on their side, despite ourselves."[95]

During the first eight decades of the nineteenth century, the peoples of Esulalu witnessed the rapidly increasing penetration of French and other non-Diola influences within the lower Casamance. French officials negotiated land concessions, intervened in intertownship disputes, and worked to exclude other European powers. Traders associated with French commercial houses established stranger villages on Esulalu territory and brought with them the religious traditions of Islam and Christianity. Still, neither the French nor the non-Diola traders sought to establish direct authority over the Esulalu townships. Village chiefs served primarily as liaisons with the French rather than as executors of a French colonial mandate. The stranger villages had to continue to ask for land rather than take it. Despite the growing non-Diola presence, the people of Esulalu continued to perceive of themselves as independent communities who had allowed small groups of powerful allies to trade with them and assist them in repelling their enemies.

During this period of relative equality, the people of Esulalu were exposed in a more sustained way to the traditions of Christianity and Islam. While there was virtually no Christian missionary activity in Esulalu during this period and the Muslim traders did not actively proselytize, the people of Esulalu gained some direct experience of religious life within these traditions. However, in an era of continued autonomy and freedom, the people of Esulalu showed little interest in conversion. Rather, they were receptive to selective borrowing of ideas that could be incorporated into their own tradition. They were particularly interested in spiritual protection against injury in war or by accident and against disease. These were major concerns of Diola, Christian, and Muslim alike. The people of Esulalu acquired saints' medals and crucifixes and Muslim gris-gris. However, they were reluctant to abandon their own system of thought, which continued to provide an effective explanation of the changing world experienced by the people of Esulalu.

Selective borrowing from other traditions was not restricted to the Diola. Christians and Muslims at Carabane, Elinkine, Pointe Saint-Georges, and Djeromait welcomed the introduction of Diola cults associated with male initiation, the procurement of rain, women's fertility, and fishing. Whether these were people who actually abandoned their identification with Christianity or Islam remains unclear, but there were certainly strong Diola influences within religious life in most of the stranger villages. In these communities, Diola religion appeared to dominate, while certain Christian rites like the All Souls' Day razza and the use of maraboutic divination to address a variety of problems enriched community religious life. In the absence of a missionary challenge to the awasena path or a sustained assault on Diola autonomy, the religious traditions of Esulalu continued to flourish, taking root even at Carabane, the French administrative center of the lower Casamance.

7

The Elaboration of Tradition
Esulalu Religion, 1800–1880

While the nineteenth century was a period of increasing interaction with the French and with other African groups, the people of Esulalu preferred to contact these newcomers at Carabane or the stranger villages, rather than in the townships. They were suspicious of French and Muslim Senegambian motives for entering the region and sought to control the influences of their new neighbors. They carefully protected the autonomy of Esulalu community institutions, while adapting to new conditions associated with cross-cultural contact. They limited their involvement in the religions of the newcomers to the purchase of saints' medals and gris-gris to ensure good health, good luck, or safety in war. Furthermore, they steadfastly refused to plant such cash crops as peanuts, which the French suggested, but which had the potential of undermining Esulalu's elaborate system of rice cultivation.

The increasing availability of European trade goods provided more of an impetus for change in Esulalu thought and values than did Esulalu's still limited contact with Christians and Muslims. The growing availability of iron and trade guns affected the way the Esulalu farmed and hunted and gave new prominence to the economic and ritual position of Esulalu's blacksmiths and several new spirit shrines they controlled. The increasing movement of people throughout the region generated a higher incidence of communicable diseases and facilitated Esulalu acceptance of a new series of healing shrines. Frequent droughts and crop failures and a growing concern about problems of infertility facilitated the introduction of a cluster of women's shrines called Ehugna. Increased commercial demand for Diola agricultural production intensified a system of domestic slavery that had been relatively unimportant in Esulalu until the nineteenth century. This, too, had to be understood within a changing awasena tradition. Finally, "stranger" styles of dress and concepts of modesty began to shape Esulalu fashions and notions of propriety.

For most of the nineteenth century, however, the people of Esulalu were also concerned with the elaboration of a relatively new awasena tradition and with fully integrating its continually evolving system of spirit shrines. Drawing on a tradition that had only recently brought together the divergent religious paths of Koonjaen and Floup, the people of Esulalu borrowed new ideas and practices from neighboring Diola, from other Africans, and from Europeans to explain and control both long-standing problems and the challenges that they encountered, for the first time, in the nineteenth century. Drawing on a tradition that stressed the capacity of individuals to have visionary experiences that could lead to the creation of spirit shrines, the Esulalu developed new cults that offered to address the challenges they encountered in the last decades of their political independence.

This chapter focuses on changes within the townships as the people of Esulalu continued to adapt the awasena tradition to meet their concerns effectively during the nineteenth century. During this era, they confronted the difficult task of maintaining township unity in the face of frequent warfare, increasing social stratification generated by the growth of domestic slavery, and the mushrooming number of witchcraft accusations brought on by new social tensions. By examining the histories of a series of new spirit shrines, I also examine the ways in which new methods of addressing these problems were elaborated and their impact on the development of the awasena path as a whole.

The Limits of Unity

Despite the incorporation of the Koonjaen into the townships and the power of such townshipwide institutions as Hutendookai and the priest-kings, the people of Esulalu were unable to sustain peaceful relations between neighboring communities. Warfare between individual quarters of the same township, between townships within Esulalu, and against other Diola groups continued to be a source of social tension. These conflicts posed a serious challenge to the efficacy of those institutions that were responsible for the protection of all the inhabitants of each township and made it easier for French or other African strangers to secure concessions from the people of Esulalu.

Violent skirmishes erupted in the townships when disputes over control of rice paddies, palm groves, or cattle could not be settled by the mediation of lineage elders or the leaders of the town council shrine of Hutendookai.[1] Each side would gather at its war shrine of Cabai or at a quarter shrine to prepare for battle and to gain spiritual protection. Interquarter skirmishes were usually of short duration because the priest-king would quickly stop any fighting within his township. During the nineteenth century, violent altercations occurred several times between the Sergerh quarter of Kadjinol and its neighbors in Kagnao and Kafone. Disputes focused on control of palm groves, rice paddies, and Sergerh's refusal to pay a fine levied by the elders of the Hutendookai shrine.[2] In each confrontation, several people were killed, some of Sergerh's houses were destroyed, and livestock were seized. In one battle, a man who had been born at Sergerh and had moved to Kagnao joined in the attack against his birthplace. As punishment for warring against his kin, it is said that witches attacked him and ate the essence of his knees, leaving him lame.[3] The evil that witches perform is occasionally seen as the result of Emitai's or lesser spirits' desires to punish wrongdoers. Similar struggles over rice paddies, palm groves, and fishing areas occurred several times between Kadjinol's quarters of Kandianka and Hassouka and Mlomp's quarters of Kadjifolong and Djicomole. At Kagnout, there were armed confrontations between Ebrouwaye and Bruhinban and between Ebrouwaye and Eyehow.[4]

During the nineteenth century, there were frequent wars between various Esulalu townships. Kagnout and Samatit fought several wars. Both Kagnout and Djicomole waged war against Eloudia, gradually pushing them further south into the forest and seizing large areas of rice paddies. As the only predominantly Koonjaen township remaining in Esulalu, Eloudia may well have been a victim of a limited resumption of the Koonjaen wars. Much of Eloudia's population took refuge in Kabrousse, thirty kilometers to the south. According to one elder, "the [arrival of] the Europeans is why Eloudia remains alive." The cessation of inter-township warfare was one of the first objectives of the French after their attainment of treaty rights over the region.[5]

To lessen the frequency of such wars, elders within Esulalu established alliances between individual quarters of independent townships. These alliances were often accompanied by the giving of a Cabai war shrine to the other quarter. These Cabai shrines were also given as thanks for assistance in war. Elders of Kadjinol-Kafone rewarded the Hassouka quarter for its help in its 1858 war against the Huluf community of Boukitingor, thereby creating an alliance between two often disharmonious quarters.[6] The presentation of the Cabai shrine lessened the likelihood of war because warfare between sharers of the same shrine would be invoking the same spirit to assist both sides. Then neither group would enter battle with the assistance of its most powerful war shrine. As the source of Cabai shrines for most of Esulalu, Kadjinol did not engage in warfare against any of the other Esulalu townships during the nineteenth century.

Warfare between the Esulalu townships and their neighbors in Huluf, Djougoutes, and Karones persisted throughout the nineteenth century. This form of warfare, fueled by the desire for cattle and captives, continued to undermine the security of Esulalu life.[7] Protection from north shore Diola attacks was a major factor in convincing the Esulalu townships to sign treaties with the French and in allowing the creation of stranger villages along their coast. Beginning in the 1850s, the French allied themselves with Esulalu and launched a series of punitive expeditions against Djougoutes, Karones, and other areas that persisted in raiding for captives. As late as 1889, the French resident at Carabane complained of warfare and slave raiding between Diola communities on both shores of the Casamance.[8]

Peaceful relations with townships outside Esulalu were developed through a system of treaties and alliances based on mutual self-interest but strengthened by religious sanctions. One such alliance existed between Thionk Essil of Djougoutes and Kagnout. These alliances gained strength because of the rituals used to link the townships, which had the effect of making the possibility of war between them gnigne (absolutely forbidden). While it is unclear which spirit shrines were invoked to establish treaties with non-Esulalu communities, the violator of such an agreement would be punished by those spirit shrines.[9]

Bertrand-Bocandé observed a ritual designed to establish a lasting peace between Thionk Essil and Itou. Similar ceremonies were probably held to cement other alliances, such as the one between Thionk Essil and Kagnout:

> A steer was sacrificed in front of the Residence at Carabane, and watered with libations of palm wine. After all the customary ceremonies of their countries, on the victim's entrails, the two peoples swore as they lifted the beverage of alliance, in their name and in the name of their compatriots, to maintain between them a perpetual peace, calling down all the curses of the heavens against any individual of either people against his friends and neighbors who would commit any action against this sworn peace.[10]

Religious sanctions were seen as certain and not contingent upon the relat'.ve power of the two parties involved. Such alliances were of a quite different order than the temporary lulls that characterized relations between townships involved in long-term raiding against one another. In the act of drinking palm wine and eating sacrificial meat together, the participants became bound to the words of alliance and peace enunciated during the ritual. In performing a treaty ritual, they became one community. Sambouway Assin described how people from Kagnout could go to Thionk Essil and take livestock as a result of their treaty: "This is why if you go there and you [someone of Kagnout] see a pig, you can kill it. Then you give it to them to cook for you." They had the same privilege at Kagnout. Such privileges are normally reserved for kin.[11]

The Incorporation of Sandianah and Elou Mlomp

In the midnineteenth century, two Diola communities within Esulalu were forcibly incorporated into the Esulalu townships. Little is known of the first of these, Sandianah, which was located about one kilometer southeast of Samatit. It had been settled by people from Ediamat at about the same time as Samatit. According to Samatit accounts, they attacked Sandianah and destroyed their homes because the men of Sandianah would seize Samatit women as captives when they went to get water at a spring. Samatit attacked them and burnt their houses. A portion of Sandianah settled at Kagnout-Bruhinban, others settled in the Kekenin quarter of Samatit, and the remainder fled to Diembering. They had their own priest-king, but there was no mention of what happened to him after the conquest by Samatit or of still extant shrines of Sandianah origin. This war probably occurred between 1830 and 1850.[12]

Elou Mlomp was a larger settlement, located in a forested area called the Hamak, several kilometers north of present-day Mlomp. The people of Elou Mlomp had their own rice paddies and palm groves. They were also skilled at fishing. They had close ties to the Djougoutes township of Mlomp, which was probably settled by people from Elou Mlomp.[13] Elou Mlomp had its own priest-king, who controlled a royal shrine called Sembini. Unlike the Esulalu Coeyi shrine, Elou Mlomp's Sembini did not depend on the priest-king of Oussouye. It had ties to Mlomp-Djougoutes's Sembini but was the senior shrine. There are still rice paddies in the Hamak that are dedicated to the priest-king of Elou Mlomp, though the office has been vacant since before World War I. Selection was by a process of spiritual election: "The one chosen, Emitai will reveal him."[14] This identification would occur through an illness linked to the shrine or through a certain aura about the person who was to be initiated as the new priest-king. Frequently, there were long interregna until someone manifested the appropriate signs. Sembini was brought to the township of Mlomp when Elou Mlomp was conquered, and it continued to have rituals performed.[15]

There had been intermittent conflict between Elou Mlomp and Djicomole (the largest quarter of what became the township of Mlomp) for much of the early nineteenth century. Disputes arose over access to palm groves, fishing areas, and rice paddies; over cattle raiding; and over the kidnapping of women. In the 1850s, Djicomole was able to overcome Elou Mlomp and force a substantial portion of the community into the township that became Mlomp.[16] The final attack came when a large portion of Elou Mlomp's population had gone to Mlomp-Djougoutes, either for a funeral or for the festival before the male circumcision ritual, Bukut. Only old men, women, and children were left behind. A woman who was originally from Elou Mlomp, but who had married someone from Djicomole, informed her husband's kin of Elou Mlomp's departure. Djicomole attacked and destroyed the village, forcing its inhabitants to seek asylum either in Mlomp of Djougoutes or the Djibetene and Etebemaye quarters of Mlomp-Esulalu.[17]

The people of Elou Mlomp were allowed to install their own spirit shrines, including Sembini, within the new township of Mlomp, a community dominated by Djicomole through its control of the office of priest-king and the office of the priest of Hutendookai. Once Sembini was established at Mlomp, its elders adopted rules limiting the people who were allowed to attend to those who were born into an Elou Mlomp patrilineage. People with maternal kin from an Elou Mlomp lineage were specifically excluded from participation because a woman born at Elou Mlomp was the one who told her husband at Djicomole when it was a good time to attack. She showed greater loyalty to her husband and his community than she did to her own relations.[18] The conquest and incorporation of Elou Mlomp, like Sandianah, did not create long-term social divisions comparable to those between Koonjaen and Diola. This suggests that they were already regarded as Diola; intermarriage was common, and their spirit shrines were similar enough to be incorporated into the new township.

Domestic Slavery in Esulalu

While warfare between townships persisted through most of the nineteenth century, the outbreak of large-scale warfare between Diola and Mandinka in northern Casamance dramatically increased the number of prisoners of war that could be sold into slavery. Additional prisoners of war, seized in wars between Mandinka Muslims and Mandinka non-Muslims (Soninké), also entered the slave trade in the lower Casamance. In sharp contrast to slaves seized in Esulalu's wars with neighboring communities in Huluf or Djougoutes, these new captives, who began arriving in the 1840s, came from Fogny, the middle Casamance, and the Gambia, areas that were a considerable distance from Esulalu. Most of these captives were resold to other Diola at Diembering and Kabrousse or to Mandinka traders who carried them to the interior.[19] A small number of captives were kept within Esulalu.

There had been some slaves and refugees in Esulalu before 1800, but they became a significant social factor by the 1840s. Unlike captives from Huluf or the coastal region of Djougoutes, who could readily escape and return to their homes, the new captives came from areas that were distant enough to discourage thoughts of escape. This distance allowed the use of slaves to become a viable option for the people of Esulalu.[20] During this same period, there was a growing demand for Diola rice. The increasing French presence in northern Senegal and the British presence in the Gambia generated active competition between such long-standing buyers as the Portuguese and Mandinka and the newcomers.[21] Finally, increased population mobility contributed to a higher incidence of infectious diseases, which may have aggravated existing labor shortages within Esulalu.[22]

Esulalu slaves lived in the family compounds of their masters, where they were treated as junior relations. Childless families would occasionally purchase boys, adopt them, and make them their heirs. A team of researchers who toured the lower Casamance in the 1890s described how the Diolas' few slaves "were purchased when they were young and became house slaves, treated as members of the family and quickly enjoying the same privileges, and able to marry free women, and only sold in cases of absolute necessity."[23] Older captives lived with their master's families, where they would assist in rice cultivation and household chores. After a while, male captives would be given rice paddies of their own, though not the best ones. Furthermore, they were assisted in providing the large quantities of palm wine that were essential gifts to a bride's family before marriage. Marriages for slave men were generally limited to fellow slaves, though Eheleterre Sambou claimed that slave men could marry free women (houbook, people born in Esulalu) if they paid their masters seven cattle, thereby purchasing their freedom.[24] Female slaves could marry either free or slave men, but their masters controlled their bridal gifts (buposs) and performed the ritual obligations required before a woman married. Masters retained the right to take rice from their slaves because they had given them land. Masters who needed to perform animal sacrifices could also take their slaves' livestock.[25]

Although there is little evidence about the number of slaves in Esulalu, clearly the numbers were sufficient to influence the development of Diola oral traditions. Thomas has collected several proverbs about the misfortunes of slaves. Diola historians refer to the important contributions of a slave woman named Kubettitaw, who was seized from Djougoutes and brought to a home at Kadjinol-Kandianka. She could not bear the way the people of Kadjinol ate their rice. It is said that they did not husk it first but merely boiled it until it was a soft mush. She taught the people of Kadjinol how to make a mortar and pestle, how to pound the rice and thresh it, and the proper ways of cooking it. Regardless of the historicity of this event, its place within oral traditions reflects the importance of keeping slaves within Esulalu society.[26]

Kubettitaw is also credited with the introduction of a major spirit shrine called Kanalia, which she brought from her home village of Affiniam in Djougoutes. She established the shrine at a spring in the rice paddies north of Kadjinol-Kandianka. When she married a man of Kandianka, she passed the shrine over to him. Since then, it has been a shrine controlled by male elders. Through rituals performed before the planting, Kanalia ensures the fertility of Kandianka's rice paddies and protects them against theft. It also serves as a major confession shrine, where people who have committed offenses against the community can purify themselves. It is said to seize wrongdoers with diarrhea, which can be cured only after confession and sacrifices are performed at the shrine. Kanalia was also associated with war; the men of Kandianka would perform rituals there before going into battle.[27]

Slaves, like other groups within Esulalu, were protected against unnecessary violence and physical abuse. Antoine Djemelene Sambou related an account of a master who killed his slave's children. The master sent a male slave off to tend some cattle, then brutally killed the slave children, and crippled their mother when she tried to resist. The master was forced to pay a fine of six cattle to be sacrificed at the Houle, a shrine associated with Bukut. While there is no confirmation of this story, it does indicate that Esulalu communities strongly condemned violence against slaves within their community and how the spirit shrines were invoked for the protection of slaves. After paying his fine, the murderous master was forced to move from the Sergerh quarter to the Hassouka quarter of Kadjinol.[28]

Despite the relatively benign treatment of slaves within Esulalu, there was a stigma attached to their status. They could be insulted as "amiekele" (slave) or "Agoutch" (a person from Djougoutes), and they had little influence in community life. The maintenance of this social distinction generated a certain discomfort within a relatively egalitarian community that had deep-seated suspicions of those who wielded power. Reflecting back on the families who kept slaves, Esulalu historians have suggested that slave owners tended to lose their natural-born heirs through disease or accidents, spiritually inflicted upon them as punishment for their assuming the role of masters. As Kapooeh Diedhiou described it: "But if you have many slaves, after a long long time, a slave will take your land. Emitai does not like it. It will strike you."[29]

If slaves were fortunate enough to find themselves in a family with few heirs, they might inherit not only the rice paddies of their masters but also some of their spirit shrines. In the absence of natural heirs, slaves could become elders of Hupila, Bukut, and Hoohaney, though they remained excluded from the cluster of black-smith, priest-king, and women's fertility shrines.[30] In some cases, giving shrines to slaves was considered a good way of keeping them from running away because they would not want to shirk their ritual responsibilities or surrender their religious authority. Furthermore, the spirit associated with the shrine might seize a runaway slave with an illness as punishment for deserting his or her ritual obligations.

During the nineteenth century, Esulalu elders established two special shrines that regulated the social status of slaves in Esulalu. One was created to provide ritual protection for slaves who were excluded from those shrines most associated with fertility of the family and of the crops. This shrine, called Dewandiahn, was introduced from the Diola township of Diembering. Slaves had their heads shaved and were presented at the shrine and placed under its protection in a ritual that paralleled the oeyi's ritual presentation of newborn children and in-marrying wives at the shrine of Coeyi. Locally born, free men controlled this shrine; its priest was always chosen from this group, not from the descendants of slaves.

By the mid-nineteenth century, at least at the time of Haieheck Diedhiou, a shrine called Huwyn, "to play," became associated with slaves and other strangers. It was used to mark the social distinction between freeborn (houbook) and slave or stranger (amiekele, *agoutch*). Masters brought their slaves, as many as forty at a time, to the shrine in the Ebankine quarter of Kadjinol. Masters fired guns near the captives to show them that they were strangers. Slaves who did not attend were fined ten head of cattle.[31] Clearly, this was a shrine of masters, not of slaves.

Funeral rituals marked the clearest differentiation between the houbook, or the native-born Esulalu, and amiekele, or slaves. Amiekele could be buried only in separate cemeteries. The houbook had spiritual ties to the land and to the cemetery, which was the visible symbol of that bond. Slaves, who had no such ties, had to be set apart and were buried in separate cemeteries. This liminal status, shorn of kin and shorn of ties to the land, was the essence of the Esulalu concept of slavery. That distinction was most carefully guarded at death.[32]

Witchcraft: Crimes of the Night and Accusations of the Day

Increasing social stratification brought on by the growth of domestic slavery and by the continuing profitability of the slave trade, frequent droughts and crop failures, and a growing insecurity about the ambitions of the French and other newcomers to the region contributed to a rising concern about the activities of witches (kusaye) in Esulalu. Growing disparities between rich and poor and between slave and free, in a society that saw itself as relatively egalitarian, generated suspicions that the newly wealthy had used illicit powers to obtain their success, at the expense of their kinsfolk and neighbors. What I suspect were higher mortality rates, brought on by increased population mobility and more frequent epidemics, also fueled fears of witchcraft activities. The withholding of rain, which became increasingly frequent after 1850, was often attributed to Emitai's displeasure at the practice of witchcraft.

During the nineteenth century, many Diola thought that certain people had special powers to see into the spiritual world, to travel at night without their bodies, and to transform themselves into animals. These people were said to be witches (kusaye). Motivated by jealousy or a lust for meat, they were said to eat people's life force, causing them to wither away and die. In 1852, Emmanuel Bertrand-Bocandé described the conceptions of witchcraft that he found at Carabane, a town that included many people from Esulalu: "All the inhabitants of Carabane . . . are extremely superstitious. They believe that several deaths in succession here . . . were not all by natural causes, but were produced by witches who, like vampires, come invisibly to suck the blood of people and to enter into their bodies to devour them, or rather to eat their souls, even though they see that the bodies of the dead remain intact."[33] Esulalu elders described witches in a similar way. Siopama Diedhiou described the way in which a witch would attach a rope around the victim's neck and then fly off like a bird carrying away the victim: "Perhaps you think its the body of someone that you carry. No, you carry the soul." The soul, which is said to reside in the blood, contains the life force of the individual; without it, a person has no will to live.[34] Both Bertrand-Bocandé and Esulalu elders described witches who traveled in the night, invisibly, while their bodies remained in their beds, to eat the life force of their victims. Their victims would fall ill and eventually die if their attackers were not revealed.

According to nineteenth-century European accounts, the Diola used two methods to identify witches: interrogating the corpse and a poison test. In 1864, Father Lacombe observed a Diola funeral at Carabane in which the widow asked her deceased husband why he had died:

> Several times, in a loud voice, she asks her dear spouse to reveal the cause of his death. Several times they carried the coffin near her and several times she pushed it back, continuing with her questioning. Finally when her husband responded that it was a witch who had eaten his soul, she broke the calabash against the cattle horns attached to the coffin and pointed with her finger the route to the cemetery.[35]

Only after the cause of death was determined could someone be buried. An affirmative response by the deceased to the suggestion that witchcraft had caused his or her death would lead to a series of questions designed to identify the guilty witch. Any increase in mortality rates was readily associated with the nocturnal attacks of witches.

Anxious Diola also used a poison test to identify witches. Accused witches were forced to drink *brilen* (also called *tali* and *mançone*), a poison made from the bark of a redwood tree, *Erythrophleum Guincense*. If they were innocent, they would vomit up the poison; if guilty, they would die.[36] In the stranger villages, marabouts used special potions, which suspects had to drink, and various divination techniques to discover the identity of witches.

In the late nineteenth century, two new Esulalu shrines, Gilaite and Ehugna, became involved in the witch-finding process. At Gilaite, people troubled by witchcraft would bring their problems to the shrine without naming specific suspects. Gilaite was said to seize the guilty parties with leprosy. Certain women elders of Ehugna were thought to have the power to identify witches. Publicly identified witches could be fined several head of cattle by the elders of Hutendookai and face a period of social ostracism.[37]

Witchcraft accusations had an extraordinarily corrosive effect on the Esulalu townships. Because witches acted only at night, in the world of the spirit, friends would not know if the accused was guilty or innocent. The same was true of spouses, who could not tell whether an apparent deep sleep was only that or the sleep of a person whose soul traveled to attack other people. Witchcraft accusations were usually made against relatives of the victims. Witches supposedly acted out of jealousy or spite, emotions that were encouraged by the growing economic stratification of nineteenth-century Esulalu. In an effort to control this problem, people in Esulalu invited Muslim marabouts to find witches, and they turned to new spirit shrines to seize witches with illnesses or disasters as punishment for their wrongdoing.

The Centrality of the Spirit Shrines

During the nineteenth century, Esulalu men and women continued to create spirit shrines in order to address new community problems, to address persistent problems more effectively, and to provide new groups of people with access to spiritual power. Virtually every economic activity had a spirit shrine associated with it. Other shrines addressed concerns about healing, the fertility of crops and women, war, and community welfare. For each type of problem, there were several types of shrines. This multiplicity of shrines helped to ensure that at least one path could resolve the problem of a supplicant individual or group. It also encouraged a broad diffusion of ritual authority; with so many shrines, chances were excellent that any individual would become a responsible elder or priest of at least one shrine during his or her lifetime. The importance of the ukine among the Diola was recognized by Father Sene, a northern Senegalese missionary based at Carabane, who described the spirit shrines in 1880:

> Near each village, in the center of the forest, and almost always around an ordinary tree, that was made sacred, are raised a palisade enclosing a sanctuary: it is the residence of the tutelary spirit called by the name "boekine." The men have theirs, the women as well. . . . The boekine is the supreme resource: for the farmer who wishes an abundant harvest, for the young woman who wishes to become a mother. . . . A Diola who is sick or threatened by a fatal portent quickly has recourse to the boekine.[38]

While most of the ukine were not associated with sacred forests, many of them were located near a consecrated tree or cluster of trees.

An individual could become an adept of a spirit shrine by inheriting a shrine associated with his or her lineage; through spiritual calls of afflictions, dreams, or visions; or by being selected by the elders of a particular cult. Parents could establish a relationship between their child and a spirit shrine, which would protect the child. Father Sene described this as well: "the children are consecrated at birth to one of the local spirits; the ceremony is done through the offering of a steer, or a pig, a dog, or a chicken, according to the resources of the family. The victim is sacrificed and the blood is spread over a kind of butte in the sacred sanctuary, with libations of palm wine."[39] Afterward, the participants drank the palm wine and ate a portion of the sacrificial meat at the shrine, while the remainder was distributed to the participants to take home. Drinking and eating together bound the participants to the central purpose of the sacrifice, the protection of the child. Children dedicated to the boekine would periodically "greet" the shrine with palm wine and small sacrifices over the course of their lives, especially at such major rites of passage as male circumcision, marriage, and the birth of their children.

Reflecting their close involvement in economic activities and daily problems, ukine were given new responsibilities, or new ones were created, in response to changes within Esulalu. In the eighteenth and nineteenth centuries, as Esulalu participation in trade increased, European cloth, firearms, and iron became increasingly available. This was especially true in the nineteenth century as stranger traders established permanent settlements in Esulalu. While the increasing availability of cloth may have influenced the clothing used in Diola ritual, it does not appear to have created new cults, as it did in the case of firearms or iron.[40]

As a result of the increasing availability of muskets, a new hunting shrine was developed to address the particular problems of hunting with a firearm. While the origin of this shrine, called Houpoombene, "the musket," remains unclear, it was an important cult by the midnineteenth century. Given the importance of hunting in early Esulalu, it probably displaced an earlier type of hunting shrine. Before going hunting, men performed rituals at Houpoombene, to ensure their success. Warriors also performed its rituals before going off to war, though Cabai remained the more important war shrine. Only successful hunters could become priests of Houpoombene. The process of becoming a priest of the shrine required furnishing game, rice, and fish for a community feast after the performance of the necessary rituals.[41]

Haieheck Djabune and the Forging of New Blacksmith Shrines

The expanding availability of iron strengthened the wealth and influence of blacksmith lineages throughout Esulalu. Greater access to iron increased local demand for holopucs, the iron tip of the Diola hand plow (cadyendo), while continuing warfare maintained a high demand for spears and knives. The overwhelming majority of blacksmiths lived in the Kafone quarter of Kadjinol, though there were a few blacksmith compounds in other parts of Kadjinol, Mlomp, Kagnout, and Eloudia. Most of the non-Kadjinol blacksmiths could trace their families back to Kafone. Thus, Kafone dominated what was becoming a vital craft both to Diola economic activity and to warfare. Kafone also had the greatest concentration of Silapoom, "the hammer" shrines that provided spiritual protection for blacksmiths and enforced guild rules concerning the spread of the technical knowledge of the forge.[42] One of the Kafone blacksmiths, a man named Haieheck, had acquired substantial wealth from his smithing and from his seizure of captives. He also became an important ritual leader, as elder at Hoohaney, Silapoom, Cayinte, and Hupila. By 1860, he had gained sufficient influence in the community to negotiate a treaty with the French, recognizing their regional sovereignty. He is also credited with introducing the major spirit shrines associated with the blacksmiths, Duhagne and Gilaite.[43] While his career was exceptional, his entire compound of Kumbogy prospered, as did many other blacksmith families.

With the growing influence of the blacksmith families and the heightened economic importance of their work, it is not surprising that two new blacksmith shrines were introduced into Esulalu in the nineteenth century. Just as slave raiders had begun to invest in cults in the mideighteenth century, the blacksmith families began to invest their wealth in two new spirit shrines. Duhagne, "the anvil," is the older of the two shrines and, while sometimes credited to Haieheck, it was probably introduced by Haieheck's father, Abindeck. Like Silapoom, Duhagne protected the blacksmith while he worked at the forge, but it also protected the Djabune (Diedhiou) lineages and the community as a whole against theft. Offenders against Duhagne, who violated the rules of the smithy, who stole, or who infringed the rights of the blacksmith lineages, were said to be seized with leprosy.[44]

In the midnineteenth century, Haieheck introduced a second major blacksmith shrine, Gilaite, to Kadjinol-Kafone. According to his descendant, Antoine Diedhiou, Haieheck became interested in Gilaite at a time when there was a serious outbreak of leprosy at Kadjinol: "Each house had maybe two or three [stricken by leprosy]."[45] During this affliction, Haieheck heard of Gilaite's reputed power to protect people from leprosy and set off for a village in Ediamat to bring back the shrine to Kadjinol. He took two head of cattle to sacrifice at the shrine. In Ediamat he learned that he required a third steer, so he had to make a second trip. He performed the necessary sacrifices and brought the shrine back to Kadjinol. The bringing back of this shrine was seen as a task that only a spiritually powerful individual, a man with a special "head," could do. According to participants at the shrine, Gilaite is fire itself, and only a blacksmith with special powers could control such a powerful boekine and bring it back to Kadjinol.[46]

When Haieheck returned to Kadjinol, he established the altar of Gilaite within the sanctuary of Duhagne at Kafone. Because of its close proximity to a footpath, uninitiated people could hear and see rituals that they did not have a right to witness. It is said that Gilaite seized these people with leprosy for violating his sanctuary. To reduce the possibility of such incidents, the shrine elders moved Gilaite to a sacred forest near the rice paddies.[47] At first, the rituals of Gilaite were performed by Haieheck, but after a few years, he initiated an elder of the Kalainou compound of Kafone as oeyi, high priest of Gilaite. He and his family, the Kumbogy compound of Kafone, retained ownership of the shrine with the right to select and initiate future oeyi-Gilaite. The decision to transfer the ritual responsibilities of Gilaite is usually justified by claiming that Haieheck wanted to strengthen a ritually weak compound.[48] A more plausible justification would be that the Kalainou concession, descendants of Koonjaen, had dominated the rituals of Silapoom, as well as the blacksmithing craft. Haieheck probably wished that the lineage with the strongest ties to the forge serve as the intermediary between the blacksmith shrines and the community. Simultaneously, Haieheck created a council of elders, including representatives from all the blacksmith lineages of Kadjinol, which would supervise the workings of the cult. This arrangement resembled that between the priest-king of each Esulalu community, also of Koonjaen descent, and the council of elders who owned the shrine.

Like Duhagne, Gilaite protected the work of blacksmiths as well as the lives and property of blacksmith lineages. It protected the community against theft and leprosy, though it also seized violators of its rules with leprosy.[49] Houben medicines made of palm fibers consecrated at the Gilaite shrine were placed near valuable goods to keep them from being stolen. People who were victims of theft or witchcraft, but who did not know the identity of the offender, would come to Gilaite and swear out the events that had occurred. Gilaite was said to seize the wrongdoers with leprosy. "This is why we have no thieves here."[50] Kadjinol's Gilaite became one of the most powerful shrines, attracting supplicants from throughout the lower Casamance.

According to Siopama Diedhiou, the sacred forest of Gilaite also served as a sanctuary for the animal doubles (siwuum) of the blacksmith lineages and those who these had maternal kin from these lineages. Individuals would perform rituals to protect their animal doubles from accidental harm. "This is why, if you don't go to perform the sacrifice, they [the siwuum] will all die." The animal doubles drink water in the sacred forest of Gilaite. "If you do not go to perform sacrifices, they won't let your animal doubles drink." Both you and your children will then fall ill.[51]

From Kadjinol, relatives of the Kafone blacksmiths took lesser shrines of Gilaite to Mlomp, Kagnout, and Eloudia.[52] All of Esulalu's Gilaite originated with the one that was introduced by Haieheck. Gilaite quickly assumed a position of dominance over the other shrines of the forge, though cattle continued to be sacrificed at the senior shrine of Duhagne. Unlike Silapoom, these new blacksmith shrines excluded women from participation, though women could have rituals performed on their behalf. Silapoom became a guild shrine taken on by only a few master craftsmen.

Healing Shrines

Esulalu's low sandy ridges covered by forests and surrounded by rice paddies were breeding grounds for a wide variety of tropical diseases, ranging from malaria and yellow fever to trypanosomiasis, dysentery, and myiasis, all of which were endemic along the West African coast. In the nineteenth century, greater population mobility brought on by increased trade with Europeans and their agents accelerated the spread of diseases. Increasing population density provided additional hosts for parasites to reproduce and spread. While witchcraft offered one type of explanation for higher incidence of diseases, the ukine offered both diagnostic methods and ways of curing these illnesses.[53]

In the early nineteenth century, many types of spirit shrines could be consulted for the healing of specific maladies. Three shrines were of particular importance: Bruinkaw, Eboon, and Kalick. A person who was afflicted by an illness that resisted ordinary cures would seek out a male or female priest of Bruinkaw, a divinatory shrine. Bruinkaw could determine the spiritual cause of one's affliction in one of two ways; either it could speak through its priest, or it could reveal the causes to the priest in a dream. While traveling through the Casamance in 1871, Alfred Marche heard of a spirit shrine that could talk and was involved in healing. He described the way in which the priest would take "two bamboo poles, moving one inside the other so that it stuck and produced with it a raucous sound that he said was the voice of the boekine, then he translated the message to the person who came there to consult." The second way of ascertaining the cause of someone's illness was to give the priest of Bruinkaw a sprig of unhusked rice for the priest to place under his or her pillow. That night, through the priest's dreams, Bruinkaw would reveal the nature of the subject's problem, its causes, and its remedy.[54]

Bruinkaw was a shrine of affliction that seized people with an illness as a way of summoning them to its priesthood. The illness itself was seen as a particularly dangerous one. The process of taking on the shrine and of becoming a priest was not only expensive, requiring the sacrifice of several pigs and a dog, but also regarded as dangerous because Bruinkaw could attack its adepts with a recurrence of the illness for minor violations of ritual rules.[55]

Unlike the divination shrine of Bruinkaw, Eboon was an important shrine for the healing process itself, once the cause of the illness had been identified. The Kalick shrine was closely associated with women's fertility problems, though its priesthood was exclusively male. Both these shrines lost much of their influence after the introduction of the women's fertility shrine of Ehugna.[56]

The Women's Shrine of Ehugna

In the midnineteenth century, people from Esulalu introduced two types of Ehugna into Esulalu. Men brought the type of Ehugna that originated at Thionk Essil, giving it to their wives, who established it in Kadjinol-Kafone. From there it spread to the Haer quarter of Mlomp, to Eloudia, and to parts of Kagnout and Samatit. At a later date, men who had immigrated from Kadjinol-Kafone to Siganar-Kataka brought Ehugna to the Huluf townships of Siganar, Karounate, and Nyambalang.[57] Women introduced a second type of Ehugna from Niomoun, via the villages of Carabane and Elinkine, to Samatit and Kagnout. Each type of Ehugna had its own rules governing access to the shrines and the performance of rituals, though they addressed similar types of spiritual concerns.

A man named Djibalene Diedhiou, nicknamed Adio Boukhan, brought the first type of Ehugna to his compound at Kadjinol-Kafone. He had observed the shrine's rituals at Thionk Essil and been impressed by the power of the women's shrine. It is said that he decided to bring the shrine because Kadjinol's women had no shrine exclusively their own. However, recurring drought, problems with women's infertility, and witchcraft concerns may have also led to his decision.[58] To obtain such a boekine, Djibalene had to use special powers. As Amelikai Diedhiou suggested: "It is not everyone who can see the boekine, one with head only . . . he stole it." That night he left, carrying the spirit of the Ehugna shrine in a sack.[59] Having decided to take on the shrine, Djibalene stole some goats from Kafone, which he sacrificed to create an Ehugna shrine. Ehugna was said to have eaten the inside of the goats, all the flesh and organs, while leaving the skin and bones intact. This power is usually attributed to witches.

He summoned his brother and a man from the Sergerh quarter and revealed the spirit to them. Then he called a meeting of the people of Kafone. They were angry because of the theft of the goats, and they wanted to know what Djibalene had done with them. He replied that he had sacrificed them at a new shrine,

Ehugna. Then he named his brother's wife, Ayncabadje Sambou, as the chief priest of the shrine, instructed her in its use, and gave her the shrine.[60]

The office of oeyi Ehugna (also called *oeyi analai* or women's priest-king) belongs to the wives of Djibalene's brothers in the Elinjahn compound of Kafone. Thus, Ehugna's priests are seized because of the status of the men they marry. However, they spend the subsequent two years training to become priests, including ritual sacrifices at Coeyi and instruction in the analysis of their dreams. Dreams were viewed as powerful ways of communicating with spirits at Ehugna and as a method of divining the causes of illness. Once chosen as priests of this shrine, women could no longer divorce or be divorced from their husbands. The men of Kadjinol were forbidden to eat or drink at the shrine, though Djibalene and his descendants performed the sacrifices of cattle, pigs, and goats as they were needed at Ehugna. Following the shrine's installation, women from neighboring quarters, from Mlomp-Haer, from Eloudia, and from parts of Kagnout and Samatit requested that Ehugna shrines be established in their communities as well.

In some ways Ehugna is comparable to the male elders' shrine of Hoohaney. These women address the spiritual concerns of women in the community and seek to direct feminine power toward issues of general concern. Central to Ehugna's concerns was the problem of fertility; only women who had given birth to children could participate in its rituals. Rituals were performed at Ehugna to ensure the fertility of women and crops and to eliminate forces that would work against natural increase in the community, including drought, witchcraft, and disease. Barren women were not permitted to attend or perform the rituals because their lack of fertility could lessen the efficacy of ritual action.[61]

The power of Ehugna, whose name is derived from *hugna* (menstruation), stemmed from the fertile power of Diola women who sought to rid themselves and their communities of evil, life-destructive forces. Childless women or barren women could have rituals performed for them to aid them in conceiving a child. Before the planting of rice, women took some of their seed rice to the Ehugna of the rice paddies, called Agebuhl at Kadjinol, to be blessed for a good harvest. Odile Journet described this ritual, which involved "dances with a strong sexual connotation, in the middle of the rice paddies and diving into the mangrove swamps to expel the destructive spirits that threatened children and harvests, and long vigils at the boekine." In the fall, before any rice was brought back from the fields, women brought small amounts of rice to the Ehugna to perform a firstfruits ritual. This ritual involves cooking some of the new rice and sharing a common meal among the women of the community.[62]

When the rains were late, women would perform rituals at Ehugna to obtain this life-giving force. When witchcraft reappeared as a community problem, women performed rituals to protect against witches and to expel evil from the community. Certain elders of Ehugna were said to have the power to see witches in the night, through dreams. Then they would make their accusations public at the Ehugna shrine. Marie Assin, oeyi of an Ehugna at Samatit, claimed that Ehugna could actually trap witches, forcing them to confess publicly. Healing diseases was also an important part of the functions of the shrine. Ehugna upheld the proper relations between the sexes by seizing men who abused women or violated menstrual avoidances with a variety of diseases, including one whose symptom of a distended stomach was said to resemble pregnancy. Men who were afflicted with diseases attributed to Ehugna or who had difficulties finding a wife might have had rituals performed for them, but they could neither enter the shrine precincts nor eat or drink anything offered in ritual.[63]

The second type of Ehugna can be traced back to the north shore communities of Itou and Niomoun. A woman nicknamed Ayou Ahan brought the shrine from Carabane to Elinkine; Kagnout and Samatit also received it from Elinkine.[64] At this type of Ehugna, men can partake of the palm wine and meat of sacrifice after the rituals have been concluded. In 1889, Father Kieffer observed an Ehugna ritual of this type at the village of Itou:

> On the days of major celebrations, a pig is sacrificed to the fetishes; and all mothers are obligated to take part in the festivities; while rice is being cooked in the courtyard of the priestess, it is the chants that continue during the day and night with quite bizarre accompaniments. Then the worshippers gather together, dressed for the occasion in red pagnes, adorned by three or four strings of bells around their waists. Carrying cow's tails they stir in rhythm and jump. The skill with which they perform the movement is some-how diabolical; one would say it is the demon that gives them the power that is necessary for them not to tire.[65]

The emphasis on mothers, rather than women as a whole, is clear evidence that Kieffer observed an Ehugna ritual. Judging from my observations of such rituals, the red cloth is associated with the high priest, indicating the possibility that Father Kieffer observed the end of the initiation of an oeyi of Ehugna. Cows' tails are symbols of wealth.

By the late nineteenth century, women had obtained ritual authority over what was regarded as one of the most powerful shrine clusters within Esulalu. The spiritual power of women, as embodied in the cult of Ehugna, rested upon their unique role as givers of life. Their power to bestow life was seen as an effective weapon against the life-destructive forces of infertility and witchcraft. In this sense, their power was akin to the power of the Koonjaen and the priest-king, whose intimate ties to the life-giving properties of the soil gave them power over the life-diminishing forces that continuously threatened Esulalu. However, they activated this power differently. In sharp contrast to most men's rituals, women's rituals at Ehugna stressed the spiritual power of dance, both to activate the unique power of women and to heal, and the importance of a ritual meal shared among all the women of the community.

Cloth, Modesty, and Morality

Early-nineteenth-century visitors to the Casamance were struck by the sharp con-trast between Diola styles of dress and the Sudanic styles that prevailed in north-ern Senegambia. Descriptions of Diola dress included none of the kaftans, cloth shirts, or baggy trousers (chaya) that were so common among the Wolof of that period and the Diola in the twentieth century. Instead, both men's and women's clothes consisted of a short cloth apron covering the groin and buttocks. Women wore large quantities of copper bracelets and necklaces and decorated their bodies with scar patterns and tattoos. In 1822, John Morgan, a Wesleyan missionary in the Gambia, visited the Casamance and noted that Diola "are very near naked, men and women. Some have a narrow strip of cloth a little wider than your hand which is fashioned to a string round the middle and hangs down behind and before."[66] According to Esulalu historians, this was a time when cloth was in such short supply that wearing *pagnes* wrapped around the hips was reserved for special occasions. Before cloth became readily available, people would make skirts from a type of palm frond called *badjak* or from goat skins.[67] Uncircumcised boys wore loin cloths called *hupip*, while young girls wore strings of beads or cowries called *epell sossou* (genital shame or modesty) or simply *basossou* (shame). Only after menarche did girls begin to wear the cloth apron.[68] In the early nineteenth century, sexual modesty, for both men and women, appeared to focus on the covering of the genitalia and did not extend to thighs or breasts.

By the end of the nineteenth century, Diola women had abandoned the apron for the more extensive covering of the pagne or wrap-around cloth. Father Wintz described Diola dress at the end of the century:

> The clothing that the Diola adult wears is very simple. A light cloth passed around the loins and between the legs makes up the clothing of the man. The woman wears that piece of cloth around her loins and lets it reach just to the knee. The children often wear nothing. Boys start to cover themselves after circumcision. Little girls around eight years of age, add a piece of cloth to the belt of fake pearls that they wear around their loins.[69]

The increasing availability of cloth that accompanied the expansion of Esulalu trade, as well as exposure to northern Senegambian styles of dress, led to the adoption of the pagne by both men and women and the extension of sexual modesty among women to include covering the thighs. This new modesty in dress may have resulted from the influence of Muslim and Christian traders, who were their prime source of cloth.

Despite John Morgan's complaints about the inadequacy of Diola dress, Esulalu sexual mores stressed premarital chastity and monogamous marriage. Esulalu informants claim that premarital intercourse was absolutely forbidden and that unwed mothers would be driven out of their townships to seek refuge in strangers' villages or Diola communities outside Esulalu. While they remained in the villages, unwed mothers would have insulting songs sung about them. Whether they were forced out of the village or shamed out by the insulting songs remains uncertain.[70] The rarity of premarital sexual relations among the south shore Diola was commented on by a Frenchman, Captain Lauque, who visited Esulalu in 1905: "Generally girls do not allow themselves to be easily corrupted, being in great fear of their mother and their aunts, it is generally only after marriage that they become mothers."[71]

As part of the final marriage preparations, both bride and groom received instruction on sexual relations between men and women, thereby indicating a customary ignorance of such matters before marriage. Unmarried men received such

instruction at their homes prior to the arrival of the bride. Unmarried women received instruction about sex and birth from a group of mothers, who would take
them to the maternity house for discussion of these matters away from the ears of
men.[72]

Throughout the nineteenth century, monogamous marriages were the norm in
Esulalu. Polygny, while permitted, was extremely rare.[73] Marriage partners usually came from within Esulalu; marriages contracted with non-Diola or non-Esulalu
were frowned upon. When a boy and a girl were quite young, it was not uncom-
mon for their parents to enter into an engagement on their behalf. As the children
grew up, the boy would periodically visit his prospective in-laws and bring them
gifts of palm wine. In this way, he could become acquainted with his future bride
and her family over a long period of time. As the prospective couple neared marriageable age, approximately fifteen for a girl and eighteen for a boy, they could
decide whether to go ahead with the marriage. Either partner could refuse, though
there were some cases of parents forcing their children to marry.[74]

Wrestling matches and social dances provided the major opportunities for girls
and boys to meet and to court. Wrestling teams competed by township quarter
against other quarters and other townships. Both boys and girls wrestled and observed the others' skills in wrestling, while providing support through songs and
dances of encouragement. Afterward, an *acconkone* social dance was held in which
boys and girls danced in separate circles facing one another. Girls of a particular
quarter would occasionally hold *heleo* dances, which were attended by boys from
within Esulalu. They would bring a two-stringed guitar called an *econtine* and
sing about the girls who interested them.[75]

Marriages involved a complex exchange of gifts between the bride and groom's
families. Most attention has focused on buposs, the vast quantities of palm wine
and a large pig that the groom had to provide for the bride's family. The palm
wine was used not only for entertainment but also for ritual libations at various
shrines associated with the bride's patrilineage, her mother's patrilineage and her
grandmothers' patrilineages.[76] These rituals were designed to gain the blessing
of all the bride's ancestors before she left for her new home and family. The pig
provided by the groom's family would be sacrificed at the bride's family Hupila
to protect her powers of fertility in her new home. The bride's family, however,
also provided substantial gifts. The bride arrived at her new home with a full set
of cooking pots and sufficient rice to last the couple until the next harvest. This
large quantity of rice offered by the bride's family exceeded the value of the palm
wine offered by the groom. The Diolas' practice of exchanging gifts between the
two families being linked in marriage was not a "bride price" but a series of exchanges that brought the two families together ritually and in terms of economic
interdependence.

Within the Esulalu townships, people worried about the perennial problems of
security and order, of fertility of women and crops, of physical well-being, and of
protection from witchcraft, but as the nineteenth century wore on, these problems
seemed to take on a new urgency. French military actions against Kagnout,

Karones, Thionk Essil, and Seleki raised the specter of European interference in Esulalu's internal affairs, while the persistence of raiding for captives did little to alleviate anxieties about community security. A prolonged drought, beginning in 1851, and the increasing incidence of disease threatened the life-giving powers of both land and women, while contributing to an actual decline in the physical well-being of the community. Increasing social inequality aggravated this sense of insecurity within the Diola townships.

These problems were not, however, seen in isolation. All of these problems could be seen to reflect increasing moral decay as Esulalu became further removed from the time of the first ancestors. This anxiety was often reflected in accusations of witchcraft, which occurred frequently throughout the century. Thus, witchcraft was identified as the cause of disease, infertility, and miscarriages. Furthermore, Emitai could well be punishing the townships for their toleration of witches by withholding rain or by imposing French hegemony. Therefore, one way to resolve the problems that Esulalu confronted in the nineteenth century was to identify and remove witches from the townships.

The Diola of Esulalu, however, did not limit their response to these problems to the socially corrosive process of witchcraft accusations. The blacksmiths of Kafone introduced a new series of shrines to protect against theft, witchcraft, and leprosy. Through the creation of the women's shrines of Ehugna, Esulalu gave institutional recognition to the distinctive spiritual power of women. Esulalu women were able to make their new shrine of Ehugna vital to the ritual life of the region by focusing its distinct spiritual power on the protection of the fertility of crops and women and the enhancement of community security against witchcraft and other forces of evil. Finally, the search for security led Esulalu elders to forge alliances through the exchanges of such spirit shrines as Cabai, while religious sanctions were provided to give power to preserve treaties between previously hostile townships.

In the nineteenth century, Esulalu religious institutions continued to provide a path for community understanding and control over the problems that beset them. New challenges were met by a reaffirmation of ritual authorities, their extension into new areas, and the creation of new spirit shrines as intermediaries between the people of Esulalu and Emitai. There was a new emphasis, however, on gendered concepts of spiritual power and the spiritual energy embodied in fire. Even these were fluid, however. A man introduced the shrine of Ehugna for the exclusive use of women. A female slave introduced the shrine of Kanalia for the men of the Kandianka quarter of Kadjinol. Still, the separation of gendered types of spiritual power became increasingly important during this period. Throughout the nineteenth century, the awasena path relied on its capacity for innovation to continue to find ways of bestowing meaning on an uncertain and rapidly changing world.

8

Conclusion

In this study I have sketched the broad outlines of the religious and social history of the Diola-Esulalu, beginning with the gradual joining together of distinct Koonjaen and Floup traditions and concluding with an examination of Diola traditions on the eve of the establishment of colonial rule and a permanent missionary presence. Written sources, primarily from travelers, traders, colonial administrators, and missionaries, provided useful descriptions of the Diola past but were too removed from Diola community life, too fragmentary in scope, and too lacking in historical perspective to provide more than supplementary evidence concerning Esulalu religious history. The core of this study had to be based on Esulalu oral traditions, which I gathered from community elders and other interested people during the course of nearly four years of field work.

Through the analysis of Esulalu oral traditions, it becomes clear that many scholars have underestimated the richness of oral traditions and the ability of oral historians to reflect on the history of their religious traditions. Change is remembered, if not in the traditions readily presented to outsiders, at least in the more private discussions among elders of particular shrines and with other parties who are able to earn their trust. From this study it becomes clear that African traditional religions do not conform to the static image perpetuated by scholars from Mbiti to Beidelman. Nor do oral traditions necessarily emphasize magical or mythical ideas of causality, as suggested by Goody and Miller.[1] On the contrary, these traditions are recounted by historians who draw on a variety of possible explanations for significant change. Rather than being unconcerned about history, as Louis Vincent Thomas suggests, many Diola are guarded about sharing their history with outsiders or the uninitiated precisely because it is so important to the community.[2] Researchers with limited time in the field may never get past the ideology of absolute continuity with the time of the first ancestors, which generates community support for awasena traditions and reinforces the authority of the spirit shrines.

Diola traditions focus primarily on the history of religious institutions rather than on changes in central elements of a Diola system of thought. The origins of specific spirit shrines, their influence within Esulalu, their rules, and their adaptations to the continuing process of socioeconomic change provide the core of remembered religious history. In the absence of formal political institutions, ukine became the primary institutions of community life, regulating such diverse activities as slave trading and community labor relations. As upholders of a moral order, the spirit shrines became a major source of cultural continuity. Shrine histories reveal far more than the nature of specific cults; they reveal the relationships among various families that control shrines and the nature of their claims to spiritual power. Frequently, the origins of particular spirit shrines shed light on the ways in which Esulalu communities sought to explain and control specific types of historical forces.

From the intricate detail of shrine histories, the historian of religions can glean evidence of their broader significance and their implications it has for the development of a Diola system of thought. In certain cases, changes in shrine structures indicate changes in the Diola conceptualization of the relationships among Emitai, the spirit shrines, and the people of Esulalu. In other instances, such changes may indicate shifting concepts of a Diola priesthood. Such interpretations are not always offered in the recounting of oral traditions, however, and the student of Diola religious history must infer from the nature of the institutional change the broader significance within a Diola history of ideas. Almost inevitably, the subtler types of changes remain elusive, concealed by the tendency to refine oral traditions in accordance with contemporary needs or lost beyond the limits of human memory. Still, the absence of fixed oral traditions in Esulalu and the existence of a multiplicity of free traditions, reflecting the diversity of spirit shrines, preserve a broader range of testimony on significant changes than the more routinized and centralized traditions of societies with more restricted access to ritual authority.

Diola religious historians often associate the creation of spirit shrines with particular problems within community life. Certain shrines are described as being created during specific crises within Esulalu history or in response to persistent environmental, economic, social, or political problems. This should not be taken to suggest, however, that the awasena path merely reflects changes within Diola community life. It is a Diola system of thought that interprets and gives meaning to those forces for change within a Diola society. Rather than an indication of the primacy of temporal experience over structures of thought, the close association of historical forces with the creation of spirit shrines is evidence of a Diola paradigm that stresses the importance of spiritual causes of many forms of change and sees the various types of spiritual beings associated with shrines as created by Emitai for the express purpose of resolving such problems. The instrumental aspect of spirit shrine worship is central to the definition of the spirits associated with these shrines. It then follows logically that historical forces for change influence the activities of certain shrines, encourage some to gain new powers, and are an impetus for the creation of new shrines and the abandonment of those that are no longer seen as efficacious.

Despite the dramatic changes within Diola society and ritual practice during the eighteenth and nineteenth centuries, the paradigm that spirit shrines serve as intermediaries between the Diola and their supreme being, in order to resolve various types of problems, was not altered. New spirit shrines were created and old ones were modified, but they continued to be approached to resolve specific types of individual, family, and community problems. Such endurance reflects the continued ability of this basic tenet of a Diola tradition to explain the changing circumstances in which the Esulalu found themselves.

The close association of the spirit shrines with changing temporal conditions allows the historian of religions to understand the ways in which the paradigm of spiritual intermediaries operates in specific contexts. By examining Esulalu religious responses to various types of temporal change, one begins to uncover the nature of the dialogue between changing social and economic conditions and their system of thought. Each shapes the other. Socioeconomic forces determine the range of phenomena to which Diola thought must respond, while the system of thought determines the ways in which such changes are perceived, explained and, controlled.

In this chapter, I explore the nature of this dialogue and the ways in which Esulalu responses to change are structured according to an Esulalu worldview. Then I discuss the broader implications of such changes and the structures within the awasena path that permit and encourage continuing innovation within a Diola religious system.

From Shrine Histories to Religious History

In normal years, the people of Esulalu could expect sufficient rainfall to ensure a good rice harvest, enough to feed a family and buy some needed goods while leaving an adequate reserve for the leaner years. Yet droughts were frequent during the eighteenth and nineteenth centuries. In a drought, most of the rice paddies do not flood; only a small portion are suitable for planting, and the yields are smaller. The failure of the rains, which often occurred in successive years, was associated not only with crop failure but also with the ebbing of life forces within the community. Adequate rainfall demonstrated the efficacy of Diola rituals designed to carry community prayers, by way of the spirit shrines, to Emitai, who gave this vital gift of life.[3]

Inadequate rainfall was a clear sign that something was wrong in the relationship of people, the spirit shrines, and Emitai. The withholding of rain was often seen as a sign of Emitai's displeasure. Perhaps the drought was caused by inadequate or poorly conducted rituals at the specific spirit shrines associated with rain or fertility. Perhaps it was due to widespread witchcraft activity or other forms of misconduct. The nature of the problem had to be discerned and ritually removed to ensure adequate rainfall and community well-being, often with a community–wide invocation of Emitai through the elaborate ritual of nyakul emit. When the rains failed to come, men and women would perform rituals at all the spirit shrines of the community, asking them to carry prayers to Emitai to send rain. Then they performed a funeral dance—in a sense a funeral dance for the entire community—imploring Emitai to pity them and to provide life-giving rain.

Prolonged drought provoked a serious questioning of the efficacy of existing spirit shrines and rain rituals and often resulted in the modification of such rituals and the introduction of new shrines. The severe drought in the late eighteenth century encouraged Diola elders to question the legitimacy of priest-kings within Esulalu whose ancestors had been involved in the conquest of the autochthonous Koonjaen. The crisis brought on by this drought was an important factor in overcoming the elders' resistance to recognizing the spiritual preeminence of the conquered Koonjaen. This allowed members of the Koonjaen royal lineage, Gent, to assume the office of priest-king and to restore its royal shrine of Egol so that prayers for the fertility of the land and the procurement of water would be offered by the most spiritually powerful people within Esulalu. The threat of drought also led to the introduction of Cayinte shrines, which were explicitly linked to rain, and, in the nineteenth century, may have influenced the spread of Ehugna, where women offered prayers for rain. Esulalu's desperate search for rain in a time of drought became a powerful force for the creation of new spirit shrines and for redefining the priesthoods that performed such rituals. It did not, however, lead to the abandonment of their fundamental idea that rainfall was dependent on the community's correct relationship with Emitai and the efficacy of Emitai's intermediaries in conveying their prayers for rain.

Epidemics were another powerful force for change within Esulalu religious life. The people of Esulalu suffered under the debilitating and often fatal effects of a host of diseases. With greater population mobility resulting from increased trade and with higher population density providing more hosts for the spread of parasitic diseases, ill health became an increasingly serious problem within Esulalu. Such diseases were often seen as having spiritual causes, ranging from witchcraft to punishment for offenses against an Esulalu moral code, from neglect of ritual obligations to a summons to become a priest of a shrine of affliction. Increasing disease rates gave rise to witch-finding movements, especially in the nineteenth century. It also encouraged the adoption of shrines with important healing roles. Thus, a high incidence of leprosy helped open the way for community acceptance of the blacksmith shrine of Gilaite, a shrine said to have the power to inflict and heal leprosy. Other diseases may have encouraged Esulalu to accept the women's shrine of Ehugna, which was said to be able to tap women's life-giving powers to promote good health. The general increase in the incidence of disease or the persistence of certain specific diseases may have contributed to the decline of such healing and women's fertility shrines as Eboon and Kalick.

Esulalu's persistent problem of township unity was also addressed through ritual activity, specifically the establishment of spirit shrines that specialized in problems of community governance and moral leadership. In the eighteenth century, Esulalu elders introduced a town council shrine, Hutendookai, where representatives of every lineage could gather and discuss community problems ranging from land disputes to enforcement of community work obligations to the searching out of witches. Hoohaney was created as a shrine for the elders who assisted the priest-king that empowered them to supervise the affairs of the cemetery and to discuss issues requiring spiritual leadership in the community. The introduction of these shrines was accompanied by the removal of the priest-king from the regulation of community affairs and his exclusion from the deliberations of Hutendookai. Stripped of what we would consider his secular powers, the priest-king was elevated above all factions and became a powerful symbol of the spiritual unity of the community. As the embodiment of township unity, the priest-king could stop all intratownship wars and also tap the power of the community as a whole to offer prayers for the protection of township fertility and welfare.

The frequency of warfare, however, resulted in the creation of a series of shrines that strengthened township quarters and individual members' martial prowess when fighting in a just cause. In the eighteenth and nineteenth centuries, a series of quarter shrines such as Elenkine-Sergerh and Kanalia, as well as Samatit's township shrine of Enac, provided spiritual protection and power for the warriors who gathered in their precincts. The threat of Kadjinol-Kafone's defeat by its neighboring quarter of Hassouka created a favorable environment for Kooliny Djabune to have visions of Emitai. His soul was said to have risen to Emitai, where he received instructions about the use of a new shrine, Cabai, which strengthened Kafone in war and allowed it to defeat its enemies. The giving of Cabai to Kafone's allies became a powerful way of providing sanctions against the breakdown of such alliances by creating a situation in which the same spirit could not assist two antagonists in a single war.

The most dramatic changes within the awasena path occurred under the influence of increasing Diola participation in trade during the eighteenth and nineteenth centuries. In the absence of a centralized state, the slave trade was regulated and legitimated through a series of cults and their priests. As the market for Diola captives dramatically increased in the eighteenth century, Diola slave traders were given new opportunities to amass wealth, especially in cattle and rice paddies. Within this relatively egalitarian society, the primary socially acceptable use of wealth was the acquisition of priestly offices. There were no specialized political offices to desire, and hoarding wealth was seen as a form of witchcraft. Wealthy slave raiders began to create new spirit shrines and to transform older cults to emphasize the role of wealth in their priestly offices. Charismatic elements in Diola ritual life became less important, and the spiritual powers associated with shrine elders were seen as being in sharp decline.

This process can best be illustrated by examining the transformation of the cults that were involved in the slave trade. Diola slave trading had its origins in the ransoming of war captives and cattle thieves seized from neighboring Diola subgroups. Captives were taken to the homes of their captors and placed in wooden fetters at the family shrine of Hupila. Only unransomed captives could be sold into slavery. Any premature sale or abuse would be punished by Hupila, who was believed to seize wrongdoers with a disease that made them feel like their bodies were bound in ropes. This type of slave trade was regarded as legitimate and was carefully regulated by one of the most basic cults of the awasena path.

As the wealth and influence of the slave traders increased, they began to use their power to dominate Esulalu ritual life. In the late eighteenth century, new forms of Hupila were introduced within Esulalu. Only men who had seized a slave could gain the right to perform rituals at this Hupila. It also imposed more costly material requirements for becoming a priest. By a process that remains unclear, participants in the slave trade gradually gained control of one of the most central shrines of the Esulalu community. They became the intermediaries in prayers for the well-being and fertility of most of the families of Esulalu. Wealth as a requirement for the acquisition of ritual office became increasingly important at the town council shrine of Hutendookai, as well as at a new form of circumcision shrine called Bukut and the new elders' shrine of Hoohaney. An increasing emphasis on animal sacrifice at these cults reflected the augmented supply of livestock, especially cattle, and the importance of this wealthier livestock-holding elite.

As seizing slaves in the Diola areas of Senegambia became more difficult, a small group of slave raiders created a secret society to seize children from their own and neighboring villages. These captives were kept at a secret shrine, hidden in the granary of the kidnappers. A new shrine, Hupila Hugop, protected the slavers from the sanctions of Hupila and other shrines that protect the community. Here one finds a spirit shrine that was established to ward off punishments imposed by other spirit shrines for what was regarded as wrongdoing and its use for the regulation of an illicit slave trade.

The slave trade and the growing availability of trade goods, however, became more than a catalyst for the introduction of new shrines and changing definitions of priests. Growing social stratification between rich and poor and between Esulalu-born and enslaved persons led to a concentration of religious authority and social influence in the hands of a slave-trading elite. As the importance of shrines that emphasized wealth as a means of access to ritual office became increasingly important, the poorer population, both slave and free, felt increasingly marginalized. Tension developed between ideas of social equality and the spiritual dangers of wealth, on the one hand, and the growing reality of privileged groups in Esulalu on the other. Such a contrast between shared values and social practice became increasingly obvious during the eighteenth and nineteenth centuries.[4]

In examining the histories of the ukine, the three primary methods of introduction appear to be based on borrowing, giving, and visions or dream experience. Some of the shrines were borrowed from neighboring communities when circumstances suggested their need and when other communities seemed to have a particularly desirable way of addressing specific problems or performing rituals. The perceived greater efficacy of Koonjaen shrines related to rain and fertility led the people of Esulalu to incorporate the Koonjaen priest-king shrine of Egol and to adopt the Koonjaen form of circumcision, Kahat. Hutendookai, Gilaite, and the new form of Hupila were all borrowed from neighboring Diola groups when individuals from Esulalu observed the efficacy of these cults in other communities. At times, these individuals performed the necessary sacrifices, brought the spirit associated with the cult back to Esulalu, together with such ritual objects as soil from the senior shrine precincts, and then established a shrine. In such instances, the initiator of the shrine had to use special powers to control the spirit associated with the shrine. More frequently, elders of the senior shrine came to Esulalu, created a new shrine, and initiated a local priest to perform its rituals. At times, the junior shrine could exceed the power of the senior shrine because of the reputed powers of its priests or a perceived greater need for its services. Thus, Kadjinol-Kafone's Gilaite, though introduced from Ediamat, became the most powerful blacksmith shrine of the south shore Diola.

Sometimes cult leaders modified the ritual rules to meet the needs of the Esulalu townships more efficaciously. Thus, the women of Ehugna-Djakati decided to exclude men from drinking palm wine at their shrine, though they were well aware that men could do so at many other forms of Ehugna.

The giving of a shrine by one community to another provides a second method of introducing new spirit shrines within Esulalu. Thus Kadjinol-Kafone's war shrine of Cabai was given to Haer in gratitude for Haer's assistance in a war between Kafone and Hassouka. Haer also received an Ehugna shrine from Kafone for its assistance in a war against Huluf. The north shore Diola community of Niomoun was given a Cayinte shrine by Kadjinol, partially in recognition of the friendship between the two communities. This method, like that of borrowing shrines from other communities, required the performance of certain rituals by the senior shrines' elders to allow for the creation of a shrine in a new community. It differs from the borrowing process in its emphasis on cult elders' desires to spread their particular shrines and their desires to utilize them to forge lasting alliances. It is also distinguished from the visionary process by its lack of emphasis on the display of spiritual powers in the shrine transfer process.

A third method of creating new shrines depended neither on borrowing from Esulalu's neighbors nor on giving shrines to neighboring communities. This method stressed the creation of new shrines within Esulalu by people who were said to have spiritual gifts. The founders of these shrines, which originated in Esulalu, were said to have special powers of the head and special powers to see in the world of the spirit. Their dreams and visions of Emitai or lesser spirits led them to create new shrines and to introduce them into Esulalu townships.

Esulalu historians have suggested that several shrines were created as a result of people's visions of Emitai. In each case, the souls of the individuals were said to leave their bodies and ascend to Emitai, where they were taught the rituals of the new cult before they returned to earth and reentered their bodies. In several instances their wives were said to have feared that the apparently lifeless bodies left behind were dead, and the visionary was forced to stop his instruction before it was complete and return to his body to avert a funeral.[5] Atta-Essou, the founder of Eloudia, provides the earliest example of visions from Emitai, a series of visions that led to his creation of Egol and the institution of the priest-king.[6] Kooliny Djabune's vision during the war between Kafone and Hassouka, in the eighteenth century, resulted in the creation of the war shrine of Cabai. Emitai's summons of Kooliny to assist his quarter in a war against another quarter provides the clearest example of the Diola supreme being's ability to intervene in the microcosm and of Its role in supporting a moral order.[7]

Visions and dreams about lesser spirits, the ammahl, are far more common within Diola oral traditions. Both men and women were said to encounter spiritual beings who taught them how to communicate with them and perform rituals to convey the needs of their communities. Spiritual experiences resulted in the creation of Elenkine-Sergerh at Kadjinol-Sergerh and other quarter shrines throughout Esulalu. These types of experiences can also be seen as a summons to the priesthood for already existing shrines and as a call to antisocial behavior when individuals strike bargains with individual ammahl to secure wealth or power at the expense of community welfare.

Esulalu elders provided several models for religious innovation. Two involve drawing on the experience of other communites, including the conquered Koonjaen, neighboring Diola, and other ethnic groups. These methods can be distinguished according to who initiates the transfer of cult knowledge: between requests to receive from these outside groups and offers from them to share a cult with an Esulalu township. The third method focuses on those individuals who claim the power to see into the world of the spirit, communicate with Emitai or lesser spirits, and then convey their teachings to the Esulalu townships.

Another form of innovation focused on the growing importance of gendered concepts of spiritual power. While the Koonjaen seemed more open to the inclusion of women in ritual life than the incoming Floup, and both communities welcomed women as diviners and spiritual healers, neither group appears to have had shrines associated with the distinctive spiritual power of women. As the Diola-Esulalu placed growing emphasis on male initiation rites, first in Kahat, then in the more elaborate Bukut, they seemed to embrace the idea of a distinctive male spiritual power. With the introduction of Ehugna, in the midnineteenth century, the people of Esulalu introduced a shrine that celebrated the distinctive power of women. At Ehugna, women performed rituals to heal the sick, identify witches, enhance the fertility of women and the land, and seek life-giving rain. It provided a structure for women to deliberate about matters of community concern and a series of shrine elders to share their decisions with the township as a whole. With the introduction of Ehugna, women gained control of a boekine that quickly became central to the religious life of Esulalu.

Another source of innovation within Esulalu was less dependent on specific shrine histories. This force for religious change drew on the creative tension within three areas of Esulalu thought in which two theoretical models competed for community adherence. These three issues were the nature of the spirit shrines, the nature of the cult priests, and the nature of the awasena tradition itself. These need to be addressed in turn.

While Diola elders generally agree that the spirit shrines serve as intermediaries between people and Emitai, they are not in agreement about the degree of independence that they possess. Some would argue that the spirits merely relay human prayer to Emitai and carry out the will of the supreme being. Others see them as less predictable and capable of exercising their own wills and deciding whether, or how to, carry such messages. Some of these differences reflect the differences between various types of ukine. Such shrines as Hutendookai and Bukut stress the intermediary role, while others, like Hupila and Elenkine-Sergerh, are seen as capable of more independent action. Still, the existence of two theories about the nature of lesser spirits allows both a greater diversity and a source of innovation within Esulalu traditions. Shrines created from visions of Emitai reaffirm the intimate role of the supreme being in the creation of channels of communication; they gain a centrality that ordinarily their newness would deny.

Furthermore, the teachings that accompany the creation of what is regarded as a divinely inspired cult could supercede contradictory rules from much older cults. However, the uncertainties of prayer through more independent spirit cults provides avenues for the possibility of negotiation with spiritual powers and helps to explain the occasional failure of properly addressed prayer. Simultaneously, it allows for the intervention of spiritual forces in matters that are regarded as still too manageable to require the intervention of Emitai. Neither model disappears, though one often appears to be ascendant until there is need for the other mode of perceiving the essential nature of the spirit shrines.

Another enduring tension in Esulalu traditions focuses on the nature of the ritual specialist. Is the priest of a shrine merely the one who knows the correct ritual techniques and possesses the wherewithal to perform required initiation rituals? Or should the specialist have received some kind of spiritual calling through an affliction associated with a specific cult or through dreams and visions? In the former case, the priest becomes a mere "technician of the sacred," a ritual expert not necessarily endowed with great wisdom or spiritual powers. In the latter case, however, the priests have been chosen by and are often seen as able to communicate with the spirits of the shrines, not only through ritual actions but also through special powers associated with the eyes and the head.

This tension between technical mastery and spiritual authority is not unique to Diola traditions, but the continuing tension between these two visions of a priest provides a source of diversity and innovation. Shrines at which elders select their membership and their priests by the criteria of family and wealth are ensured of maintaining their priesthoods without long interregna. When vacancies occur, successors are easily chosen. Communication with the spirits of the shrine is fairly routinized, through the correct performance of rituals. Such shrines become an important source of continuity and stability within Esulalu ritual life. Still, such shrines' stress on ritualism, regularity, lineage, and wealth may become too rigid, resistant to change, and incapable of utilizing personal spiritual experience within an overly routinized structure.

Shrines that stress charismatic selection of priests have certain problems and advantages. The office of the priest could fall vacant for long periods of time if the proper disease does not seize a potential priest or the proper spirit does not reveal itself in dreams or visions.[8] There is comparatively less community input into the selection of such priests. Priests deemed inappropriate by virtue of their youth, moral character, or general knowledge could undermine the authority of a cult. Still, the stress in such cults on dreams, visions, and the ability to communicate with the spirits associated with the shrine allows a continuing renewal of spiritual experience, a greater flexibility in ritual rules and guidelines for community behavior, and the harnessing of the spritual power of those who are said to receive a calling to offer prayer on behalf of the community.

In the face of continuing tension between technicians and seers, Esulalu drew on both the routinized power of the elective shrines and the internal religious experience of the more charismatic shrines. The relative importance of these two visions of leadership have fluctuated over time. During the period of increasing wealth and stratification, the elective principle and the technical mastery of the priest were stressed. Yet, in times of crisis, the shrines of priests who claimed a spiritual calling were there to provide leadership based on their spiritual gifts.

The third source of tension focuses on the nature of the awasena tradition itself, whether Koonjaen or Diola. Beginning in the eighteenth century, when the people of Esulalu began to regard the Koonjaen as members of their community and not just a conquered minority, the newcomers to Esulalu began to draw on the spiritual power of the older inhabitants that grew out of their positions as owners of the land. Because of this power, the Diola newcomers embraced the Koonjaen form of circumcision and the Egol shrine of the Koonjaen priest-king and turned over their office of priest-king to the Koonjaen descendants of Atta-Essou. They recognized the spiritual power of being rooted in the land through one's attachment to ancestors who had died there over many generations, and they turned to that power when their own cult institutions seemed ineffective. To reconcile their incorporation of Koonjaen cults and priests, however, they embraced the Koonjaen oral traditions and made their own the accounts of Atta-Essou and his many children. With the incorporation of the traditions of Atta-Essou, they also embraced a tradition of direct revelations from Emitai, a force that became increasingly important to a developing Esulalu awasena tradition. The people of Esulalu gradually bridged the tension between Koonjaen and Diola visions of history by making the shrines Koonjaen and priests Diola, while maintaining the memory of the Koonjaen's true ancestry primarily as a check on their potential abuse of power.

In examining the tension between conflicting theories in Diola thought during the eighteenth and nineteenth centuries, there appears to be significant change, but no revolutions. One theory does not seem to disappear; rather, it wanes, only to be revived when it seems to be more effective. More dramatic theoretical shifts, like the scientific revolutions described by Thomas Kuhn, tend to occur during a time of community crisis, when the dominant paradigm seems less able to explain and control the forces of change that confront it. "So long as the tools a paradigm supplies continue to prove capable of solving the problems it defines, science moves fastest and penetrates most deeply through confident employment of those tools. . . . The significance of crisis is the indication they provide that an occasion for retooling has arrived."[9]

In the history of Esulalu in the eighteenth and nineteenth centuries, there does not appear to be a time when Esulalu theories lose their power to interpret the forces that confront them. Consequently, within Esulalu, there was no need to relegate one theoretical model to the memories of a few masters of oral tradition. Crisis situations seem to emphasize the most appropriate theory, while conserving the other as a viable alternative in another time or for a different type of problem. Two visions of the nature of lesser spirits, priests, and, to a lesser extent, of the tradition itself continue to coexist, offering a greater flexibility and range of answers to the challenges of rendering intelligible a rapidly changing world. The shift of paradigms, like the process of religious conversion or revolutions, rarely results in the elimination of past ways of perceiving and explaining the world. Rather, it brings new structures of thought into greater prominence. People continue to draw on those resources within their worldview that are still effective in explaining and influencing their world. The memories of older paradigms reemerge in new crises and endure when they are able to bestow the world with meaning.

Esulalu thought about the importance of religious change and their ability to live with continued ambiguity about the nature of spirits and priests raises serious questions about descriptions of African traditional throught as closed and rigid. Robin Horton has argued that the fundamental difference between African traditional thought and Western science is the absence in the former of a "developed awareness of alternatives to the established body of theoretical tenets."[10] Precolonial Esulalu does not fit within Horton's idea of a traditional system. Adherents of Esulalu "religion" were quite receptive to borrowing new types of cults from their neighbors while modifying their ritual rules to meet their needs. Under the pressures of environmental uncertainty, the people of the townships were willing to incorporate the traditions of the Koonjaen within their own developing tradition. They were willing to abandon one form of male initiation and embrace another because of a series of advantages of the new ritual form. Moreover, the Esulalu continued to tolerate the unresolved tension between two conflicting visions of the spirit shrines and their priesthoods and drew on one in particular when it more appropriately explained their community's experience.

The awasena path's emphasis on personal religious experience, through dreams and visions, as well as the broad diffusion of shrines and priestly offices, encouraged a continuing diversity of interpretations of major issues in Esulalu thought. This diversity of interpretation, each supported by its own spiritual authority, protected and nurtured the creative tension between conflicting visions of the fundamental nature of an Esulalu spiritual order. Deeply rooted structures of innovation in Diola ritual forms, combined with a critical stance in relation to their system of thought, provided Esulalu's awasena path with the richness and versatility to adapt to the rapidly changing circumstances of precolonial Senegal.

Appendix

Chronology in Diola-Esulalu Oral Traditions

Throughout this study, oral traditions have provided the core of evidence for the analysis of Diola-Esulalu religious history. In this appendix, I describe my methods for establishing a chronological framework within the oral traditions that I collected and some of the problems inherent in such an analysis.

Western historians have tended to assume an absolute and quantifiable sense of chronology as central to their discipline. However, this approach is not universal; many societies stress the importance of a relative chronology as central to their idea of history. In a highly useful study, *The Chronology of Oral Tradition*, David Henige claims: "The memory of the past in oral societies seldom included its abstract quantification. Traditional accounts were designed to develop and transmit those aspects of the past which were deemed important, and absolute dating was never, nor could it ever be, one of these."[1] Absolute dating of the relatively distant past within the chronicles of a particular society depends on the existence of a quantifiable system of naming or numbering years, of remembering chronology in abstract terms, shorn of its relation to major events in that society's history. In societies that do not stress a quantitative concept of time, neither oral nor written traditions provide this type of chronology.

Part of the task of a Western-trained historian is to translate other ideas of chronology into the absolute chronology to which Western readers are accustomed. To do this, however, oral traditions' rich sense of relative chronology must be supplemented by other forms of data, including written documents from outside that society that can be related to events recounted in oral traditions, archaeological evidence, and evidence of ecological changes. All of these can be utilized in the quest for an absolute chronology that is not provided within the oral traditions themselves.[2]

Rather than providing exact dates, oral traditions are concerned with identifying historical events that are roughly contemporaneous and with establishing a sequence of events. This relative chronology is important because it reveals the relative seniority of social groups; legal, social, and economic rights; and ritual

185

precedence that structure contemporary human activity.[3] Obviously, when chronologies are used to legitimate a variety of social relations in contemporary society, they can be used to advance the positions of certain groups. In the mediation of land and succession disputes, for example, oral evidence can be developed in a "creative" fashion. This type of evidence, in which the recounter of an oral tradition has something to gain from her or his particular use of chronology, must be used with great caution.

Of far greater value is the type of oral traditions in which relative chronology is suggested, but there are no motives for distortion or there are motives for distortions that are not being made. Take the example of the history of a Diola spirit shrine. Suppose an elder of that shrine suggests that it was created by an ancestor of his four generations ago, when he has already recounted to you a genealogy eight generations deep. For him to claim that his shrine was created four generations ago, when eight are remembered, is to suggest that there was a time when this spirit shrine did not exist and the people of his community used other means to resolve the problems associated with that shrine. Given that many Diola associate the longevity of a cult with its power, the informant is saying that this shrine is senior to some and junior to others. It did not exist since the time of the "first ancestors." This evidence can be more readily relied on than claims of antiquity that are self-serving.

Admitting the historicity of the creation of a spirit shrine and placing it within remembered relative chronologies run counter to the public presentation of Diola traditions, which suggests that all cults existed since the first ancestors. In fact, such dating of shrines was rarely offered in initial interviews, when the more official "ahistorical" presentations were made. A reliance on the historical accounts of the establishment of such shrines is supported by Jan Vansina's claim: "When features which do not correspond to those commonly attributed to an ideal type nevertheless persist in a tradition, they may usually be regarded as trustworthy."[4]

One technique for the establishment of relative chronologies within a society as a whole is through the analysis of king lists. In a society with a tradition of centralized kingship, detailed lists of rulers in chronological order are carefully maintained. Various types of political, economic, religious, and environmental changes are said to have occurred during the reign of a particular monarch or chief. Sometimes there is even greater specificity, for example, that a particular event occurred early in a ruler's reign. Such linkages provide a sense of which events are roughly contemporaneous, or which events occurred before or after other events. They do not provide an absolute chronology, however. Royal reigns vary radically in length; some successions may be collateral rather than lineal, and there may be long interregna.[5] Similar problems exist in societies without centralized kingship, that maintain lists of priests and priest-kings of major shrines. In my research on the Diola-Esulalu, I used these priest-king lists as an aid in determining the temporal relation of one event to another.

Of far greater significance in my research on Diola-Esulalu history was the use of Bukut circumcision lists. Beginning about 1790, the men of Esulalu adopted a form of male initiation ritual called Bukut. It was said to have been held once every twenty years, though drought, poor crops, or other disruptions often caused substantial delays in the enactment of the ritual. In these rites, all males (approximately three to twenty-three years of age) who had been weaned since the last Bukut were circumcised together. These circumcision rituals were named, and men who were initiated together were said to belong to the same generation. Although this practice did not take on the full organizational structure of an age grade, Bukut initiation rites are used to mark the different generations. The names of men's circumcision rituals are well known and are used by the Esulalu themselves to establish relative seniority in social relations. Some of these circumcision rituals can be dated in absolute terms by French visitors who wrote descriptions of these elaborate events. Eight circumcision rituals have been described to me. The methods of dating each Bukut are cited in the appropriate footnote. Dates are for Kadjinol's Bukuts. Other township Bukuts would lag four to ten years behind Kadjinol and do not include Cata Seleki. Kadjinol gave Bukut to the other townships.

Waite	1990
Batchakuale	1948, Hassouka; 1952, Kalybillah[6]
Djambia	1923[7]
Badusu	1900[8]
Batingalite	1875
Soiybac	1850[9]
Bagungup	1830[10]
Ane Ebané	1810
Cata Seleki	1790

"Cata Seleki" refers to the introduction of Bukut into Esulalu from the Diola-Bandial township of Seleki. Elders from Seleki conducted this initiation of Kadjinol males and then initiated a Bukut priesthood at Kadjinol.[11] From this list one can obtain an approximate date for the introduction of the Bukut form of circumcision into Esulalu of 1790. Because the dates of all the circumcision rituals before 1900 are approximations, the earliest Bukut circumcision could have been slightly earlier or later. The translation of a Diola relative chronology into a Western absolute form cannot be done exactly, even with the aid of outside observations of more recent rituals. I have to add a qualification to this date, that it could vary by as much as twenty years in either direction.

The time of the introduction of the Bukut form of circumcusion and the replacement of the Kahat form marks a major event in the history of Esulalu. A number of other shrines are said to be either older or younger than Bukut. Thus the shrines associated with the priest-king, the town council shrine of Hutendookai, the healing shrine of Bruinkaw, the blacksmith shrine of Silapoom, and even the newer forms of Hupila that are linked to the slave trade are said to be older than Bukut. The powerful blacksmith shrines of Gilaite and Duhagne and the women's fertility shrine of Ehugna are all said to have been introduced after the establishment of Bukut, though before the living memory of any of my informants.

Using the introduction of Bukut as a major milestone in Esulalu history, I could then establish more specific categories within the way Esulalu periodize their

history. In chapter 1, I described three categories of Diola history: a time of the
first ancestors, beyond the reach of genealogical reckoning; the time of the ancestors, included within the genealogies; and the period lived through by at least some
of the elders within the community. The approximate date of the introduction of
Bukut and the use of that date to establish the age of various Diola spirit shrines
allow the historian to separate accounts of eighteenth-century history (pre-Bukut)
from descriptions of the nineteenth century (post-Bukut).

Within the nineteenth century, I can use the names of specific circumcision
rites to devise an approximate age of people who have introduced certain shrines
and thus to calculate an approximate date for their introduction. Take, for example,
the actions of Haieheck Djabune. I know from French records and from Esulalu
oral traditions that Haieheck signed a treaty with the French in 1860. He was circumcised in the Bukut called Bagungup. He would have had to have been of
elder status before signing such a treaty. He is also credited with the introduction
of Gilaite, which allows us to approximate the date of that introduction to a time
when Haieheck had already achieved elder status. Given that he was initiated about
1830, he probably would not have been in a position to introduce such a powerful shrine before 1850. He probably would have been too old to have introduced
it later than 1870. Thus, I concluded that Haieheck brought the Gilaite cult to
Kadjinol in the midnineteenth century, more precisely between 1850 and 1870.[12]

Dating events that occurred during the eighteenth century is more difficult.
There are no named circumcision rituals to provide chronological markers, only
the indication that such an event occurred before the adoption of Bukut. For this
period I was forced to rely on genealogies and the nature of the changes that were
described during the eighteenth century. Again I turn to the Kumbogy lineage of
Haieheck Djabune.

Heohow
Djimindene
Kamayen (Cata Seleki)
Abindeck (Ane Ebané)
Haieheck (Bagungup)
Kulimpodia (Soiybac)
Kunone (Batingalite)
Antoine (Djambia, though his brothers were Badusu)
Pierre (a Christian, he would have been Batchakuale)

Note that there are two generations with no Bukut circumcision. Thus Djimindene
had to have been an adult, already initiated at Kahat and a father, before the introduction of Bukut. Thus he was probably born between 1740 and 1760. According
to this genealogy his father, Heohow, could have been born as recently as 1730.

The acceptance of a 1730 birthdate for Heohow, however, creates serious problems in explaining the incorporation of the Koonjaen into the Esulalu communities. Using a 1730 birthdate for Heohow, the Koonjaen could not have been
conquered before 1745, since Heohow was a participant in that war. This dating
would allow a period of only forty-five years for the Koonjaen to be assimilated

sufficiently to accept their form of circumcision, Kahat; to use this form of circumcision for a sufficient period for its rituals to be considered vital for the blessing of a newer circumcision form, Bukut; and the abandonment of Kahat in favor of Bukut.

To explain the persistence of these Kahat rituals as essential preliminaries in the present Bukut, as well as the centrality of the circumcision rite transition in Esulalu oral traditions, it had to have persisted for more than one generation, that of Djimindene Djabune. Using a conservative estimate of three generations undergoing Kahat initiations and twenty years between generations, I would place the birth of Heohow at about 1680 and the Koonjaen war in which he fought, at about 1700. This dating would allow for a minimal amount of time to explain the importance of Kahat in Esulalu society.[13] In the streamlining of oral traditions, it is quite common for some generations to be forgotten, though it is rare to forget the name of a person such as Heohow, who was seen as the founder of his lineage. Jan Vansina has recognized this problem in genealogical chronology: "Ancestors who are not founders of lineages are omitted because they are of no importance in explaining the relations obtaining between the various existing social groups, and although this occurs most commonly with distant ancestors, it can occur anywhere in the genealogy."[14] This would be particularly true in recalling those generations for whom the mnemonic assistance of named circumcision rituals were not available. I would suggest that a minimum of two generations have been forgotten.

Working from the date of the introduction of Bukut, I could project back the introduction of Kahat by the Koonjaen and establish an approximate date for the conquest of the Koonjaen, an event which is said to have occurred at the time of the first ancestors recorded in most Esulalu genealogies. From this analysis of circumcision, genealogies, and a sense of how changes in initiation may have taken place, I established an approximate date of 1700 for the beginning of what Diola-Esulalu traditions refer to as the time of the ancestors. This period, roughly from 1700 to 1880, is the subject of this study.

While Diola-Esulalu oral traditions stress relative chronologies, there is a certain amount of quantifiable material within circumcision lists and genealogies. Circumcision rituals of the Bukut type are held once every twenty years, but those observed by outsiders were often held less freqently. Genealogies, which often include information in circumcision rituals, not only provide chronologies in marking generations within a family, but also, through their particular circumcision rites, situate them within relative chronologies for the entire community. Genealogies and initiation lists, accompanied by some written descriptions of circumcision rituals that were dated in Western forms of absolute chronology, allow the historian to move from the relative chronologies of Diola-Esulalu oral tradition to approximate dates within the historian's concept of absolute chronology.

Notes

Introduction

1. I use the term *traditional religion* to indicate a religion that was developed by a particular people that is closely associated with their sense of ethnic identity. By using this term, I do not embrace the contrast of "traditional" versus "modern" religion or an ahistorical vision of traditional societies. On the contrary, following the important work of the Rudolphs on South Asia, I see mechanisms for change as integral to any "traditional" religion. Lloyd I. Rudolph and Susanne H. Rudolph, *The Modernity of Tradition: Political Development in India*, Chicago: University of Chicago Press, 1967. For a description of the traditional-versus-modern dichotomy in religious studies, see John Skorupski, *Symbol and Theory: A Philosophical Study of Theories of Religion in Social Anthropology*, Cambridge: Cambridge University Press, 1983, pp. 1–2.

2. This number is somewhat higher than estimates by other scholars who suggest a total Diola population between 250,000 and 350,000. The 1988 census claims that there are 357,666 Diola in Senegal alone. This number does not include the approximately 65,000 Diola in the Gambia or the approximately 16,000 Diola in Guinea-Bissau. Adding in population growth since the 1970s for Gambia and Guinea-Bissau and for Senegal since 1988, one reaches a number of approximately 500,000. More general evaluations of the Diola population of Senegal suggest that it is 9 percent of a total population of 7,740,000 (1990 estimate). Thus, a figure of 500,000 remains a conservative one. Jean N'Dong, *Memento des Resultats definitifs du recensement general de la population et de l'habitat du Senegal/ 1988*, Dakar: Bureau d'Etudes et de Recherches Documentaires Sur le Sénégal, 1992, p. 5. Central Statistics Department, Ministry of Economic Planning and Industrial Development, *Population and Housing Census 1983: General Report Volume I*, Banjul, The Gambia, 1987, p. 115. Departamente Central de Recensemento, *Recensemento Geral da populaçaô e da habitaçaô, 1979*, Bissau, 1981, p. 130. *The World Almanac and Book of Facts, 1991*, New York: Pharos Books, 1990, p. 397, 401, 748.

3. Peter Mark, "Urban Migration, Cash-Cropping, and Calamity: The Spread of Islam among the Diola of Boulouf (Senegal), 1900–1940," *The African Studies Review*, 1978, vol. 21, pp. 1–12; and *A Cultural, Economic, and Religious History of the Basse Casamance since 1500*, Stuttgart: Franz Steiner Verlag, 1985, pp. 93–115.

4. For a discussion of southern Diola religious change during the colonial era, see Robert M. Baum, "The Emergence of a Diola Christianity," *Africa*, 1990, vol. 60, pp. 370–398.

5. Precolonial religion of northern Diola communities has not been adequately studied, but it appears that many of their most powerful shrines come from the south. The lack of evidence of precolonial northern Diola religious traditions stems from the fact that most historical and ethnographic studies in the area were conducted after a majority of the populace had embraced Christianity or Islam. Chapters 3, 4, and 7 discuss Esulalu shrines associated with priest-kingship that were introduced into the northern area of Bliss-Karones. Mark, *Cultural*, pp. 77–81.

6. For a discussion of the importance of life experience in the construction of systems of meaning, see Alfred Schutz, *The Phenomenology of the Social World*, Evanston, Ill.: Northwestern University Press, 1967, pp. 78–86.

Chapter 1

1. John Mbiti, *African Religions and Philosophy*, Oxford: Heinemann, 1990, pp. 4, 211.

2. Jean Girard, *Genèse du Pouvoir Charismatique en Basse Casamance (Sénégal)*, Dakar: IFAN, 1969, p. 19 and passim.

3. V. Y. Mudimbe, *The Invention of Africa: Gnosis, Philosophy, and the Order of Knowledge*, Bloomington: Indiana University Press, 1988, p. 70.

4. I am indebted to Eric Wolf for the term "people without history." See his *Europe and the People without History*, Berkeley: University of California Press, 1982. G. W. F. Hegel, *The Philosophy of History*, New York: Dover, 1956, pp. 91, 93, 99.

5. Charles Long, *Significations: Signs, Symbols, and Images in the Interpretation of Religion*, Philadelphia, Fortress Press, 1986, p. 91. Mudimbe, *Invention*, pp. 30–32. Robert M. Baum, "Graven Images: Scholarly Representations of African Religions," *Religion*, 1990, vol. 20, passim; Robert M. Baum, "The Myth of Ahistorical African Traditional Religions," forthcoming.

6. Mudimbe, *Invention*, p. 177. See, for example, Jan Vansina, *Oral History: A Study in Historical Methodology*, Harmondsworth: Penguin, 1973. Wyatt MacGaffey would attribute a similar importance to the use of oral traditions by Vansina and an increasing number of Africanist historians in the past thirty years. See Wyatt MacGaffey, "African History, Anthropology and the Rationality of Natives," *History in Africa*, 1978, vol. 5, p. 103 and passim.

7. Eliade's *Patterns in Comparative Religion* (New York: New American Library, 1974 [1958]) is full of examples from the Americas, Australasia, Siberia, and, to a lesser extent, Africa, but his three-volume *History of Religious Ideas* (Chicago: University of Chicago Press, 1978–1986) barely mentions these areas.

8. E. E. Evans-Pritchard's work on the Nuer was an early influence in the development of this historical approach. E. E. Evans-Pritchard, *Nuer Religion*, Oxford: Oxford University Press, 1974 (1956). Terence Ranger and I. Kimambo, eds., *The Historical Study of African Religion*, Berkeley: University of California Press, 1972. Robin Horton, "A Hundred Years of Change in Kalabari Religion" in John Middleton, ed., *Black Africa: Its Peoples and Their Cultures Today*, New York: Macmillan, 1970. Iris Berger, *Religion and Resistance: East African Kingdoms in the Pre-Colonial Period*, Tervuren: Musée Royal de l'Afrique Central, Annales, 1981. W. M. J. van Binsbergen, *Religious Change in Zambia: Exploratory Studies*, London: Kegan Paul, 1981.

9. The annual Satterthwaite Colloquium on African Religion and Ritual, organized by the anthropologist Richard Werbner, is an important example of the new understanding of African religions that can be derived from sharing the insights of anthropological, historical, and literary approaches to the study of African re-

ligions. This work has benefited by the rich discussions that I participated in during those colloquia in 1989 and 1991. Representative of these more historical studies by anthropologists include Richard Werbner, editor, *Regional Cults*, London: Academic Press, 1977. J. M. Schoffeleers, "The History and Political Role of the M'bona Cult among the Mang'anja," in Ranger and Kimambo, *Historical*, pp. 73–94. Roy Willis, *A State in the Making: Myth, History, and Social Transformation in Pre-Colonial Ufipa*, Bloomington: Indiana University Press, 1981. For a discussion of the growing importance of historical approaches in anthropology, see George E. Marcus and Michael M. J. Fischer, *Anthropology as Cultural Critique: An Experimental Moment in the Social Sciences*, Chicago: University of Chicago Press, 1986, pp. 34–39 and 95–108. Jonathan D. Hill, ed., *Rethinking History and Myth: Indigenous South American Perspectives on the Past*, Urbana: University of Illinois Press, 1988.

10. Geoffrey Parrinder, *West African Religion*, New York: Barnes and Noble, 1970 (1961), p. 8. Robin Horton and D. J. E. Maier have conducted research on precolonial religious history in coastal areas of southeastern Nigeria and the Gold Coast. See Horton, "Kalabari Religion," and D. J. E. Maier, *Priests and Power: The Case of the Dente Shrine in Nineteenth Century Ghana*, Bloomington: Indiana University Press, 1983.

11. Jack Goody, *The Logic of Writing and the Organization of Society*, Cambridge: Cambridge University Press, 1986, pp. 7–8.

12. Michel Foucault, *The Archaeology of Knowledge and the Discourse of Language*, New York: Harper and Row, 1972, pp. 4–6, 9. Fredrik Barth, *Cosmologies in the Making: A Generative Approach to Cultural Variation in Inner New Guinea*, Cambridge: Cambridge University Press, 1987, pp. 6, 20, 27, 45.

13. For a critical discussion of the secondary works on the Diola and on southern Senegal, see Robert M. Baum, "A Religious and Social History of the Diola-Esulalu in Pre-Colonial Senegambia," Ph.D. diss., Yale University, New Haven, 1986, pp. 12–15.

14. The Holy Ghost Fathers began work in the Casamance region of Senegal in the 1850s but did not establish a mission in Diola areas until 1880. Nevertheless, they were frequent visitors to the French administrative center of Carabane and occasional visitors to Diola communities. Portions of their letters and reports were published in *Bulletin de la Congrégation de Saint Esprit*, Paris.

15. Jan Vansina, *Oral Tradition as History*, Madison: University of Wisconsin Press, 1985, p. 3. David Henige offers a narrower definition of oral traditions as "those recollections of the past that are commonly or universally known in a given culture," which limits oral traditions to the public recitations of hegemonic groups, excluding less powerful ethnic, class, or women's traditions. It would not include the work of historians like Mamadou Diawara, who has done important work on the oral traditions of Malian slave women. David Henige, *Oral Historiography*, London: Longman, 1982, p. 2. Mamadou Diawara, "Women, Servitude, and History: The Oral Historical Traditions of Women of Servile Condition in the Kingdom of Jaara (Mali) from the Fifteenth to the Mid-Nineteenth Century," in Karin Barber and P. F. de Moraes-Farias, *Discourse and Its Disguises: The Interpretation of African Oral Texts*, Birmingham: Centre for West African Studies, University of Birmingham, England, 1989, pp. 109–137.

16. Fixed oral traditions are performed by a specialized group of oral historians, who emphasize carefully defined narrative forms and exact replication of certain passages of the narrative in their performances. Vansina, *Oral History*, pp. 22–23.

17. Recent studies of civil religion would suggest that the "mythic" representation of the past is by no means limited to oral cultures. Jack Goody, *The Domestication of the Savage Mind*, Cambridge: Cambridge University Press, 1986 (1977), p. 27. On mythic representations of the past in literate societies, see Leonard M.

Thompson, *The Political Mythology of Apartheid*, New Haven: Yale University Press, 1986, pp. 144–188. Frederick Merk, *Manifest Destiny and Mission in American History*, New York: Random House, 1963, pp. 124, 158.

18. Goody, *Domestication*, p. 14. See also Walter Ong, *Orality and Literacy: The Technologizing of the Word*, London: Metheun, 1982, p. 46.

19. Jan Vansina, *The Children of Woot: A History of the Kuba Peoples*, Madison: University of Wisconsin Press, 1978, p. 197. He reiterates that position in "History of God among the Kuba," *Africa*, 1983, vol. 28, p. 17.

20. Jan Vansina, "Oral Tradition and Its Methodology," in J. Ki-Zerbo, ed., *Unesco General History of Africa, vol. 1, Methodology and Prehistory*, Berkeley: University of California Press, 1981, pp. 152–153.

21. Wyatt MacGaffey, "Oral Tradition in Central Africa," *Journal of African Historical Studies*, 1975, vol. 7, p. 417.

22. Steven Feierman, *Shambaa Kingdom*, Madison: University of Wisconsin Press, 1974, p. 4. See also Joseph Miller, ed., *The African Past Speaks: Essays on Oral Tradition and History*, Folkestone: Wm. Dawson, 1980. Vansina, *Oral Tradition as History*, passim. The Miller anthology is a collection of essays by oral historians that are focused precisely on this problem. One of the major differences between Vansina's 1985 work and his earlier *Oral Tradition* is the emphasis on the social and cosmological contexts for such oral traditions.

23. T. O. Beidelman, "Myth, Legend, and Oral History: A Kaguru Traditional Text," *Anthropos*, 1970, vol. 65, p. 95.

24. While there are hints of social change involving the incorporation of diverse groups into Kaguru and an attempt to address this problem in the oral traditions, Beidelman will not acknowledge that the metaphors that are so pervasive in Kaguru oral traditions may be ways of interpreting historical changes. The presentation of Kaguru thought, throughout the monograph, fails to employ any diachronic analysis. T. O. Beidelman, *Moral Imagination in Kaguru Modes of Thought*, Bloomington: Indiana University Press, 1986, pp. 72, 82.

25. Robert Harms, "Oral Tradition and Ethnicity," *Journal of Interdisciplinary History*, 1979, vol. 10, p. 66.

26. Randall M. Packard, "The Study of Historical Process in African Traditions of Genesis: The Bashu Myth of Muhiyi," in Miller, ed., *The African Past Speaks*, p. 174.

27. Vansina, *Oral Tradition as History*, p. 107.

28. Scholars who work with hand-copied manuscripts confront a similar problem: Original texts are altered by additions, deletions, or errors of transcription. In many cases, these copies are all that remain. At this point, the similarities of written and oral texts may outweigh their differences. Marilyn Waldman pointed out the difficulties of working with written traditions in which manuscripts are the primary sources.

29. Vansina, *Oral Tradition as History*, p. 29. Harms, "Oral," p. 67.

30. It should be added, however, that the different texts on a medieval parchment need not have any relation to one another. They are more likely to have some relation within an oral tradition. Jan Vansina, "Comment: Traditions of Genesis," *Journal of African History*, 1974, vol. 15, p. 320.

31. For a discussion of the problem of chronology, see the Appendix.

32. Louis Vincent Thomas, *Les Diola: Essai d'Analyse fonctionelle sur une population de Basse Casamance*, Dakar: IFAN, 1959, p. 489.

33. There is a parallel here between levels of historical teaching and levels of ritual instruction in other cultures. Barth's important study of the seven stages of Baktaman initiation in highland New Guinea reveals a process of unfolding new levels of "truth" at higher stages of initiation that contradict earlier levels of "truth," as initiates mature. Fredrik Barth, *Ritual and Knowledge among the Baktaman of New Guinea*, New Haven: Yale University Press, 1975, pp. 81, 234,

and passim. This idea of higher truths is particularly pronounced in Vajayrana Buddhism.

34. Vansina, *Oral Tradition*, p. xiv.

35. At least in contemporary Esulalu, Diola specialists in religious and historical knowledge have not restricted their sources to the elders of their own compound but consulted the elders from several compounds, quarters, and townships. For example, it is difficult to talk about a Kumbogy or Kalainou tradition within Kadjinol's quarter of Kafone. It is more than likely that a Kalainou elder also heard traditions of the Kumbogy compound and drew on both in his or her teachings. There are traditions associated with particular spirit shrines, however.

36. There seem to be parallels between this type of instruction and the experience of Paul Stoller, particularly the emphasis on hearing, seeing, and asking only "appropriate" questions. Paul Stoller and Cheryl Olkes, *In Sorcery's Shadow: A Memoir of Apprenticeship among the Songhay of Niger*, Chicago: University of Chicago Press, 1987, p. 37.

37. Anthony Giddens, *The Constitution of Society: Outline of a Theory of Structuration*, Berkeley: University of California Press, 1984, p. 281. For a critique of structural anthropology's marginalization of indigenous exegesis, see Pierre Bourdieu, *In Other Words: Essays towards a Reflexive Sociology*, Stanford, Calif.: Stanford University Press, 1991, p. 20.

38. Interview with Sikakucele Diatta, Kadjinol-Kafone, 9/24/74.

39. Interview with Sihumucel Badji, Kadjinol-Hassouka, 3/5/75.

40. Vansina, *Oral Tradition as History*, pp. 135 and 111–112. See also Bennetta Jules-Rossette, *African Apostles: Ritual and Conversion in the Church of John Maranke*, Ithaca, N.Y.: Cornell University Press, 1975.

41. Paul Rabinow, *Reflections on Fieldwork in Morocco*, Berkeley: University of California Press, 1977, p. 79.

42. Ibid. p. 80. For a discussion of my fieldwork techniques, which sought to minimize the distance between researcher and community, see the final section of this chapter.

43. Ibid., pp. 38–39.

44. Fernand Braudel's focus on the longue durée, of structures of history that change so slowly over time that they are difficult to describe in a chronological narrative, is one example of this type of projection. I differ from Braudel in the sense that I do not see these structures as constraining history but as elements of an overall historical framework whose subtle changes are difficult to describe. Thus, the projection back of elements that have a high degree of continuity becomes a means of establishing connections between the often fragmentary evidence of the past. F. Braudel, "History and the Social Sciences: The Longue Durée," in F. Braudel, *On History*, tr. Sarah Matthews, Chicago: University of Chicago Press, 1980, pp. 27–33.

45. Interview with Siliungimagne Diatta, Kadjinol-Kandianka, 3/2/75.

46. Louis Vincent Thomas, "Brève Esquisse sur la Pensée Cosmologique du Diola," in Meyer Fortes and Germaine Dieterlen, eds., *African Systems of Thought*, London: Oxford University Press, 1965, pp. 367–368.

47. Hoyt Alverson, *Mind in the Heart of Darkness: Value and Self-Identity among the Tswana of Southern Africa*, New Haven: Yale University Press, 1978, p. 110. See also E. E. Evans-Pritchard, *Social Anthropology and Other Essays*, New York: Free Press, 1962, p. 79.

48. Evans-Pritchard, *Nuer Religion*, p. v.

Chapter 2

1. Baum, "Emergence." Girard, *Genèse*. Marilyn R. Waldman with Robert M. Baum, "Innovation as Renovation: The 'Prophet' as an Agent of Change," in Michael

A. Williams and Martin S. Jaffee, eds., *Innovation in Religious Traditions*, Berlin: Mouton de Gruyter, 1992, pp. 241–284.

2. Feierman, *Shambaa Kingdom*, p. 4.

3. Braudel, "History," pp. 27–33. Stuart Clark, "The *Annales* Historians," in Quentin Skinner, ed., *The Return of Grand Theory in the Human Sciences*, Cambridge: Cambridge University Press, 1987, pp. 182–185.

4. These are personal estimates checked against the Archives de Sous-Préfecture de Loudia-Ouoloff 1972 census materials, which overlook the large number of migrant workers who spend a substantial part of the year in other areas of Senegambia.

5. The neighboring Manjaco of Guinea-Bissau, whose system of priest-kings and concept of township (*usok*) are related to that of the Diola, also see spirit shrines as central to the idea of township unity. The anthropologist Eve Crowley gives added emphasis to the role of spirit shrines when she translates the Manjaco term *usok* as "spirit province." Eve Crowley, "Contracts with the Spirits: Religion, Asylum, and Ethnic Identity in the Cacheu Region of Guinea-Bissau," Ph.D. diss., Yale University, New Haven, 1990, p. 215. The origins and role of the oeyi and Hutendookai are discussed in chapters 3 and 4.

6. The Baimoon quarter is often confused with Hassouka as a whole. Colonial officials identified the quarter chief of Baimoon as the chief of Hassouka and appointed a separate chief for Kandianka. Contemporary usage has shifted as a result, and people of Baimoon identify themselves as from Hassouka. In identifying informants I have followed this new practice.

7. This high-density settlement pattern was common to most Diola; the Kujaamaat or Fogny were exceptions. Paul Pélissier, "Les Diola: Etude sur l'habitat des riz cultures de Basse Casamance," Travaux du Département de Géographie, Université de Dakar, 1958, passim.

8. Interview with Sikakucele Diatta, Kadjinol-Kafone, 3/17/78.

9. Paul Pélissier, *Les Paysans du Sénégal: Les Civilisations agraires du Cayor à la Casamance*, Saint Yrieix: Imprimerie Fabrègue, 1966, p. 709.

10. Francis Snyder, "L'Evolution du Droit Foncier Diola de Basse Casamance (Republique du Sénégal)," Ph.D. diss., Sorbonne, Paris: 1973, p. 170.

11. Interview with Ramon Sambou, Kadjinol-Ebankine, 7/28/78.

12. The agronomist Roland Portères claims that the lower Casamance was one of the first places where African rice (*oryza glaberrima*) was domesticated. R. Portères, "Berceaux Agricoles sur le Continent Africain," *Journal of African History*, 1962, vol. 3, pp. 189–201. R. Portères and J. Barrau, "Origins, Development and Expansion of Agricultural Techniques," in J. Ki-Zerbo, ed., *UNESCO General History of Africa*, vol. 1. *Methodology and African Prehistory*, Paris: UNESCO, 1981, pp. 694–698. Olga Linares de Sapir, "Shell Middens of the Lower Casamance and Problems of Diola Protohistory," *West African Journal of Archaeology*, 1971, vol. 1, pp. 32–43. Pélissier, *Paysans*, p. 823. Yasmine Marzouk-Schmitz, "Instruments Aratoires, Systèmes de Culture et Différenciation Intra-Ethnique," *Cahiers Orstrom*, Série Sciences Humaines, 1984, vol. 20, p. 404.

13. Pélissier, "Les Diola," p. 7. See also Olga Linares, "Intensive Agriculture and Diffuse Authority among the Diola of West Africa," unpublished manuscript, 1979; Marzouk-Schmitz, "Instruments," passim.

14. T. Monod, A. Teixeira da Mota, and R. Mauny, eds., *Déscription de la Côte Occidentale d'Afrique (Sénégal au Cap de Monte Archipels) par Valentim Fernandes (1506–1510)*, Bissau: Centro de Estudos da Guiné Portuguesa, 1951, pp. 61–69. André Alvares de Almada, *Relação e Descrição de Guiné na Qual se trata da varia noçens de negros, que a povação*, Lisbon: Miguel Rodriques, 1733, p. 24.

15. Marzouk-Schmitz described an attempt by a European development group (ILACO) to find a faster way of converting mangrove swamps into rice paddies. They built a series of dikes near the village of Tobor and drained the saltwater

Notes to Pages 29–31 197

away but did not allow several years of fresh rainwater to cleanse the fields of their salt. The cleared land became hard laterite surfaces that were useless for agriculture. See Marzouk-Schmitz, "Instruments," p. 412.

16. Olga Linares, "From Tidal Swamp to Inland Valley: On the Social Organization of Wet Rice Cultivation among the Diola of Senegal," *Africa*, 1981, vol. 51, pp. 560, 573. Pélissier, *Paysans*, pp. 722–729. Marc Schloss, *The Hatchet's Blood: Separation and Gender in Ehing Social Life*, Tucson: University of Arizona Press, 1988, p. 116.

17. On individual paddy ownership in Esulalu, see Olga Linares, *Power, Prayer, and Production: The Jola of Casamance, Senegal*, Cambridge: Cambridge University Press, 1992, p. 15. Matrilineal inheritance of rice paddies in Esulalu represents an influence from the neighboring communities of Bandial and Seleki, where substantial numbers of rice paddies are controlled by women. Francis Snyder, *Capitalism and Legal Change: An African Transformation*, New York: Academic Press, 1981, pp. 68–76. The ransoming of captives is discussed in chapter 5.

18. Rural migration to the cities and to palm wine harvesting areas has curtailed work on the dams and dikes of Esulalu. Along with the droughts of the past thirty years, it has led to a virtual moratorium on the extension of arable land into new areas of marshland. Among Mandinguized Diola, the growth of peanut production, which men control, has led them to abandon most of the "male" tasks associated with rice farming. Women's work in rice cultivation had to be extended to the preparation of the paddies for planting, leaving little extra time for the preparation of new dikes. See Marzouk-Schmitz, "Instruments," p. 417. Linares, *Power*, pp. 180, 187; for a detailed description of Diola rice farming, see pp. 15–23.

19. It was considered cruel to subject cattle to work in flooded rice paddies, and it was considered morally wrong to use a domestic animal, which was being raised for food, to labor in the procurement of other foods for its owner. Marzouk-Schmitz suggests that the Diola will not use cattle to plow because it would result in a withholding of rain, presumably by the supreme being, Emitai. Marzouk-Schmitz, "Instruments," p. 406.

20. Linares, "Intensive Agriculture," p. 8. Thomas, *Diola*, p. 44. For a detailed study of the various types of cadyendo, see Marzouk-Schmitz, "Instruments," passim.

21. Northern Diola would have smaller yields per hectare because of the lower amounts of rainfall in the north. Olga Linares de Sapir, "Agriculture and Diola Society," in F. M. McLoughlin, ed., *African Food Production Systems: Cases and Theory*, Baltimore: Johns Hopkins University Press, 1970, p. 211. Linares, "Intensive," p. 10. Linares's estimate is too low. Thomas estimates that, during the rainy season, a man will eat as much as one kilo of rice per day. Thomas, *Diola*, p. 85. I think a closer estimate would be 180 kilos of rice per adult per year.

22. Interview with Siopama Diedhiou, Kadjinol-Kafone, 1/27/78.

23. Linares, "Intensive," p. 3.

24. Linares, "From Tidal," p. 565. Pélissier, *Paysans*, p. 726.

25. "Diola" rice, oryza glaberrima, is the rice that was first domesticated in West Africa, in the Niger, Gambia, and Casamance river valleys. Asian rice is referred to as European because it was introduced by the French and Portuguese. Portères, "Berceaux," pp. 189–201. Pélissier, *Paysans*, pp. 731, 736. Interview with Ramon Sambou, Kadjinol-Kafone, 7/28/76.

26. Interviews with Dionsal Diedhiou, Kadjinol-Kafone, 11/2/77; and Antoine Houmandrissah Diedhiou, Kadjinol-Kafone, 11/9/77.

27. Linares, "Intensive," p. 1.

28. Interviews with Antoine Houmandrissah Diedhiou, Kadjinol-Kafone, 11/9/77; Dionsal Diedhiou, Kadjinol-Kafone, 11/2/77. Linares, "From Tidal," pp. 567–568. Thomas, *Diola*, p. 29.

29. Manioc was introduced in the sixteenth century. People in Esulalu have

adopted Wolof terms for peanut, okra, bitter tomato, and sorghum. David P. Gamble, *The Wolof of Senegambia*, London: International African Institute, 1967, p. 29. On the spread of peanut production, see Linares, *Power*, pp. 98–101, 127–129. Peter Mark, "Urban Migration," passim.

30. Hutendookai's role in the settling of land disputes has been undermined by people seeking to use Senegalese land law where it suited them. There are strong social pressures against taking any land case to government authorities. Interviews with Terence Senghor, Kadjinol-Hassouka, 3/31/88; Simon Tidjane Bassin, Mlomp-Haer, 3/27/88; Sikakucele Diatta, Kadjinol-Kafone, 11/12/77. Pélissier, *Paysans*, p. 692.

31. Interview with Hilaire Djibune, Kagnout-Ebrouwaye, 10/28/78. Thomas, *Diola*, pp. 53–56, 75–76. Pélissier, *Paysans*, p. 770.

32. Pélissier, *Paysans*, p. 760.

33. Ibid., p. 761. Interviews with Anto Manga, Kadjinol-Ebankine, 7/2/75; Dionsal Diedhiou, Kadjinol-Kafone, 1/8/79.

34. Father Jean-Baptiste Labat, *Nouvelle Relation de l'Afrique Occidentale*, Paris: Théodore le Gras, 1728, pp. 43–44. While there is no clear evidence that the Diola smelted their own iron, there are bog iron deposits in the area. Linares de Sapir, "Shell Middens," passim. Oliver Davies, *West Africa before the Europeans: Archaeology and Prehistory*, London: Methuen, 1967, p. 25. Philip Curtin, *Economic Change in Pre-Colonial Africa: Senegambia in the Era of the Slave Trade*, Madison: University of Wisconsin Press, 1975, pp. 207, 210. Walter Rodney, *A History of the Upper Guinea Coast, 1545–1800*, Oxford: Clarendon, 1970, p. 184.

35. The Sambous of Kadjinol-Hassouka used to work with iron but gave it up in order to devote more time to fishing. They retain an important place among the group of elders of the blacksmith shrines. At Mlomp-Haer, a family with the name Sambou learned how to work with iron, so they changed their name to Diedhiou. Interview with Djilehl Sambou, Kadjinol-Hassouka, 4/28/78.

36. Only the Sambous who became Diedhious at Mlomp-Haer did not originate at Kadjinol. Interview with Kapooeh Diedhiou, Kadjinol-Kafone, 1/19/79.

37. Interview with Antoine Houmandrissah Diedhiou, Kadjinol-Kafone, 3/28/78. Thomas, *Diola*, p. 63. Peter Mark, "Economic and Religious Change among the Diola of Boulouf (Casamance), 1890–1940. Trade, Cash-Cropping, and Islam in Southwestern Senegal," Ph.D. diss., Yale University, New Haven, 1976, p. 41.

38. Recent droughts have eliminated the trade of livestock for rice. In the postcolonial era, the cash economy has seriously eroded the entire rice-based exchange system.

39. J. Z. Smith, *Imagining Religion: From Babylon to Jonestown*, Chicago: University of Chicago Press, 1982, p. xi. Marilyn Waldman also questions the use of the term "religion" because it "requires us to make an artificial separation between certain dimensions of human experience and others." M. Waldman, "Unity and Diversity in a Religious Tradition," in Carole Elchert, ed., *The White Lotus*, Ithaca, N.Y.: Snow Lion, 1990, p. 1.

40. Louis Brenner, "Religious Discourse in and About Africa," in Barber and Moraes Farias, eds., *Discourse and Its Disguises*, p. 87.

41. I am reminded of a debate I had with a colleague at Barnard College about on which side of the boundary we should put Freudian psychology. Winston King, "Religion," in Mircea Eliade, ed., *The Encyclopedia of Religion*, vol. 12, New York: Macmillan, 1987, p. 282.

42. In 1972 I observed several worship services at a Guilford, Connecticut, Assembly of God church, as part of an undergraduate course on "Myth, Ritual, and Social Structure."

43. Smith, *Imagining*, p. xi.

44. Kasa is a general term for southern Diola, including Esulalu. The dictionary includes some terms that have been given a Christian meaning. For example,

Wintz translates *ange* as *ahuka*, which is a term for "benevolent ancestor." Father Edouard Wintz, *Dictionnaire de Dyola-Kasa*, Paris: Pères du Saint-Esprit, 1909, pp. 94, 152.

45. John Mbiti, *African Religions* chapter 4. J. B. Danquah imposes a monotheistic image on Akan religious traditions, as does E. Bolaji Idowu for the Yoruba. J. B. Danquah, *The Akan Doctrine of God*, London: 1944. E. Bolaji Idowu, *Oludumare, God in Yoruba Belief*, London: Longman, 1962. For critiques of this approach, see Okot p'Bitek, *African Religions in Western Scholarship*, Kampala: East African Literature Bureau, 1970. Rosalind Shaw, "The Invention of African Traditional Religion," in *Religion*, vol. 20, 1990, pp. 339–353.

46. I use the genderless pronoun "It" for the supreme being because there are no gendered pronouns in West Atlantic languages and the Diola supreme being is not seen as male or female. Robin Horton, "African Conversion," *Africa*, vol. 41, 1971, p. 101.

47. He overemphasizes the localism of precolonial African life. Long-distance trade and multiethnic empires were common in many parts of Africa, from the high veldt of southern Africa to West Africa's Sudanic kingdoms. Ibid., p. 101. R. Horton, "On the Rationality of Conversion," *Africa*, vol. 45, 1975, p. 219. Turner's studies on Ndembu religion tend to support the image of a remote supreme being. Victor Turner, *The Ritual Process: Structure and Anti-Structure*, Chicago: Aldine, 1969. This is also true of Griaule's studies of Dogon religion. Marcel Griaule, *Conversations with Ogotemmeli*, London: Oxford, 1965.

48. This is based on observations of approximately twenty-five different types of spirit shrines.

49. J. David Sapir, "Kujaama: Symbolic Separation among the Diola-Fogny," *American Anthropologist*, vol. 72, 1970, p. 1331. It appears that Sapir did not pursue certain evidence pointing toward human contact with the supreme being. In a folktale that he analyzed, one of the versions begins with what he translates as "The man went away, saying, 'I'm going up into the sky.'" The original Diola, however, has the man saying "Panijaw bet emitey." While *emit* can mean "sky" or "year," *emitey* or *emitai* is a term for the supreme being. This folktale could refer to visions of the supreme being in which the soul is said to "go to Emitai." Esulalu oral traditions include several such accounts. J. D. Sapir, "The Fabricated Child," in J. D. Sapir and J. Christopher Crocker, eds., *The Social Use of Metaphor: Essays on the Anthropology of Rhetoric*, Philadelphia: University of Pennsylvania Press, 1977, pp. 196 and 222.

50. Mark, "Economic," p. 26. See also Abbé P. D. Boilat, *Esquisses Sénégalaises*, Paris: P. Bertrand, 1853, p. 431.

51. In his analysis of Lasnet's description of a Diola supreme being who "rewards good and evil," Mark assumes that this was an imposition of Christian ideas on the Diola rather than the translation of Diola ideas into a language dominated by a Christian religious tradition. Mark, *Cultural*, pp. 84–85.

52. "Dictionnaire des Langues Françoise et nègres dont on se sert dans la concession de la Compagnie Royale du Sénégal Scavoir Guilof, Foule, Mandingue, Saracolé, Séraire, Bagnon, Floupe, Papel, Bisagots, Nalous et Sapi." Fonds Orientaux, Fonds Africain, #6, Bibliothèque Nationale. There was no date for this manuscript, but the Compagnie Royale du Sénégal was active only in the late seventeenth century. Félix Brigaud, *Histoire Moderne et Contemporaine du Sénégal*, Saint-Louis du Sénégal: C.R.D.S., 1966, p. 6. K. G. Davies, *The Royal African Company*, New York: Atheneum, 1970, pp. 19–20. There was no word listed for "rain" (*pluie*) in the vocabulary list. This may well indicate that traders preferred to frequent the Diola (called Floupe) areas during the long dry season rather than risk the violent storms of the rainy season from May to October.

53. Emmanuel Bertrand-Bocandé, "Carabane et Sedhiou," *Revue Maritime et Coloniale*, vol. 16, 1856, p. 416.

54. Thomas, *Diola*, p. 588. On other aspects of creation, see interview with Indrissa Diedhiou, Kadjinol-Kafone, 11/17/74. Father Henri Joffroy, "Les Coutumes des Diola du Fogny (Casamance)," *Bulletin du Comité d'Etudes Historiques et Scientifiques de l'A.O.F.*, 1920, p. 102.

55. Interviews with Indrissa Diedhiou, Kadjinol-Kafone, 10/17/74; Siopama Diedhiou, Kadjinol-Kafone, 11/21/77 and 8/15/78; Diashwah Sambou, Kadjinol-Kafone, 10/21/78; Sinyendikaw Diedhiou, Kadjinol-Kafone, 4/2/78.

56. Interview with Attabadionti Diatta, Kadjinol-Sergerh, 5/8/78. Interview with Sikakucele Diatta, Kadjinol-Kafone, 4/20/75. Joffroy "Coutumes," p. 182.

57. Thomas, *Diola*, pp. 418 and 588.

58. Interviews with Kemehow Diedhiou, Eloudia, 11/20/78; Djiremo Sambou, Kadjinol-Ebankine, 4/9/78; Terence Galandiou Diouf Sambou, Kadjinol-Ebankine, 3/30/78; Siopama Diedhiou, Kadjinol-Kafone, 2/16/78.

59. These include Alinesitoué in the early 1940s, Agnawlen Diatta of Emaye in the 1960s, and Todjai of Djivent, who began actively teaching in 1987. The history of the Diola prophetic tradition, perhaps the richest indigenous tradition of divine revelation in all of Africa, will be the subject of my next book.

60. Atta-Essou was from the Koonjaen ethnic group, a people who were conquered by the Diola by the end of the seventeenth century. Many of their traditions were incorporated into what we now know as Esulalu religion. All accounts of revelations from Emitai that are attributed to a period before 1700 are associated with Koonjaen lineages. Atta-Essou is seen as the founder of all the Gent (priest-king) lineages. See chapters 3 and 4.

61. Interview with Ansamana Manga, Kadjinol-Ebankine, 7/9/96; Michel Djigoon Senghor, Kadjinol-Kandianka, 9/10/96; Indrissa Diedhiou, Kadjinol-Kafone, 7/10/96 and 7/7/97; Ohooliyoh Bassin, Kadjinol-Ebankine, 7/10/97. Group discussions with Ansamana Manga and Pauline Manga, Kadjinol-Ebankine, 7/27/97; Augustin Aoutah, Kagnout-Eyehow, and Francois Buloti Diatta, Kadjinol-Kafone, 9/20/96. Ansamana is the priest of Aberman.

62. It was at this time that Emitai gave Kooliny the spirit shrine, Cabai, to help his quarter in a war against another quarter of Kadjinol. See chapter 4.

63. Interviews with Rosine Rohaya Diatta, Kolobone, 5/25/96 and 7/11/97. Group discussion with Attebah Diedhiou and Koolioominyan Djabune, Oussouye, 7/1/97.

64. Interviews with Sambouway Assin, Kagnout-Bruhinban, 1/8/79, and Hilaire Djibune, Kagnout-Ebrouwaye, 12/17/78. There are other accounts for Kadjinol as well. Interview with Mungo Sambou, Kadjinol-Kafone, 5/22/78. The physical symptoms associated with these visions, an appearance of death for several days, could well be associated with African sleeping sickness. The beginning of these descriptions of visions from Emitai are quite similar to the beginning of the folk tale that is analyzed by Sapir in "The Fabricated Child." In each case, the individual goes up to "Emitai." Sapir, "Fabricated," p. 196.

65. Interview with Siopama Diedhiou, Kadjinol-Kafone, 5/21/78. Interviews with Djilehl Sambou, Kadjinol-Hassouka, 12/27/78; Paponah Diatta, Mlomp-Etebemaye, 12/27/78; Kemehow Diedhiou, Eloudia, 11/20/78.

66. I use the term *witch* in its anthropological sense to designate a type of person who uses spiritual means to attack other people. Except for the fact that anthropologists used a term that misrepresented pre-Christian, Celtic religion to designate nefarious powers cross-culturally, I am not suggesting any linkage between African witchcraft and neo-pagan or feminist witchcraft. Interview with Siliungimagne Diatta, Kadjinol-Kandianka, 11/8/78.

67. Interviews with Siopama Diedhiou, Kadjinol-Kafone, 4/19/78; Sikakucele Diatta, Kadjinol-Kafone, 11/7/78. For a discussion of similar opponents of witches in Italy, see Carlo Ginzburg, *The Night Battles: Witchcraft and Agrarian Cults in*

the Sixteenth and Seventeenth Centuries, Baltimore: Johns Hopkins University Press, 1983.

68. This is discussed in greater detail toward the end of this chapter. Interview with Paponah Diatta, Mlomp-Etebemaye, 4/27/78.

69. Thomas, *Diola*, pp. 534–535. Interview with Sikakucele Diatta, Kadjinol-Kafone, 1/20/75.

70. Interview with Agnak Baben, Samatit, 12/6/78. Thomas, *Diola*, pp. 541–542, 617.

71. As I tell my students, the American practice of holding prayer sessions to win football games would be regarded as blasphemous by people in Esulalu. The idea of invoking the supreme being for such minor matters is a sign of an arrogance akin to the Greek idea of hubris.

72. Interviews with Paponah Diatta, Mlomp-Etebemaye, 3/21/78; Mungo Sambou, Kadjinol-Kafone, 5/22/78. Charles Albinet, "Moeurs et Coutumes des Diola," Mémoire de l'Ecole Nationale de la France d'Outre Mer, 1945–1946, p. 36.

73. Again one finds the association of Emitai, water, fertility, and life. Thomas, *Diola*, p. 189.

74. This prayer was collected by Thomas in Diembering. Its gendered reference to Emitai reflects French pronoun usage rather than the original Diola. Louis Vincent Thomas, Bertrand Luneau, et Jean Doneux, *Les Religions d'Afrique Noire: Textes et Traditions Sacrée*, Paris: Fayard/Deniel, 1969, pp. 48–49.

75. Interview with Paponah Diatta, Mlomp-Etebemaye, 4/11/78. Interview with Kapooeh Diedhiou, Kadjinol-Kafone, 8/8/87. Sapir, "Kujaama," p. 1331.

76. Such statements occasionally included mention of the ukine and Jesus as children of Emitai, but the ukine were seen as older and therefore senior to Jesus. For a discussion of the development of Diola apologetics, see Baum, "Emergence," passim.

77. Ibid., p. 605. Interviews with Badjaya Kila, Eloudia, 12/23,78; Edouard Kadjinga Diatta, Kadjinol-Kafone; Antoine Houmandrissah Diedhiou, Kadjinol-Kafone, 4/25/78; Boolai Senghor, Kadjinol-Sergerh, 6/18/78; Djiremo Sambou, Kadjinol-Ebankine, 4/9/78; Asambou Senghor, Kadjinol-Sergerh, 4/7/78.

78. Each of these different types of shrines could have multiple independent shrines. For shrines associated with the family, there could be as many as one per compound. For a list of Diola shrines throughout the Casamance, see Thomas, *Diola*, pp. 591–594.

79. Ibid, pp. 597–598.

80. Ibid., p. 683.

81. General greetings of a boekine taught to me by Econdo Sambou, Gnapoli Diedhiou, and Adiabaloung Diedhiou, Kadjinol-Kafone, 4/7/75.

82. Interview with Siopama Diedhiou, Kadjinol-Kafone, 8/15/78.

83. Interview with Siliungimagne Diatta, Kadjinol-Kandianka, 6/27/76. Thomas, *Diola*, p. 168.

84. Interview with Diashwah Sambou, Kadjinol-Kafone, 5/12/78.

85. Thomas, *Diola*, p. 671.

86. This was particularly stressed by Alinesitoué. Interviews with Alphonse Diedhiou, Kadjinol-Kafone, 9/10/74; Gnapoli Diedhiou, Kadjinol-Kafone, 10/30/74; Sikakucele Diatta, Kadjinol-Kafone, 7/16/76 and 6/28/76. Thomas, *Diola*, p. 153.

87. Prayer collected by Jean Girard, *Genèse*, p. 124. Interview with Ekum-sumben Diedhiou, Kadjinol-Kafone, 2/27/75. Thomas, *Diola*, p. 153.

88. Interview with Siopama Diedhiou, Kadjinol-Kafone, 5/19/78.

89. Interview with Kapooeh Diedhiou, Kadjinol-Kafone, 8/8/87.

90. Interviews with Sooti Diatta, Samatit, 12/21/78; Sihumucel Badji, Kadjinol-Hassouka, 5/11/78; Kapooeh Diedhiou, 8/8/87. Group discussion with Hoomahey Diatta and Econdo Sambou, Kadjinol-Kafone, 5/22/75.

91. This type of ammahl is very similar to the Kujamaatay "bagum" spirits and the Manjaco's nature spirits, which offer similar Faustian bargains in exchange for personal power. Thomas, *Diola*, pp. 613, 615–616. Crowley, "Contracts," pp. 333–337. Interviews with Kapooeh Diedhiou, Kadjinol-Kafone, 8/8/87; Antoine Houmandrissah Diedhiou, Kadjinol-Kafone, 12/19/78; Asambou Senghor, Kadjinol-Sergerh, 4/7/78.

92. Interview with Terence Galandiou Diouf Sambou, Kadjinol-Ebankine, 2/13/78. David Sapir claimed that the animal doubles (siwuum) of a particular family were also summoned to the Kouhouloung shrine. J. D. Sapir, "Fragments for a Paper on Kujamaat and Kasa *Siwuum*," unpublished manuscript.

93. Thomas, *Diola*, p. 292. Interview with Siopama Diedhiou, Kadjinol-Kafone, 7/16/78.

94. While this was quite similar to the arrangements between spirits and supplicants described by Crowley as "spirit contracts" among the Manjaco, people in Esulalu stressed their gratitude for spiritual assistance over any type of legal obligations, which would motivate a return ritual after the spirit has met their requests. Crowley, "Contracts," p. 4 and passim. Thomas, *Diola*, p. 290.

95. I witnessed this dialogue of accusation and denial and subsequent confession on several occasions during healing rites by women associated with the fertility shrine of Ehugna. See Thomas, *Diola*, p. 497. Some illnesses were not considered to have spiritual significance. There were Diola healers who relied on herbs, massage, and other medical practices without reference to spiritual causes of disease, though their medical knowledge was seen as a gift of Emitai.

96. Linares, "Intensive," p. 28.

97. Interviews with Siopama Diedhiou, Kadjinol-Kafone, 11/12/78; Terence Galandiou Diouf Sambou, Kadjinol-Ebankine, 2/19/78 and 5/19/78; Paponah Diatta, Mlomp-Etebemaye, 1978. Thomas, *Diola*, p. 496. These shrines were similar to what Turner calls shrines of affliction. Victor Turner, *The Forest of Symbols: Aspects of Ndembu Ritual*, Ithaca, N.Y.: Cornell University Press, 1967, passim.

98. One often heard that a particular shrine was more powerful in the past because its priest was a seer or that one should consult a different shrine because of the wisdom of its elders.

99. One such fertility shrine was abandoned at the turn of the century but was revived in 1978. Interviews with Siopama Diedhiou, Kadjinol-Kafone, 11/11/78; Terence Galandiou Diouf Sambou, Kadjinol-Ebankine, 11/17/78; Basayo Sambou, Kadjinol-Kandianka, 11/29/77; Paponah Diatta, Mlomp-Etebemaye, 12/27/78; Indrissa Diedhiou, Kadjinol-Kafone, 10/17/74. Robin Horton noted that the Kalabari of Nigeria also abandon unhelpful shrines. R. Horton, "A Hundred Years," p. 195.

100. Thomas, "Brève Esquisse," pp. 370–371. Thomas, *Diola*, pp. 164, 171, 537.

101. Thomas, *Diola*, p. 422.

102. Ibid., p. 549. See also Boilat, *Esquisses*, p. 431.

103. Interview with Siopama Diedhiou, Kadjinol-Kafone, 11/13/78. Interviews with Eddi Senghor, Kadjinol-Sergerh, 3/9/78; Basayo Sambou, Kadjinol-Kandianka, 3/19/78. Thomas, *Diola*, p. 164.

104. Interview with Kapooeh Diedhiou, Kadjinol-Kafone, 11/27/78. Thomas, *Diola*, p. 168.

105. Interview with Siliungimagne Diatta, Kadjinol-Kandianka, 3/24/78. Interview with Siopama Diedhiou, Kadjinol-Kafone, 11/13/78. Thomas, *Diola*, p. 70.

106. Thomas, *Diola*, pp. 166, 170. Interviews with Boolai Senghor, Kadjinol-Sergerh, 7/10/78; Asenk Ahan Diedhiou, Kadjinol-Kafone, 8/14/76. Group discussion with Elizabeth Sambou and Diongany Diedhiou, Kadjinol-Kafone, 8/16/76.

107. Interviews with Dionsal Diedhiou, Kadjinol-Kafone, 6/23/78; Siliungimagne Diatta, Kadjinol-Kandianka, 6/7/76. Mamadou Gaye, "Les Bois Sacrées dans le

Département de Bignona (le Droit au Seuil des Sanctuaires)," Dakar: Mémoire de l'Ecole Nationale d'Administration, 1973–1974, pp. 12–13. Thomas, *Diola*, p. 168. For a description of a different system of animal doubles, see J. David Sapir, "Fecal Animals: An Example of Complementary Totemism," *Man*, vol. 12, 1977, pp. 1–21.

108. Ibid., pp. 2–3. Interviews with Asenk Ahan Diedhiou, Kadjinol-Kafone, 3/29/78; Siopama Diedhiou, Kadjinol-Kafone, 3/4/78; Elizabeth Sambou, Kadjinol-Kafone, 3/3/78; Siliungimagne Diatta, Kadjinol-Kandianka, 6/7/78.

109. Thomas, *Diola*, p. 168.

110. Sapir, "Fecal," p. 6. Thomas, *Diola*, p. 124.

111. Interviews with Siliungimagne Diatta, Kadjinol-Kandianka, 6/7/76; Terence Galandiou Diouf Sambou, Kadjinol-Ebankine, 12/25/78. Thomas, *Diola*, pp. 168, 619. Sapir, "Fecal," pp. 6–12.

112. Interview with Siopama Diedhiou, Kadjinol-Kafone, 3/28/78. Interviews with Elizabeth Sambou, Kadjinol-Kafone, 3/3/78; Terence Galandiou Diouf Sambou, Kadjinol-Ebankine, 12/25/78.

113. Interviews with Terence Galandiou Diouf Sambou, Kadjinol-Ebankine, 12/25/78; Indrissa Diedhiou, Kadjinol-Kafone, 10/20/74. Thomas, *Diola*, p. 691.

114. Interviews with Djilehl Sambou, Kadjinol-Hassouka, 4/28/78; Sikakucele Diatta, Kadjinol-Kafone, 6/19/76; Adiabaloung Diedhiou, Kadjinol-Kafone, 8/11/76; Indrissa Diedhiou, Kadjinol-Kafone, 10/20/78. This is confirmed by Thomas, but Father Joffroy claims it is the ancestors who judge. Thomas, *Diola*, pp. 541–542. Joffroy, "Coutumes," p. 183. "Dictionnaire des Langues Françoise et nègres."

115. Interviews with Jean-Baptiste Diatta, Mlomp-Kadjifolong, 9/16/77; Indrissa Diedhiou, 10/20/78; Eddi Senghor, Kadjinol-Sergerh, 3/9/78, Siopama Diedhiou, Kadjinol-Kafone, 11/16/77; François Buloti Diatta, Kadjinol-Kafone, 7/26/75; Boolai Senghor, Kadjinol-Sergerh, 7/10/78. See also, Joffroy, "Coutumes," pp. 182–183. Thomas, *Diola*, pp. 617, 629.

116. Interviews with Landing Diedhiou, Kadjinol-Kafone, 12/27/78; Boolai Senghor, Kadjinol-Sergerh, 7/10/78; Eddi Senghor, Kadjinol-Sergerh, 7/11/76; Diashwah Sambou, Kadjinol-Kafone, 2/2/78. Thomas, *Diola*, p. 625.

117. In fact, they would harm people from their own villages who recognized them in Housandioume. The Manjaco and Baboi of Guiné-Bissau have similar ideas about villages of the dead south of their homelands near Cacheu. Crowley, "Contracts," p. 347. Interview with Elizabeth Sambou, Kadjinol-Kafone, 6/5/96. Group discussion, Dionsal Diedhiou and Diongany Diedhiou, Kadjinol-Kafone, 6/25/78; Gnapoli Diedhiou, Njaga Diedhiou, and Dioulimagne Diedhiou, Kadjinol-Kafone, 8/8/96. Interviews with Henri Diedhiou, Kadjinol-Kafone, 7/5/76; Indrissa Diedhiou, Kadjinol-Kafone,10/20/78; Siopama Diedhiou, Kadjinol-Kafone, 11/16/78 and 4/1/78; Sikakucele Diatta, Kadjinol-Kafone, 4/7/78; Terence Galandiou Diouf Sambou, Kadjinol-Ebankine, 6/4/96; Adiabaloung Diedhiou, Kadjinol-Kafone, Kadjinol-Kafone, 6/25/96. Thomas, *Diola*, pp. 630–633.

118. Interviews with Siopama Diedhiou, Kadjinol-Kafone, 6/24/78; Sikakucele Diatta, Kadjinol-Kafone, 6/19/76; Agnak Baben, Samatit, 12/6/78; Eddi Senghor, Kadjinol-Sergerh, 3/9/78; Dionsal and Diongany Diedhiou, Kadjinol-Kafone, 6/25/76. One of the primary objections to Christian teachings encountered in Esulalu was missionary insistence on the permanence of damnation in hell.

119. Such revelations "poison the ears" of the hearer. Interviews with Terence Galandiou Diouf Sambou, Kadjinol-Ebankine, 7/31/78; André Bankuul Senghor, Kadjinol-Hassouka, 3/30/78. Thomas, *Diola*, p. 233, 535.

120. Thomas, *Diola*, p. 636.

121. Ibid, pp. 528–534.

122. Interview with Siliungimagne Diatta, Kadjinol-Kandianka, 3/2/75. Linares, "Intensive," p. 27. The growth of the slave trade in the eighteenth century weakened this egalitarianism in practice, though it remained a community value. See chapter 5.

123. Thomas interpreted this as meaning that one could not carry one's riches to heaven, but I believe his interpretation was incorrect. People were often buried with several cloths, given by friends and relatives. Also, it was thought that the cattle sacrificed during a funeral accompanied the dead into the afterlife. Thomas, *Diola*, pp. 420, 422.

124. For a sense of the elaborate ritual avoidances among the Kujamaatay Diola, see Sapir, "Kujaama," passim.

125. Until recently, only the priest-kings took more than one wife. In 1979, only two of Kadjinol's men were polygynists. In other townships, it was almost as rare, though several Muslim Diola had two wives. Interviews with Gustave Sambou, Kadjinol-Kafone, 10/12/77; Dionsal Diedhiou, Kadjinol-Kafone, 6/12/78; Elizabeth Sambou, Kadjinol-Kafone, 7/28/76; Kapooeh Diedhiou, Kadjinol-Kafone, 8/3/87. Group discussion with Bruno Gitao Diedhiou of Kadjinol-Kafone, Daniel Diatta of Kadjinol-Hassouka, and Sirku Bassin of Kadjinol-Ebankine, 1/31/75.

126. Interview with André Bankuul Senghor, Kadjinol-Hassouka, 11/18/77. Thomas, *Diola*, p. 254.

127. There was an unsuccessful attempt to do this at Mlomp in the late 1970s. Kadjinol's last boodji was in the early 1970s. Too many unmarried women stayed in the city rather than be forced to choose a husband. The Huluf township of Boukitingor had a successful boodji in 1996. Interviews with Antoine Djemelene Sambou, Kadjinol-Kagnao, 12/27/77; Siliungimagne Diatta, Kadjinol-Kandianka, 10/24/77; Kapooeh Diedhiou, Kadjinol-Kafone, 8/3/87. Pélissier, *Paysans*, p. 697. Thomas, *Diola*, p. 263.

128. Interviews with Henri Diedhiou, Kadjinol-Kafone, 7/5/76; Antoine Houmandrissah Diedhiou, Kadjinol-Kafone, 3/31/78; Kapooeh Diedhiou, Kadjinol-Kafone, 1/16/79; Siopama Diedhiou, Kadjinol-Kafone, 7/31/78; Econdo Sambou and Sikakucele Diatta, Kadjinol-Kafone, 5/12/75.

129. Group discussion with Econdo Sambou, Adiabaloung Diedhiou, and Gnapoli Diedhiou, Kadjinol-Kafone, 4/27/75. Interviews with Gilippe Diedhiou, Kadjinol-Kafone, 6/8/75; Kapooeh Diedhiou, Kadjinol-Kafone, 7/28/78.

130. The sixth cow was kept by the priest-king. Interviews with Siliungimagne Diatta, Kadjinol-Kandianka, 7/30/78; Boolai Senghor, Kadjinol-Sergerh, 6/8/78; Kapooeh Diedhiou, Kadjinol-Kafone, 7/28/78.

131. Interviews with Diashwah Sambou, Kadjinol-Kafone, 4/13/78; Siopama Diedhiou, Kadjinol-Kafone, 4/10/78; Asssamboulay Diatta, Kadjinol-Kandianka, 12/12/78; Boolai Senghor, Kadjinol-Sergerh, 11/17/78; Jean-Baptiste Diatta, Mlomp-Kadjifolong, 9/16/77; Djatti Sambou, Mlomp-Haer, 1/13/79.

132. Elung was linked to the priest-king of Oussouye who was the senior oeyi of the region. Interviews with Paponah Diatta, Mlomp-Etebemaye, 11/11/78; Djatti Sambou, Mlomp-Haer, 1/13/79; Agnak Baben, Samatit, 12/6/78. Enac was Samatit's most powerful shrine. Linares, *Power*, p. 34.

133. Interviews with Boolai Senghor, Kadjinol-Sergerh, 11/17/78; Paponah Diatta, Mlomp-Etebemaye, 11/11/78; Antoine Houmandrissah Diedhiou, Kadjinol-Kafone, 4/4/78 and 1/13/79; Siopama Diedhiou, Kadjinol-Kafone, 4/10/78.

134. Interviews with Elizabeth Sambou, Kadjinol-Kafone, 11/2/78 and 11/27/78.

135. I translate the Diola term *kusaye* as "witch" following standard ethnographic usage, which distinguishes between "witches," who are said to possess spiritual powers that are used to harm others, and "sorcerers," who use objects of the material world and incantations to either help or harm others. Witches operate entirely in an immaterial world; sorcerers work in a material one. The Diola term *kusaye* (sing. asaye) comes from the root word "to dry." Kusaye dry out the life force of their victims by consuming their souls. Interviews with Sikakucele Diatta, Kadjinol-Kafone, 11/7/78 and 11/30/77; Siopama Diedhiou, Kadjinol-Kafone, 6/26/78; Djiremo Sambou, Kadjinol-Ebankine, 10/19/78.

136. The kusaye also punished murderers by hounding them until they left the township. Interviews with Siliungimagne Diatta, Kadjinol-Kandianka, 11/8/78; Boolai Senghor, Kadjinol-Sergerh, 7/2/78.

137. For a discussion of Diola eschatology, see later. Interview with Paponah Diatta, Mlomp-Etebemaye, 4/27/78.

138. This French term has entered the Diola language as a word for petty power struggles and corruption. Interviews with Indrissa Diedhiou, Kadjinol-Kafone, 10/19/78; Antoine Djemelene Sambou, Kadjinol-Kagnao, 7/25/78; Landing Died–hiou, Kadjinol-Kafone, 12/27/78; Sikakucele Diatta and Assinway Sambou of Kadjinol-Kafone, 3/4/78.

139. Interviews with Kapooeh Diedhiou, Kadjinol-Kafone, 7/28/78; Assinway Sambou, Kadjinol-Kafone, 2/2/78.

140. Elizabeth Sambou cited a case of two ahoonk who exposed some kusaye, who retaliated by driving the ahoonk to madness. Interview with Elizabeth Sambou, Kadjinol-Kafone, 11/7/78. Interviews with Siopama Diedhiou, Kadjinol-Kafone, 6/26/78; Terence Galandiou Diouf Sambou, Kadjinol-Ebankine, 7/2/78; Kapooeh Diedhiou, Kadjinol-Kafone, 7/28/78; Assinway Sambou, Kadjinol-Kafone, 7/2/78.

141. Sapir, "Fabricated," p. 210.

142. Since 1960, two maternity houses have been established in Esulalu. Since the late 1970s, government-trained midwives have staffed them. Until then, the head of the Kadjinol maternity was also the priestess of Kahoosu-Djilem, the confession shrine. Interviews with Antoine Houmandrissah Diedhiou, Kadjinol-Kafone, 1/13/79; Boolai Senghor, Kadjinol-Sergerh, 7/10/78; Jean-Baptiste Diatta, Mlomp-Kadjifolong, 9/16/77. Thomas, Diola, p. 271.

143. Interviews with Papʒnah Diatta, Mlomp-Etebemaye, 4/27/78; Siopama Diedhiou, Kadjinol-Kafone, 1/21/78; Dionsal Diedhiou, Kadjinol-Kafone, 6/30/76. Thomas, Diola, p. 269.

144. Interviews with Philip Estabo Sambou, Kadjinol-Kagnao, 8/1/76; Terence Galandiou Diouf Sambou, Kadjinol-Ebankine, 12/25/78; Alai Djikune, Kadjinol-Kagnao, 1/15/78. L. V. Thomas, "Un système philosophique Sénégalais: La cosmologie des Diola," Présence Africaine, vol. 32–33, 1960, p. 65.

145. Interviews with Josephine Badji, Mlomp-Haer, 9/25/77; Kumbumbatome Diedhiou, Kadjinol-Kafone, 1/15/75; Madeleine Diedhiou, Kadjinol-Kafone, 3/23/78; Mandiaye Diatta, Kadjinol-Kandianka, 11/21/77; Dionsal Diedhiou, Kadjinol-Kafone, 11/21/77; Gustave Sambou, Kadjinol-Kafone, 1/11/74.

146. Interviews with Grégoire Diatta and Pap Gueye Diatta, Mlomp-Kadjifolong, 11/14/78; Siliungimagne Diatta, Kadjinol-Kandianka, 8/12/78; Econdo Sambou, Kadjinol-Kafone, 5/22/75; Indrissa Diedhiou, Kadjinol-Kafone, 2/10/78. Thomas, Diola, pp. 693–694.

147. The Diola of Huluf and Bandial required circumcision prior to marriage; the Esulalu did not. There are several men, some in their sixties or seventies, who were circumcised during the same rites as their fathers, though not on the same day. In genealogies, it is common for a father and son, six initiations ago, to have been involved in the same circumcision rites. Since the establishment of the Bukut rite, circumcision rites have been held once every twenty to thirty years. In Esulalu, female circumcision is seen as an abomination; women from Esulalu who might undergo such an operation would be seized either by the women's fertility shrine or the male circumcision shrine. In Diola communities that have embraced Islam, as taught by the Mandinka, female circumcision has become the norm. Such practices among the Mandinka predate their acceptance of Islam.

148. This ritual was performed by many Diola Christians who abstained from other awasena ritual obligations. Interviews with Indrissa Diedhiou, Kadjinol-Kafone, 6/29/75; Kapooeh Diedhiou, Kadjinol-Kafone, 7/28/78; Alai Djikune, Kadjinol-Kagnao, 1/15/78.

The frequency of drought and the persistence of the secessionist movement, in the 1980s and 1990s, have eroded Diola resources, and many men are unable to perform such elaborate forms of bridal gifts and ritual greetings of the ukine.

149. The interrogation of the corpse has been described by travelers and government administrators in the midnineteenth century. Interviews with André Bankuul Senghor, Kadjinol-Hassouka, 11/5/75; Siopama Diedhiou, Kadjinol-Kafone, 3/10/78. G. G. Beslier, *Le Sénégal*, Paris: Payot, 1935, p. 59. Boilat, *Esquisses*, pp. 431–432. Thomas, *Diola*, p. 7.

150. Interview with Terence Galandiou Diouf Sambou, Kadjinol-Ebankine, 5/12/78. Interview with Kemehow Diedhiou, Eloudia, 5/18/78. Schloss reports a similar account among the neighboring Ehing. Schloss, *The Hatchet's Blood*, p. 56.

151. Interviews with Djilehl Sambou, Kadjinol-Hassouka, 4/24/78; Paponah Diatta, Mlomp-Etebemaye, 4/27/78; Siopama Diedhiou, Kadjinol-Kafone, 4/1/78.

152. Interview with Paponah Diatta, Mlomp-Etebemaye, 4/27/78.

153. In establishing the date of 1700 as the beginning of the historical accounts, I analyzed genealogies and circumcision ritual names to reach an approximate date, with a possible variation of twenty years in either direction. See the appendix for a description of these methods.

154. Linares, *Power*, pp. 23–24.

Chapter 3

1. Jan Vansina, *Kingdoms of the Savanna*, Madison: University of Wisconsin Press, 1968, p. 14.

2. Thomas, *Diola*, p. 11. Sagnia claims that the term "Diola" is of Mandinka origin and refers to the tendency of the Diola to "pay back" any wrong done to them. B. K. Sagnia, "A Concise Account of the History and Traditions of Origin of Major Gambian Ethnic Groups," Banjul: Gambia National Museum, 1984, p. 2. On the fluidity of ethnic boundaries, see Fredrik Barth, *Ethnic Groups and Boundaries: The Social Organization of Culture Difference*, Boston: Little, Brown, 1969, "Introduction." Alma Gottlieb, *Under the Kapok Tree: Identity and Difference in Beng Thought*, Bloomington: Indiana University Press, 1992, p. 1.

3. I have witnessed Wolof, Serer, Tukulor, Peulh, and Mandinka supplicants at Diola shrines. Several shrines in Esulalu were borrowed from other ethnic groups. Van Binsbergen and Crowley have noted the presence of Senegalese (non-Manjaco) supplicants at Manjaco shrines. Wim van Binsbergen, "The Land as Body: An Essay on the Interpretation of Ritual among the Manjak of Guinea Bissau," paper presented at the Satterthwaite Colloquium on African Religion and Ritual, 1986, p. 5. Eve Crowley, "Contracts with the Spirits," pp. 1–4 and passim. Richard Werbner, *Regional Cults*, pp. ix–xi.

4. Olga Linares de Sapir, "Shell Middens," pp. 32–43. Pélissier, *Paysans*, p. 823.

5. T. Monod, et al., *Description*, pp. 57–59. The Bainounk, now only about 15,000 people, occupied large areas of the Casamance until the eighteenth century. Local historians attribute their decline to a plot against their king, at Brikama, who cursed them for the deed. Felix Brigaud, *Histoire*, p. 177. Jean Boulègue, "Aux Confins du Monde Malinké: Le Royaume du Kasa Casamance," paper presented to the Congress of Manding Studies, London, 1972. Luis Silveira, Edicão Nova de *Tratado Breve dos Rios de Guiné feito pelo Capitão André Alvares d'Almada*, Lisbon: 1946, p. 39. Interview with Siliungimagne Diatta, Kadjinol-Kandianka, 6/9/78.

6. For an analysis of the methods used in establishing chronologies, see the appendix.

7. Linares has examined the ruins of the settlement near Kagnout-Bruhinban. Oral traditions that I collected did not refer to it by name. Linares de Sapir, "Shell Middens," p. 36. The ruins of Elou Mlomp, which was not abandoned until the midnineteenth century, are still visible in the forest area known as the Hamak. See chapter 7.

8. Paponah Diatta, generally one of the best informed Diola historians, claims that "Koonjaen" was a pejorative term for "newcomers" to the region. However, the discussion of the Koonjaen wars and the importance of Koonjaen descendants to most of the major shrines make this unlikely. Still, it could indicate newcomers to the townships rather than to the region. Interview with Paponah Diatta, Mlomp-Etebemaye, 12/1/77. For the interpretation of the Koonjaen as the first inhabitants, see interviews with Antoine Houmandrissah Diedhiou, Kadjinol-Kafone, 11/17/77; Kuadadge Diatta, Kadjinol-Kafone, 6/24/78; Indrissa Diedhiou, Kadjinol-Kafone, 1/27/78; Badiat Sambou, Kadjinol-Kagnao, 7/16/78; Sikarwen Diatta, Eloudia, 7/19/78 and 1/11/79; Fidel Manga, Kolobone, 5/1/78.

Estimates of Koonjaen numbers range from a substantial minority to the overwhelming majority of present-day Esulalu. Virtually all lineages have at one time been mentioned as Koonjaen, though Diedhiou, Manga, and Diatta are the most frequently cited.

9. Interviews with Adiabaloung Diedhiou, Kadjinol-Kafone, 7/13/87; Indrissa Diedhiou, Kadjinol-Kafone, 1/27/78; Kuadadge Diatta, Kadjinol-Kafone, 11/10/77 and 2/20/78; Eddi Senghor, Kadjinol-Sergerh, 7/16/78; Corrugate Bassin, Kadjinol-Ebankine, 7/15/9. Kuadadge identified himself as Faroon, which is a northern Diola term for Bainounk. Linares has confirmed that the Koonjaen are Bainounk (personal communication, 1979). Basayo Sambou describes the Koonjaen as a distinct race (het). Interview with Basayo Sambou, Kadjinol-Kandianka, 8/9/87. A few informants deny that the Koonjaen were Bainounk. Antoine Dieddhiou claims that both Bainounk and Koonjaen lived in the forest south of Esulalu and that both of them were removed. However, he describes the removal of only the Koonjaen, whom he identifies as a type of Diola. The Bainounk simply disappear from his account. It appears that the communities that he identifies as separate are one and the same. Interviews with Antoine Houmandrissah Dieddhiou, Kadjinol-Kafone, 11/11/77 and 2/8/78. Others claim that the Koonjaen were merely a group of forest dwellers who used a dialect of Diola that is no longer spoken. These latter suggestions come from people of Koonjaen descent, who may feel it is necessary to minimize Koonjaen and Floup differences. Interviews with Michel Amancha Diatta, Kadjinol-Kandianka, 12/18/78; Etienne Manga, Kadjinol-Kandianka, 2/5/78; Sikarwen Diatta, Eloudia, 1/11/79.

10. Sapir used the Swadesh "first one hundred" method of lexical counting; Huluf scored a 19 percent similarity with Banhun, one percentage point less than what Sapir required to put them into the same subgrouping within West Atlantic. Those he grouped together with Banhun had percentage similarities of 22 to 37 percent. See J. David Sapir, "West Atlantic: An Inventory of the Languages, Their Noun Class Systems, and Consonant Alternation" in Thomas Sebeok, ed., *Current Trends in Linguistics*, vol. 7, *Linguistics in Sub-Saharan Africa*, The Hague: Mouton, 1971, pp. 47–49.

11. While several studies mention the Bainounk, they have been of only minor importance in histories by Leary, Roche, Mark, and Brigaud. These historians have not speculated on the origins of the Bainounk. Dembo Kanoute, a Mandinka griot, suggests that they are a group of Mande from Gabou. However, much of Kanoute's account of West African history is inaccurate. Frances Leary, "Islam, Politics, and Colonialism: A Political History of Islam in the Casamance Region of Senegal (1850–1919)," Ph.D diss., Northwestern University, Evanston, Ill., 1970. Christian Roche, *Conquête et Résistance des Peuples de Casamance (1850–1920)*, Dakar: Les Nouvelles Éditions Africaines, 1976. Peter Mark, *Cultural.* Brigaud, *Histoire*

Traditionelle. Dembo Kanoute, *Tradition Orale: Histoire de l'Afrique Authentique,* Dakar: Impricap, 1972.

12. On the coexistence of Bainounk and Floup, see Boulègue, "Aux Confins," pp. 2–6. P. Cultru, *Premier Voyage du Sieur de la Courbe Fait à la Coste d'Afrique in 1685,* Paris: Edouard Champion, 1913, p. 207. Jean-Baptiste Labat, *Nouvelle Relation,* vol. 5, p. 318. Monod, *Fernandes,* pp. 57–59. Cissoko and Sambou have collected oral traditions among the Casamance Mandinka that claim the Bainounk are a Diola group who were pushed back "ceux qu'on a chassé (Bainounkolu)." Sekené Cissoko and Kaoussou Sambou, *Recueil des Traditions Orales des Mandingue de Gambie et de Casamance,* Dakar: IFAN, 1969, p. 193. Kanoute claims that the Diola and Bainounk are both from Gabou. Kanoute, *Tradition,* pp. 81–82. Moore describes the Bainounk as a type of Floup. Francis Moore, *Travels into the Inland Parts of Africa,* London: Edward Love, 1738, p. 24. While these accounts are dubious, they do illustrate the tendency of outsiders to lump them together.

The principal difference between Cassangas and other Bainounk is the former's greater influence from the Mandinka. Djibril Tamsir Niane, *Histoire des Mandingues de l'Ouest,* Paris: Editions Karthala, 1989, p. 32. Leary, "Islam," p. 6. André Alvares d'Almada, cited in Thomas, *Diola,* p. 310. Duarte Pacheco Pereira, *Esmeraldo de Situ Orbis,* London: Hakluyt Society, 1971, p. 88.

13. This is the earliest report of the six-day week, which became an important part of the Bainounk and the Diola calendar. Monod, *Fernandes,* pp. 69–71 and 57–59.

14. Monod, *Fernandes,* p. 71. Antonio Brasio, ed., "Relacaõ de Francisco de Andrade sobre os ilhas de Cabo Verde" (1582), in *Monumenta Missionaria Africana, Africa Ocidental (1570–1600),* ed. Antonio Brasio, second series, vol. 3, Lisbon: Agencia Geral do Utramar, 1964, p. 105. P. E. H. Hair, *An Interim and Makeshift Edition of André Alavares de Almada's Brief Treatise on the Rivers of Guinea,* unpublished manuscript, Liverpool, 1984, p. 73.

15. Lançados were Portuguese traders who left Portuguese-controlled areas and lived in African communities. Monod, *Fernandes,* p. 71. Rodney, *Upper Guinea,* p. 111. Pereira, *Esmeraldo,* p. 90. Bainounk were also enslaved during this period. Frederick Bowser, *The African Slave Trade in Colonial Peru 1524–1650,* Stanford: Stanford University Press, 1974, pp. 40–42.

16. Teté Diadhiou claimed that the ritual was designed to ensure the long life of the king, but since a ruler had to be able to procure adequate rainfall, these explanations are not contradictory. Teté Diadhiou, cited in Brigaud, *Histoire,* p. 177. One king was said to have cursed his people before his death, which caused the collapse of the Bainounk kingdom. Leary, "Islam," pp. 21–22. Diola made similar types of pilgrimages to an important rain priest and king at Enampore during the nineteenth and twentieth centuries. Mark, *Cultural,* p. 78. Girard, *Genèse,* pp. 116–130.

17. António Brásio, ed., "Tratado Breve dos Rios de Guiné do Cabo Verde Feito Pelo Capitão André Alvares de Almada, Naturel da Ilha de Santiago de Cabo Verde," in Brasio, *Monumenta,* vol. 3, pp. 296–297. Silveira, *Tratado,* p. 40.

18. Monod, *Fernandes,* pp. 71–73. The Ehing are neighbors of the southern Diola. For a detailed description of the Ehing hatchet shrine, see Marc Schloss, *The Hatchet's Blood.* For a description of it among the Bandial, see Francis Snyder, *Capitalism,* p. 38.

19. Monod, *Fernandes,* p. 73. Ninety years later, de Almada mentioned the same Cassanga term *china* for "spirit shrine." Hair, *De Almada,* p. 72. For the Ediamat term for spirit shrine, see Thomas, *Diola,* pp. 654–655. Esulalu occasionally pronounce *boekine* as *bachine; xinabu* is pronounced *chinabu.*

20. Monod, *Fernandes,* p. 73.

21. This, too, parallels Diola ritual practice. On Diola war shrines, see chapter 4. On Diola blacksmith shrines, see chapter 7. P. E. H. Hair, *An Interim Transla-*

tion of Manuel Alvares S. J. Ethiopia Menor e Descripcão Geografica da Provincia de Serra Leoa (1615), unpublished manuscript, Liverpool, 1990, p. 74.

22. Hair, *de Almada*, p. 72.

23. De Almada also mentions that this custom is followed by the Buramos (Manjaco) and Bainounk. Hair, *De Almada*, pp. 69–70, 82, 83.

24. Interview with Sikarwen Diatta, Eloudia, 7/19/78. Interviews with Antoine Houmandrissah Diedhiou, 2/27/78 and 5/23/78; Grégoire Djikune, Kadjinol-Kagnao, 7/23/78; Badiat Sambou, Kadjinol-Kagnao, 7/16/78; Sihumucel Badji, Kadjinol-Hassouka, 5/18/78; Paponah Diatta, Mlomp-Etebemaye, 6/21/78.

25. Esulalu traditions suggesting that the Koonjaen were not skilled in making dugout canoes may indicate a difference between them and the eastern Bainounk, who used canoes as a part of their trading activities. Interviews with Antoine Houmandrissah Diedhiou, Kadjinol-Kafone, 2/27/78; Edouard Kadjinga Diatta, Kadjinol-Kafone, 2/6/78.

26. Interviews with Sikarwen Diatta, Eloudia, 12/12/78; Badjaya Kila, Eloudia, 11/8/78; Antoine Houmandrissah Diedhiou, Kadjinol-Kafone, 4/4/78; Indrissa Diedhiou, Kadjinol-Kafone, 1/27/78.

27. The controversy about the Koonjaen origins of Gent and Eloudia stems from a widespread Esulalu desire to conceal Koonjaen origins, especially since the Gent lineage serves as the priest-kings of Kadjinol, Mlomp, and a part of Kagnout. Fidel Manga, a son of one of the elders of Djiguemah at Kolobone-Ekink, has linked his family directly to the Koonjaen and to all the Gent compounds of Esulalu and Huluf. Sikakucele Diatta confirms the Gent-Ekink connection. Others described the shrine as a Koonjaen shrine. Antoine Dieddhiou confirmed that Gent used to live near the Djiguemah shrine in a forest called Hena. Interviews with Fidel Manga, Kolobone-Ekink, 5/1/78; Sikakucele Diatta, Kadjinol-Kafone, 6/18/78; Eddi Senghor, Kadjinol-Sergerh, 2/12/78; Antoine Djemelene Sambou, Kadjinol-Kagnao, 6/12/78. For a discussion of the priest-kings, see chapter 4.

Thomas collected one account suggesting that Eloudia was settled by people from the Gambia, but he does not regard it as reliable. Thomas, *Diola*, p. 490.

28. Interviews with Badjaya Kila, Eloudia, 12/12/78 and 12/23/78.

29. Interviews with Ampercé Lambal, Oussouye, 1/10/79; Siliungimagne Diatta, Kadjinol-Kandianka, 3/31/78; Edouard Kadjinga Diatta, 2/4/78; Kuadadge Diatta, Kadjinol-Kafone, 2/21/78; Badjaya Kila, Eloudia, 12/12/78. This is a very different tradition than the one offered by Jean Girard, concerning Oussouye's Djoenenandé. Girard, *Genèse*, pp. 39–44.

30. Interviews with Badjaya Kila, Eloudia, 11/8/78 and 12/12/78; Indrissa Diedhiou, Kadjinol-Kafone, 2/4/78; Sikarwen Diatta, Eloudia, 12/12/78.

31. The shrine no longer receives a regular cult. It has not been used since before World War I. Interviews with Badjaya Kila, Eloudia, 12/12/78; Edouard Kadjinga Diatta, Kadjinol-Kafone, 2/14/78.

32. In fact, there is evidence to the contrary. According to Crowley, the Manjaco of Guinea-Bissau did not engage in communications with a supreme being until the late nineteenth century, and they claimed that they learned to do this from the Diola. Eve Crowley, personal communication, February 1990. Given that the Floup came from the same area as the Manjaco and borrowed several shrines from them, it appears that they began to stress the importance of the supreme being after they had settled in the Huluf-Esulalu area, rather than before they left the area adjacent to the Manjaco settlements. Such an influence probably came from the Koonjaen.

33. Bog iron has been found in archaeological digs in the region from as early as two thousand years ago. Linares, "Shell Middens," p. 33. Interviews with Sidionbaw Diatta, Kadjinol-Kafone, 2/7/78; Kapooeh Diedhiou, Kadjinol-Kafone, 7/28/78; Samuel Diedhiou and Ompa Kumbegeny Diedhiou, Kadjinol-Kafone, 7/1/78.

34. For the idea that the Koonjaen taught the Diedhious how to forge, see interviews with Indrissa Diedhiou, Kadjinol-Kafone, 2/4/78; Siliungimagne Diatta, Kadjinol-Kandianka, 5/20/78. For the idea that the Koonjaen were more skilled at smithing, see interviews with Sikarwen Diatta, Eloudia, 7/19/78; Adiabaloung Diedhiou, Kadjinol-Kafone, 7/16/76. Further evidence of Koonjaen importance is the use of the surname "Djabune" for blacksmith families. "Jabundos" was the name of a Bainounk group described in the sixteenth century. Silveira, *Tratado*, p. 38.

35. Interviews with Djilehl Sambou, Kadjinol-Hassouka, 5/23/78; Samuel Diedhiou, Kadjinol-Kafone, 12/24/78. On the special powers associated with the forge, see William Simmons, *Eyes of the Night: Witchcraft among a Senegalese People*, Boston: Little, Brown, 1971. Crowley, "Contracts," p. 67. Marcel Griaule, *Conversations with Ogotemmeli*, London: Oxford University Press, 1970, pp. 84–88. Sandra Barnes, *Ogun: An Old God for a New Age*, Philadelphia: Institute for the Study of Human Issues, 1980, passim. Patrick McNaughton, *The Mande Blacksmiths: Knowledge, Power, and Art of West Africa*, Bloomington: Indiana University Press, 1988, pp. 12–22. Eugenia Herbert, *Iron, Gender, and Power: Rituals of Transformation in African Societies*, Bloomington: Indiana University Press, 1993.

36. Interviews with Siliungimagne Diatta, Kadjinol-Kandianka, 5/20/78; Djilehl Sambou, Kadjinol-Hassouka, 5/23/78; Siliya Diedhiou, Kadjinol-Kafone, 5/22/78. Gilaite and Duhagne are said to have been brought to Esulalu in the nineteenth century. See chapter 7. Group discussion with Siliya Diedhiou and Djoolimagne Diedhiou, Kadjinol-Kafone, 8/3/78; Siliya Diedhiou and Kulappa Diatta, Kadjinol-Kafone, 9/8/78. Interview with Samuel Diedhiou, Kadjinol-Kafone, 12/24/78. Both Siliya Diedhiou and Samuel Diedhiou "finished" Silapoom.

37. The idea that Koonjaen women exercised more prominent roles in ritual life is reinforced by scattered references to women rulers among the Bainounk, who, presumably, would have controlled the major shrines associated with the procurement of rain and with kingship. B. K. Sidibe, "The Story of Kaabu: Its Extent," paper presented at the Conference on Manding Studies, School of Oriental and African Studies, London, 1972, p. 6. Mbalefele Janneh, "Jola History," Cultural Archives, Banjul, The Gambia, 1970, pp. 2, 6.

38. These reasons are frequently cited as causes of war in the lower Casamance and Guinea-Bissau region and could be considered a cliché within local traditions. It is unclear if this occurred before the removal of the Koonjaen from the Calemboekine forest; Eloukasine was destroyed before the time covered by detailed genealogies. Interviews with Paponah Diatta, Mlomp-Etebemaye, 12/1/78; Sikarwen Diatta, Eloudia, 11/20/78; Sambouway Assin, Kagnout-Bruhinban, 12/2/78; Nicholas Djibune, Mlomp-Djicomole, 7/9/97.

39. The Hawtane-Koonjaen connection was rarely made directly. Many people from Edioungou are said to be from Hawtane, and Edioungou is also said to be largely Koonjaen. Interviews with Georges Manga, Edioungou, 12/12/78; Jean-Luc Lambal, Oussouye, 6/17/94; Sidionbaw Diatta, Kadjinol-Kafone, 2/7/78.

40. Interview with Siliungimagne Diatta, Kadjinol-Kandianka, 5/20/78; Sikarwen Diatta, Eloudia, 7/19/78.

In at least one instance, the Koonjaen were prohibited by the Floup from continuing to use the shrine. Interviews with Edouard Kadjinga Diatta, Kadjinol-Kafone, 2/4/78; Sihumucel Badji, Kadjinol-Houssouka, 5/18/78; Antoine Houmandrissah Diedhiou, Kadjinol-Kafone, 5/23/78; Antoine Djemelene Sambou, Kadjinol-Kafone, 6/12/78.

41. Fidel Manga's father was one of the elders. Interviews with Fidel Manga, Kolobone, 5/1/78; Antoine Houmandrissah Diedhiou, Kadjinol-Kafone, 2/2/78 and 5/23/78; Sidionbaw Diatta, Kadjinol-Kafone, 2/7/78.

42. Kadjinol's descendants of the priest-king of Oussouye, while not part of Gayo, can also attend. See chapter 4 for a more detailed description. Interviews

with Kuadadge Diatta, Kadjinol-Kafone, 2/17/78; Terence Galandiou Diouf Sambou, Kadjinol-Ebankine, 2/19/78; Sidionbaw Diatta, 2/7/78; Edouard Kadjinga Diatta, Kadjinol-Kafone, 2/4/78.

43. Most of these accounts refer to a Coeyi boekine that was Atta-Essou's and another that came from Kerouhey. This latter shrine is the Floup Coeyi; Egol is the Koonjaen shrine. Interviews with Ampercé Lambal, Oussouye, 1/10/79; Siliungimagne Diatta, Kadjinol-Kandianka, 3/31/78; Edouard Kadjinga Diatta, Kadjinol-Kafone, 2/4/78; Kuadadge Diatta, Kadjinol-Kafone, 2/21/78; Badjaya Kila, Eloudia, 12/12/78.

44. For a discussion of the Koonjaen Calemboekine, see interviews with Djilehl Sambou, Kadjinol-Hassouka, 5/23/78; Siliungimagne Diatta, Kadjinol-Kandianka, 5/20/78; Asamayo Diedhiou, Kadjinol-Kafone, 7/26/78; Sikarwen Diatta, Eloudia, 1/11/79. Sidionbaw Diatta and Djadja Sambou have suggested that the Koonjaen Calemboekine was the Calemboekine of Kafone, a quarter of Kadjinol. The oeyi of Kafone has no Coeyi; he may perform rituals only at Egol. Furthermore, he is not dependent on Oussouye, like the other oeyi of Esulalu. Interviews with Sidionbaw Diatta, 2/7/78; Djadja Sambou, Kadjinol-Hassouka, 7/17/78; Sikakucele Diatta, Kadjinol-Kafone, 6/18/78. Sikakucele was the oeyi of Kafone until 1990.

45. Thomas, *Diola*, pp. 490–491. These traditions are also reported by Leary, Hanin, Janneh, and Antoine Diedhiou. In the 1990s, the Senegalese government has encouraged this theory as a way of combating a Diola-led secessionist movement. In 1996, the government sponsored a series of celebrations of the "common" ancestry of Diola and Serer. Leary, "Islam," p. 75. Charles Hanin, *Occident Noir*, Paris: Editions Alsatia, 1946, p. 61. Janneh, "Jola," p. 3. Interview with Antoine Houmandrissah Diedhiou, Kadjinol-Kafone, 4/23/78.

46. The coastal Serer group, called the Niominka, have certain similarities to the Diola, but this could be a result of commercial ties or of borrowing rice-growing techniques from the Diola. Pélissier, *Paysans*, pp. 491, 659.

47. I do not have specific information about the Kujamaatay, though Karones and Djougoutes are largely of southern origin. Pélissier, *Paysans*, pp. 663, 665. Mark, *Cultural*, p. 19.

48. Thomas, *Diola*, p. 119. Group discussion with Henri Gomes Diedhiou and Indrissa Diedhiou, Kadjinol-Kafone, 9/26/74. Interview with Indrissa Diedhiou, 1/27/78.

49. Group discussion with Dionsal Diedhiou and Diongany Diedhiou, Kadjinol-Kafone, 6/25/76; and Gnapoli Diedhiou, Njaga Diedhiou and Dioulimagne Diedhiou, Kadjinol-Kafone, 8/8/96. Interviews with Terence Galandiou Diouf Sambou, Kadjinol-Ebankine, 6/5/96; Adiabaloung Diedhiou, Kadjinol-Kafone, 6/25/96. Crowley's work on the Manjaco suggests a long-standing process of mutual borrowing of spirit shrines between Diola and Manjaco and strong similarities between their respective religious systems. Crowley, "Contracts," pp. 65–67, 606, and passim.

50. Ediamat is the area along the Senegal–Guinea-Bissau border, extending as far south as the São Domingo River. Group discussion with Wuuli Assin, Abel Assin, Cyriaque Assin, Baengoon Assin, and Agnak Baben, Samatit, 4/26/78. Interviews with Terence Galandiou Diouf Sambou, Kadjinol-Ebankine, 11/7/78; Sikarwen Diatta, Eloudia, 7/5/78.

51. Interview with Eheleterre Sambou, Kadjinol-Hassouka, 1/4/79.

52. Interview with Kemehow Diedhiou, Eloudia, 1/28/78. Migration traditions' stress on finding new hunting areas is shared by the Floup's southern neighbors, the Manjaco. Crowley, "Contracts," pp. 65–66.

53. Thomas has found the ruins of the original Seɩghalene. Thomas, *Diola*, p. 178. According to Boolai Senghor, the area was called Hutongat. A single homestead remains on the former location. Interview with Boolai Senghor, Kadjinol-Sergerh, 8/14/78.

54. Some of the descendants of the men who went to Kerouhey settled in Kadjinol-Hassouka after the defeat of Senghalene. Samouli Senghor was descended from one of them. Interviews with Samouli Senghor, Kadjinol-Hassouka, 6/13/78; Antoine Houmandrissah Diedhiou, Kadjinol-Kafone, 5/23/78 and 6/18/78; Michel Djigoon Senghor, Kadjinol-Kandianka, 7/20/78; Antoine Djemelene Sambou, Kadjinol-Kagnao, 6/12/78; Alouise Manga, Mlomp-Djicomole, 12/27/78; Sebeoloute Manga, Mlomp-Djicomole, 7/12/78.

55. This is only one account of Oussouye's and Huluf's seniority to Esulalu, but it is echoed by Badjaya Kila, who claims that Huluf stole its royal shrines from Esulalu. Others claim that Oussouye went to Kerouhey first and that the oeyi of Oussouye was appointed as the senior oeyi. Kolobone is a Huluf township that has important shrines associated with the Huluf priest-king. Interviews with Sidionbaw Diatta, Kadjinol-Kafone, 4/13/78; Badjaya Kila, Eloudia, 12/23/78; Alouise Sambou, Kadjinol-Ebankine, 7/27/96.

56. Siliungimagne Diatta is the present priest-king of Kadjinol. Interview with Siliungimagne Diatta, Kadjinol-Kandianka, 3/31/78. Interviews with Antoine Houmandrissah Diedhiou, Kadjinol-Kafone, 5/23/78 and 6/25/78; Sebeoloute Manga, Mlomp-Djicomole, 4/24/78; Alouise Manga, Mlomp-Djicomole, 12/27/78.

57. Interviews with Antoine Houmandrissah Diedhiou, Kadjinol-Kafone, 5/23/78; Ampercé Lambal, Oussouye, 1/10/79; Sebeoloute Manga, Mlomp-Djicomole, 4/24/78; Jacques Lopi, Djeromait, 7/14/78; Basayo Sambou and Silokolai Sambou, Kadjinol-Kandianka, 8/10/87. Ampercé, Basayo, and Silokolai suggest a Manjaco origin for the Huluf oeyi as well.

58. The oeyi has to avoid women other than his wives; he may talk with them, but he may not come in close contact. Material on Manjaco religion is scanty. The principal ethnography by Antonio Carreira emphasizes political and social structures. Two recent doctoral dissertations on Manjaco religious life suggest that the priest-king's prohibitions on entry into the rice paddies were eased during the colonial period as the stability of spirit provinces was weakened. Antonio Carreira, *Vida Social des Manjacos*, Bissau: Centre de Estudo da Guiné Portuguesa, 1947. Crowley, "Contracts," pp. 82–88. Eric Gable, "Modern Manjaco: The Ethos of Power in a West African Society," Ph.D. diss., University of Virginia, Charlottesville, 1990, pp. 236–238.

59. Many people would flee one community and seek the sanctuary of another to avoid the onerous obligations of certain shrines. The Cayinte shrines of Huluf required priests to remain celibate, leaving the priests with no one to carry on their names and provide new offspring for their reincarnations. The ancestors of Sikakucele Diatta, Assinway Sambou, and André Kebroohaw Manga fled Huluf for this reason. Interviews with Sikakucele Diatta, Kadjinol-Kafone, 6/18/78; Assinway Sambou, Kadjinol-Kafone, 7/12/75; André Kebroohaw Manga, Kadjinol-Sergerh, 4/17/78.

Murderers were required to leave their own villages. Other criminals and those subject to malicious gossip (e.g., unwed mothers) would often flee as well.

The date of 1700 is derived from nine- to ten-generations-deep genealogies for several families within Kadjinol and the presence of one of them, a man named Haieheck, three generations before a man in his eighties, who signed a treaty with the French in 1861. See the appendix. Only Eloudia of the Koonjaen settlements still exists, though with many Diola settlers in the community.

60. On droughts, see Philip Curtin, *Economic Change. Supplementary Evidence*, pp. 3–6. George Brooks, "Ecological Perspectives on Mande Population Movements, Commercial Networks, and Settlement Patterns from the Atlantic Wet Phase (ca. 5500–2500 B.C.) to the Present," *History in Africa*, vol. 16, 1989, p. 23; and *Landlords and Strangers: Ecology, Society, and Trade in Western Africa, 1000–1630*, Boulder, Colo.: Westview Press, 1993, p. 7.

61. Fear of witchcraft was an important factor in the decision of some people to settle north of the Casamance. Interview with Kapooeh Diedhiou, Kadjinol-Kafone, 1/6/79. On Kasa's role in populating Djougoutes, see Mark, *Cultural*, p. 31. Pélissier, *Paysans*, p. 853. Thomas, *Diola*, p. 13. The ties between the Bliss-Karones area and Esulalu are still maintained. Niomoun received its ukine of Coeyi and Cayinte from Kadjinol, and Kadjinol elders still initiate the priests of Niomoun. Interview with Basil Diedhiou, Niomoun, 3/28/88.

62. Group discussion with Indrissa Diedhiou and Edouard Kadjinga Diatta, Kadjinol-Kafone, 2/4/78. This is supported by Rodney, who noted a growing population pressure on coastal areas throughout upper Guinea in the seventeenth century. Rodney, *Upper Guinea*, pp. 109–110.

63. Jean Boulègue, Walter Rodney, and T. Monod, as well as many others, rely on Fernandes. Pereira visited the southern fringe of the Floup domains but described only trade. Pereira, *Esmeraldo*, p. 91. There are no direct descriptions of this kingdom in the oral traditions that I collected.

64. Fernandes claims the Mansa Floup received one quarter of all livestock, palm products, and rice produced in his kingdom. Monod, *Fernandes*, pp. 63–65. The large canoes described by early travelers are still in use. Throughout the eighteenth and nineteenth centuries, such canoes were used to transport war parties and traders transporting cattle.

65. Ibid., p. 65.

66. Jan Vansina, "A Comparison of African Kingdoms," *Africa*, vol. 32, 1962, p. 375.

67. Monod, *Fernandes*, p. 63.

68. Thomas, *Diola*, pp. 203–204.

69. After the conquest of the Koonjaen, the Senghalene-Djikune lineage of Kadjinol and the Lambal lineage of Oussouye turned over the office of priest-king to members of the Gent lineages, who were seen as "owners of the soil." See chapter 4. Interviews with Sebeoloute Manga, Mlomp-Djicomole, 7/12/78 and 12/27/78; Antoine Houmandrissah Diedhiou, Kadjinol-Kafone, 6/18/78; Ampercé Lambal, Oussouye, 1/10/79.

70. Interview with Michel Anjou Manga, Kadjinol-Kafone, 12/11/78. Group discussion with Djadja Sambou, Kadjinol-Hassouka; Elyse Sambou, Titis Sambou, Paul Sambou, Kadjinol-Kagnao. Interviews with Albidihaw Diatta, Kadjinol-Kafone, Ka Diatta, Mlomp-Kadjifolong; Djejoe Manga, Mlomp-Djicomole, 7/17/78.

71. Interviews with Antoine Houmandrissah Diedhiou, Kadjinol-Kafone, 2/2/78 and 2/27/78; Sikarwen Diatta, Eloudia, 7/19/78; Indrissa Diedhiou, Kadjinol-Kafone, 1/27/78; Diashwah Sambou, Kadjinol-Kafone, 2/2/78; Sihumucel Badji, Kadjinol-Hassouka, 5/18/78; Siopama Diedhiou, Kadjinol-Kafone, and Asambou Senghor, Kadjinol-Sergerh, 3/5/78.

72. Rape of women is cited as a cause of many Esulalu wars and may represent an attempt to describe the enemy as violators of the most basic tenets of what Diola regard as civilized society. Interviews with Kapooeh Diedhiou, Kadjinol-Kafone, 3/9/78, 7/17/87, and 7/27/87; Djiremo Sambou, Kadjinol-Ebankine, 7/21/78; Boolai Senghor, Kadjinol-Sergerh, 6/10/78 and 12/21/78.

73. Among the wars fought by Kadjinol against the Koonjaen, there are two that may be remembered within the time span of detailed genealogies. An elder, Antoine Diedhiou, sometimes claims that his ancestor Abeohow, at least eight generations ago (born sometimes between 1680 and 1730) participated in such a war and sometimes claims that it was before Abeohow's time. It could well be that he participated in one of the last of these wars. Two families are cited by name, one from Kafone and one from Kagnao, as being Koonjaen who sought refuge at Kadjinol. But in the case of the Kafone case, the genealogy of a far younger man is only five generations deep and was probably too recent to reflect a full geneal-

ogy. Interview with Antoine Houmandrissah Diedhiou, Kadjinol-Kafone, 2/2/78 and 2/8/78.

74. Interviews with Sihumucel Badji, Kadjinol-Hassouka, 5/18/78 and Kapooeh Diedhiou, Kadjinol-Kafone, 7/17/87.

75. Interviews with Diashwah Sambou, Kadjinol-Kafone, 2/2/78 and 4/25/78; Terence Galandou Diouf Sambou, Kadjinol-Ebankine, 2/19/78; Antoine Houmandrissah Diedhiou, Kadjinol-Kafone, 6/18/78; Michel Anjou Manga, 12/11/78; André Bankuul Senghor, Kadjinol-Hassouka, 6/15/78.

76. Interviews with Antoine Houmandrissah Diedhiou, Kadjinol-Kafone, 2/27/78, 2/2/78, and 5/8/78; Asambou Senghor, Kadjinol-Sergerh; Siopama Diedhiou, Kadjinol-Kafone, 2/3/78; Kapooeh Diedhiou, Kadjinol-Kafone, 7/17/87.

77. Interview with Badiat Sambou, Kadjinol-Kagnao, 7/16/78.

78. This removal of Senghalene probably occurred during the course of the Koonjaen wars, not afterward. This is based on their more complete integration into Esulalu than most of the Koonjaen groups. For a discussion of the war, see interviews with Michel Djigoon Senghor, Kadjinol-Kandianka, 7/20/78; Siliungimagne Diatta, Kadjinol-Kandianka, 7/15/78; André Bankuul Senghor, Kadjinol-Hassouka, 6/15/78.

79. Rodney, *Upper Guinea*, pp. 109–113. Pereira, *Esmeraldo*, p. 88. Boulegue, "Kasa," p. 6. Monod, *Fernandes*, pp. 57–58. Sieur Vincent LeBlanc, *Les Voyages Fameux du Sieur Vincent LeBlanc*, Paris: Pierre Bergeron, 1649. pp. 28–31. For a discussion of Mandinka expansion, see Rodney, *Upper Guinea*, chap. 2; Leary, "Islam," pp. 39–43; Charlotte Quinn, *Mandingo Kingdoms of the Senegambia: Traditionalism, Islam and European Expansion*, Evanston, Ill.: Northwestern University Press, 1972. pp. 9–10.

80. André Alvares de Almada quoted in Thomas, *Diola*, pp. 309–310.

81. Cultru, *de la Courbe*, pp. 207–208.

82. Rodney, *Upper Guinea*, pp. 95, 111. Monod, *Fernandes*, p. 69. Pereira, *Esmeraldo*, p. 90.

83. Monod, *Fernandes*, p. 69. Pereira, *Esmeraldo*, pp. 89–90.

84. Alvares de Almada quoted in Thomas, *Diola*, pp. 309–310. Hair, *de Almada's*, p. 61. George Brooks, "Perspectives on Luso-African Commerce and Settlement in the Gambia and Guinea-Bissau Region, 16th–19th Centuries," Paper presented at the Fourth International Congress of Africanists, Kinshasa, December 1978, p. 11. Brooks, *Landlords*, pp. 23, 59, 79, 89. Pélissier, *Paysans*, p. 65. Rodney, *Upper Guinea*, p. 65.

85. Hair, *The Almada*, p. 63.

86. Olfert Dapper, *Description de l'Afrique*, Amsterdam: Wolfgang Waesbroge, 1686, p. 242.

87. Buramos is a general term for the coastal peoples of Guinea-Bissau and usually refers to the Mancagne and Manjaco peoples, who inhabited an area southeast of the Floup. Hair, *De Almada*, p. 63. Such attacks on Portuguese travelers is also mentioned by Father Manuel Alvares. Hair, *Alvares*, pp. 42–43.

88. Hair, *De Almada*, p. 64.

89. Group discussion with Wuuli Assin, Neerikoon Assin, Cyriaque Assin, Samatit, 5/11/78. Interviews with Antoine Houmandrissah Diedhiou, Kadjinol-Kafone, 3/2878; Attabadionti Diatta, Kadjinol-Sergerh, 7/13/76 and 6/10/78.

90. Interviews with Indrissa Diedhiou, Kadjinol-Kafone, 7/31/76; Sikarwen Diatta, Eloudia, 7/19/78; Grégoire Diatta, Mlomp-Kadjifolong, 7/5/76.

91. André Donelha, *An Account of Sierra Leone and the Rivers of Guinea of Cape Verde (1625)*, edited by Avelino Teixeira da Mota, tr. P. E. H. Hair, Lisbon: Junta de investigacoes cientificas do ultramar, 1971, p. 161. De Almada noted that there were several koranic schools frequented by Mandinka along the lower and middle Gambia. Hair, *De Almada*, p. 46.

92. Walter Rodney, *A History of the Upper Guinea Coast, 1545–1800*, Oxford: Clarendon, 1970, p. 117. Hair, *De Almada*, p. 117. George Brooks also suggests that acephalous societies were usually reluctant to participate in the slave trade. Brooks, *Landlords*, p. 139.

93. Francisco de Lemos Coelho, *Description of the Coast of Guinea* (*1684*), tr. P. E. H. Hair, unpublished manuscript, Liverpool, 1985, vol. 1, chap. 3, 7:12.

94. Rodney, *Guinea*, p. 98. Duncan agrees with Rodney, suggesting that Portuguese traders regularly overloaded slave ships in the region. T. Bentley Duncan, *Atlantic Islands: Madeira, the Azores, and the Cape Verdes in Seventeenth Century Commerce and Navigation*, Chicago: University of Chicago Press, 1972, pp. 201–206. In 1595, de Almada claimed that the Rio São Domingo supplied more slaves than "any other river in Guinea." Cacheu was the main slave-trading port on that river. Hair, *De Almada*, p. 86. By 1687, the Senegal Company estimated that it was exporting 12,000 to 15,000 slaves per year from the region between the Casamance and the Rio Nunez. Abdoulaye Ly, *La Compagnie du Sénégal*, Paris: Présence Africaine, 1958, p. 286.

95. Tito Augusto de Carvalho, *As Companhis Portuguesas de Colonizacôo*, Lisbon: Impresena Nacional, 1902, pp. 34–35.

96. Lemos Coehlo quoted in Rodney, *Upper Guinea*, p. 136.

97. Dierek Ruiters quoted in Jean Boulègue, *Les Luso-Africains de Sénégambie*, *XVIe-XIXe siécle*. Dakar: Université de Dakar, 1972. p. 39. De Almada noticed a similar hardening of African attitudes toward Europeans in sixteenth-century Gambia. Hair, *De Almada*, p. 58.

98. Azevedo de Coehlo quoted in Thomas, *Diola*, pp. 310–311. De Almada had noted this potential in the late sixteenth century. Hair, *De Almada*, p. 64.

99. Thomas, *Diola*, p. 310.

100. George Brooks, "The Observance of All Souls' Day in the Guinea-Bissau Region: A Christian Holy Day, an African Harvest Festival, or an African New Year's Celebration?" *History in Africa*, vol. 7, pp. 12–17.

101. Cultru, *de la Courbe*, p. 192–193. Father Balthasar Barreira quoted in Brooks, "Observance," pp. 18. Monseigneur Cónego Francisco Xavier Gomes Catåo, "A diocese de Cabo Verde et o clero de Goa," in *Studia Revista Quadrimestral*, vol. 19, December 1966, pp. 98–100. Hair, *De Almada*, p. 77. Coelho, *Description*, vol. 1, chap. 2, 32:70.

102. Labat, *Nouvelle*, vol. 2, p. 20. Nothing came of this because the Spaniard who broached the subject with the king of Gereges could not gain the support of the Portuguese traders there, most of whom were New Christians who feared the spread of the Inquisition to West Africa. Labat, *Nouvelle*, vol. 2, p. 20. Azevedo de Coelho in Thomas, *Diola*, p. 311.

103. Hecquard describes this as having been an important and long-standing trade between Afro-Portuguese and the Diola, but his account is from the mid-nineteenth century. Hyacinthe Hecquard, *Voyages sur la côte et dans l'intérieur de l'Afrique Occidentale*, Paris: Imprimerie de Benaud, 1853. p. 110.

104. Hair, *De Almada*, pp. 79–80.

105. Coelho, *Description*, vol. 1, chap. 9, 36:74.

106. Goody describes a bow and arrow and spear weaponry as "democratic" because these weapons were easily obtainable. It stands in sharp contrast to the weaponry of the Sudan's slave raiders, who relied on horses and firearms. The expense and high mortality of horses and the scarcity of muskets and gunpowder made it easier for trading states to limit their availability within their domains. Jack Goody, *Technology, Tradition, and the State in Africa*, London: Oxford University Press, 1971, passim.

107. For example, see John Fage, "Slavery and the Slave Trade in the Context of West African History," *Journal of African History*, vol. 10, 1969, pp. 393–404.

Chapter 4

1. The ransoming of war captives probably developed independently of European influence. However, there is no clear evidence of the use of slaves within Esulalu before the development of a European market for slaves. See chapter 5.

2. Examples include the Kolobone lineage (originally from Huluf), most of whom presently bear the family name of Manga. Families with the name of Senghor or Djikune are members of the Djisenghalene-Djikune lineage, which traces its origins to the Huluf town of Senghalene.

3. The problem of interquarter unity has remained a serious one. Interquarter divisions and violent confrontations were reported as recently as 1979. For a discussion of a parallel process among the Diola-Bandial, see Snyder, "L'Evolution," p. 55.

4. The linguist Pierre-Marie Sambou translated the term as "there where you find yourselves," with the implication of a "region that is poorly known." Sambou, *Phonologie du nom en Diola Kasa Esuulaalu*, Dakar: Centre de Linguistique Appliqué de Dakar, 1977, p. 1.

5. For a discussion of the way in which religious systems interpret the world and endow it with meaning, see Peter Berger, *The Sacred Canopy: Elements of a Sociological Theory of Religion*, Garden City, N.Y.: Anchor, 1969, pp. 42–44. Clifford Geertz, *The Interpretation of Cultures*, New York: Basic Books, 1973, pp. 87–141.

6. Interviews with Indrissa Diedhiou and Edouard Kadjinga Diatta, Kadjinol-Kafone, 2/4/78; Sidionbaw Diatta, Kadjinol-Kafone, 2/7/78.

7. There is some disagreement about whether there was intermarriage with the Koonjaen, but judging from the collected genealogies and asylum-seeking procedures, it appears that it did occur. Indrissa Diedhiou of Kadjinol-Kafone (2/10/78) claimed that intermarriage with the Koonjaen developed only after they were brought into the townships. Badiat Sambou of Kadjinol-Kagnao (7/16/78) suggested that intermarriage was common before the conquest. This claim is supported by the exogamous marriage patterns of the Koonjaen lineages.

8. The Diola term *adjati* is translated by French-speaking Diola as *tuteur*. Interviews with Badiat Sambou, Kadjinol-Kagnao, 7/16/78; Antoine Houmandrissah Diedhiou, Kadjinol-Kafone, 2/27/78.

9. Many Koonjaen refugees settled in Kadjinol's quarter of Kafone and Kagnout's quarter of Ebrouwaye. In some cases, Koonjaen families retained ownership of their old rice paddies near the Calemboekine forest. They also retained rights to harvest palm wine in these areas. Interview with Sidionbaw Diatta, Kadjinol-Kafone, 2/7/78.

10. For a discussion of Esulalu domestic slavery, see chapter 7. Suzanne Miers and Igor Kopytoff emphasize the role of stranger as an integral part of a slave's status. However, it should be seen as more than a social category; it is a religious idea separating out those people who have no spiritual link to the community. See Miers and Kopytoff, *Slavery in Africa: Historical and Anthropological Perspectives*, Madison: University of Wisconsin Press, 1977, pp. 15–16. See also interview with Antoine Houmandrissah Diedhiou, Kadjinol-Kafone, 8/1/76, who makes a similar distinction. On humiliating rituals for slaves, see Antoine Houmandrissah Diedhiou, Kadjinol-Kafone, 7/17/78. On separate slave cemeteries, see interviews with Eheleterre Sambou, Kadjinol-Hassouka, 1/4/79; Michel Amancha Diatta, Kadjinol-Kandianka, 12/18/78; Kapooeh Diedhiou, Kadjinol-Kafone, 7/28/78; Siopama Diedhiou, Kadjinol-Kafone, 1/26/79; Sihendoo Manga, Kadjinol-Kafone, 7/15/78; Terence Galandiou Diouf Sambou, Kadjinol-Ebankine 6/19/75 and 5/12/78; Antoine Djemelene Sambou, Kadjinol-Kagnao, 6/23/78.

11. Interviews with Sidionbaw Diatta, Kadjinol-Kafone, 2/7/78; Antoine Houmandrissah Diedhiou, Kadjinol-Kafone, 5/23/78; Sihumucel Badji, Kadjinol-Hassouka, 5/18/78; Kapooeh Diedhiou, Kadjinol-Kafone, 7/27/87.

12. Interview with Kapooeh Diedhiou, Kadjinol-Kafone, 3/9/78. Interview with Sihumucel Badji, Kadjinol-Hassouka, 7/3/78. For a description of the Egol shrine and its role in Koonjaen society, see chapter 3. I have not learned what happened to the priests of Egol during the Koonjaen wars. Interviews with Sihumucel Badji, Kadjinol-Hassouka, 5/18/78; Siliungimagne Diatta, Kadjinol-Kandianka, 5/20/78; Djilehl Sambou, Kadjinol-Hassouka, 5/23/78.

13. There is evidence that Kadjinol temporarily established its Coeyi at the Koonjaen site in the forest of Calemboekine. Interview with Sidionbaw Diatta, Kadjinol-Kafone, 2/7/78. Many Christian shrines were established at the site of older shrines in Europe and Latin America for similar reasons.

14. Outside of the Gayo lineage, only two families can attend its rites, the adjunct (*kayille*) to the oeyi of Oussouye and the oeyi's relations in Kadjinol. The Oussouye adjunct is the major priest of the cult. This linkage between the Koonjaen and the priest-kingship will be discussed later. Interviews with Kuadadge Diatta, Kadjinol-Kafone, 2/26/78; Sidionbaw Diatta, Kadjinol-Kafone, 2/7/78; Kapooeh Diedhiou, Kadjinol-Kafone, 3/9/78 and 7/21/87. Kuadadge is one of the few non-Gayo men who can attend the ritual, based on his descent from a priest-king of Oussouye.

15. Interviews with Fidel Manga, Kolobone, 5/1/78; Antoine Houmandrissah Diedhiou, Kadjinol-Kafone, 2/2/78, 2/27/78, 5/31/78, and 6/18/78; Sidionbaw Diatta, Kadjinol-Kafone, 2/7/78.

16. Interviews with Kuadadge Diatta, Kadjinol-Kafone, 11/10/77; Mungo Sambou, Kadjinol-Kafone, 4/15/78; LeBois Diatta, Kadjinol-Hassouka, 1/26/78; Wuuli Assin, Cyriaque Assin, and Neerikoon Assin, Samatit, 5/11/78; Sooti Diatta, Samatit, 12/21/78. The raiders from Djougoutes who figure so prominently in Esulalu oral traditions are probably the same people whom Francisco de Azevedo de Coehlo describes as Saccaletes. Coelho quoted in Thomas, *Diola*, p. 310.

17. This process may have been aided by the erosion of Bainounk power during the eighteenth century. Interview with Antoine Houmandrissah Diedhiou, Kadjinol-Kafone, 2/27/78. George Brooks, "Perspectives."

18. I have gathered no evidence of a Floup blacksmith shrine that was created before the adoption of Silapoom.

19. Interview with Basayo Sambou, Kadjinol-Kandianka, 7/3/78. Interview with Djilehl Sambou, Kadjinol-Hassouka, 5/23/78. For a discussion of Gent's special status, the concept of the "owners of the soil," and Esulalu's role in the lives of the "first ancestors," see chapter 2.

20. The Diola-Esulalu have three different forms of Hupila. Two of these were developed under the influence of the slave trade and were not of Koonjaen origin. The third form, usually referred to as the "old Hupila," does not have the slave fetters on the shrine. It is this type of Hupila that would most likely be of Koonjaen origin or influenced by Koonjaen traditions. Both the Diola Kouhouloung and the old Hupila were described as existing since the "time of the first ancestors" and were among the very oldest Diola shrines. Because of their age, I was unable to obtain origin accounts of Kouhouloung or the old Hupila.

21. Kapooeh Diedhiou is one of the few elders who openly said that Kahat was of Koonjaen origin. This is supported by the fact that the family that controlled Kahat was of Koonjaen descent, and one of the reasons for eventually abandoning Kahat was that, by doing so, they restricted Koonjaen influence. Interviews with Kapooeh Diedhiou, Kadjinol-Kafone, 7/21/87; Basayo Sambou, Kadjinol-Kandianka, 7/3/78 and 11/7/78; Kuadadge Diatta, Kadjinol-Kafone, 2/20/78; Antoine Houmandrissah Diedhiou, Kadjinol-Kafone, 11/11/77.

22. None is mentioned in the oral traditions, and early travelers' accounts do not specifically mention southern Floup. In the sixteenth century, Valentim Fernandes claimed that the Balangas (Balanta) practiced circumcision. Monod, *Fernandes*, p. 61. A document circulated by the Holy Ghost Fathers, "Annales

Religieuses de la Casamance (Groupement Diola)," suggests that the Diola have practiced circumcision since approximately 1730. PSE Archives, 164B, p. 34. On the Koonjaen origin of Kahat, see interview with Kapooeh Diedhiou, Kadjinol-Kafone, 7/17/87. On communitas in initiation rites, see Turner, *Ritual Process.*

23. B. K. Sagnia, "Social and Religious Significance of Traditional Jola Male Initiation (Extract)," Banjul: Occasional Publications of the Gambia National Museum, vol. 6, 1984, p. 5.

24. Interviews with Asambou Senghor, Kadjinol-Sergerh, 10/24/77; Badiat Sambou, Kadjinol-Kagnao, 12/21/78; Basayo Sambou, Kadjinol-Kandianka, 11/7/78; Kuadadge Diatta, Kadjinol-Kafone, 2/21/78.

25. Interviews with Djiremo Sambou, Kadjinol-Ebankine, 2/17/78; Antoine Houmandrissah Diedhiou, 11/28/77; Indrissa Diedhiou, Kadjinol-Kafone, 7/31/76; Kuadadge Diatta, Kadjinol-Kafone, 2/21/78; Basayo Sambou, Kadjinol-Kandianka, 7/3/78. I am being deliberately vague on the nature of the operation and the activities that occurred during the ritual seclusion at the request of the elders of the present circumcision shrine, Bukut. Kahat is still practiced in several Huluf and Ediamat towns. For a description of Kahat in the 1950s, see Thomas, *Diola,* pp. 702–703. Most Bainounk, strongly influenced by the Mandinka and the Diola, presently use the Bukut form of male initiation rather than Kahat.

26. The term "Koonjaen" remains a strong ethnic slur in contemporary Diola usage. Interviews with Paponah Diatta, Mlomp-Etebemaye, 12/1/78; Antoine Houmandrissah Diedhiou, Kadjinol-Kafone, 5/8/78; Kapooeh Diedhiou, Kadjinol-Kafone, 7/17/87.

27. Curtin, *Economic,* vol. 2, pp. 3–7. Sharon E. Nicholson, "A Climatic Chronology for Africa: Synthesis of Geological, Historical, and Meteorological Information and Data," Ph.D. diss., University of Wisconsin, Madison, p. 124.

28. Interviews with Sebeoloute Manga, Mlomp-Djicomole, 7/12/78 and 12/27/78. Interviews with Alouise Manga, Mlomp-Djicomole, 6/18/78; Nicholas Djibune, Mlomp-Djicomole, 7/9/97.

29. Interview with Antoine Houmandandrissah Diedhiou, Kadjinol-Kafone, 6/18/78. At Eloudia, the office of priest-king was passed from the Kila lineage, which claims descent from Atta-Essou, to a different Koonjaen lineage from Eloukasine. This change was done fairly recently, after the war between Djicomole and Eloudia, and reflects the declining numbers of the Kila lineage. The priest-king of Samatit is also from this Eloukasine lineage. Interviews with Badjaya Kila, Eloudia, 12/12/78 and 12/23/78.

30. Francis Snyder reports a similar dualism in the royal shrines of the neighboring Bandial region. Personal communication, September 1983.

31. Interviews with Siliungimagne Diatta, Kadjinol-Kandianka, 11/15/77; LeBois Diatta, Kadjinol-Hassouka, 1/29/78; Sihumucel Badji, Kadjinol-Hassouka, 5/11/78. Some of these restrictions are probably older than the joining of Koonjaen and Floup shrines. The Manjaco priest-king, whose shrines are the source of the newer Floup ones, had even more restrictions than the priest-kings of the Floup. Interview with Jacques, Lopi, Djeromait, 7/14/78.

32. Interview with Father Earnest Sambou, Kadjinol-Kagnao, 8/18/78.

33. This is supported by evidence that the Manjaco of Guinea-Bissau, who live in an area from which the Floup migrated into the lower Casamance, did not have a tradition of direct prayer to or revelations from a supreme being until the beginning of the twentieth century. They claim to have gotten the idea of direct prayer and the cult associated with it from the Diola, who probably got it from the indigenous inhabitants of the lower Casamance, the Koonjaen. Personal communication from Eve Crowley.

34. Interview with Indrissa Diedhiou, Kadjinol-Kafone, 7/7/97.

35. Rituals are still performed there, but it is no longer used to pray for rain. Rather, it focuses on Aberman's fertility; it serves as a lineage shrine for the pro-

tection of children. Whether its role as a shrine of the supreme being was abandoned after Alinesitoué's introduction of her rain shrine of Kasila remains unclear. Group discussions with Ansamana Manga and Pauline Manga, Kadjinol-Ebankine 7/27/96; Terence Galandiou Diouf Sambou and Vincent Manga, Kadjinol-Ebankine, 8/20/96; Augustin Aoutah, Kagnout-Ebrouwaye, and Francois Buloti Diatta, Kadjinol-Kafone, 9/25/96. Interviews with Ansamana Manga, Kadjinol-Ebankine, 7/9/97; Michel Djigoon Senghor, Kadjinol-Kandianka, 9/10/96; Prosper Kwangany Diatta, Kadjinol-Kafone, 7/10/97; Elizabeth Sambou, Kadjinol-Kafone, 7/20/97; Indrissa Diedhiou, Kadjinol-Kafone, 7/10/96 and 7/11/97. Ansamana is the priest of Aberman.

36. Virtually everyone has Koonjaen ancestry on the maternal side, though one is described as Koonjaen only on the basis of paternal descent.

37. Fredrik Barth, "Introduction," in *Ethnic Groups*. For a discussion of Diola antipathy to the hoarding of wealth, see chapter 2. Hoarders of power and wealth were often thought to be witches.

38. Scattered incidents of violence resulting from land disputes have occurred as recently as the 1960s in Esulalu and the 1970s in other Diola areas. Interviews with André Kebroohaw Manga and Musampen Diatta, Kadjinol-Sergerh, 4/18/78; René Djabune, Oukout, 1/30/78. On proverbs see Abbé Nazaire Diatta, *Les Joolas: Proverbes et Expressions, Contribution à l'elaboration de la charte culturelle Sénégalaise*, Youtou, Senegal: published by the author, 1985, vol. 2, 49-1. For a description of warfare over land in other Diola areas, see Snyder, "Droit Foncier," pp. 50–51. Peter Mark, "Economic," p. 16.

39. Interview with Sikakucele Diatta, Kadjinol-Kafone, 3/17/78.

40. Such houses were being built in Esulalu as recently as the 1960s. Jean Baptiste Labat, *Nouvelle Relation*, vol. 2, p. 32. While Labat wrote his account in the early eighteenth century, it is plagiarized from a seventeenth-century work by Sieur de la Courbe, of which only fragments are available. Cultru, *de la Courbe*.

41. Interview with Sinyendikaw Diedhiou, Kadjinol-Kafone, 7/11/78. This is confirmed by Sebikuan Sambou, oeyi of Mlomp. Interview with Sebikuan Sambou, Mlomp-Djicomole, 6/14/94.

42. Interviews with Anto Manga, Kadjinol-Ebankine, 8/15/78; Sikakucele Diatta, Kadjinol-Kafone, 3/17/78; Yerness Manga, Mlomp-Djicomole, 21/2/77.

43. For a detailed discussion of the relationship between warfare, spirit shrines, and the awasena way, see Robert M. Baum, "Shrines, Medicines, and the Strength of the Head: The Way of the Warrior among the Diola of Senegambia," *Numen*, vol. 40, 1993, pp. 274–292. Elenkine-Sergerh represents the Kalybillah half of Kadjinol. The shrine predates the Hassouka-Kafone war of the late eighteenth century, which resulted in the transfer of Ecuhuh from Hassouka to Kafone. Some quarter shrines, such as Dehouhow, include women as participants; Elenkine-Sergerh excludes them. For Kadjinol-Kandianka, the shrine of Elucil allows men from all part of Kandianka, except Batendu, to attend. Interview with Basayo Sambou, Kadjinol-Kandianka, 11/29/77.

44. The spring called Kanalia is closely linked to the Elucil shrine of Kandianka. Interview with Etienne Manga, Kadjinol-Kandianka, 8/17/76. The spring called Cassissilli is linked to a shrine of the same name at Kagnout-Ebrouwaye. Interviews with Pakum Bassin, Kagnout-Ebrouwaye,12/17/78; Djikankoulan Sambou, Kagnout-Ebrouwaye, 1/8/79.

45. Interview with Boolai Senghor, Kadjinol-Sergerh, 6/10/78. Interviews with Kapooeh Diedhiou, Kadjinol-Kafone, 8/5/87 and 8/8/87; Siopama Diedhiou, Kadjinol-Kafone, 12/4/77; Etienne Manga, Kadjinol-Kandianka, 8/17/76.

The women's fertility shrine, Ehugna, was introduced by men, but participation at its rituals is limited to women. See chapter 6. Odile Journet has also noticed this gender complementarity, suggesting that several women's shrines are seen as "essentially masculine" and several male shrines are seen as "essentially feminine." Odile Journet, "Les Hyper-Mères n'ont plus d'enfants: Maternité et ordre social chez les Joola de Basse-Casamance," in Nicole-Claude Mattieu, editor, *L'Arraisonment des Femmes: Essais en Anthropologies des Sexes*, Paris: Editions de l'Ecole des Hautes Etudes en Science Sociales, 1985, p. 18.

46. Samatit's townshipwide shrine of Enac could also refuse to allow a war. There is a green mamba snake that is associated with the Enac shrine. Interviews with Sooti Diatta, Samatit, 12/21/78; Boolai Senghor, Kadjinol-Sergerh, 6/10/78; Kapooeh Diedhiou, Kadjinol-Kafone, 3/9/78; Sinyendikaw Diedhiou, Kadjinol-Kafone, 4/7/78.

47. The Portuguese were already at Ziguinchor, and muskets were already being used in battle. The late-eighteenth-century date is also derived from an analysis of Diedhiou genealogies, the diffusion of the Cabai shrine, and the fact that it was introduced before the Bukut form of male initiation at the end of the eighteenth century. Interviews with Antoine Houmandrissah Diedhiou, Kadjinol-Kafone, 8/1/77 and 2/27/78; Diaswah Sambou, Kadjinol-Kafone, 12/12/77.

48. Interviews with Antoine Houmandrissah Diedhiou, Kadjinol-Kafone, 8/1/76 and 2/27/78; Diashwah Sambou, Kadjinol-Kafone, 7/7/76 and 12/12/77. Some people claimed that a dispute over burial rites was also involved. The townships excluded men born outside Esulalu from burial in the main cemetery. They may have tried to extend this to those of Koonjaen descent. Group discussion with Ompa Kumbegeny Diedhiou and Edouard Kadjinga Diatta, Kadjinol-Kafone, 6/13/78.

49. Interview with Sinyendikaw Diedhiou, Kadjinol-Kafone, 4/7/78. Interview with Siopama Diedhiou, Kadjinol-Kafone, 3/20/78. The vision could have occurred during a bout with African sleeping sickness, which was common in the area until well into the twentieth century. Other descriptions of visions were said to have occurred during a deep sleep. Interviews with Etienne Abisenkor Sambou, 4/15/78; Kapooeh Diedhiou, Kadjinol-Kafone, 8/5/87. J. C. Ene, *Insects and Man in West Africa*, Ibadan: Ibadan University Press, 1963, p. 12.

50. Interview with Antoine Houmandrissah Diedhiou, Kadjinol-Kafone, 2/27/78. This is confirmed in interviews with Diashwah Sambou, Kadjinol-Kafone, 9/25/78; Ompa Kumbegeny Diedhiou, Kadjinol-Kafone, and Boolai Senghor, Kadjinol-Sergerh, 6/13/78.

51. Interviews with Antoine Houmandrissah Diedhiou, Kadjinol-Kafone, 2/27/78 and 6/25/78; Etienne Abbisenkor Sambou, Kadjinol-Kafone, 4/15/78; Siopama Diedhiou, Kadjinol-Kafone, 3/20/78; Kapooeh Diedhiou, Kadjinol-Kafone, 8/3/87.

52. For a more detailed discussion of the visions of Atta-Essou, see chapter 3. In the early 1940s Alinesitoué claimed an ongoing series of revelations from Emitai. Girard, *Genèse*, pp. 214–269. Waldman with Baum, "Innovation."

53. Interviews with Sinyendikaw Diedhiou, Kadjinol-Kafone, 4/7/78; Kapooeh Diedhiou, Kadjinol-Kafone, 8/3/87 and 8/8/87.

54. Interviews with Sikakucele Diatta, Kadjinol-Kafone, 3/17/78; Antoine Houmandrissah Diedhiou, Kadjinol-Kafone, 8/1/76, 2/27/78, and 6/25/78.

55. Interview with Djatti Sambou, Lampolly Sambou, and Edouard Sambou, Mlomp-Haer, 1/9/79.

56. For a description of the confessional rite associated with Djimamo, see chapter 2. Interviews with Diashwah Sambou, Kadjinol-Kafone, 4/13/78; Mungo Sambou, Kadjinol-Kafone, 4/15/78; Attabadionti Diatta, Kadjinol-Sergerh, 7/13/76; Diashwah Sambou, Isador Sambou, and Mungo Sambou, Kadjinol-Kafone, 6/26/76.

57. Katapf is closely linked to Cabai in many quarters and protects against wounds by metal objects at work, as well as in war. Interview with Sikakucele Diatta, Kadjinol-Kafone, 3/17/78. Personal observations of Katapf rituals.

58. Muslim amulets (gris-gris) were in common use by the midnineteenth century. On Diola war medicines see interviews with Diashwah Sambou, Kadjinol-Kafone, 7/7/76; Kuadadge Diatta and Ompa Kumbegeny Diedhiou, Kadjinol-Kafone, 6/24/76.

59. Interviews with Cyriaque Assin and Neerikoon Assin, Samatit, 6/20/78; Antoine Houmandrissah Diedhiou, Kadjinol-Kafone, 6/25/78; Diaswah Sambou, Kadjinol-Kafone, 7/7/76; Boolai Senghor, Kadjinol-Sergerh, 8/14/78; Siopama Diedhiou, Kadjinol-Kafone, 6/25/78.

60. Interviews with Djatti Sambou, Mlomp-Haer, 1/13/79; Sihumucel Badji, Kadjinol-Hassouka, 7/8/78; Sebeoloute Manga, Mlomp-Djicomole, 4/24/78. There was a similar rite called Hounillo, which was performed to purify those Esulalu who had fought in the world wars. Interview with Terence Galandiou Diouf Sambou, Kadjinol-Ebankine, 10/19/78.

61. Interviews with Kuadadge Diatta, Kadjinol-Kafone, 11/10/77; Siliungimagne Diatta, Kadjinol-Kandianka, 11/25/78; Antoine Houmandrissah Diedhiou, Kadjinol-Kafone, 11/28/78; Diashwah Sambou, Kadjinol-Kafone, 7/7/76; Asambou Senghor, Kadjinol-Sergerh, 12/12/77; Sooti Diatta, Samatit, 12/12/78.

62. While we lack detailed priest lists or detailed accounts of its origin, informants all insist that Hutendookai is extremely old. Specific priests are mentioned in the early nineteenth century, but informants generally suggested a greater antiquity, invoking the term "since the time of the first ancestors" or comparing its longevity to that of the priest-kingship itself. Interviews with Kuadadge Diatta and Antoine Houmandrissah Diedhiou, Kadjinol-Kafone, 2/16/78; Djiremo Sambou, Kadjinol-Ebankine, 4/9/78; Sikarwen Diatta, Eloudia, 7/19/78; Songatebeh Diatta, Mlomp-Kadjifolong, 6/29/78.

For its introduction from Seleki, see interview with Assinway Sambou, Kadjinol-Kafone, 11/11/77. The Bandial-Seleki area appears to be the only other Diola area that has Hutendookai. Francis Snyder, "Legal Innovation and Social Disorganization in a Peasant Community: A Senegalese Village Police," *Africa*, vol. 48, 1978, pp. 231–247.

63. Interviews with Yerness Manga, Mlomp-Djicomole, 12/2/77; Assinway Sambou, Kadjinol-Kafone, 4/25/78.

64. Interviews with Boolai Senghor, Kadjinol-Sergerh, 6/29/78; Assinway Sambou, Kadjinol-Kafone 1/1/77. I was initiated into this organization in 1977 and patroled the rice paddies with its members. Snyder, "Legal Innovation," passim.

65. Interviews with Kuadadge Diatta and Antoine Houmandrissah Diedhiou, Kadjinol-Kafone, 2/16/78; Assinway Sambou, Kadjinol-Kafone, 11/11/77 and 2/2/78; Sikarwen Diatta, Eloudia, 1/11/79.

66. References to people who "eat human flesh" could refer to two different types of witches, an asaye or an assanga. The asaye was said to travel about at night as a soul leaving its body behind. While traveling it might consume the soul of another person. This was described as eating human flesh. There was also said to be a secret society called kussanga whose members ate human flesh. While some believe that this happens in the temporal world (i.e., Father Henri Joffroy and the French colonial authorities), I would contend that these, too, were acts of the spiritual world. See Robert M. Baum, "Crimes of the Dream World: French Trials of Diola Witches," Paper presented at the University of Warwick Conference on the History of Law, Labor, and Crime, 1983.

67. Certain lands were reserved for the office of the priest-king. The township as a whole cultivated these paddies and provided rice for the priest-king's household. Interviews with LeBois Diatta, Kadjinol-Hassouka, 4/24/78; André Bankuul Senghor, Kadjinol-Hassouka, 11/18/77; Siliungimagne Diatta, Kadjinol-Kandianka, 11/15/77. Snyder, "Droit Foncier," p. 49.

68. Interviews with Alouise Manga, Mlomp-Djicomole, 12/27/78; Sebeoloute Manga, Mlomp-Djicomole, 4/24/78.

69. Interviews with Siliungimagne Diatta, Kadjinol-Kandianka, 6/21/78; Antoine Houmandrissah Diedhiou, Kadjinol-Kafone, 6/18/78; Diashwah Sambou, Kadjinol-Kafone, 4/26/78; Mungo Sambou, Kadjinol-Kafone, 4/15/78.

70. For a discussion of the role of wealth in the selection of Hoohaney elders, see chapter 5. Interview with Kapooeh Diedhiou, Kadjinol-Kafone, 7/17/87.

71. Interviews with Djatti Sambou, Mlomp-Haer, 11/9/78 and 1/13/79; Antoine Houmandrissah Diedhiou, Kadjinol-Kafone, 6/18/77; Kapooeh Diedhiou, Kadjinol-Kafone, 2/7/78; Siliungimagne Diatta, Kadjinol-Kandianka, 8/12/78; Samouli Senghor, Kadjinol-Hassouka, 6/25/75.

72. Hoohaney is described as extremely old, but not as old as those created at the time of the "first ancestors." It is said to be older than the Bukut form of circumcision, which was introduced in the waning years of the eighteenth century. Interviews with Siopama Diedhiou, Kadjinol-Kafone, 6/9/78; Djiremo Sambou, Kadjinol-Ebankine, 6/29/78; Paponah Diatta, Mlomp-Etebemaye, 8/7/78. That it did not precede Bukut by many years is suggested by the rule that no man may hold priestly office in both Bukut and Hoohaney. On its being limited to Esulalu, see interviews with Antoine Houmandrissah Diedhiou, Kadjinol-Kafone, 6/18/77 and Kapooeh Diedhiou, Kadjinol-Kafone, 7/10/87. Thomas, *Diola*, p. 595.

73. According to Kapooeh Diedhiou, Hassouka's Hoohaney elders used their authority to seize pigs from Kalybillah, which they sacrificed at the shrine. Based on Diedhiou-Djabune lineages, Penjaw was born in the mideighteenth century and could have represented his compound at the Hoohaney shrine as early as 1790. There have been a total of eight priests of the Kalybillah shrines, though there often are long interregna between priests. Interviews with Kapooeh Diedhiou, Kadjinol-Kafone, 7/28/78 and 7/21/87; Siliungimagne Diatta, Kadjinol-Kandianka, 8/12/78; Djatti Sambou, Mlomp-Haer, 1/13/79.

74. Interviews with Kapooeh Diedhiou, Kadjinol-Kafone, 7/28/78; Basayo Sambou, Kadjinol-Kandianka, 7/3/78; Djatti Sambou, Mlomp-Haer, 1/13/79.

75. Dating of the switch from Kahat to Bukut is based on initiation lists of eight Bukut initiations. These were said to be held every twenty years, though for Kadjinol in the twentieth century, they were held less frequently (Badusu, 1901; Djambia, 1923, Batachakuale, 1952; and the most recent, Waite, in 1990). The third oldest Bukut, Bagangup, was the circumcision rite of Haieheck, who signed a peace treaty with the French in 1860. By 1860, he would have been an elder and was probably circumcised by 1820. Interviews with Kubaytow Diatta, Kadjinol-Kandianka, 5/20/78; Antoine Houmandrissah Diedhiou, Kadjinol-Kafone, 8/1/76, 11/9/77, and 11/28/77; Kuadadge Diatta and Djisenghalene Sambou, Kadjinol-Kafone, 2/14/78; Indrissa Diedhiou, Sinyendikaw Diedhiou, Edmund Diedhiou, Ompa Kumbegeny Diedhiou, 6/18/75; Terence Galandiou Diouf Sambou, Kadjinol-Ebankine, 5/15/78; Eddi Senghor, Kadjinol-Sergerh, 11/6/77; Etienne Manga, Kadjinol-Kandianka, 2/5/78.

Peter Mark claims that the Bukut form entered the Djougoutes area no later than 1800. Mark, *Cultural*, pp. 19–20. Girard has argued that Bukut was introduced in the early twentieth century by the Mandinka, as part of a modernization process. This is not supported by any of the evidence. Girard, *Genèse*, p. 66.

76. Mandinka circumcision rituals are held whenever there are a group of boys of an appropriate age. Where they are most similar is in their lengthy ritual seclusion in shelters on the edge of settlement and in their announcement of deaths of initiates by the display of their ceremonial cloths. Matt Schaffer and Christine Cooper, *Mandinko: The Ethnography of a West African Holy Land*, New York: Holt, Rinehart and Winston, 1980, pp. 95–99. Abdoulie Bayo, "Interview with Muhammed Jebate," unpublished manuscript, Cultural Archives, The Gambia, November 1980. On the introduction of Bukut, see interviews with Amymoh Manga, Enampore, 7/14/97; Agnauti Senghor, Kadjinol-Sergerh, 7/20/97; Eddi Senghor, Kadjinol-Sergerh, 2/12/75 and 11/6/77; Indrissa Diedhiou, Sinyendikaw Diedhiou, Edmund Diedhiou, Ompa Kumbegeny Diedhiou, 6/18/75; Kuadadge Diatta, Kadjinol-Kafone, 2/21/78; Indrissa Diedhiou, Kadjinol-Kafone, 7/31/78; Yerness Manga, Mlomp-Djicomole, 6/20/76.

77. I have refrained from naming informants on this point because some elders would not be pleased that this information was revealed. Although I have the permission of my sources, I think it is advisable to protect their identities. Interview in Kadjinol, 2/17/78. This was confirmed in Kadjinol, 5/22/78; Kadjinol, 4/9/78; Kadjinol 7/3/78.

78. Interview with Alouise Sambou, Kadjinol-Ebankine, 6/11/87. Kapooeh Diedhiou insists that the elders came from Djirikanao or Seleki. Bandial is a collective term for a cluster of Diola townships east of Esulalu, as well as a name for a specific township. Djirikanao is a township within the Bandial area. Interview with Kapooeh Diedhiou, Kadjinol-Kafone, 7/10/87.

79. Interviews with Djiremo Sambou, Kadjinol-Ebankine, 2/17/78; Antoine Houmandrissah Diedhiou, 11/28/77 and 4/23/78; Indrissa Diedhiou, Kadjinol-Kafone, 7/31/78; Boolai Senghor, Kadjinol-Sergerh, 7/10/78; Kuadadge Diatta, Kadjinol-Kafone, 2/21/78.

80. Interview with Boolai Senghor, Kadjinol-Sergerh, 7/10/78. Secrecy is important in most shrines. Abbé Diatta has collected a proverb that supports that: "The shrine elder should know when to be silent." Diatta, *Joolas*, vol. 5, p. 95-1. Beryl Bellman has noted a similar attitude toward secrecy among the Kpelle of Liberia. He noted that women elders possess a considerable knowledge of the men's secret society, Poro, while male elders know a considerable amount about the women's secret society, Sande. Diola women have a similar knowledge of male initiation. Publicly, both Kpelle and Diola elders act as if they have no such knowledge of the other gender's secrets. See Beryl Bellman, *The Language of Secrets: Symbols and Metaphors in Poro Ritual*, New Brunswick, N.J.: Rutgers University Press, 1984, passim.

81. Girard, *Genèse*, p. 90.

82. Interviews with Siliungimagne Diatta, Kadjinol-Kandianka, 5/20/78; LeBois Diatta, Kadjinol-Hassouka, Antoine Djemelene Sambou, Kadjinol-Kagnao, and Djalli Bassin, Kadjinol-Ebankine, 4/16/78.

83. This did not involve any form of female circumcision, a practice that is absolutely forbidden in Esulalu. Women midwives would complete the ritual initiation of women at the time when they gave birth for the first time. This was followed by several days of seclusion.

84. The elaborate celebrations are central to Alouise Sambou's account of the introduction of Bukut into Esulalu. Interviews with Alouise Sambou, Kadjinol-Ebankine, 6/11/87; Kuadadge Diatta, Kadjinol-Kafone, 2/21/78; Djiremo Sambou, Kadjinol-Ebankine, 2/17/78; Boolai Senghor, Kadjinol-Sergerh, 7/10/78; Badjaya Kila, Eloudia, 12/12/78; Djibandial Diedhiou, Kadjinol-Kafone, 5/29/75; Antoine Houmandrissah Diedhiou, 11/28/77. For a description of Bukut in the neighboring Diola community of Niomoun, see L. V. Thomas, "Mort Symbolique et Naissance Initiatique (Bukut chez les Diola-Niomoun)," *Cahier des Religions Africaines*, 1970, pp. 41–71. The emphasis on animal sacrifice in the celebration and in the taking on of ritual office is discussed in greater detail in chapter 5.

85. This cannot be discussed in any detail at the request of the elders of Bukut. Interviews with Djibandial Diedhiou, Kadjinol-Kafone, 5/29/75; Indrissa Diedhiou, Kadjinol-Kafone, 7/31/76; Malanbaye Sambou, Mlomp-Djicomole, 11/7/78; Boolai Senghor, Kadjinol-Sergerh, 7/10/78; Antoine Houmandrissah Diedhiou, Kadjinol-Kafone, 11/11/77; Ekusumben Diedhiou, Kadjinol-Kafone, 7/23/87; Landing Diedhiou and Kapooeh Diedhiou, Kadjinol-Kafone, 7/10/87.

86. They moved from Kadjinol-Ebankine to Kadjinol-Kafone in the early 1960s. Corrugate Diedhiou claims that their lineage, Elou Sangene, was forcibly removed from Sergerh because of their refusal to adopt Bukut. Interviews with Kapooeh Diedhiou, Kadjinol-Kafone, 7/17/87 and 7/10/87; Tibor Diedhiou, Kadjinol-Kafone, 8/8/87; Corrugate Gilbert Diedhiou, Kadjinol-Kafone, 8/8/96.

87. The Ewang shrine at Kolobone, controlled by the priest-king of Oussouye,

is the most powerful shrine associated with the resolution of land disputes for Huluf and Esulalu. Interview with Jonas Sina Diatta, Mlomp-Etebemaye, 7/7/87. Personal communication, Klaus de Jonge, 1/13/75.

88. Interviews with Kuadadge Diatta, 2/21/78; Indrissa Diedhiou, Kadjinol-Kafone, 7/31/76; Asenkahan Diedhiou, Kadjinol-Kafone, 8/14/76; Anto Manga, Kadjinol-Ebankine, 4/17/75; Djiremo Sambou, Kadjinol-Ebankine, 4/9/78. Girard, *Genése*, p. 44.

89. Interviews with Sikakucele Diatta, Kadjinol-Kafone, 11/7/78; Boolai Senghor, 8/14/78; Paponah Diatta, Mlomp-Etebemaye, 12/27/78.

90. Interviews with Songatebeh Diatta, Mlomp-Kadjifoling, 12/19/78; Boolai Senghor, Kadjinol-Sergerh, 11/17/78; Terence Galandiou Diouf Sambou, Kadjinol-Ebankine, 6/19/75; Siopama Diedhiou, Kadjinol-Kafone, 6/9/78; Kapooeh Diedhiou, Kadjinol-Kafone, 11/28/78.

91. Interviews with Paponah Diatta, Mlomp-Etebemaye, 12/27/78; Hoosooli Diedhiou, Kadjinol-Ebankine, and Diongany Diedhiou, Kadjinol-Kafone, 1/20/78. Victor Turner, *The Drums of Affliction*, Oxford: Clarendon, 1968, passim. For the only historical study of a cult of affliction, see John M. Janzen, *Lemba, 1650–1930: A Drum of Affliction in Africa and the New World*, New York: Garland, 1982, pp. 3–4.

92. Robin Horton, "African Traditional Thought and Western Science," *Africa*, vol. 37, 1967, pp. 155–156. A similar contrast is made by Lévi-Strauss when he compares the *bricoleur* and the engineer. Claude Lévi-Strauss: *The Savage Mind*, Chicago: University of Chicago Press, 1968, pp. 17–19.

93. For a fuller discussion of his basic African cosmology, see chapter 2. Horton, "African Conversion," p. 101.

94. Interview with Paponah Diatta, Mlomp-Etebemaye, 11/11/78. Sapir, "Kujaama," p. 1331. Thomas, *Diola*, p. 537.

95. Joseph C. Miller, "The Dynamics of Oral Tradition in Africa," in B. Bernardi, C. Poni, and A. Triulzi, eds., *Fonti Orali—Oral Sources—Sources Orales. Antropologiae Storia—Anthropology and History—Anthropologie et Histoire*, Milan: F. Angeli, 1978, pp. 89–90.

Chapter 5

1. This may have helped to overcome Diola resistance to participation in the slave trade. Jean Boulègue, *Les Luso-Africains*, p. 39. Rodney, *Upper Guinea*, p. 98. For discussion of the Portuguese prohibition on the firearms trade and its dramatic increase once other Europeans entered the slave trade, see Joseph Miller, *Way of Death: Merchant Capitalism and the Angolan Slave Trade, 1730–1830*, Madison: University of Wisconsin Press, 1988, pp. 76, 88. For a description of pre-eighteenth-century slave trading in Casamance, see chapter 3 and Mark, *Cultural*, pp. 11–32.

2. Charlotte Quinn bases this on statistics from the Royal African Company. Slave trading along the Gambia peaked at six to seven thousand slaves per annum in 1677. Quinn, *Mandingo Kingdoms*, p. 8.

3. Alvares de Almada in Thomas, *Diola*, pp. 309–310. Rodney, *Upper Guinea*, pp. 103, 105, 111. P. Cultru, *Premier Voyage*, p. 208. Labat, *Nouvelle Relation*, vol. 4, p. 271.

4. On Aetingah raids see interviews with Antoine Houmandrissah Diedhiou, Kadjinol-Kafone, 3/28/78; Attabationti Diatta, Kadjinol-Sergerh, 7/13/76 and 6/10/78. Frederick Bowser estimates that 387 slaves of Diola (Falupo) origin were brought to Peru by 1650. F. Bowser, *The African Slave Trade in Colonial Peru, 1524–1650*, Stanford: Stanford University Press, 1974, pp. 40–42. John Thornton, *Africa and Africans in the Making of the Atlantic World, 1400–1680*. Cambridge:

Cambridge University Press, 1993, pp. 159, 198–199. Gilberto Freyre, *The Masters and the Slaves: A Study in the Development of Brazilian Civilization*, New York: Alfred A. Knopf, 1964, p. 412.

5. Claude Meillassoux, *The Anthropology of Slavery: The Womb of Iron and Gold*. Chicago: University of Chicago Press, 1991, pp. 85–86.

6. Rodney, *Upper Guinea*, p. 117.

7. Olfert Dapper describes some incidents in which Floup slave traders were sold into slavery. Dapper, *Description*, p. 242. Thornton argues that such incidents were common when slave traders were not protected by powerful African states. Thornton, *Africa*, p. 70.

Francisco de Lemos Coelho claims that some Floup traded directly with the Portuguese at Cacheu. See Coelho, *Description*, 3:7:12. De Almada emphasized the use of African middlemen. Silveira, *Tratado*, p. 135.

8. *Grumetes* were West Africans who embraced Portuguese culture and dress while working with the Portuguese trading companies. Cultru, *de la Courbe*, p. 205. Group discussion with Wuuli Assin, Neerikoon Assin, Cyriaque Assin, Samatit, 5/11/78. George Brooks, "Perspectives," passim. Dapper, in Boulègue, *Luso-Africans*, p. 46.

9. Captain Philip Beaver, *African Memoranda: Relative to an Attempt to Establish a British Settlement on the Island of Bulama, on the Western Coast of Africa, in the Year 1792*, London: C. and R. Baldwin, 1805, p. 322.

10. Interview with Indrissa Diedhiou, Kadjinol-Kafone, 7/31/76. Interviews with Sikarwen Diatta, Eloudia, 7/19/78; Grégoire Diatta, Mlomp-Kadjifolong, 7/5/76.

11. Walter Rodney, *Upper Guinea*, p. 117; and "African Slavery and Other Forms of Social Oppression on the Upper Guinea Coast in the Context of the Atlantic Slave Trade," *Journal of African History*, vol. 7, no. 3, 1966, p. 432. Claude Meillassoux, "Correspondence," *Economy and Society*, vol. 7, 1978, p. 322; and *Anthropology*, pp. 36, 43, 85–86.

12. Interviews with Sikarwen Diatta, Eloudia, 7/19/78; Antoine Houmandrissah Diedhiou, Kadjinol-Kafone, 2/2/78 and 2/27/78; Indrissa Diedhiou, Kadjinol-Kafone, 1/27/78; Kuadadge Diatta, 11/10/78; Diashwah Sambou, Kadjinol-Kafone, 2/2/78; Sihumucel Badji, Kadjinol-Hassouka, 5/18/78. Group discussion with Asambou Senghor, Kadjinol-Sergerh, and Siopama Diedhiou, Kadjinol-Kafone, 3/5/78.

De Almada, cited in Thomas, *Diola*, pp. 309–310. George Brooks, personal communication, 1979.

13. Slaves were buried in a separate "strangers' cemetery." Koonjaen were buried in the main cemetery. Robert M. Baum, "Incomplete Assimilation: Koonjaen and Diola in Pre-Colonial Senegambia," Paper presented to the ninety-eighth annual meeting of the American Historical Association, San Francisco, 1983, p. 13.

14. This tends to confirm Rodney's and Linares's contentions that a slave trade was not common among the coastal peoples of upper Guinea before the arrival of Europeans. Rodney, "African Slavery," pp. 432–434. Olga Linares, "Deferring to Trade in Slaves: The Jola of Casamance, Senegal in Historical Perspective," *History in Africa*, vol. 14, 1987, pp. 114–116.

15. Interviews with Anto Manga, Kadjinol-Ebankine, 6/4/76; Badiat Sambou, Kadjinol-Kagnao, 7/16/78; Grégoire Djikune, Kadjinol-Kagnao, 7/23/78; Antoine Houmandrissah Diedhiou, Kadjinol-Kafone, 2/27/78; Kuadadge Diatta, Kadjinol-Kafone, 11/10/77; André Manga, Kadjinol-Sergerh, 4/18/78; René Djabune, Oukout, 1/30/78; Wuuli Assin, Neerikoon Assin, Cyriaque Assin, Samatit, 5/11/78.

16. Coelho in Thomas, *Diola*, p. 310. The Sacaletes are probably the seventeenth-century ancestors of the Diola of Djougoutes. On the Ekabliane or Aetingah, see interview with Kuadadge Diatta, Kadjinol-Kafone, 11/10/77.

17. Thornton, *Africa*, p. 99.

18. This did not exclude occasional cattle raids between Esulalu townships during periods of tension. Captives were not seized within Esulalu because they were of one land (essouk). Ideally, this should have prevented interquarter and intertownship wars, but it did not. However, the priest-kings of Esulalu would stop any warfare within Esulalu. Interview with Kubaytow Diatta, Kadjinol-Kandianka, 4/26/78.

19. Interview with Sinyendikaw Diedhiou, Kadjinol-Kafone, 2/9/78.

20. Group discussion with Cyriaque Assin and Neerikoon Assin, Samatit, 6/20/78.

21. Interview with Edouard Kadjinga Diatta, Kadjinol-Kafone, 3/3/78. Robert M. Baum, "Shrines," pp. 274–292.

22. Muskets and gunpowder, as foreign trade goods, could be more readily subjected to control by a ruler or a warrior class. Jack Goody, *Technology*, p. 43.

23. Kopytoff and Miers, "Introduction," in Miers and Kopytoff, *African Slavery*.

24. Group discussion with Cyriaque Assin, Wuuli Assin, and Neerikoon Assin, Samatit, 5/11/78. Interviews with Antoine Houmandrissah Diedhiou, Kadjinol-Kafone, 8/1/76, 2/27/78, and 6/8/78; Edouard Kadjinga Diatta, Kadjinol-Kafone, 3/3/78; Anto Manga, Kadjinol-Ebankine, 6/4/76; Sirkimagne Diedhiou, Kadjinol-Kafone, 7/12/87; Kapooeh Diedhiou, Kadjinol-Kafone, 7/17/87; Ekusumben Diedhiou, Dionsal Diedhiou, and Diongany Diedhiou, Kadjinol-Kafone, 7/22/78.

25. Interviews with Indrissa Diedhiou, Kadjinol-Kafone, 7/31/76; Moolaye Bassin, Kadjinol-Ebankine, 11/1/78. Abdoulaye Ly reports that, in 1685, French and British traders were purchasing slaves for sixteen to thirty cattle apiece. The lower price in Esulalu could be readily explained by its distance from the major trade factories. Abdoulaye Ly, "Un Navire de Commerce sur la Côte Sénégambienne en 1685," IFAN, *Catalogues et Documents*, vol. 17, 1964, p. 26. Interviews with Antoine Houmandrissah Diedhiou, Kadjinol-Kafone, 2/27/78; Antoine Djemelene Sambou, Kadjinol-Kagnao, 6/12/78.

26. Interviews with Boolai Senghor, Kadjinol-Sergerh, 7/2/78; Antoine Houmandrissah Diedhiou, Kadjinol-Kafone, 6/8/78; Edouard Kadjinga Diatta, Kadjinol-Kafone, 3/3/78; Moolaye Bassin, Kadjinol-Ebankine, 11/1/78; Sidionbo Diatta and Simingkennah Diatta, Kadjinol-Kafone, 1/18/79.

27. Claire Robertson and Martin Klein, editors, *Women and Slavery in Africa*, Madison: University of Wisconsin Press, 1983, p. 3 and passim. For a discussion of Diola slavery, as opposed to the slave trade, see chapter 6.

28. This linking of economic activities with ukine did not end with the slave trade. In the nineteenth century, a new hunting shrine, Houpoombene, was named after the Diola word for "musket." In the twentieth century, the women's fertility shrine of Ehugna became associated with the protection of urban palm wine vendors and was invoked to safeguard public transportation.

29. Research by Donatus Ibe Nwoga has raised questions about whether Aro Chukwu was an oracle of the Igbo supreme being or just the most important oracle of the Aro community of southeastern Nigeria. In either case, its spiritual prestige legitimated its priests' seizure of slaves and protected slave traders associated with the shrine while they traveled in the region. Nwoga, *The Supreme God as Stranger in Igbo Religious Thought*, Ekwereazu, Nigeria: Hawk Press, 1984, passim. On the Aro Chukwu shrine's involvement in the slave trade, see K. Onwuka Dike, *Trade and Politics in the Niger Delta, 1830–1885*, Oxford: Clarendon Press, 1966, pp. 37–40. David Northrup, *Trade without Rulers: Pre-Colonial Economic Development in South-Eastern Nigeria*, Oxford: Clarendon Press, 1978, chap. 5.

30. John Janzen, *Lemba*, pp. 3–4 and passim.

31. Bernard Belasco, *The Entrepreneur as Culture Hero: Preadaptations in Nigerian Economic Development*, New York: J. F. Begin, 1980, pp. 22, 52, 95, 131–132.

32. Interview with Sikarwen Diatta, Eloudia, 7/19/78.

33. Interview with Badjassaw Senghor, Kadjinol-Kandianka, 8/5/87.

34. Each new child has a ritual greeting performed on its behalf. In-marrying wives also have such a rite performed. These rituals ensure that Calemboekine assumes responsibility for the well-being of all the inhabitants of the township.

35. In the nineteenth and twentieth centuries, a newer blacksmith shrine would seize such people with leprosy.

36. The same thing happened to her sister some years later. Interview with Nuhli Bassin, Kadjinol-Ebankine, 7/13/76. A similar relationship exists between certain Diedhious and certain Sambous. Using the term *gnigne* (absolutely forbidden) to describe such actions and describing the custom as existing since the "time of the first ancestors" suggest a spiritual sanction. Interview with Badiat Sambou, Kadjinol-Kagnao, 7/16/78.

37. Group discussion with Cyriaque Assin, Neerikoon Assin, and Wuuli Assin, Samatit, 5/11/78. Interviews with Badiat Sambou, Kadjinol-Kagnao, 7/16/78; Sooti Diatta, Samatit, 12/21/78; Edouard Kadjinga Diatta, Kadjinol-Kafone, 3/3/78; Boolai Senghor, Kadjinol-Sergerh, 7/2/78. Murder was seen as a grave sin (*cahofor*) and usually led to the forfeiture of rice paddies and expulsion of the murderer. Also, witches would attack the murderer in his sleep.

38. Interviews with Sikarwen Diatta, Eloudia, 7/19/78; Grégoire Djikune, Kadjinol-Kagnao, 7/23/78; Boolai Senghor, Kadjinol-Sergerh, 7/2/78; Moolaye Bassin, Kadjinol-Ebankine, 11/1/78; Joseph Salinjahn Diedhiou, Kadjinol-Kafone, 6/8/75. Meillassoux noted that the ransoming of hostages was a common West African practice between societies that maintained some type of social interaction despite frequent warfare. Meillassoux, *Anthropology*, pp. 103–104.

39. There are no gendered pronouns in the Diola language. This quotation applies equally to male and female captives. Interview with Siopama Diedhiou, Kadjinol-Kafone, 1/26/79.

40. Interviews with Bipah Senghor, Mlomp-Kadjifolong, 7/10/87; Antoine Houmandrissah Diedhiou, Kadjinol-Kafone, 2/27/78; Badjassaw Senghor, Kadjinol-Kandianka, 7/3/78 and 11/8/78; Grégoire Djikune, Kadjinol-Kagnao, 7/23/78. Djougoutes apparently paid a ten-cattle ransom. Whether a longer mourning period was the justification remains unclear. Fines for starting a war between the quarters of the same Esulalu township were also seven cattle. Interview with Sinyendikaw Diedhiou, Kadjinol-Kafone, 7/11/78.

41. Interview with Badjassaw Senghor, Kadjinol-Kandianka, 11/8/78.

42. Interview with Badjassaw Senghor, Kadjinol-Kandianka, 7/31/78 and 11/8/78. In eighteenth-century Esulalu, few captives were kept permanently as slaves. Captives were usually from areas that were too close to Esulalu to discourage escape. Some children were adopted into childless families, but they were fully assimilated into the Esulalu townships. See chapter 6. Pélissier, *Paysans*, pp. 681–682. Interviews with Boolai Senghor, Kadjinol-Sergerh, 7/2/78; Badiat Sambou, Kadjinol-Kagnao, 7/16/78; Cyriaque Assin, Wuuli Assin, and Neerikoon Assin, Samatit, 5/11/78.

43. In Fogny, Hupila is called Caneo, "rope." Many diseases that are considered to be caused by moral wrongs have symptoms closely related to the offense that was committed. Interview with Antoine Houmandrissah Diedhiou, Kadjinol-Kafone, 6/18/78. Interviews with Antoine Djemelene Sambou, Kadjinol-Kagnao, 5/17/78; Siliungimagne Diatta, Kadjinol-Kandianka, 3/31/78; Paponah Diatta, Mlomp-Etebemaye, 8/7/78.

44. Interviews with René Djabune, Oukout, 1/30/78; André Kebroohaw Manga, Kadjinol-Sergerh, 4/18/78; Siopama Diedhiou, Kadjinol-Kafone, 11/17/77.

45. Interviews with Siliungimagne Diatta, Kadjinol-Kandianka, 7/30/78; Siopama Diedhiou, Kadjinol-Kafone, 1/26/79.

46. Interviews with Moolaye Bassin, Kadjinol-Ebankine, 11/1/78; Siopama Diedhiou, Kadjinol-Kafone, 1/26/79.

47. Certain Esulalu quarters have seven-day mourning periods for both men and women, though most have a six-day mourning period for women.

48. The idea that the keeping of slaves was spiritually dangerous is discussed in chapter 6.

49. Interviews with Sikakucele Diatta, Kadjinol-Kafone, 3/17/78; Edouard Kadjinga Diatta, Kadjinol-Kafone, 3/3/78; Eddi Senghor, Kadjinol-Sergerh, 11/6/77. Sikakucele received his shrine of Katapf because he successfully seized some cattle thieves in the 1940s.

50. Interview with Antoine Djemelene Sambou, Kadjinol-Kagnao, 6/12/78. Offerings were made at Elenkine Sergerh before waging war. See chapter 4.

51. Interview with Siopama Diedhiou, Kadjinol-Kafone, 11/17/78. Interview with Adjobin Bassin, Kadjinol-Ebankine. The disease was identified by certain symptoms seen as characteristic of the disease "hupila." It afflicted only men. The victim would be taken to Bruinkaw, a divinatory shrine, which would identify the cause of his malady. On shrines of affliction, see Turner, *Forest*, p. 10.

52. Interviews with Paponah Diatta, Mlomp-Etebemaye, 7/19/78; Antoine Houmandrissah Diedhiou, Kadjinol-Kafone, 1/13/79; Musasenkor Diedhiou, Kadjinol-Kafone, 6/14/78; Terence Galandiou Diouf Sambou, Kadjinol-Ebankine, 8/3/87; Badjassaw Senghor, Kadjinol-Kandianka, 8/5/87.

53. I have not conducted sufficient research in these areas to trace the new Hupilas back further than Ediamat, Diembering, or Niomoun. They were created there or borrowed from slave-trading neighbors. Interviews with Badjassaw Senghor, Kadjinol-Kandianka, 7/31/78; Terence Galandiou Diouf Samobu, Kadjinol-Ebankine, 1/27/79; Kapooeh Diedhiou, Kadjinol-Kafone, 7/28/78; Siopama Diedhiou, Kadjinol-Kafone, 7/24/78; Moolaye Bassin, Kadjinol-Ebankine, 11/1/78; Sidionbaw Diatta and Simingkennah Diatta, Kadjinol-Kafone, 1/8/79.

54. A precise date for the introduction of this shrine is extremely difficult. There is some confusion in the oral traditions between the first to introduce a shrine and the first to finish it. Finishing a shrine refers to the most elaborate sacrifices possible for that shrine. The first to finish this shrine in Esulalu and therefore the first to assume the right to install others as full priests may not have done so until the late nineteenth century. Before that, they would have been dependent on priests from Niomoun or Bouyouye for the initiation of new priests, though Esulalu priests could have performed ordinary rituals. For the interpretation of an early introduction and a late finishing, see interviews with Antoine Houmandrissah Diedhiou, Kadjinol-Kafone, 1/13/79; Sidionbaw Diatta and Simingkennah Diatta, Kadjinol-Kafone, 1/18/79.

This could also refer to a return to finishing the shrine after a lapse, when a generation or so had not completed the final rites. It could also refer to an expansion of the sacrifices necessary to take on the shrine, a change that might have occurred in the late nineteenth century. Some of the oral traditions suggest that the shrine itself was not introduced before the time of their grandfathers, in the late nineteenth century, but this is contradicted by the close links between slave raiding and this form of Hupila. Such a close association would no longer have made sense in the waning years of the nineteenth century. Interviews with Basayo Sambou, Kadjinol-Kandianka, 4/3/78; Paponah Diatta, Mlomp-Etebemaye, 7/19/78; Sooti Diatta, Samatit, 1/4/79; Moolaye Bassin, Kadjinol-Ebankine, 11/1/78; Badjassaw Senghor, Kadjinol-Kandianka, 7/3/78.

Others suggest that this form of Hupila was already present at the end of the Koonjaen wars. This is too early because slave raiding was not of sufficient importance at that time. Interviews with Indrissa Diedhiou, Kadjinol-Kafone,

7/9/78; Antoine Houmandrissah Diedhiou, Kadjinol-Kafone, 11/28/77. Based on the broad diffusion of the shrine and its linkages to captive raiding, I would place the installation of the shrine at about 1750, though the completion of its most elaborate rituals could have waited until the nineteenth century.

55. Interviews with Indrissa Diedhiou, Kadjinol-Kafone, 7/9/78; Moolaye Bassin, Kadjinol-Ebankine, 11/1/78; Terence Galandiou Diouf Sambou, Kadjinol-Ebankine, 1/27/79; Badjassaw Senghor, Kadjinol-Kandianka, 7/31/78; Paponah Diatta, Mlomp-Etebemaye, 7/19/78. On the Ediamat form of Hupila, see interviews with Siopama Diedhiou, Kadjinol-Kafone, 7/31/78; Basayo Sambou, Kadjinol-Kandianka, 7/31/78.

56. Interview with Moolaye Bassin, Kadjinol-Ebankine, 11/1/78. Interviews with Antoine Houmandrissah Diedhiou, Kadjinol-Kafone, 1/13/79; Badjassaw Senghor, Kadjinol-Kandianka, 11/8/78; Siopama Diedhiou, Kadjinol-Kafone, 11/17/78. Group discussion with Hounakaw Diatta, Simatellihaw Leon Sambou, Assalawbaw Sambou, Jaimala Assin, and Mien Julien Sambou, Mlomp, 12/15/78.

57. The shrine itself was named after the slave, not the spirit associated with the shrine. For example, in Kadjinol's quarter of Ebankine the slave at Moolaye Bassin's Hupila was named Amoody; at Terence Sambou's, Bookanbon; at Alanbissay Bassin's, Adjagi; at Djisahl Sambou's, Djumba. Interviews with Moolaye Bassin, Kadjinol-Ebankine, 11/1/78; Terence Galandiou Diouf Sambou, Kadjinol-Ebankine, 1/27/79; Acanediake Sambou, Kadjinol-Kagnao, 1/21/79; Antoine Houmandrissah Diedhiou, Kadjinol-Kafone, 6/7/76; Sirkimagne Diedhiou, Kadjinol-Kafone, 7/12/87; Badjassaw Senghor, Kadjinol-Kandianka, 8/5/87.

58. Some Hupilas without slave fetters still exist, but the priests who perform their rituals are the same ones who control Hupila Hudjenk. Interviews with Antoine Houmandrissah Diedhiou, Kadjinol-Kafone, 1/13/79; Paponah Diatta, Mlomp-Etebemaye, 7/19/78 and 8/7/78; Terence Galandiou Diouf Sambou, Kadjinol-Ebankine, 8/3/87.

59. Interview with Siopama Diedhiou, Kadjinol-Kafone, 11/17/77. Turner, *Forest*, pp. 10–13.

60. Interview with Badjassaw Senghor, Kadjinol-Kandianka, 11/8/78. Interviews with Boolai Senghor, Kadjinol-Sergerh, 7/2/78; Group discussion with Lampolly Sambou and Sigondac Edouard Sambou, Mlomp-Haer, 1/12/79.

61. Interview with Paponah Diatta, Mlomp-Etebemaye, 7/19/78. Interview with Siopama Diedhiou, Kadjinol-Kafone, 11/17/77.

62. The quantity of livestock has been verified by personal observation. Interviews with Antone Houmandrissah Diedhiou, Kadjinol-Kafone, 1/13/79; Indrissa Diedhiou, Kadjinol-Kafone, 7/31/78 and 7/9/78; Siopama Diedhiou, Kadjinol-Kafone, 11/17/77 and 7/31/78; Paponah Diatta, Mlomp-Etebemaye, 7/19/78; Malanbaye Sambou, Mlomp-Djicomole, 11/7/78. On the suspicions focused on rich people, see Thomas, *Diola*, pp. 613–614.

63. The people who introduced this shrine are said to be grandfathers of elders with whom I talked, which would place the introduction of this shrine in the nineteenth century. This appears to be unlikely because the sale of captives was already important a century earlier and this shrine stressed the slavery connection. The man usually credited with introducing the shrine was called Hunome Boukhan, which means "Seller of People." It is unlikely that this was his given name. Rather, it appears to have been a nickname (casell), which could have been applied to several of the people within his ancestral line. Once again, this could refer to the completion of the shrine rather than its introduction.

64. Thomas, *Diola*, p. 223. Christian Schefer, *Instructions Générales Données de 1763 à 1870 aux Gouverneurs et Ordonnateurs des Etablissements Français en Afrique Occidentale*, Paris: Librairie Honoré Champion, 1921. J. Machat, "Documents sur les établissements français de l'Afrique Occidentale au XVIII siècle," Ph.D. diss., University of Paris, 1905. p. 106.

65. Interview with Kapooeh Diedhiou, Kadjinol-Kafone, 7/28/78. Boolai Senghor claims that they killed slaves at the shrine and buried them near the Hupila shrine. Interview with Boolai Senghor, Kadjinol-Sergerh, 7/2/78. Group discussion with Hounakaw Edouard Diatta, Simatellihaw Leon Sambou, Assalabaw Sambou, Jainaba Assin, and Mien Julien Sambou, Mlomp, 12/15/78. Interviews with Francois Diedhiou, Niomoun and Ziguinchor, 7/6/96; Badjassaw Senghor, Kadjinol-Kandianka, 7/31/78; LeBois Diatta, Kadjinol-Hassouka, 1/29/78; Antoine Houmandrissah Diedhiou, Kadjinol-Kafone, 6/7/76 and 2/8/78; Basayo Sambou, Kadjinol-Kandianka, 7/3/78; Sikarwen Diatta, Eloudia, 7/19/78. Beating of captives was forbidden by the "old Hupila" and Hupila Hudjenk.

66. There are three at Mlomp-Kadjifolong, two at Mlomp-Djicomole, and several others in the other quarters of Mlomp and Kagnout, but none in Kadjinol, Eloudia, or Samatit. Interviews with Tidjane Diatta, Mlomp-Kadjifolong, 7/20/87; Badjassaw Senghor, Kadjinol-Kandianka, 7/31/78 and 8/5/87.

67. Interview with Kapooeh Diedhiou, Kadjinol-Kafone, 7/28/78 and also 7/17/87. Interviews with Siopama Diedhiou, Kadjinol-Kafone, 7/31/78; Kapooeh Diedhiou, Kadjinol-Kafone, 1/16/79.

68. Group discussion with Hounakaw Edouard Diatta, Simatellihaw Leon Sambou, Assalabaw Sambou, Nainaba Assin, Mien Julien Sambou, Mlomp, 12/15/78. Interviews with Paponah Diatta, Mlomp-Etebemaye, 7/19/78 and 8/7/78; Sikarwen Diatta, Eloudia, 7/19/78.

69. Interviews with Boolai Senghor, Kadjinol-Sergerh, 7/2/78; Antoine Djemelene Sambou, Kadjinol-Kagnao, 6/17/78; Kapooeh Diedhiou, Kadjinol-Kafone, 7/17/87.

70. Interview with Siliungimagne Diatta, Kadjinol-Kandianka, 7/11/75.

71. Group discussion with Sidionbaw and Simingkennah Diatta, Kadjinol-Kafone, 1/18/79. Labat, *Nouvelle Relation*, vol. 5, p. 32. This is a description of north shore fortress houses. On south shore houses, see interview with Samedymolly Diedhiou, Kadjinol-Kafone, 6/22/75. From 1974 to 1979, I lived in a house that was constructed in this fortress style.

72. Interview with Nuhli Bassin, Kadjinol-Ebankine, 7/13/76. Interviews with Antoine Djemelene Sambou, Kadjinol-Kagnao, 6/17/78; Moolaye Bassin, Kadjinol-Ebankine, 11/1/78; Nuhli Bassin, Kadjinol-Ebankine, 6/16/75.

73. Interview with Sikarwen Diatta, Eloudia, 7/19/78.

74. Curtin, *Economic*, pp. 328–333.

75. The Diola's southern neighbors, the Manjaco, sold people accused of witchcraft as slaves to the Portuguese at Bissau. Beaver, *African Memoranda*, p. 178. Eve Crowley, "Contracts," p. 120. On the role of judicial authorities in the enslavement process in Zaire and southeastern Nigeria, see Dike, *Niger*, pp. 40–41. Northrup, *Trade*, p. 153. Robert Harms, *River of Wealth, River of Sorrow: The Central Zaire Basin in the Era of the Slave and Ivory Trade, 1500–1891*, New Haven: Yale University Press, 1981, pp. 33–35. On the absence of such judicial abuses among the Diola, see Rodney, *Upper Guinea*, p. 260. This is supported by the silence of Diola sources.

76. Interviews with Kubaytow Diatta, Kadjinol-Kandianka, 4/26/78; Sikarwen Diatta, Eloudia, 7/19/78.

77. I first attended this shrine in June, 1975, when I visited a friend in the Ebankine quarter of Kadjinol. The entire family was assembled in the granary, where his father was completing the rituals necessary to become a priest of Hupila Hugop. Because of my closeness to the family, I was allowed to attend.

78. Interviews with Eddi Senghor, Kadjinol-Sergerh, 11/6/77; Antoine Houmandrissah Diedhiou, Kadjinol-Kafone, 6/8/78; Bipah Senghor, Mlomp-Kadjifolong, 7/10/87. Kadjinol had strong commericial and religious ties with Niomoun. Kadjinol gave a rain shrine, Djalangoo, and a priest-king shrine, Coeyi, to Niomoun.

79. Cult members stole livestock as well as children. Interviews with Eddi Senghor, Kadjinol-Sergerh, 2/17/78; Djisambouway Diedhiou, Kadjinol-Kafone, 12/26/78; Moolaye Bassin, Kadjinol-Ebankine, 11/1/78; Babackar Manga, Loudia-Ouloff, 7/13/78; Bipah Senghor, Mlomp-Kadjifolong, 7/10/87; Badjassaw Senghor, Kadjinol-Kandianka, 8/5/87; Ekusumben Diedhiou, Dionsal Diedhiou, and Diongany Diedhiou, Kadjinol-Kafone, 7/22/78.

80. Such descriptions of children being seized and hidden away may be the source of African-American folk traditions about the "boogie man." Interviews with Siopama Diedhiou, Kadjinol-Kafone, 8/10/78; Ekusumben Diedhiou, Kadjinol-Kafone, 5/21/76; Badiat Sambou, Kadjinol-Kagnao, 7/16/78; Djisambou-way Diedhiou, Kadjinol-Kafone, 12/26/78; Joseph Salinjahn Diedhiou, Kadjinol-Kafone, 7/19/76; Nuhli Bassin, Kadjinol-Ebankine, 7/13/76; Antoine Djemelene Sambou, Kadjinol-Kagnao, 6/17/75.

81. Interview with Djisambouway Diedhiou, Kadjinol-Kafone, 12/26/78.

82. Joffroy, "Coutumes," p. 91. Thomas, *Diola*, p. 545.

83. Interviews with Ekusumben Diedhiou, Kadjinol-Kafone, 5/21/78; Badiat Sambou, Kadjinol-Kagnao, 7/16/78; Anto Manga, Kadjinol-Ebankine, 6/14/76; Siopama Diedhiou, Kadjinol-Kafone, 11/17/77; Bipah Senghor, Mlomp-Kadjifolong, 7/10/87. Mark describes a similar process in Djougoutes. Mark, "Economic," p. 15. L. Berenger-Feraud, *Les Peuplades de la Sénégambie*, Paris: LeRoux, 1879, p. 292.

84. Interviews with Nuhli Bassin, Kadjinol-Ebankine, 1/13/76; Eddi Senghor, Kadjinol-Sergerh, 2/12/78, Antoine Houmandrissah Diedhiou, Kadjinol-Kafone, 6/8/76; Joseph Salinjahn Diedhiou, Kadjinol-Kafone, 6/8/76; Siopama Diedhiou, Kadjinol-Kafone, 8/10/78; Antoine Djemelene Sambou, Kadjinol-Kagnao, 6/17/75 and 7/15/75; Badiat Sambou, Kadjinol-Kagnao, 7/16/78.

85. Interview with Kubaytow Diatta, Kadjinol-Kandianka, 4/26/78. Interview with Djisambouway Diedhiou, Kadjinol-Kafone, 12/26/78.

86. Interviews with Boolai Senghor, Kadjinol-Sergerh, 7/2/78; Kubaytow Diatta, Kadjinol-Kandianka, 4/26/78.

87. Interviews with Boolai Senghor, Kadjinol-Sergerh, 7/2/78; Antoine Djemelene Sambou, Kadjinol-Kagnao, 5/17/78, 6/5/76, and 6/17/75; Nuhli Bassin, Kadjinol-Ebankine, 6/16/75; Djisambouway Dieddhjiou, Kadjinol-Kafone, 12/26/78; Anto Manga, Kadjinol-Ebankine, 7/14/76; Joseph Salinjahn Diedhiou, Kadjinol-Kafone, 7/19/76.

88. Interviews with Babackar Manga, Loudia-Ouloff, 7/13/78; Siopama Diedhiou, Kadjinol-Kafone, 8/10/78; Ekusumben Diedhiou, Dionsal Diedhiou, and Diongany Diedhiou, Kadjinol-Kafone, 7/22/78.

89. Iron was in short supply in the eighteenth century. Old iron cadyendo tips were melted down and reforged, but they rusted more quickly and did not hold their sharpness. Those who could not afford to purchase iron hardened their wooden cadyendo blades in the fire.

90. On the social prestige of cattle, see Pélissier, *Paysans*, p. 760. Cattle were required for sacrifice at the new Hupila, at various shrines of the priest-kings, and for rites of purification.
Interviews with Sikarwen Diatta, Eloudia, 7/19/78; Dionsal Diedhiou, Kadjinol-Kafone, 1/8/79; Anto Manga, Kadjinol-Ebankine, 7/2/75; Siliungimagne Diatta, Kadjinol-Kandianka, 7/30/78; Kapooeh Diedhiou, Kadjinol-Kafone, 11/28/78.

91. Interview with Eddi Senghor, Kadjinol-Sergerh, 11/6/77. Interviews with Antoine Houmandrissah Diedhiou, Kadjinol-Kafone, 11/28/77; Boolai Senghor, Kadjinol-Sergerh, 7/10/78; Djibandial Diedhiou, Kadjinol-Kafone, 5/29/75; Kuadadge Diatta, Kadjinol-Kafone, 2/21/78; Djiremo Sambou, Kadjinol-Ebankine, 2/17/78.

92. Interview with Yerness Manga, Mlomp-Djicomole, 12/2/77.

93. Interview with Ramon Sambou, Mlomp-Haer, 6/28/78.

94. On the creation of Hoohaney, see chapter 4. Interviews with Sinyendikaw Diedhiou, Kadjinol-Kafone, 4/7/78; Kapooeh Diedhiou, Kadjinol-Kafone, 2/7/75 and 7/28/78; Siliungimagne Diatta, Kadjinol-Kandianka, 8/12/78. Dating of this shrine's creation is based on the priest-king lists of Kadjinol, which extend back to the late eighteenth century. Priest lists of Hoohaney's Kalybillah shrine include seven priests. Estimating 20 years per priest, this would mean that 140 years has passed since the split between Hassouka's and Kalybillah's Hoohaney, which was already fairly old.

95. There are many intermediate stages of initiation as well. Interviews with Kapooeh Diedhiou, Kadjinol-Kafone, 7/10/87, 7/28/78 and 12/7/77. See also Thomas, *Diola*, p. 606. On the difficulties of finishing Hoohaney, from a financial point of view, see Interview with Salomon Ompa Kembegeny Diedhiou, Kadjinol-Kafone, 2/18/78.

There are parallels between southeastern Nigeria's system of titles based on wealth and the series of levels of initiation associated with Hoohaney. It is no coincidence that both systems of linking wealth and power developed in decentralized societies during the era of the slave trade. These similarities are strongest with the Kalabari Ekpe society and with the Igbo *nri* title system. David Northrup, *Trade without Rulers: Pre-Colonial Economic Development in Southeastern Nigeria*, Oxford: Clarendon Press, 1978, pp. 108–112, 134. Elizabeth Isichei, *The Ibo People and the Europeans: The Genesis of a Relationship to 1906*, New York: St. Martins, 1973, p. 56. Simon Ottenberg, *Boyhood Rituals in an African Society: An Interpretation*, Seattle: University of Washington Press, 1989, p. xx.

96. Interview with Kapooeh Diedhiou, Kadjinol-Kafone, 3/9/78. Kapooeh was a Lingona.

97. Belasco has noted a similar increase in witchcraft accusations among the Kalabari, Edo, Itsekiri, Ondo, and Ijebu communities in coastal Nigeria as they became increasingly involved in the slave trade. Belasco, *Entrepreneur*, p. 103.

98. Diola cattle, mostly of the *ndama* type, have some resistance to African sleeping sickness, but they are not immune. In Esulalu, there is a widespread idea that a wealthy man who fails to share or boasts of his charity to the poor will soon find himself impoverished, and the humiliated person will find himself rich.

99. Belasco, *Entrepreneur*, p. 70.

100. This wealth differential was greatly diminished by French colonial policies of taxing Diola livestock. Each village quarter was commanded to supply a certain amount of livestock. This burden tended to fall on the cattle-wealthy elite. In this limited sense, colonial rule encouraged a certain type of economic leveling.

101. Interviews with Siopama Diedhiou, Kadjinol-Kafone, 5/2/78; Djilehl Sambou, Kadjinol-Hassouka, 12/27/78; Kemehow Diedhiou, Eloudia, 11/20/78; Paponah Diatta, Mlomp-Etebemaye, 12/27/78.

102. Horton, "African Conversion," passim.

103. Interview with Siliungimagne Diatta, Kadjinol-Kandianka, 7/11/75.

Chapter 6

1. Mandinka attempts to occupy Diola areas south of the Gambia River and along the Soungrougrou River are major exceptions to this general tendency but had little impact among south shore Diola, including Esulalu. Charlotte Quinn, *Mandingo*, p. 10; and "Relations between Mandingo Rulers and Stranger Groups along the Gambia River during the Nineteenth Century," Paper presented to the Conference on Manding Studies, School of Oriental and African Studies, London 1972, p. 1. Donald Wright, *The Early History of Niumi: Settlement and Founda-*

tion of a Mandinka State on the Gambia River, Athens: Ohio University Center for International Studies, 1977, p. 63. Mungo Park, *Travels of Mungo Park*, edited by Ronald Miller, London: J. M. Dent, 1960, pp. 3–4.

2. M. Le Brasseur, "Détails historiques et politiques sur la religion, les moeurs et le commerce des peuple qui habitent la côte occidentale d'Afrique depuis l'Empire de Maroc jusqu'aux rivière de Casamanse et de Gambie," 1778, Bibliothèque Nationale, Manuscrits Français, 12080. "Lettre de M. Raymeral, le 3 juin, 1777 demandent que M. le Ministre des Bloies sois de nouveau autorisé à faire des demandes pour obtenir la restitution de la Cargaison du navire le St. Jean Baptiste avec le indemnité," Ministre des Affaires Etrangères, Mémoires, Documents, Afrique et Colonies Françaises, no. 12, Sénégal et Côtes Occidentales, 1670–1790, p. 32.

3. In 1778, a severe yellow fever epidemic took the lives of 80 percent of the French at Gorée. Curtin, *Economic*, vol. 2, p. 5. The French Revolution diverted the energies of the French from their West African holdings, and the Napoleonic wars prevented them from embarking on maritime expeditions. For other reports of the trade potential of the Casamance, see Citizen Blanchot, in Schefer, *Instructions*, p. 187. De LaJaille, *Voyage au Sénégal Pendant les années, 1784–1785*, Paris: LaBarthe, 1802. Jean-Baptiste Durand, *Voyage au Sénégal*, Paris: Henri Agasse, 1802, pp. 68, 74. Silvester Golberry, *Travel in Africa, Performed by Silvester Meinrad Xavier Golberry*, vol. 2, London: Jones and Bunford, 1808, p. 156.

4. French slave traders were regular visitors to the Casamance, with at least six such vessels loading slaves between 1819 and 1823. Serge Daget, *Répertoire des Expéditions Négrières Françaises à la Traite Illégale (1814–1850)*, Nantes: University of Nantes, 1988, pp. 84, 138, 158, 195, 282. "Lettre de Gouverneur Roger, 31 mars, 1826," Archives Nationales du Sénégal (ANS), 13G 360. Eugène Saulnier, Les Français en Casamance et dans l'Archipel des Bissagos (Mission d'Angles, 1828), Institut de France, Manuscrits, pp. 130–131. Christian Roche, *Conquête et Résistance des Peuples de Casamance (1850–1920)*, Dakar: Les Nouvelles Editions Africaines, 1976, p. 76.

5. "Fifteenth Report of the African Institute," 1821, quoted in William Fox, *A Brief History of the Wesleyan Mission on the Western Coast of Africa*, London: Aylott and Jones, 1851, p. 263. On French interest in slave trading in the Casamance, see Leary, "Islam," pp. 82–83.

6. Itou received its office of the priest-king and accompanying shrines from Kadjinol. "Mission Dangles, 1828" Archives Nationales d'Outre Mer (ANOM), Sénégal III Dossier 3. Saulnier, "Français," pp. 132–138. Jacques Foulquier, "Les Français en Casamance de 1826 à 1854," Mémoire, Faculté des Lettres, Université of Dakar, 1966, pp. 34–35. Roche, *Conquête*, p. 75.

7. "Traité avec Coulaubousse, chef de village d'Itou, le 31 mars, 1828," in ANOM, Sénégal III Dossier 3, "Mission Dangles 1828."

8. Foulqiuer, "Français," p. 58. Roche, *Conquête*, p. 77.

9. "Traité de Cession de l'île de Carabane au Gouvernment Français, 12 janvier, 1836," ANS, "Copies des Traités Contenus dans le registre #1 de 1 à 109 inclus," p. 93. Roche, *Conquête*, p. 79. Foulquier, "Français," p. 38. Interviews with Hilaire Djibune, Kagnout-Ebrouwaye, 10/28/78; Djikankoulan Sambou, Eina Sambou, and Amangbana Diatta, Kagnout-Ebrouwaye, 6/26/78.

10. The Baudin family served as residents of Carabane until 1848. "Copies des Rapports de M. Penaud, Lieutenant de Vaisseau, Commandant le Malavoise sur la prise possession des terres acquis par la France à l'entré de la rivière Casamance," 9/2/1837, ANOM, Sénégal IV Dossier 25.

On the unhealthy condition of Carabane, see Pierre Baudin: "Rapport sur l'Ile de Carabane ou des Eléphants en la Rivière Casamance, Note de M. M. Baudin, 1836, janvier," Archives Nationales de France (ANF), Archives Privés Noirot, 185 Mi, "Papiers de Gouveneur Ballot," #48.

11. Golberry, *Voyage*, p. 156. On the decline of Portuguese trade, see Ernest Fallot, *Histoire de la Colonie Française du Sénégal*, Paris: Challarmel Ainé, 1884, p. 80. Pierre-Xavier Trincaz, *Colonisation et Régionalism: Ziguinchor en Casamance*, Paris: Editions de l'ORSTROM, 1984, p. 27. By 1840, French trade had exceeded the Portuguese by 50 percent. Roche, *Conquête*, pp. 37–38. Brooks, "Observance," p. 21. Dagorne, "Rapport de la Commission d'exploration," Bordereau des Pieces annexés à la lettre du Gouvernment en date de ler juillet, 1837, no. 139, ANOM, Sénégal IV, Dossier 25, "Expansion Français, Casamance, 1829–1854."

12. The Portuguese attempted to tax French commerce in the Casamance but were unable to collect it. On African revolts in the Casamance-Guinea-Bissau region, see "Extrait d'une lettre du Ministre de France en Portugal, addressée, le 21 janvier, 1879 au ministre des Affaires Etrangères," ANOM, Serie Géographique Afrique IV, Colonies Portugueses, 1835–1939. The Portuguese garrison at Bolor, at the southern edge of Diola territory, was destroyed in one such revolt. On Portuguese diplomatic protests, see ANOM, Série Geographique Afrique VI Dossier 4, 1836–1858. Ministre des Affaires Etrangères, Memoires et Documents d'Afrique, Sénégal et Dependences, Tome 40 (Sénégal), Letters of Viscount de Carreira. Saulnier, "Français," p. 131. Foulquier, "Français," p. 68. While British traders visited the Casamance in the 1820s and 1830s, they did not try to establish a permanent presence. Roche, *Conquête*, pp. 88–90. "Lettre du l'Amirail Pair de France à Monsieur le Ministre des Affaires Etrangères, le 17 janvier, 1840," Mémoire et Documents d'Afrique: Sénégal et Dependences, Tome 41 (Sénégal), 1840–1841. Ministre des Affaires Etrangères.

13. Hecquard, *Voyages*, p. 109; and "Rapport de M. Hecquard, sous-lieutenant de Spahis sur son voyage dans l'interieur," ANOM, Sénégal III Dossier 8, 1851. Brooks, "Observance," p. 18. Lieutenant A. Vallon, "La Casamance, Dépendance du Sénégal," *Revue Maritime et Coloniale*, vol. 6, 1862, pp. 463–465. Christian Roche, "Ziguinchor et son passé (1645–1920)," *Boletim Cultural da Guiné Portuguesa*, vol. 28, 1973, p. 38.

14. Hecquard, *Voyage*, p. 110. Brooks, "Observance," pp. 16–18.

15. "Lettre de 27 mars, 1856, M. R. Ribade Barbosa Morra, curé de Cacheo," Archives des Pères de Saint Esprit (PSE) Archives 154. "Voyages de P. Aragon à Sedhiou," April 1848, PSE Archives 153:136. "Annales Religieuses de la Casamance," PSE Archives 164 B, Sénégambie-Casamance.

16. Brooks, "Observance," passim. This emphasis on All Souls' Day was also common in the Spanish Philippines.

17. It still is an important holiday among Afro-Portuguese Catholics in Ziguinchor but a relatively minor event among Diola Catholics. This further supports the idea that All Souls' Day was important to Portuguese traders, rather than just an African emphasis within the Catholic liturgical calendar.

18. Brooks, "Observance," p. 12.

19. Ibid., p. 9.

20. Hecquard, *Voyage*, p. 110.

21. "Ile de Carabane" Sénégal et Dépendences: État Nominative de la population de Casamance," 4/15/1842. ANS 136:360. Vallon, "Casamance," p. 471. Interview with Juliette N'diaye, Carabane, 9/3/78.

22. "Rapport sur l'Ile de Carabane ou des Eléphants en la Rivière Casamance; note de M. M. Baudin, 1836 janvier à Gouverneur Malavois," ANF, Archives Privés Noirot 5, 185 Mi, Papiers du Gouverneur V. Ballot, no. 48. "Rapport de la Commission d'exploration, Dagorne," "Bordereau des Pièces annexés à la lettre du Gouvernment," July 1, 1837, #139, ANOM, Sénégal IV Dossier 25. Foulquier, "Français," p. 58. Roche, *Conquête*, pp. 77, 81, 82.

23. Leary, "Islam," pp. 82–83. Interview with Jean-Baptiste Manga, Kagnout, 11/23/77. Roche, *Conquête*, pp. 88–89, 181. François Renault, *Liberation d'esclaves et nouvelle servitude*, Abidjan: Les Nouvelles Editions Africaines, 1976, p. 62 and

passim. Renault describes French trade in ransomed slaves, which continued into the early twentieth century. Many captives were ransomed to government and private employers in French Guiana, Martinique, and Guadeloupe. Some of these "ransomed" slaves were taken from Carabane.

24. His predecessor, Jean Baudin, was removed from office because he owned slaves. Jean Bertrand-Bocandé, Gabriel Debien, and Yves Saint Martin, "Emmanuel Bertrand-Bocandé (1812–1881), Un Nantais en Casamance," *Bulletin d'IFAN*, vol. 31, Serie B no. 1, 1969, pp. 280–285. Roche, *Conquête*, p. 82.

25. Hecquard, *Voyage*, p. 109. Foulquier, "Français," pp. 60–63, 116. Roche, *Conquête*, pp. 82–83. Jean Bertrand-Bocandé, et al., "Emmanuel," pp. 285–294. Emmanuel Bertrand-Bocandé, "Carabane," pp. 399–400.

26. "Voyages de P. Aragon à Sedhiou," April 1848, PSE Archives 153: 136. Roche, *Conquête*, p. 83. Foulquier, "Français," pp. 63–64.

27. For a discussion of Diola domestic slavery, see chapter 7. Banishment was a common punishment for murder and other serious crimes. Mark, *Cultural*, p. 64. Interview with Paponah Diatta, Mlomp-Etebemaye, 1/24/78.

28. Roche, *Conquête*, p. 181. There was also a Manjaco shrine called Khameme at Carabane. Interview with Jacques Lopi, Djeromait, 7/14/78.

29. The name of the shrine Ehugna is closely linked to the Diola term for menstruation (*hugna*). Carabane's Ehugna are still used. The most recent Bukut initiation was performed at Carabane in 1993. Interviews with Dyaye Babu Faye, Elinkine, 12/6/78; Adama Touré, Carabane, 2/7/79; Abdoulaye Gueye, Carabane, 6/22/96; Hadi Lambal, Carabane, 6/22/96. Pierre-Marie Sambou, Kagnout-Ebrouwaye, 11/10/78; Sawer Sambou, Kagnout-Ebrouwaye, 10/28/78; Eina Sambou, Kagnout-Ebrouwaye, 1/14/79; Girard Senghor, Kadjinol-Hassouka, 7/26/87.

30. E. Bertrand-Bocandé, "Carabane," p. 413.

31. Hecquard, "Rapport sur les voyages dans la Casamance," 1850, Sénégal III, Dossier 8, Hecquard, 1851, ANOM. For an abbreviated account, see Hecquard, *Voyage*, pp. 108–109. Father Gabriel Sène, "Annales Religieuses, Casamance," Pères du Saint Esprit, (ANFOM), 14 Mi 1610, p. 32.

32. Interviews with Paponah Diatta, Mlomp-Etebemaye, 3/21/78; Gnimai Diatta, Kadjinol-Kafone, 5/9/78; Mungo Sambou, Kadjinol-Kafone, 5/22/78; Econdo Sambou, Kadjinol-Kafone, 8/13/78; Antoine Djemelene Sambou, Kadjinol-Kagnao, 2/5/78. Such a public display of "immodesty" is also done by barren women seeking to conceive during certain public healing rituals associated with Ehugna and Ehugnalene.

33. Father Lacombe in "Annales Religieuses," PSE Archives 164 B, p. 10, of a Carabane funeral. Charles Bour, *Étude sur la fleuve Casamance*, Paris: Berger-Levrualt, 1883, p. 30. Captain Brosselard-Faidherbe, *Casamance et Mellacorée: Pénétration au Soudan*, Paris: La Librairie Illustrée, no date, approximately 1892.

34. Lacombe, cited in "Annales." Within the Esulalu townships, a door is used for a funeral bier, rather than a canoe fragment. The cattle skulls provide a tangible reminder of those cattle sacrificed for members of the deceased's patrilineage at the time of their deaths and may provide a means of summoning their spirits to witness the funeral of their kin.

35. Baum, "Crimes." Henri Gravand, "'Naq' et Sorcellerie dans les Conceptions Serères," *Psychopathologie Africaines*, vol. 11, 1975, pp. 179–216. M. C. and Ed. Ortigues, *Oedipe Africain*, Paris: Union Generales d'Editions, 1973, pp. 240–267. Simmons, *Eyes of the Night*, passim.

36. "E. Bertrand-Bocandé à Monsieur le Commandant du poste de Sedhiou" 4/23/1852, ANS 13G 455.

37. Ibid.

38. "E. Bertrand-Bocandé à Monsieur Felix Baudin," Carabane, 4/21/1852, ANS 13G 455. Bertrand-Bocandé's opposition to the marabout's witch finding reflected not only his skepticism about witchcraft but also his concern with influential

Muslim leaders, such as Al Haji Umar Tall and Ma Ba Diakhou. See Martin Klein, *Islam and Imperialism in Senegal, Sine-Saloum, 1847–1914*, Stanford, Calif.: Stanford University Press, 1968, p. 67.

39. "E. Bertrand-Bocandé à Monsieur le Commandant du poste de Sedhiou," Carabane, 4/23/1852, ANS 13G 455.

40. Father Lacombe, in "Annales Religieuses," PSE Archives 164 B-2.

41. This is confirmed by an examination of the names of the first settlers, which included Wolof names like Djow and Diouf, Serer names like Faye, and Aku names like Bruce. Interview with Dyaye Babu Faye, assisted by Fatou Coly of Elinkine and Houmissa Djinna of Samatit, 12/6/78. Interview with Abel Assin, Cyriaque Assin, Baengoon Assin, Wuuli Assin, and Agnak Baben, Samatit, 4/26/78. "Emmanuel Bertrand-Bocandé à Monsieur le Commandant de Gorée," Carabane, December 1849, ANS 13G 453. After their annexation by the French, Elinkine's leaders petitioned the Carabane resident, in English, for protection against mistreatment by the Diola. Signatories included Wari Diow and three Akus, "Letter to the French Commander," Carabane, 11/29/1856, ANS 13G 455. Vallon, "Casamance," pp. 465, 471.

42. Interview with Cyriaque Assin, Wuuli Assin, and Neerikoon Assin, Samatit, 5/11/78. According to French records, Elinkine helped repel raiders from Thionk Essil. Bertrand-Bocandé, December 1849, ANS 13G 453. Interviews with Dyaye Babu Faye, Elinkine, assisted by Fatou Coly of Elinkine and Houmessie Djinna of Samatit, 12/6/78; Dyaye Babu Faye assisted by Fatou Coly and Jean Francois Djemé, Elinkine, 6/20/78; Cyriaque Assin, Wuuli Assin, Abel Assin, Baengoon Assin, and Agnak Baben, Samatit, 4/26/78. "Calendrier des Evenements Historiques du village d'Elinkine," Archives de sous préfecture de Loudia-Ouloff (ASPLO).

43. This was the same family that the French appointed as the first chiefs at Samatit. Interviews with Antoine Houmandrissah Dieddhiou, Kadjinol-Kafone, 7/12/75, 6/7/76, 8/1/76, 11/9/77, and 3/21/78; Cyriaque Assin and Neerikoon Assin, Samatit, 6/20/78; Cyriaque Assin, Abel Assin, Wuuli Assin, and Neerikoon Assin, Samatit, 5/11/78; Sooti Diatta, Agnak Baben, Abel Assin, Eemonah Assin, and Sisseman Diatta, Samatit, 12/6/78; Kuadadge Diatta, Kadjinol-Kafone, 7/9/76. "Correspondances échangés entre la Commandant de Carabane et le Commandant Particulier de Gorée, 1839–1859, Letters of M. Boudeny to the Commandant of Gorée, 1857. ANS 13G 455. Vallon, "Casamance," p. 467.

44. "E Bertrand-Bocandé à Monsieur le Commandant Particulier de Gorée," Carabane, October 30, 1853, ANS 13G 455. Interviews with Cyriaque Assin and Neerikoon Assin, Samatit, 6/20/78; Djikankoulan Sambou, Kagnout-Ebrouwaye, 6/26/78.

45. "Bertrand-Bocandé à Monsieur le Commandant Particulier a Gorée," 1850, ANS 13G 361. "Bertrand-Bocandé à M. le Commandant Particulier de Gorée," March 28, 1851, ANS 13G 455. French officials continued to complain about this "English hamlet." In 1887, the people of Elinkine invited Wesleyan missionaries to establish a school, whose language of instruction was English. It was shut down after protests by the Holy Ghost Fathers because it was not Catholic and by French officials because of its use of English. "Journal du Père Kieffer," 1890, PSE, Boite, "Carabane et Sedhiou, 1880 à 1892," Journals de la Mission. "Letter of William Thomas Cole to the Honorable F. Corker, Berwick Town, Barra Point, May 21, 1887," Wesleyan Missionary Archives, Sierra Leone and Gambia, Box 288, 1885–1900 Correspondence File, 1887–1889. "Letter to the Lieutenant Governor," Gorée, May 12, 1887, ANS 13G 422: 17. Despite Elinkine's maintenance of ties to Britain, the Colonial Office refused to protect them. Quinn, *Mandingo*, p. 145. "Rapport sur l'exploration dans le Marigot de Cagnout par Gourlier (Second du Rubris), 1850," ANF Papiers Bayol, 185 Mi 2, #65.

46. In Senegambia, strangers, both African and European, often married local women to establish trade alliances. Interviews with Jean-Baptiste Chiam, Elinkine,

5/11/78; Joseph N'diaye and Dyaye Babu Faye, Elinkine, 12/6/78. On the regional importance of such marriages, see George Brooks, "A Nhara of the Guinea-Bissau Region: Mae Aurelia Correia," in Claire Robertson and Martin Klein, eds., *Women and Slavery in Africa*, Madison: University of Wisconsin Press, 1983, pp. 295–319. Intermarriage was also a way to obtain rice paddies from neighboring villages.

47. At this shrine you could not sacrifice a bull, but at Carabane you could. This indicated the subordinate status of Elinkine's Ehugna. At Elinkine, men could not attend the ritual but could drink palm wine afterward. This is not allowed at Esulalu's Ehugna. Elinkine's Ehugna, like most of its shrines, are no longer used. The village is predominantly Christian and Muslim. Interviews with Jean-Baptiste Chiam, Elinkine, 5/11/78 and 6/20/78; Dyaye Babu Faye, Elinkine, 12/6/78.

48. Interviews with Dyaye Babu Faye, Elinkine, 6/20/78 and 12/6/78; Jean-Baptiste Chiam, Elinkine, 6/20/78; Paponah Diatta, Mlomp-Etebemaye, 5/19/78; Jean-Baptiste Chiam and Joseph N'diaye, Elinkine, 5/11/78.

49. Roche, *Conquête*, pp. 199–214.

50. The first systematic attempt to impose colonial rule lasted from 1880 to 1914 and resulted in armed resistance by many Diola. I will examine that in a subsequent study. Roche, *Conquête*. In 1886, the Portuguese ceded the Ziguinchor area to the French.

In the 1860s, French Protestant missionaries affiliated with the Paris Evangelical Society operated a mission at Sedhiou. It closed in 1867 and did not work in the Esulalu area. A Catholic mission opened at Sedhiou in 1876. See Jean Faure, "Histoire de la Mission Evangelique au Sénégal, 1862–1914," Societé des Missions Evangeliques de Paris.

51. Djibamuh's rituals on behalf of Kagnout involved nocturnal sacrifices of cattle. Interviews with Hilaire Djibune, Kagnout-Ebrouwaye, 7/11/78 and 10/28/78; Bernard Ellibah Sambou, Kagnout-Ebrouwaye, 6/28/78 and 10/13/78; Girard Senghor, Kadjinol-Hassouka, 7/26/87. On French trade at Kagnout, see "Correspondances échangés entre la Commandant de Carabane et le Commandant Particulier de Gorée," 1839–1859 and 1861–1864, ANS 13G 455.

52. "E. Bertrand-Bocandé à M. le Commandant Particulier de l'Ile de Gorée," Carabane, 10/4/1850, ANS 13G 455. Cattle raiding was a common activity of young Diola men against hostile communities and was especially frequent between Esulalu and Huluf.

53. Ibid. According to the governor of Senegal, the elders of Kagnout agreed to pay an indemnity of ten times the value of the cattle but claimed that they needed a delay of one month to pay. This was refused by Bertrand-Bocandé. Then Kagnout renounced the agreement and said that they had made it only out of fear. "Gouverneur de Sénégal et Dependences au Monsieur le Ministre de la Marine et des Colonies," January 8, 1851, ANOM, Sénégal I Dossier 37.

54. Diola estimated the value of one head of cattle at twenty bushels of rice. Thus the payment represented only half the value of the stolen cattle and did not include an indemnity. "E. Bertrand-Bocandé à M. le Commandant Particulier de Gorée," Carabane, February 11, 1851, ANS 13G 455. "E. Bertrand-Bocandé au Commandant du poste de Sedhiou," Carabane, October 6, 1850, ANS 13G 361. Lettre de Capitaine de 'Rubis de Perulo,'" November 16, 1850, ANS 13G 361.

55. Interviews with Djikankoulan Sambou, Eina Sambou, and Amangbana Diatta, Kagnout, 6/26/78; Djisambouway Assin, Kagnout-Bruhinban, 12/2/78; Oumar Assin and Sawer Sambou, Kagnout, 3/2/78. "E. Bertrand-Bocandé à Monsieur le Commandant Particulier de Gorée," 3/28/1851, ANS 13G 455. Roche, *Conquête*, p. 99. According to Fallot, Kagnout repulsed the French twice, causing them to use artillery before launching a third assault. Fallot, *Histoire*, p. 82.

56. "Traité conclu le 25 mars, 1852 avec les chefs de Cagnut," ANOM, Traité, Carton II, 253.

57. "E. Bertrand-Bocandé à Monsieur le Commandant Particulier de Gorée," 3/28/1851, ANS 13 G 455.

58. "Calendrier des Evenements Historique de village de Cagnout Bouhinbane," "Calendrier des Evenements Historiques de village de Cagnout Houyaha," ASPLO.

59. Only a "finished" Hupila would have a separate house for the shrine. Partially finished or older forms of Hupila would be attached to the home. Simendow was from the Gent lineage of Kagnout, which controls their sacred forest of Calemboekine. Interviews with Djisambouway Assin, Kagnout-Bruhinban, 12/2/78; Djikankoulan Sambou, Kagnout-Ebrouwaye, 6/26/78; Terence Galandiou Diouf Sambou, Kadjinol-Ebankine, 2/19/78.

60. "Traité conclu le vingt-cinq mars mil huit cents cinquante et un avec les chefs de Samatite," ANOM, Traité, Carton II, 252. Samatit asked for French protection against excessive demands by Elinkine traders and against raiders from Djougoutes. "Capitaine command la poste de Carabane, Limomine au Commandant de Gorée," April 21, 1860, ANS 13G 366. "Grazim au Commandant Carabane," August 27, 1856, ANS 13G 455.

61. "E. Bertrand-Bocandé à Monsieur le Commandant de Gorée et Dépendences," Carabane, May 29, 1855, ANS 13G 455.

62. Kadjinol offered twenty-two head of cattle to Bertrand-Bocandé as part of its request for protection. Haieheck's name is spelled Heêke on the treaty. Kadjinol also accepted the right of the French resident to mediate all disputes with neighboring communities. "Commandant Superieur Carabane, Mailhetard au Commandant Particulier de Gorée," April 29, 1865, ANS 13G 367. "Traités avec Cadjinol, 19 mai, 1860," ANS 13G 4. Haieheck is remembered for his wealth in slaves, cattle, and rice paddies, as well as his control of a major Hupila, Hoohaney, and Cabai. Interviews with Antoine Houmandrissah Diedhiou, Kadjinol-Kafone, 8/1/76, 11/28/77, and 2/8/78; Indrissa Diedhiou, Kadjinol-Kafone, 7/31/76 and 2/10/78; Siopama Diedhiou, Kadjinol-Kafone, 6/15/78; Sinyendikaw Diedhiou, Kadjinol-Kafone, 12/1/77; Grégoire Djikune, Kadjinol-Kagnao, 11/27/77.

63. Simembo Sambou assumed the chiefship after 1865 and was still chief in 1890. "Calendrier des Evenements Historique du Village de Cadjinolle-Kagnao," ASPLO. Interviews with Attabadionti Diatta, Kadjinol-Sergerh, 7/13/76 and 5/8/78; Eddi Senghor, Kadjinol-Sergerh, 7/11/76; Boolai Senghor, Kadjinol-Sergerh, 6/6/78; Sihendoo Manga, Kadjinol-Kafone, and Pierre Marie Diatta, Kadjinol-Kandianka, 7/15/78.

64. "Rapport Politique, Agricole et Commercial sur la Casamance," 1867, ANS 133G 368. See also "Rapport de la Tournée faite dans le marigot à Kadjinol, 21 mars, 1865," ANS 13G 440.

65. The dispute involved Djicomole's scavenging of shipwrecked trade canoes that belonged to merchants at Carabane. "Rapport de Bertrand-Bocandé Resident à Carabane, sur les courses qui presentent dans leur état actual les comptoirs français sur les bords de la Casamance," ANS 2DS 7. "E. Bertrand-Bocandé à Monsieur le Commandant Particulier à Gorée," Carabane, July 4, 1852, ANS 13G 455.

66. E. Bertrand-Bocandé à Monsieur le Commandant Particulier à Gorée," 1855, ANS 13G 455. The raids did not stop with the establishment of a trading post. "Rapport du Bertrand-Bocandé," ANS 2D5 7. "Rapport," Carabane, 10/2/1857, ANS 13G 455. In 1860, Pinet-Laprade attacked Karones and Thionk Essil in retaliation for their attacks on "our nationality and allies." *Annales Sénégalaises de 1854–1885*, Paris: Maisonneuve Frères, 1888, p. 215.

67. "Traité de Jicomole," April 6, 1860, ANS 13G 4. The relationship between Mlomp and Pointe Saint-Georges is discussed later. Eloudia, which does not border a major channel of the Casamance River, did not sign a treaty with France or develop extensive contacts before 1880.

68. On French attempts to persuade or force the Diola to sell cattle to French traders, see *Moniteur de Sénégal*, August 9, 1859, ANS 13G 300. "Expedition de la Basse Casamance par Pinet-Laprade, 1860," ANS ID 16. On French efforts to maintain the peace, see Snyder, "L'evolution," p. 391. "Traité de Paix entre le Village de Ytou et le Village de Kion par le médiation du Resident Français à Carabane," June 9, 1853, ANS 13G 4. Interviews with Antoine Houmandrissah Dieddhiou, Kadjinol-Kafone, 11/28/77; Hassouka Elders, Kadjinol-Hassouka, 6/28/75. Efforts to collect rice were sporadic. Within Esulalu, only Elinkine and Carabane were paying taxes regularly during this period. Roche, *Conquête*, p. 182.

69. Diola domestic slavery is discussed in chapter 7. Roche, *Conquête*, p. 110. Leary, "Islam," pp. 82–83. Bérenger-Feraud, *Peuplades*, p. 292.

70. "Procureur Imperial, Ch. De Roboeuf à Monsieur le Commandant," December 7, 1855, ANS 13G 455. Leary, "Islam," pp. 82–83. Interview with Jean Baptiste Manga, Kagnout, 11/23/77. Philip Curtin, *The Atlantic Slave Trade: A Census*, Madison: University of Wisconsin Press, 1969. Renault, *Liberation*, pp. 14, 176–177. Roche, *Conquête*, pp. 88–89. That Diola were among those seized (and freed by the British antislavery squadrons) can be documented through Koelle's linguistic analysis of liberated captives in Sierra Leone. Philip Curtin and Jan Vansina, "Sources of the Nineteenth Century Atlantic Slave Trade," *Journal of African History*, vol. 2, 1964, pp. 185–208.

71. Mark, *Cultural*, pp. 66, 70. Vallon, "Casamance," p. 463. Bérenger-Feraud, *Peuplades*, p. 463. Foulquier, "Français," p. 106. Bertrand-Bocandé, "Carabane," p. 402.

72. The stranger village of Badjigy was not founded until after 1880. The stranger village of Santiaba, population fifty, is not discussed because its history is quite similar to Efissao, Loudia-Ouloff, and Sam Sam. Carabane and Ziguinchor are not "stranger villages"; they are *essouk ehloumo*, "places of Europeans," because Europeans and Euro-Africans lived there.

73. Dominga Lopez was a Luso-African Christian whom Bertrand-Bocandé had met in Ziguinchor before becoming Carabane's resident. "E. Bertrand-Bocandé à Monsieur le Commandant Particulier à Gorée," 1853, ANS 11G 3. On the relationship between Bertrand-Bocandé and Dominga Lopez, as well as their son, see "H. Boudeny, Resident à Monsieur de Commandant de Gorée," Carabane, September 22, 1857, ANS 13G 455. "Ch. de Roboeuf," ANS 13G 455. "P. Alexis Huchard à Monsieur le Resident de France à Carabane," July 11, 1858, ANS 13G 455.

74. She is remembered in oral accounts as Puntavina. Interview with Terence Galandiou Diouf Sambou, Kadjinol-Ebankine, 10/20/77. Edouard Sagna and Ramon Diatta describe the founding of Pointe Saint-Georges by a man from Carabane and his wife, though neither of them was ethnically identified. Interview, Punta, 12/18/78. "Copie d'une lettre le M. le Commandant de Carabane addressé à M. le Commandant du Cercle de Sedhiou," Carabane, 1/22/1866, ANS 13G 368. "Lettre du Directeur des affaires politique à administrateur, Casamance, Sedhiou," 12/26/1891, ANS 13G 466. "Annexes à la lettre #11, Le Lieutenant de vaisseau, L. Arnaud à M. le Capitaine de vaisseau, chef de la Division navale de l'Atlantique Sud," 2/12/1886, ANOM, Sénégal IV Dossier 107. Thomas, *Diola*, p. 95. Brosselard-Faidherbe, *Casamance et Mellacorée*, p. 15.

75. Interviews with Antoine Houmandrissah Diedhiou, Kadjinol-Kafone, 5/23/78; Tomis Senghor, Mlomp-Kadjifolong, 11/18/78; Edouard Sagna and Ramon Diatta, Pointe Saint-Georges, 12/18/78. "Registre des Baptêmes," Archives de la Mission d'Oussouye, 1880–1883. "Direction des affaires politiques á l'administrateur Casamance," December 26, 1891, ANS 13G 466. There was also a small group of slaves of diverse origins. Pélissier, *Paysans*, pp. 681–682.

76. Vallon, "Casamance," pp. 464, 471–472. Interview with Edouard Sagna and Ramon Diatta, Pointe Saint-Georges, 12/18/78. The acting resident, Boudeny com-

plained of the embarrassment to French authority brought on by this raid: "It was necessary to pay enormous ransoms, thus that of Dominga Lopez was raised to a sum of over 500 francs because she is the wife of the Commandant of the Casamance." "J. H. Boudeny à M. le Commandant de Gorée," Carabane, July 20, 1858, ANS 13G 455. It was this incident that provoked Pinet-Laprade's 1860 attack against Thionk Essil and Karones. Charles Albinet, *Moeurs et Coutumes des Diolas*, Memoire, École Nationale de la France d'Outre Mer, Paris, 1945–1946, p. 5.

77. Father Kieffer, *Bulletin de la Congregation*, PSE, vol. 13, no. 167-1, 1883–1885, p. 709. Father Gabriel Sene noted the enthusiasm with which people flocked to church once one opened (p. 710).

78. None of these emphases was uniquely African. They were also common in rural Portugal. The cult of Saint Anthony was practiced wherever the Portuguese went in Africa.

79. Pointe Saint-Georges's Ehugna is still used. It was probably brought from Carabane. Bukut is no longer used. Interviews with Edouard Sagna and Ramon Diatta, Pointe Saint-Georges, 12/18/78; Paul Diatta, Pointe Saint-Georges, 12/18/78; Antoine Houmandrissah Dieddhiou, Kadjinol-Kafone, 6/8/78.

80. Both shrines are still used. Paul Diatta is their priest. Interview with Paul Diatta, Jacques Lopi, and Mother Victoire Ehemba, Pointe Saint-Georges, 12/8/78. Interview with Ramon Diatta, Pointe Saint-Georges, 12/8/78.

81. Djeromait was founded by the Djiba and Diouf families. Interviews with Antoine Houmandrissah Dieddhiou, Kadjinol-Kafone, 2/27/78, 4/4/78, and 5/23/78; Siliungimagne Diatta, Kadjinol-Kandianka, 11/15/77; Kuadadge Diatta, Kadjinol-Kafone, 7/9/76; Grégoire Djikune, Kadjinol-Kagnao, 11/27/77 and 7/23/78; Jacques Lopi, Djeromait, 11/1/77, 7/14/78, and 6/27/94; Emmanuel Corryea, Djeromait, 7/21/76; Djangi Diatta and Sebeoloute Diatta, Kadjinol-Sergerh, 8/1/76; Henri Djikune, Samuel Djikune, and Sina Djikune, Kadjinol-Kagnao, 6/26/94. "Calendrier des Evenements Historiques de Village de Djeromait," ASPLO. This protection was not sufficient. In 1857, raiders from Thionk Essil attacked Djeromait, as well as Pointe Saint-Georges. "Baudeny à Monsieur le Commandant Gorée," Carabane, 10/8/1857, ANS 13G 455.

82. Interviews with Jean Coly, Djeromait, 8/4/87; Antoine Houmandrissah Dieddhiou, Kadjinol-Kafone, 4/4/78; Soolai Diatta and Jacques Lopi, Djeromait, 1/5/79. "L'administrateur de la Basse Casamance à Monsieur le Gouverneur de Sénégal," 1889 ANS 13G 464.

83. Initially, this new group settled in a separate area called Sitotok, but they were integrated into Djeromait when they helped the earlier settlers repel an attck from the Diola of Seleki. Interviews with Jacques Lopi, Djeromait, 7/14/78; Jacques Lopi and Soolai Diatta, Djeromait, 1/5/79. The two villages were joined well before 1889, when the French established a customs post at Djeromait. "Monographe du Cercle," 1911, ANS 1G 343. Jacques Lopi's grandfather, Pasena Lopi, fled to Djeromait to avoid becoming a Manjaco priest-king.

84. Prayers are offered at Djeromait's Khameme in Portuguese Creole, Wolof, Diola, and Manjaco. This reflects Djeromait's diverse origins. Interviews with Jacques Lopi and Soolai Diatta, Djeromait, 1/5/79; Jacques Lopi, Djeromait, 11/1/77, 7/14/78, and 6/27/94; Jean Coly, Djeromait, 4/17/78.

85. Interviews with Jean Coly, Djeromait, 4/17/78; Martha Corryea and Jacques Lopi, Djeromait, 1/5/79; Gilbert Ousman Diatta, Djeromait, 8/3/87.

86. The persistence of women's cults in Muslim communities has attracted substantial interest among Islamicists. Janice Boddy, *Wombs and Alien Spirits: Women, Men and the Zar Cult in Northern Sudan*, Madison: University of Wisconsin Press, 1989. Margaret Strobel, *Muslim Women in Mombasa*, New Haven: Yale University Press, 1979, pp. 78–80. Ortigues, *Oedipe*, p. 151. I have not discussed Christians at Djeromait because they did not become significant until after missionary work began in the 1880s.

87. Initially Wolof settlers did not know how to cultivate rice; they raised peanuts and millet. Their wives and in-laws instructed them in rice agriculture. Interviews with Sikarwen Diatta, Eloudia, 7/19/78; Babackar Manga, Loudia-Ouloff, 6/12/78 and 7/13/78; Boolai Cissoko, Loudia-Ouloff, 11/18/78; LeBois Diatta, Kadjinol-Hassouka, 7/5/75. In 1896, only thirty people lived there. "G. Adam, administrateur Superieur de la Casamance à Monsieur le Directeur des Affaires Indigènes," 1896, ANS 13G 485.

88. Interview with Babackar Manga, Loudia-Ouloff, 6/12/78; Bakary Dembo Cissoko, Loudia-Ouloff, 4/27/78; Ekusumben Dieddhiou, Kadjinol-Kafone, 2/20/78.

89. Interviews with Bakary Dembo Cissoko, Loudia-Ouloff, 4/27/78 and 11/12/78.

90. "Calendrier des Evenements Historiques de Fissao," ASPLO. Interviews with Constance Bassin, Efissao, 1/3/79; Sambouway Sambou, Kagnout-Eyehow and Efissao, 1/3/79. Group discussion, Hyacinthe Dieddhiou, Attikelon Sambou, Thomas Sambou, and Sambouway Sambou, Efissao, 5/9/78. In recent years, there has been a substantial movement of Diola from Kagnout and other Esulalu townships to Efissao. As a result, there are now several spirit shrines there, and it has a Diola majority.

91. Interviews with Alfa Sakho, Sam Sam, 12/6/78 and 1/6/79; Djak Ba, Prefect of Oussouye, 1/6/79. Group discussion with Cyriaque Assin, Wuuli Assin, and Neerikoon Assin, Samatit, 5/11/78. "Calendrier Historique: Arrondissement de Loudia Ouloff," ASPLO. "Calendrier des Evenements Historiques du Village de Sam-Sam," ASPLO.

92. Followers of the Tijanniyya do not accept non-Tijanniyya Sufi teachers. They regard al-Tijani as the "seal of the saints." Jamil Abun-Nasr, *The Tijanniyya: A Sufi Order in the Modern World*, London: Oxford University Press, 1965, p. 38.

93. Interviews with Indrissa Diedhiou, Kadjinol-Kafone, 7/31/78; Siliungimagne Diatta, Kadjinol-Kandianka, 7/30/76; Antoine Houmandrissah Diedhiou, Kadjinol-Kafone, 6/7/76; Michel Anjou Manga, Kadjinol-Kafone, 7/2/78; Paponah Diatta, Mlomp-Etebemaye, 4/27/78 and 10/21/78. Roche, *Conquête*, pp. 132–138.

94. Jacques Waille, *La Penetration et l'Installation Française en Casamance, 1855–1883*, Paris: Institut International d'Administration Publique, Memoires, 1946–1947, no. 21, p. 4. Interview with Antoine Houmandrissah Dieddhiou, Kadjinol-Kafone, 11/11/77 and 7/17/78.

95. "F. Jalibert à Monsieur le Gouverneur du Sénégal," Carabane 1889, ANS 13G 464. The resident at Carabane also complained about a Muslim interpreter at Carabane: "Birama Gueye is a stranger to the lower Casamance, who is from Cayor and not Diola, marabout and not fetishist, that is to say a marabout exploiter of the fetishist, exploiter of the naivete, the fears of the Diolas." He was relieved of his duties.

Chapter 7

1. Interviews with Siopama Diedhiou, Kadjinol-Kafone, 12/4/77; Kuadadge Diatta, Kadjinol-Kafone, 7/9/76; Michel Amancha Diatta, Kadjinol-Kandianka, 12/18/78; Edouard Signondac Sambou, Mlomp-Haer, 1/5/79.

2. Interviews with Eddi Senghor, Kadjinol-Sergerh, 7/11/76; Attabadionti Diatta, Kadjinol-Sergerh, 7/13/78; Abbas Senghor, Kadjinol-Sergerh, 8/1/76, 7/24/78, and 11/5/78; André Kebrouha Manga, Kadjinol-Sergerh, 5/6/78.

3. Group discusssion with Abbas Senghor, Kadjinol-Sergerh, and Sooti Diatta and Djibune Baben, Samatit, 7/24/78.

4. Group discussion with Sihumucel Badji and Samoully Senghor, Kadjinol-Hassouka, 7/29/76. Interviews with Michel Amancha Diatta, Kadjinol-Kandianka,

12/8/78; Kuadadge Diatta, Kadjinol-Kafone, 7/9/78; Etienne Manga, Kadjinol-Kandianka, 8/17/78; Basayo Sambou, Kadjinol-Kandianka, 7/3/78; Sambouway Assin, Kagnout-Bruhinban, 11/15/78; Kuhlappa Manga, Mlomp-Djibetene, 12/27/90. Armed conflicts between quarters of the same townships still occur. For example, Mlomp's dispute between Kadjifolong and Djicomole erupted in violence in 1952 and has nearly recurred several times. Thomas, *Diola*, p. 337.

5. Interview with Lampolly Sambou, Mlomp-Haer, 1/12/79. "Traité de Paix entre le village d'Itou et le village de Kion, par le mediation du résident français à Carabane." June 9, 1853, ANS 13G 4. Roche, *Conquête*, pp. 110, 183, and passim. Berenger-Feraud, *Peuplades*, p. 287. Interviews with Thomas Diatta, Eloudia, 6/17/78; Lomé Diedhiou, Eloudia, 8/11/78; Jean Diatta, Kagnout, 11/23/77; Antoine Houmandrissah Diedhiou, Kadjinol-Kafone, 1/13/79; Diashwah Sambou, Kadjinol-Kafone, 12/12/77; Sikarwen Diatta, Eloudia, 7/5/78; Kemehow Diedhiou, Eloudia, 12/8/77 and 1/28/78; Sambouway Assin, Kagnout-Bruhinban, 11/15/78.

6. Interviews with Siopama Diedhiou, Kadjinol-Kafone, 6/25/78; Ramon Sambou, Mlomp-Haer, 1/9/79. "Gruzin au Commandant Carabane, 1858," ANS 13G 455. Mlomp's quarter of Haer received a Cabai shrine in the eighteenth century for helping Kafone against Hassouka. This alliance still exists.

7. This has been discussed in chapter 5. On Esulalu's wars with Huluf, see interviews with Diashwah Sambou, Kadjinol-Kafone, 7/7/76; Asambou Senghor, Kadjinol-Sergerh, 12/12/77; Antoine Houmandrissah Diedhiou, Kadjinol-Kafone, 1/23/78 and 2/27/78; Siopama Diedhiou, Kadjinol-Kafone, 6/25/78. "H. Boudeny à M. le Commandant Gorée," Carabane, 7/20/1858, ANS 13G 455. On wars with Djougoutes and Karones, see interviews with Paponah Diatta, Mlomp-Etebemaye, 12/1/78; Sambouway Assin, Kagnout-Bruhinban, 11/15/78; Sooti Diatta, Samatit, 12/21/78; Amakobo Bassin, Kadjinol-Ebankine, 6/8/76; Attabadionti Diatta, Kadjinol-Sergerh, 6/10/78; Sidionbaw Diatta, Kadjinol-Kafone, 1/8/79; Tomi Senghor, Mlomp-Kadjifolong, 11/18/76. On French complaints about Karones and Djougoutes and the punitive expeditions, see "Rapport de Bertrand-Bocandé, Resident à Carabane, sur les sources qui presentent dans leur état actuel les comptoirs français sur les bords de la Casamance," ANS 13G 366. "E. Bertrand-Bocandé à Monsieur le Commandant Particulier de Gorée," Carabane, 12/1/1849, ANS 13G 455. R. Touze, *Bignona en Casamance*, Dakar: Editions Sepa, 1963, p. 27. Roche, *Conquête*, p. 109. Fallot, *Histoire*, p. 82.

8. "L'Administrateur de la Basse Casamance, F. Galibert à M. le Gouverneur de Sénégal et Dépendences," ANS 13G 464, 1889.

9. "Rapport à M. le Commandant Particulier de Gorée et Dépendences sur le Basse Casamance," July 1856, ANS 13G 361. Interview with Sambouway Assin, Kagnout-Bruhinban, 11/15/78. These same accounts included descriptions of wars within Esulalu as "diakoute" (bad).

10. "Traité de Paix entre le village d'Itou et le village de Kion, par le médiation du résident français à Carabane," June 1853, ANS 13G 4. The transfer of Cabai shrines was used to arrange alliances within Esulalu, but there is no evidence to suggest that it was used in similar fashion beyond Esulalu.

11. Interview with Sambouway Assin, Kagnout-Bruhinban, 11/15/78. The privilege of taking livestock is of major significance. Someone can go to his or her maternal kin and seize chickens at any time. When I was adopted by my host family at Kadjinol, my adoptive brother Dionsal Diedhiou said, "What's mine is yours. If you need a chicken, you take it" (November 1974).

12. Group discussion with Cyriaque and Wuuli Assin, Samatit, 1/6/79. Interview with Sooti Diatta, Samatit, 1/6/79. Interview by Olga Linares with Assenbasen, Samatit, 1/6/66, and with Sambujati, Samatit, 2/6/66. The war took place at the time of the great-grandfather of an elder of Samatit. It also occurred before the establishment of Elinkine and Sam Sam, both of which would have had to negotiate with Sandianah for land cessions. The ruins of Sandianah are still visible.

13. Mark, *Cultural*, p. 19. Pélissier, *Paysans*, p. 853. Thomas, *Diola*, pp. 13, 311.

14. Itou also has a Sembini shrine, which it received from Elou Mlomp. Interviews with Paponah Diatta, Mlomp-Etebemaye, 5/19/78, 1/24/78, and 6/21/78; Sebeoloute Manga, Mlomp-Djicomole, 7/12/78; Malanbaye Sambou, Mlomp-Djicomole, 8/8/78. Group discussion with Salinjahn Diatta and Djonker, Mlomp-Etebemaye, 1/9/79.

15. The last priest-king of Elou Mlomp's Sembini died around 1920, but there are still elders who perform the rituals. Since the 1920s, no one has manifested the necessary signs to be seized as the priest-king. Interview with Paponah Diatta, Mlomp-Etebemaye, 6/21/78.

16. Before 1850, the main part of Mlomp was called Djicomole by the French. French maps of the period showed a place called Mlomp in the Hamak area. On more recent maps, it is several kilometers to the south. By 1860, when the French signed a treaty with Djicomole, the latter was able to cede a portion of the Hamak area to the French for the establishment of Pointe Saint-Georges.

17. Interviews with Paponah Diatta, Mlomp-Etebemaye, 1/24/78 and 6/21/78; Siopama Diedhiou, Kadjinol-Kafone, 6/25/78; Emmanuel Sambou, Mlomp-Djicomole, 10/8/78; Malanbaye Sambou, Mlomp-Djicomole, 8/8/78; Etienne Manga, Kadjinol-Kandianka, 2/5/78; Asaye Manga and Kuhlappa Manga, Mlomp-Djibetene, 12/27/78. "Calendrier des Evenements Historiques du village de Mlomp Etebemaye," ASPLO.

18. Interviews with Ramon Sambou, Mlomp-Haer, 6/28/78; Malanbaye Sambou, Mlomp-Djicomole, 8/8/78; Etienne Manga, Kadjinol-Kandianka, 2/5/78; Robert Manga, Mlomp-Djibetene, 3/1/78. "Calendrier des Evenements Historique du village de Mlompe Etebemaye," ASPLO.

19. Kabrousse and Diembering had large slave populations. The division between slave and free remains strong in both communities. Interviews with Teté Diadhiou, Ziguinchor, 8/5/78; Alouise Diedhiou, Kabrousse, 4/29/78; Sheriff Baye, Diembering, 5/1/78. "Eiffon, Chef de poste de Carabane au Lieutenant Gouverneur à Gorée," March 30, 1884, ANOM Sénégal VI, Dossier 14.

20. North shore slave traders carried their slaves to such south shore areas as Esulalu primarily because the Casamance River was an effective barrier to escape by northern captives. Slaves who could readily escape had no economic value. On the increasing number of slaves from these wars, see interviews with Antoine Houmandrissah Diedhiou, Kadjinol-Kafone, 6/7/76, 8/1/76, and 5/8/78; Paponah Diatta, Mlomp-Etebemaye, 4/27/78; Siliungimagne Diatta, Kadjinol-Kandianka, 7/30/76. On warfare between the Mandinka and the Diola, see Leary, "Islam," p. 95. Schaffer and Cooper, *Mandinko*, pp. 78–79. Mark, *Cultural*, pp. 67–68. Quinn, *Mandingo*, pp. 67–70. J. M. Gray, *History of the Gambia*, London: Frank Cass, 1966, p. 388. In the 1870s, captives from Fodé Kabba's wars against the Diola became increasingly important. "Annales Religieuses," PSE Archives 164 B, p. 22.

21. In the 1850s, Bertrand-Bocandé complained bitterly about the growing competition for Diola rice. "E. Bertrand-Bocandé à Monseiur le Commandant Particulier de Gorée," Carabane, October 30, 1853, ANS 13G 455. James Searing has noted that a growing demand for grain in European-dominated coastal towns also contributed to an increase in domestic slavery in northern Senegal. James Searing, *West African Slavery and Atlantic Commerce: The Senegal River Valley, 1700–1860*, Cambridge: Cambridge University Press, 1993, passim.

22. While there are no reliable statistics on disease in nineteenth-century Esulalu, there are records of a yellow fever epidemic in 1866 and a cholera epidemic in 1868. Quinn, *Mandingo*, pp. 77, 136. Philip Curtin, *Economic* vol. 2, p. 5. The creation of a major new women's fertility shrine in the nineteenth century may also reflect growing problems of infertility among Esulalu women. Slave children were often incorporated into families that lacked heirs, as discussed later.

23. Dr. Lasnet, A. Cligny, Aug. Chevalier, and Pierre Rambaud, *Une Mission au Sénégal*, Paris: Augustin Challamel, 1900, p. 170. Interviews with Abbas Ciparaw Senghor, Kadjinol-Sergerh, 11/5/78; Sirkimagne Diedhiou, Kadjinol-Kafone, 7/12/87. This is supported by a colonial report of 1907, "Note sur le captivité dans les territoires de la Casamance". "The purchased captive for the most part is a child who will not be delayed in being assimilated as a house captive" (ANS K18: 295). Eve Crowley notes a similar practice of adopting young slaves within the masters' families among the diverse peoples of northeastern Guinea-Bissau. Crowley, "Contracts," p. 238.

24. Interviews with Kapooeh Diedhiou, Kadjinol-Kafone, 7/17/87 and 8/5/87; Ehleterre Sambou, Kadjinol-Hassouka, 1/4/79. Lasnet's team suggested that slave men could marry free women. Lasnet et al., *Mission*, p. 170.

25. This would make it extremely difficult for a male slave to purchase his freedom. Interviews with Kemehow Diedhiou, Eloudia, 5/8/78; Antoine Houmandrissah Diedhiou, Kadjinol-Kafone, 8/1/76 and 7/12/75; Attabadionti Diatta, Kadjinol-Sergerh, 6/10/78; Abbas Ciparaw Senghor, Kadjinol-Sergerh, 11/5/78; Siopama Diedhiou, Kadjinol-Kafone, 11/17/77; Antoine Djemelene Sambou, Kadjinol-Kagnao, 7/1/78; Amakabaw Bassin, Kadjinol-Ebankine, 6/8/76; Anto Manga, Kadjinol-Ebankine, 6/4/76; André Bankuul Senghor, 11/18/77; Siliungimagne Diatta, Kadjinol-Kandianka, 7/11/75; Oumar Assin, Kagnout-Bruhinban, 3/2/78.

26. On Diola proverbs relating to slavery, see Thomas, *Diola*, p. 420. On Kubettitaw's contribution of a new method of rice cooking, see Thomas, *Diola*, p. 432. Interviews with Paponah Diatta, Mlomp-Etebemaye, 1/24/78; Antoine Houmandrissah Diedhiou, 11/18/77; Siopama Diedhiou, Kadjinol-Kafone, 12/4/77; Eddi Senghor, Kadjinol-Sergerh, 3/5/78; Djiremo Sambou, Kadjinol-Ebankine, 4/9/78; LeBois Diatta, Kadjinol-Hassouka, 7/5/75; Kubaytow Diatta, Kadjinol-Kandianka, 4/16/78 and 4/26/78; Michel Amancha Diatta, Kadjinol-Kandianka, 12/18/78; Etienne Manga, Kadjinol-Kandianka, 8/17/76.

27. This shrine is also called Elucial and Ayimp (the spring). Only people from Kandianka can attend its rituals. Interviews with Kubaytaw Diatta, Kadjinol-Kandianka, 5/20/78; Etienne Manga, Kadjinol-Kandianka, 8/17/78; Siopama Diedhiou, Kadjinol-Kafone, 12/4/77; Kapooeh Diedhiou, Kadjinol-Kafone, 6/10/78; Basayo Sambou, Kadjinol-Kandianka, 11/29/77.

28. If he had killed a free person, he would have been banished from the entire township, not just his quarter. Interview with Antoine Djemelene Sambou, Kadjinol-Kagnao, 6/17/78.

29. Interview with Kapooeh Diedhiou, Kadjinol-Kafone, 7/17/87. Interview with Terence Galandiou Diouf Sambou, Kadjinol-Ebankine, 5/4/78.

30. Interviews with Siliungimagne Diatta, Kadjinol-Kandianka, 7/30/76; Antoine Houmandrissah Diedhiou, Kadjinol-Kafone, 8/1/76; Badjassaw Senghor, Kadjinol-Kandianka, 7/31/78.

31. The Dewandiahn shrine was abandoned before World War I. The Huwyn shrine was suppressed by the French in the early twentieth century. Interviews with Antoine Houmandrissah Diedhiou, Kadjinol-Kafone, 7/17/78 and 8/1/76; Kapooeh Diedhiou, Kadjinol-Kafone, 7/21/87.

32. Slaves were often referred to as Agoutch because they were brought to Esulalu from Djougoutes, though they were usually brought to Djougoutes from other communities to the north or east. Wealthy slaves could, by sacrificing a large number of cattle (seven to ten), be considered free and eligible for burial in the main cemetery. Interview with Terence Galandiou Diouf Sambou, 5/12/78. There were at least two stranger cemeteries within Kadjinol alone. These cemeteries were abolished by Paul Sambou, canton chief in Esulalu during the 1920s. Interviews with Siliungimagne Diatta, Kadjinol-Kandianka, 7/30/78; Eheleterre Sambou, Kadjinol-Hassouka, 1/4/78; Michel Amancha Diatta, Kadjinol-Kandianka, 12/18/78; Antoine Djemelene Sambou, Kadjinol-Kagnao, 6/23/78; Terence Galandiou Diouf

Sambou, Kadjinol-Ebankine, 6/19/75, 2/19/78 and 5/12/78; Antoine Houmandrissah Diedhiou, Kadjinol-Kafone, 5/20/78; Sihendoo Manga, Kadjinol-Kafone, 4/9/78; Abbas Ciparan Senghor, Kadjinol-Sergerh, 11/5/78. People from Elou Mlomp and Sandianah, like Koonjaen, were considered houbook and could be buried in the main cemeteries. On stranger status and African concepts of slavery, see Miers and Kopytoff, *Slavery*, pp. 15–17.

33. "E. Bertrand-Bocandé à Monsieur le Commandant du poste de Sedhiou," April 23, 1852, ANS 13G 455.

34. Interview with Siopama Diedhiou, Kadjinol-Kafone, 11/13/78 and 6/26/78. Group discussions with Sikakucele Diatta and Assinway Sambou, Kadjinol-Kafone, 3/4/75; Dionsal Diedhiou and Elizabeth Sambou, Kadjinol-Kafone, 7/1/78. Interviews with Econdo Sambou, Kadjinol-Kafone, 10/22/77; Dadu Aowa Sambou, Kadjinol-Kagnao, 5/22/75; Djiremo Sambou, Kadjinol-Ebankine, 10/19/78; Terence Galandiou Diouf Sambou, Kadjinol-Ebankine, 7/2/78.

35. Father Lacombe, in "Annales Religieuses," PSE Archives 164 B, p. 11. The interrogations of the corpses that I first observed in the 1970s were almost identical. The stretcher was an old door instead of an old canoe, and senior kinsmen of the deceased, not just the widow, interrogated the corpse.

36. E. Bertrand-Bocandé, "Carabane," p. 408. Bérenger-Feraud, *Peuplades*, p. 291. Interviews with Assinway Sambou, Kadjinol-Kafone, 2/2/78; Moolaye Bassin, Kadjinol-Ebankine, 3/21/78; Siopama Diedhiou, Kadjinol-Kafone, 3/28/78; Dionsal Diedhiou and Elizabeth Sambou, Kadjinol-Kafone, 7/1/78. Although Maclaud noted in 1907 that Diola were no longer administering poison test ordeals, as recently as 1978 witch finders administering nonpoisonous potions were conducting such activities in Esulalu. Maclaud, "La Basse Casamance et ses Habitants," *Bulletin de la Société de Géographie Commerciale de Paris*, 1907, p. 199.

Similar poison ordeals were administered by the Balanta and Serer. C. Maclaud, "Empoissonnements rituels chez les Balantes 1911–1912," ANOM, Sénégal VIII Dossier 33, Casamance, no. 373. Henri Gravand, *Visage Africaine de l'Eglise: Une Expérience au Sénégal*, Paris: Editions de L'Orante, 1961, p. 50.

37. Interviews with Kapooeh Diedhiou, Kadjinol-Kafone, 7/28/78; Siopama Diedhiou, Kadjinol-Kafone, 3/28/78; Assinway Sambou, Kadjinol-Kafone, 2/2/78; Sooti Diatta, Samatit, 12/21/78. These new shrines are discussed more fully later.

38. Father Sene, 1880, in "Annales Religieuses," PSE Archives 164 B.

39. Ibid. Interview with Elizabeth Sambou, Kadjinol-Kafone, 8/13/78. I have attended such rituals at Houle, Gilaite, and Cahite shrines on several occasions. The type of animal sacrificed depended more on the shrine rules than on the family's wealth. Cattle were sacrificed only at very powerful shrines, for matters of great import.

40. On the availability of European iron in regional commerce, see interviews with Silingimagne Diatta, Kadjinol-Kandianka, 5/20/78; Patrice Sambou, Mlomp-Djicomole, and Adiabaloung Diedhiou, Kadjinol-Kafone, 8/9/76. Curtin, *Economic*, p. 210. Park, *Travels*, p. 217. Roche, *Conquête*, p. 84. On the increasing availability of guns see group discussion with Cyriaque Assin, Wuuli Assin, and Neerikoon Assin, Samatit, 5/11/78. Bérenger-Feraud, *Peuplades*, p. 290. On the expanding availability of iron within Esulalu, see interviews with Samuel and Ompa Kumbegeny Diedhiou, Kadjinol-Kafone, 7/1/78; Paponah Diatta, Mlomp-Etebemaye, 10/21/78.

41. Interviews with Ramon Sambou, Mlomp-Haer, 6/28/78 and 11/11/78; Babackar Manga, Loudia-Ouloff and Eloudia, 7/13/78; Boolai Senghor, Kadjinol-Sergerh, 8/14/78; Corrugate Bassin, Kadjinol-Ebankine, 7/17/78. Group discussions with Silokolai Sambou, Basayo Sambou, and Houmouneh Diatta, Kadjinol-Kandianka, 3/18/75; the elders of Mlomp-Kadjifolong-Badiat, 7/5/76.

42. Interviews with Kapooeh Diedhiou, Kadjinol-Kafone, 1/19/79 and 7/23/87; Siliungimagne Diatta, Kadjinol-Kandianka, 5/20/78; Djilehl Sambou, Kadjinol-Hassouka, 5/23/78; Siliya Diedhiou, Kadjinol-Kafone, 5/22/78.

43. His importance in Esulalu history is attested to by the discussion of his life in seventeen interviews with Antoine Houmandrissah Diedhiou, Kadjinol-Kafone; and numerous interviews with Indrissa Diedhiou, Kadjinol-Kafone; Sinyendikaw Diedhiou, Kadjinol-Kafone; Siopama Diedhiou, Kadjinol-Kafone; Sikakucele Diatta, Kadjinol-Kafone; Michel Anjou Manga, Kadjinol-Kafone; and Paponah Diatta, Mlomp-Etebemaye. All these interviews stress his wealth and ritual authority. On his role in negotiating the treaty with the French, see chapter 6.

44. This association of leprosy with blacksmiths probably arises from the similarity of the festering wounds caused by leprosy and those inflicted by fire. Interviews with Antoine Houmandrissah Diedhiou, Kadjinol-Kafone, 11/18/77; Indrissa Diedhiou, Kadjinol-Kafone, 1/27/78; Siopama Diedhiou, Kadjinol-Kafone, 11/27/77; Terence Galandiou Diouf Sambou, Kadjinol-Ebankine, 4/19/78.

45. This is probably overstated, though "house" here may refer to a compound of several houses. Interviews with Antoine Houmandrissah Diedhiou 3/1/78 and 2/2/78. Interview with Kapooeh Diedhiou, Kadjinol-Kafone, 7/23/87.

46. Interviews with Siopama Diedhiou, Kadjinol-Kafone, 6/15/78 and 6/14/78; Henri Diedhiou, Kadjinol-Kafone, 7/5/76; Gnapoli Diedhiou, Adiabaloung Diedhiou, and Econdo Sambou, Kadjinol-Kafone, 3/1/78, 3/28/78 and 5/23/78; Kapooeh Diedhiou, Kadjinol-Kafone, 8/5/87. Dating of this shrine is based on analysis of the Kumbogy and Kalainou lineage genealogies. Haieheck was a community leader during the period 1850 to 1870. The first priest of Gilaite, besides Haieheck, died before 1900. Interviews with Antoine Houmandrissah Diedhiou, Kadjinol-Kafone, 8/1/76, 11/18/77, 3/4/78, and 11/2/78; Musasenkor Diedhiou, Kadjinol-Kafone, 6/14/78.

47. Interviews with Sidionbaw Diatta, Kadjinol-Kafone, 2/7/78; Antoine Houmandrissah Diedhiou, Kadjinol-Kafone, 3/1/78, 3/28/78, and 5/23/78.

48. Interviews with Antoine Houmandrissah Diedhiou, Kadjinol-Kafone, 8/1/76; Antoine Djemelene Sambou, Kadjinol-Kagnao, 6/12/78.

49. Interview with Antoine Houmandrissah Diedhiou, Kadjinol-Kafone, 3/1/78.

50. Group discussions with Gnapoli Diedhiou, Adiabaloung Diedhiou, and Hubert Econdo Samobu, Kadjinol-Kafone, 4/27/75; Gilippe Diedhiou, Gnapoli Diedhiou, and Adiabaloung Diedhiou, Kadjinol-Kafone, 6/18/75. Interviews with Ekusumben Diedhiou, Kadjinol-Kafone, 4/29/78; Antoine Houmandrissah Diedhiou, Kadjinol-Kafone, 3/4/78; Gilippe Diedhiou, Kadjinol-Kafone, 6/15/75; Henri Diedhiou, Kadjinol-Kafone, 7/5/76; Kapooeh Diedhiou, Kadjinol-Kafone, 7/28/78.

51. Interview with Siopama Diedhiou, Kadjinol-Kafone, 3/28/78. On the Esulalu concept of animal doubles, see chapter 2.

52. Interviews with Sinyendikaw Diedhiou, Kadjinol-Kafone, 2/9/78; Sidionbaw Diatta, Kadjinol-Kafone, 2/7/78; Kapooeh Diedhiou, Kadjinol-Kafone, 1/16/77. Samatit acquired a small Gilaite recently, but it has no blacksmiths. Group discussion with Cyriaque Assin and Neerikoon Assin, Samatit, 6/20/78.

53. For a description of diseases prevalent along the coast of West Africa, see Ene, *Insects*. On the increasing incidence of disease, see Davies, *West Africa*, p. 21. He claims: "The vectors, mosquito, tsetse, and semulium, have probably been indigenous: but so long as there were very few human hosts, the parasites could not easily complete their life cycles. It is not known when malaria, sleeping-sickness (trypanosomiasis) and fly blindness (onchocerciasis) became endemic in West Africa. Is is likely that until recent times they existed only in limited areas." Curtin noted that there was a major cholera epidemic in 1868 and 1869. Curtin, *Economic*, vol. 2 p. 5. A yellow fever epidemic swept through the area in 1878. "Les Camps de dissemination au Sénégal, 2 Avril, 1891," manuscript, Institut de France.

54. Alfred Marche, *Trois Voyages dans l'Afrique Occidentale: Sénégal-Gambie, Casamance, Gabon Ogoué*, Paris: Librairie Hachette, 1982, p. 76. Sikakucele Diatta claims that Bruinkaw could reveal what type of spirit has seized a sick person

and what actions that person had done to provoke it. Interview with Sikakucele Diatta, Kadjinol-Kafone, 3/17/78. I often heard that Bruinkaw could speak, though I never witnessed it at the rites that I attended. Interviews with Dionsal Diedhiou, Kadjinol-Kafone, 11/2/77; Boolai Senghor, Kadjinol-Sergerh, 8/14/78; Songatebeh Diatta, Mlomp-Kadjifolong, 12/19/78. Thomas, *Diola*, p. 497.

55. Interviews with Paponah Diatta, Mlomp-Etebemaye, 12/27/78; Siopama Diedhiou, Kadjinol-Kafone, 11/17/77; Dionsal Diedhiou, Kadjinol-Kafone, 11/2/77. Group discussion with Paponah Diatta and Homère Diedhiou, Kadjinol-Kafone, 12/13/78.

56. Eboon is quite rare now. In 1979 there was only one left at Kadjinol. Interviews with Boolai Senghor, Kadjinol-Sergerh, 11/17/78; Kapooeh Diedhiou, Kadjinol-Kafone, 11/18/78. On Kalick, see interviews with Edouard Kadjinga Diatta and Indrissa Diedhiou, Kadjinol-Kafone, 2/4/78; Kuadadge Diatta and Ompa Kumbegeny Diedhiou, Kadjinol-Kafone, 6/24/76. This shrine probably dates back to the early eighteenth century because the Ecuhuh section of Kafone is excluded from participation in its rites; Ecuhuh was a part of Hassouka during the Hassouka-Kafone war (see chapter 4). Interview with Kuadadge Diatta, Kadjinol-Kafone, 7/9/76.

57. The Mlomp quarters of Djicomole and Kadjifolong have a similar type of Ehugna, but they did not receive it from Kadjinol. Group discussion with Musasenkor Diedhiou and Lolene Diatta, Kadjinol-Kafone, 2/20/78. Interview with Djisambouway Diedhiou, Kadjinol-Kafone, 12/26/78; Corrugate Gilbert Diedhiou, Kadjinol-Kafone, 8/8/96; Elizabeth Diedhiou, Nyambalang, 8/13/96. In August 1996, more than fifty people from Siganar came back to Kadjinol to participate in the initiation of a new priest of Kafone's Ehugna because it was the senior shrine. Another women's shrine, associated with problems of women's infertility, Ehugnalene, was introduced in the early twentieth century and will be discussed in a future study.

58. There are no statistics on nineteenth-century fertility rates, only the shift in fertility rituals from Kalick to Ehugna. Declining fertility rates could be linked to migrant labor at Carabane and the increasing presence of French and African traders within Esulalu, both of which could be implicated in the spread of venereal disease. Such a linkage is not suggested by the oral traditions that I collected. It is interesting to note that Djibalene Diedhiou had no children. Djibalene was also an important slave trader and had a Hupila Hugop. Interviews with Kuadadge Diatta, Kadjinol-Kafone, 2/21/78; Boolai Senghor, Kadjinol-Sergerh, 12/21/78; Corrugate Gilbert Diedhiou, Kadjinol-Kafone, 8/10/96.

59. Interview with Amelikai Diedhiou, Kadjinol-Kafone, 8/7/96.

60. Djibalene was a contemporary of Haieheck and was circumcised in the same Bukut. Ayncabadje was the grandmother of Sambou Bakual Diedhiou, who was born in 1906. Interviews with Ekusumben Diedhiou, Kadjinol-Kafone, 5/19/78; Djisambouway Diedhiou, Kadjinol-Kafone, 12/26/78; Boolai Senghor, Kadjinol-Sergerh, 12/21/78; Musasenkor Diedhiou and Lolene Diatta, Kadjinol-Kafone, 2/20/78; Elizabeth Sambou, Kadjinol-Kafone, 6/12/94; Corrugate Gilbert Diedhiou, Kadjinol-Kafone, 8/7/96; Amelikai Diedhiou, Kadjinol-Kafone, 3/26/78; Matolia Manga and Amelikai Diedhiou, Kadjinol-Kafone, 11/7/77. Matolia was the priest of Ehugna until her death in the early 1990s. Djisambouway and Amelikai are descendants of Djibalene's brother and Amelikai is Matolia's husband. Linares noted that in Samatit, the priest of Ehugna is chosen from the wives married to men of the Sitohong compound. Letter from Olga Linares, 2/20/81. Olga Linares, *Power*, p. 45. There is a small Ehugna at Kadjinol-Kafone's Gent compound, which is said to be of an older and different type than Djakati. This Ehugna is presided over by the high priest of Djakati, but it belongs to the wives of the Gent lineage, which is linked to the priest-king of Oussouye and to certain Koonjaen shrines. Whether this is a Koonjaen form of Ehugna is unclear. Interviews with Kuadadge

Diatta, Kadjinol-Kafone, 2/20/78 and 2/21/78; Musasenkor Diedhiou and Lolene Diatta, Kadjinol-Kafone, 2/20/78.

61. Interview with Elizabeth Sambou, Kadjinol-Kafone, 1/4/78. Linares, *Power*, p. 47.

62. Journet, "Hyper-Mères," p. 21. Linares, *Power*, pp. 48–49. Field notes of Olga Linares, Samatit, 11/19/76. Interviews with Amelikai Diedhiou, Kadjinol-Kafone, 3/26/78; Georgette Dukema Bassin, Kadjinol-Kafone, 2/28/78; Antoine Djemelene Sambou, Kadjinol-Kagnao, 6/23/78; Ekusumben Diedhiou, Kadjinol-Kafone, 12/14/78; Elizabeth Sambou, Kadjinol-Kafone, 6/12/94.

63. Interviews with Dionsal Diedhiou, Kadjinol-Kafone, 11/2/77; Ekusumben Diedhiou, Kadjinol-Kafone, 3/26/78; Indrissa Diedhiou, Kadjinol-Kafone, 10/19/78 and 10/20/78; Siopama Diedhiou, Kadjinol-Kafone, 12/21/78; Elizabeth Sambou, Kadjinol-Kafone, 11/13/77. Field notes of Olga Linares, 11/20/76, 11/24/76 and 11/26/76. Eve Crowley describes a similar Baboi-Bainounk ritual performed by women during periods of drought. Crowley, "Contracts," p. 244.

64. Samatit and Kagnout have both types of Ehugna. Samatit's Ehugna Djakati has the same exclusion of men as is found in Kadjinol. Field notes, Olga Linares, interview with Jagesa, 11/21/76. Samatit's Ehugna Tengo has the same rules as Elinkine and Carabane.

65. The strings of bells are still worn by the women at Ehugna rituals. Father Kieffer, *Bulletin de la congrégation du Saint Esprit*, Tome XII, 1881–1883, p. 477.

66. "Extract from John Morgan's Journal, August 17, 1822" in Wesleyan Mission Archives (WMA), Gambia Correspondence, 1821–1852, Box 293, File 1821 to 1837. M. Perrotet, cited in Amedée Tardieu, *Sénégambie et Guinéé*, Paris: Firmis Didet Frères, 1847, p. 137.

67. Interviews with Basayo Sambou, Kadjinol-Kandianka, 11/29/77; Sihendoo Manga, Kadjinol-Kagnao, 10/25/78; Michel Amancha Diatta, Kadjinol-Kandianka, 1/28/79; Grégoire Diatta, Mlomp-Kadjifolong, 7/5/76. On the wearing of their pagnes for festivals, see Boilat, *Esquisses*, p. 431.

68. Group discussion with Antoine Djemelene Sambou, Kadjinol-Kagnao, and LeBois Diatta, Kadjinol-Hassouka, 4/16/78. Interview with Basayo Sambou, Kadjinol-Kandianka, 11/29/77.

69. Father Wintz in "Annales Religieuses," PSE Archives 164 B, p. 36. Lasnet, et al., *Mission*, p. 156. Interview with Siliungimagne Diatta, Kadjinol-Kandianka, 5/20/78. "Rapport de Bertrand-Bocandé, Resident à Carabane sur les sources qui presentent dans leur état actuel les comptoir français sur les bords de la Casamance." ANS 2D5-7.

70. Interviews with Basayo Sambou, Kadjinol-Kandianka, 11/29/77; Assinway Sambou and Amperoot Diedhiou, Kadjinol-Kafone, 3/17/78; Songant Ebeh Diatta, Mlomp-Kadjifolong, 11/7/78.

71. Despite the military nature of his mission, Captain Lauque provides detailed descriptions of south shore Diola social relations. "Rapport special sur les operations militaire executés en Casamance," 1905, ANS 1D 170.

72. Men would instruct the groom during a social event called *hukwen*, when the groom's kin gather around and engage in sexually explicit joking. This practice was observed in 1977. At Kadjinol, girls were taken to a place called Agabuhl, a shrine of Ehugna located in the rice paddies. Interview with Econdo Sambou, Kadjinol-Kafone, 8/13/78.

73. Group discussion with Yerness Senghor and Edouard Kadjinga Diatta, Kadjinol-Kafone, 7/11/76. Father du Palquet, "Notes sur la Mission des Deux Guinées," 1848 PSE Archives 146 B, Dossier B. This is confirmed by Father Wintz in 1909, in "Annales Religieuses," PSE Archives 164 B, p. 35. This is not the case for the north shore communities of Djougoutes and Fogny, where polygyny is more common.

74. Interviews with Dionsal Diedhiou, Kadjinol-Kafone, 6/12/78 and 11/13/77; Basayo Sambou, Kadjinol-Kandianka, 11/29/77; Gustave Sambou, Kadjinol-Kafone, 10/12/77; Bruno Gitao Diedhiou, Kadjinol-Kafone, Daniel Diatta, Kadjinol-Hassouka, and Alexandre Sirku Bassin, 1/31/75; Elizabeth Sambou, Kadjinol-Kafone, 7/28/76. Pélissier, *Paysans*, p. 684. Lauque, "Rapport," ANS 1D 170.

75. This type of dance is no longer held, though a few men still play the econtine. Interviews with Boolai Senghor, Kadjinol-Sergerh, 8/15/78; Songant Ebeh Diatta, Mlomp-Cadjifolong, 6/29/78. Alfred Marche noted the importance of wrestling among the south shore Diola. Marche, *Trois Voyages*, p. 78. In 1905 Captain Lauque described the elaborate preparations and dancing that accompanied Esulalu wrestling matches, ANS ID 170.

76. These shrines would include cults associated with ancestors of particular lineages, including such shrines as Elenkine, Hoolinway, and Ebalass, as well as shrines at which important members of the lineage hold ritual office. Interview with Acanediake Sambou, Kadjinol-Kagnao, 1/21/79. The gifts themselves are confirmed by Father Sene, 1880, in "Annales Religieuses," PSE Archives 164 B, as well as Captain Lauque, ANS 1D 170, in 1905. Acanediake claims that the groom's cost and the size of buposs has increased rapidly since his father's time.

Chapter 8

1. Mbiti, *African*, p. 283. Beidelman, *Moral*, pp. 72, 82. Goody, *Domestication*, pp. 14–15. Miller, "Dynamics," pp. 89–90.

2. Thomas, *Diola*, p. 489.

3. This close association of rain and the supreme being is common to many West African religions. The Diola term for rain, *emitai ehlahl*, invokes the name of the supreme being, Emitai. A part of Emitai's life-giving force is said to fall with rain.

4. Ironically, the French conquest and its imposition of taxes in cattle became a heavier burden on the wealthy, but this growing social inequality was not directly addressed until Alinesitoué challenged the linkage of wealth and ritual authority in 1942.

5. This was the case with Kooliny Djabune and his visions relating to Cabai, as well as the visions that led to the creation of Kagnout's shrine of Cassissilli.

6. Atta-Essou was said to have never died. His name means "birdlike." He was said to have made wings of palm fibers and flown up to join Emitai and to continue to appear to his descendants, the Gent lineages of Esulalu. This is probably a Koonjaen tradition.

7. In his essay "African Conversion," Robin Horton described a basic African cosmology in which the supreme being is associated with the macrocosm and lesser spirits with the microcosm. He claimed that African communities, until recently, were focused on the microcosm, making lesser spirits the primary ritual focus and the primary upholder of a moral order. Horton, "African," passim.

8. This has been the case with the priest-king of the Sembini shrine of Elou Mlomp. It has been vacant for at least seventy years.

9. Thomas Kuhn, *The Structure of Scientific Revolutions*, Chicago: University of Chicago Press, 1970, p. 76. Kuhn describes a scientific revolution as one in which a new paradigm first becomes ascendant and then causes the other to virtually disappear (p. 17). Such a dramatic shift may have occurred as a result of the spiritual crisis of conquest, which, for the Diola, reached its peak in the 1940s. This resulted in a prophetic movement led by Alinesitoué, who introduced new theoretical models for the explanation of the awasena path, and in the emergence of a

significant Christian community within Esulalu. Baum, "Emergence." For an application of Kuhn's theories to the study of African religions, see Dan Bauer and John Hinnant, "Normal and Revolutionary Divination: A Kuhnian Approach to African Traditional Thought," in Ivan Karp and Charles Bird, editors, *Explorations in African Systems of Thought*, Washington: Smithsonian Institution, 1987, pp. 213–236.

10. Horton, "African Traditional Thought," p. 155.

Appendix

1. David Henige, *The Chronology of Oral Tradition: Quest for a Chimera*, Oxford: Clarendon, 1974, pp. 1–2.

2. Henige has described this process quite effectively in *Oral Historiography*, pp. 96–105. Vansina, *Oral Tradition: A Study*, p. 100.

3. Feierman, *Shambaa*, p. 4.

4. Vansina, *Oral Historiography*, p. 107.

5. Henige, *Chronology*, pp. 6, 34, 145–165.

6. In the Batchakuale Bukut, Kadjinol-Hassouka was ready for the initiation in 1948, but Kalybillah was not and decided to wait until 1952. Mlomp's quarter of Kadjifolong performs its Bukut a few years after Kadjinol. In this case it was held in 1956. This was followed by the rest of Mlomp, Kagnout, Eloudia, and Samatit in 1962.

7. This circumcision ritual was held approximately four years after World War I veterans returned from France (1919). Three years is the usual time between the Kabomen preparatory ritual and the actual circumcision ritual of Bukut. Several men initiated in Djambia had fathers who returned from the service and then fathered them. Since they would have had to been weaned before the circumcision ritual and Diola women nurse their children for three years, the circumcision could not have been held before 1923.

8. Father Wintz described Kagnout's Badusu Bukut, which was held in 1904. The rules of transmission of Bukut require that Kadjinol's Bukut be held several years before the rest of Esulalu. "Carabane, Journal de la Communauté, 1898–1920," PSE Archives.

9. These two Bukut are dated together. Bertrand-Bocandé observed a circumcision ritual at Kagnout in 1854. Since Kagnout's were held four to ten years after Kadjinol's, I approximate the date of Kadjinol's as 1850. All such dates are approximate. Batingalite refers to a mumps epidemic. "Lettre à Monsieur le Commandant Particulier Gorée, 1855," ANS 13G 455.

10. Bagangup was the Bukut of Haieheck who signed a treaty with the French in 1860. For him to be in such a position of authority, he would already have had to be middle-aged. Being circumsised in 1830, he would have been between thirty-three and fifty-three at the time of the treaty signing. Bagangup could have been as much as ten years earlier than 1830.

11. Peter Mark has found that Bukut has a similar longevity among the north shore communities of Djougoutes. He collected names of thirteen Bukut, which he also estimates were held at twenty-year intervals. Bukut is probably older in Djougoutes. See Mark, *Cultural*, p. 20; and "Economic," p. 34. For a further discussion of Bukut, see chapter 4.

12. See chapter 7.

13. See chapter 3.

14. Vansina, *Oral Historiography*, p. 102.

Glossary

Aberman. Spirit shrine of Kadjinol-Ebankine, named after Aberman Manga.

Acconkone. Social dance often performed after wrestling matches in Esulalu.

Adonai. Destruction of the world by Emitai. It is said to have occurred many times.

Aetingah. Afro-Portuguese from Ziguinchor and Portuguese Guinea.

Agoutch. Literally, "a person from Djougoutes," a term for slaves.

Ahoeka. A benevolent ancestor, someone who has received a good afterlife.

Ahoelra. A phantom, someone who has received a bad afterlife.

Ahoonk. A person with special mental powers who uses them to combat witches.

Aje. Yoruba spirit cult increasingly associated with the acquisition of wealth.

Alkati. Term of Arabic origin, used in northern Senegal to describe officials in charge of trade.

Amachala. Young initiated men, charged with enforcing the decrees of Hutendookai shrine.

Amiekele. Slave.

Ammahl. Spirit associated with water who may reveal itself at shrines or independently to individuals.

Analai. Woman.

Aro Chukwu. Igbo oracle of Chukwu, usually described as an oracle of the supreme being.

Asandioume. Deceased person, neither ancestor or phantom, exiled to a village far to the south.

Asaye. Witch.

Ata-Emit. The Diola supreme being, usually called Emitai.

Avi. The Diola-Bandial term for *oeyi*, priest-king.

Awasena. Diola term for their religion, referring to one who performs rituals.

Badian Kasall. One of the women's spirit shrines at Carabane.

Boekine. Spirit shrine.

Boodji. A form of marriage in which widowed or divorced women choose new spouses.

Bouboon. Medicines.

Boutine. Path. This term has come to refer to specific religious traditions.

Brilen. Synonym for *tali*, a poison used in witchcraft ordeals.

Bruinkaw. A divinatory shrine, important for healing.

Bruinom (Buhinum). Mind or spirit of a human being, but it can refer to animals.

Bukut. The newer form of male initiation, prevalent in Esulalu.

Buposs. Bridal gifts provided by the groom before marriage.

Cabai. The "spear," a shrine associated with war, founded by Kooliny Djabune.

Cadyendo. Diola fulcrum shovel used primarily for rice cultivation.

Calau. Diola male initiation ritual related to the rites of the dead and of the priest-king.

Calemboekine. The sacred forest of the priest-king and the shrines that are located within the forest (Coeyi and Egol).

Casell. Nickname or epithet, often alluding to distinguishing characteristics of the person.

Casine. A Manjaco spirit shrine, found at Carabane and Djeromait.

Casop. A part of funeral rituals in which the corpse is interrogated as to the cause of death.

Cayinte. Rain shrines controlled by the priest-king through neighborhood priests.

Chaya. Northern Senegalese style of loose-fitting pants.

Coeyi. A major shrine of the priest-king.

Dehouhow. A quarter shrine for the Kalybillah half of Kadjinol.

Depah. A village shrine of Pointe Saint-Georges.

Dewandiahn. A spirit shrine related to the keeping of slaves in Esulalu.

Djicomole. An independent township in the eighteenth century, eventually the dominant quarter of Mlomp.

Djikamhoukaw. A men's spirit shrine at Carabane.

Djiguemah. A Koonjaen shrine associated with the Gent lineage of Kolobone.

Djilem. Women's spirit shrine, also known as Kahoosu, used in ritual purification.

Djimamo. Men's spirit shrine, associated with the priest-king and used in ritual purification.

Djoenenandé. A men's spirit shrine, associated with the priest-kings of Eloudia and Huluf.

Djougoutes. A region on the north shore of the Casamance River, also known as Buluf.

Djumpoc. A men's spirit shrine, associated with warfare.

Duhagne. An important blacksmith shrine, introduced in the nineteenth century.

Duhow. A spirit shrine of Kadjinol-Kafone, associated with community decision-making.

Ebila. Men's spirit shrine associated with circumcision and with healing.

Eboon. Spirit shrine associated with healing.

Econtine. Stringed musical instrument used to accompany Diola singing.

Ediamat. A Diola area along the Guinea-Bissau border.

Ediumpo. A spirit in animal form, a type of *ammahl*, often associated with spirit shrines.

Egol. The Koonjaen shrine of the priest-king, established by Atta-Essou.

Ehugna. Women's fertility shrine, introduced in the nineteenth century. There are several different types.

Ekabliane. Afro-Portuguese from Ziguinchor and Portuguese Guinea, also known as Aetingah.

Ekisumaye. Spirit shrine associated with healing.

Ekunga. A spirit shrine associated with the protection of children.

Eleng. A stage of initiation for the spirit shrine Hoohaney.

Elenkine. A spirit shrine associated with the Gent lineage in Esulalu and Huluf.

Elenkine-Sergerh. A quarter shrine for the Kalybillah half of Kadjinol.

Elucil. A spirit shrine at Kadjinol-Kandianka, introduced by a slave woman, also known as Kanalia.

Elung (Ewang). A shrine of the land, associated with the priest-king of Oussouye and Kahat.

Embottai. A social organization that often supports itself by hiring itself out as farm labor.

Emitai. The supreme being in Diola religion.

Enac. Important township shrine of Samatit.

Engagé à temps. Indentured servitude.

Essouk. Country or place.

Ewang. Shrine of the land, associated with the priest-king of Oussouye and with the Kahat form of circumcision.

Ewe. Reincarnation.

Ewuum. An animal double.

Floup. Portuguese term for Diola, used here to indicate the ancestors of the Diola before they conquered the Koonjaen.

Gent. The descendants of Atta-Essou.

Gilaite. The most powerful Esulalu blacksmith shrine, introduced in the mid-nineteenth century by Haieheck Djabune.

Gnigne. Something that is absolutely forbidden.

Grumetes. African soldiers and traders who identified themselves with the Afro-Portuguese.

Hank. A family compound.

Heleo. A girls' social dance.

Holopuc. The iron tip of the *cadyendo*.

Hoohaney. Shrine associated with the elders and the cemetery.

Hoolinway. A spirit shrine associated with the Diedhiou, blacksmith lineages.

Hoonig. A Huluf war shrine.

Houbook. Someone born in the community where he or she resides or in a neighboring township.

Hougendone. Spirit shrine of the Kadjinol-Kafone's subquarter of Ecuhuh.

Hougounayes. Purification ritual for those who had taken a life or who had handled a corpse.

Houkaw. Literally, "head," it refers to special mental powers associated with the head.

Houlang. A spirit shrine that selects its priests by seizing them with mental illness.

Houle. A spirit shrine important to male initiation.

Hounig. A Huluf spirit shrine associated with the waging of war.

Houpoombene. The "musket," a spirit shrine associated with hunting.

Housandioume. The place where some deceased go to live, before they die again and are reborn.

Housenghalene. A spirit shrine associated with the Djisenghalene-Djikune lineage.

Houssana. A primarily urban spirit shrine, associated with the protection of maternity houses.

Houssiquekou. A ritual greeting of lineage shrines by maternal kin in the family compound.

Huasene. A general term for ritual.

Hudjenk. Wooden fetters used in the slave trade and placed at certain types of Hupila shrines.

Huluf. The cluster of townships around Oussouye, south of Esulalu.

Hupila. The family shrine of the Diola. It has several forms.

Hupila Hugop. Hupila of the rice granary, a secret spirit shrine designed to protect slave traders.

Hutendookai. The town council shrine of Esulalu and Bandial.

Huwyn. "To play," a spirit shrine associated with the keeping of slaves in Esulalu.

Huyaye. The Diola day of rest, every sixth day, revived by Alinesitoué Diatta in 1942.

Ignebe. A dance, performed by women at the Ehugna shrine and by men and women socially.

Kagalen. The "inquiry," when the family of captives seeks to locate and ransom their relatives.

Kahat. The Koonjaen form of male circumcision, initially adopted by the Esulalu townships.

Kahit. Spirit shrine associated with the protection of children and the enhancement of fertility.

Kahlayoh. A Koonjaen family shrine at Kadjinol.

Kahoeka. Benevolent ancestors (plural form of *ahoeka*) and the place where they reside.

Kahoosu. Ritual purification for offenses against women's spirit shrines.

Kainoe. Thought.

Kalick. A spirit shrine associated with women's fertility, but controlled by men.

Kanalia. A rain shrine at Kadjinol-Kandianka, introduced by a female slave, also known as Elucil.

Kanoken. A stage of initiation at the spirit shrine of Hoohaney.

Kasick. A women's spirit shrine at Carabane.

Kasila. A spirit shrine and ritual used to ask Emitai for rain.

Katapf. A spirit shrine that protects people from being wounded by metal weapons or tools.

Khameme. Manjaco spirit shrine at Djeromait and Carabane.

Kikillo. The first stage of initiation at the spirit shrine of Hoohaney.

Koonjaen. Early inhabitants of the forest area south of Esulalu, a type of Bainounk.

Kouhouloung. Family shrine of the dead.

Kuasene. Rituals (plural form of *huasene*).

Kumachala. Male enforcers of decisions of Hutendookai (plural of *amachala*).

Kusaye. Witches (plural form of *asaye*).

Lingona. An elder of Hoohaney with the right to perform rituals at the shrine.

Magne mahité. Ilmenite.

Makanaye. Customs or traditions.

Mancone. A synonym for *tali*, a poison used to detect witches.

Mlomp. Now the largest township in Esulalu, created when Djicomole conquered Elou Mlomp and incorporated them into their township.

Ndama. Type of cattle with some resistance to African sleeping sickness.

Nyakul. Funeral dance performed by men in honor of other men or elderly women.

Nyakul emit. Ritual supplication of Emitai and all the spirit shrines during a severe drought.

Oeyi. The Diola priest-king.

Ousanome. "Give me some," in the imperative, and Diola term for rich person.

Pagne. French term for wrap-around cloth, used by men and women as skirts.

Pite. Special mental powers.

Punkus aye. A northern Diola practice of seizing children and selling them into slavery.

Razza. Afro-Portuguese festival honoring the dead on the eve of All Saints Day.

Sembini. Shrine of the priest-king of Elou-Mlomp.

Sihinna. Sacred forest of the Bukut form of circumcision.

Silapoom. The Koonjaen shrine of the forge, adopted by Esulalu.

Sissouk. Countries, communites (plural form of *essouk*).

Situbai Sihan. The first ancestors.

Siwuum. Animal doubles (plural form of *ewuum*).

Tali. Poison used in witchcraft ordeals among the Diola and the Balanta.

Tariqa. Arabic term for a Sufi brotherhood.

Ukine. Spirit shrines. (The plural form of *boekine*.)

Yahl. The soul.

Bibliography

I. Published Books and Dissertations

Abun-Nasr, Jamil (1965). *The Tijanniyya: A Sufi Order in the Modern World.* London: Oxford University Press.

Albinet, Charles (1945–1946). *Moeurs et Coutumes des Diolas.* Mémoire, École Nationale de la France d'Outre-Mer, Paris.

Alvares d'Almada, André (1733). *Relaçåe Descripçåo de Guiné na Qual se trata das varia noçens de negros, que a povaçåo,* Lisbon: Miguel Rodrigues.

Alverson, Hoyt (1978). *Mind in the Heart of Darkness: Value and Self-Identity among the Tswana of Southern Africa.* New Haven: Yale University Press.

Annales Sénégalaises de 1854–1885 (1888). Paris: Maisonneuve Frères.

Badets, Jacques (1954). "Du Problème Foncier en Pays Diola Casamançais: Tentative d'Application du decret du 8 octobre, 1925." Mémoire, Institut International d'Administration Publique, Paris.

Barber, Karin, and P. F. de Moraes Farias, eds. (1989). *Discourse and Its Disguises: The Interpretation of African Oral Texts.* Birmingham: Centre for West African Studies, University of Birmingham.

Barnes, Sandra. (1980). *Ogun: An Old God for a New Age.* Philadelphia: Institute for the Study of Human Issues.

Barth, Fredrik (1987). *Cosmologies in the Making: A Generative Approach to Cultural Variation in Inner New Guinea.* Cambridge: Cambridge University Press.

——— (1969). *Ethnic Groups and Boundaries: The Social Organization of Culture Difference.* Boston: Little, Brown.

——— (1975). *Ritual and Knowledge among the Baktaman of New Guinea.* New Haven: Yale University Press.

Baum, Robert M. (1986). "A Religious and Social History of the Diola-Esulalu in Pre-Colonial Senegambia." Ph.D. diss., Yale University, New Haven.

Beaver, Captain Philip (1805). *African Memoranda: Relative to an Attempt to Establish a British Settlement on the Island of Bulama, on the Western Coast of Africa, in the Year 1792.* London: C. and R. Baldwin.

Beidelman, T. O. (1986). *Moral Imagination in Kaguru Modes of Thought.* Bloomington: Indiana University Press.

Belasco, Bernard (1980). *The Entrepreneur as Culture Hero: Preadaptations in Nigerian Economic Development.* New York: J. F. Begin.

Bellman, Beryl (1984). *The Language of Secrecy: Symbols and Metaphors in Poro Ritual.* New Brunswick, N.J.: Rutgers University Press.

Bérenger-Feraud, L. B. (1879). *Les Peuplades de la Sénégambie.* Paris: LeRoux.

Berger, Iris (1981). *Religion and Resistance: East African Kingdoms in the Pre-Colonial Period.* Tervuren: Musée Royal de l'Afrique Centrale, Annales.

Berger, Peter (1969). *The Sacred Canopy: Elements of a Sociological Theory of Religion.* Garden City, N.Y.: Anchor.

Beslier, G. G. (1935). *Le Sénégal.* Paris: Payot.

Boddy, Janice (1989). *Wombs and Alien Spirits: Women, Men and the Zar Cult in Northern Sudan.* madison: University of Wisconsin Press.

Boilat, Abbé P. D. (1853). *Esquisses Sénégalaises.* Paris: P. Bertrand.

Boulègue, Jean (1972). *Les Luso-Africaines de Sénégambie, XVIe-XIXe siècles.* Dakar: University of Dakar.

———(1968). "La Sénégambie du Milieu du XVe siècle au début du XVIIe siècle." Ph.D. diss., University of Paris.

Bour, Charles (1883). *Étude sur la fleuve Casamance.* Paris: Berger-Levrault.

Bourdieu, Pierre (1991). *In Other Words: Essays towards a Reflexive Sociology.* Stanford, Calif.: Stanford University Press.

———(1977). *Outline of a Theory of Practice.* Cambridge: Cambridge University Press.

Bowser, Frederick (1974). *The African Slave Trade in Colonial Peru, 1524–1650.* Stanford, Calif.: Stanford University Press.

Brasio, Antonio (1958). *Monumenta Missionaria Africana, Africa Ocidental (1570–1600).* Lisbon: Agencia Geral do Ultramar.

Brigaud, Félix (1962). *Histoire Traditionnelle du Sénégal, Etudes Sénégalaises 9.* Saint-Louis du Sénégal: C.R.D.S.

———(1966). *Histoire Moderne et Contemporaine du Sénégal.* Saint-Louis du Sénégal: C.R.D.S.

Brooks, George (1993). *Landlords and Strangers: Ecology, Society, and Trade in Western Africa, 1000–1630.* Boulder, Colo.: Westview Press.

———(1970). *Yankee Traders, Old Coasters, and African Middlemen: Legitimate Trade with West Africa in the Nineteenth Century.* Boston: Boston University Press.

Brosselard-Faidherbe, Captain (1892). *Casamance et Mellacorée: Pénétration au Soudan.* Paris: La Librairie Illustrée.

Carreira, Antonio (1947). *Vida Social des Manjacos.* Bissau: Centre de Estudo da Guiné Portuguesa.

Carvalho, Tito Augusto de (1902). *As Companhis Portuguesas de Colonizacâo.* Lisbon: Impresena Nacional.

Central Statistics Department Ministry of Economic Planning and Industrial Development (1987). *Population and Housing Census 1983: General Report Volume I.* Banjul, The Gambia.

Cissoko, Sekené, and Kaoussou Sambou (1969). *Receuil des Traditions Orales des Mandingue de Gambie et de Casamance.* Dakar: IFAN.

Coelho, Francisco de Lemos (1985). *Description of the Coast of Guinea (1684).* Vol. 1, tr. P. E. H. Hair. Unpublished manuscript, Liverpool: University of Liverpool.

Crone, G. R., ed. (1937). *The Voyages of CadaMosta.* London: Hakluyt.

Crowder, Michael (1962). *Senegal: A Study of French Assimilation Policy.* London: Methuen.

Crowley, Eve L. (1990). "Contracts with the Spirits: Religion, Asylum, and Ethnic Identity in the Cacheu Region of Guinea-Bissau." Ph.D. diss., Yale University, New Haven.

Cultru, P. (1913). *Premier Voyage du Sieur de la Courbe Fait à la Côte d'Afrique en 1685.* Paris: Edouard Champion.

Curtin, Philip (1969). *The Atlantic Slave Trade: A Census*. Madison: University of Wisconsin Press.
——— (1975). *Economic Change in Pre-Colonial Africa: Senegambia in the Era of the Slave Trade*. 2 volumes. Madison: University of Wisconsin Press.
Daget, Serge (1988). *Répertoire des Expéditions Négrières Françaises à la Traite Illégale (1814–1850)*. Nantes: University of Nantes.
Daneel, M. L.(1970). *The God of the Matopo Hills*. The Hague: Mouton.
Danquah, J. B. (1968). *The Akan Doctrine of God*. London: Frank Cass.
Dapper, Olfert, (1686). *Description de l'Afrique*. Amsterdam: Wolfgang Waesbroge.
Davies, K. G. (1970). *The Royal African Company*. New York: Atheneum.
Davies, Oliver (1967). *West Africa before the Europeans: Archaeology and Pre-history*. London: Methuen.
Deherme, Georges (1908). *L'Afrique Occidentale Française*. Paris: Librairie Blond et Cie.
DeLajaille, André (1802). *Voyage au Sénégal Pendant les années 1784–1785, d'après les Mémoires du DeLajaille, ancien officier de la Marine*. Paris: P. LaBarthe.
Delcourt, Jean (1976). *Histoire Religieuse du Sénégal*. Dakar: Clairafrique.
Departamento Central de Recensemento (1981). *Recensemento Geral des popu-lação e da habitação, 1979*. Bissau.
Diatta, Abbé Nazaire (1988). *Les Joolas: Proverbes et Expressions, Contribution à Charte Culturelle Sénégalaise*. Vols. 1–5. Youtou: by the author.
Dike, K. Onwuka (1966). *Trade and Politics in the Niger Delta, 1830–1885*. Ox-ford: Clarendon.
Donelha, André (1971). *An Account of Sierra Leone and the Rivers of Guinea of Cape Verde (1625)*. Ed. Avelino Teixeira da Mota, tr. P. E. H. Hair. Lisbon: Junta de investigacoes cientificas do ultramar.
Donnan, Elizabeth (1930). *Documents Illustrative of the History of the Slave Trade to America*. Vol. 1, 1441–1700. Washington, D.C.: Carnegie Institute.
Duncan, T. Bently (1972). *Atlantic Islands: Madeira, the Azores, and the Cape Verdes in Seventeenth Century Commerce and Navigation*. Chicago: Univer-sity of Chicago Press.
Durand, Jean-Baptiste (1802). *Voyage au Sénégal*. Paris: Henri Agasse.
Eliade, Mircea (1978–1986). *A History of Religious Ideas*. Chicago: University of Chicago Press.
——— (1974). *Patterns in Comparative Religion*. New York: New American Li-brary.
Ellis, A. B. (1970 [1883]). *The Land of Fetish*. Westport, Conn.: Negro Universi-ties Press.
Ene, J. C. (1963). *Insects and Man in West Africa*. Ibadan: Ibadan University Press.
Evans-Pritchard, E. E. (1974 [1956]). *Nuer Religion*. New York: Oxford University Press.
——— (1962). *Social Anthropology and Other Essays*. New York: Free Press.
Fallot, Ernest (1884). *Histoire de la Colonie Française du Sénégal*. Paris: Challarmel Ainé.
Feierman, Steven (1990). *Peasant Intellectuals: Anthropology and History in Tan-zania*. Madison: University of Wisconsin Press.
——— (1974). *Shambaa Kingdom*. Madison: University of Wisconsin Press.
Fortes, Meyer, and Germaine Dieterlen, eds. (1965). *African Systems of Thought*. London: Oxford University Press.
Foucault, Michel (1972). *The Archaeology of Knowledge and the Discourse on Language*. New York: Harper and Row.
Foulquier, Jacques (1966). *Les Français en Casamance de 1826 à 1854*. Mémoire, Faculté des Lettres, University of Dakar.
Fox, William (1851). *A Brief History of the Wesleyan Mission on the Western Coast of Africa*. London: Aylott and Jones.

Freyre, Gilberto (1964). *The Masters and the Slaves: A Study in the Development of Brazilian Civilization.* New York: Alfred A. Knopf.

Froger, S. (1699).*Relation du Voyages de M. de Gennes aux Côtes d'Afrique fait in 1695, 1696, et 1697.* Amsterdam.

Gable, Eric (1990). "Modern Manjaco: The Ethos of Power in a West African Society." Ph.D. diss., University of Virginia, Charlottesville.

Gamble, David (1967). *The Wolof of Senegambia.* London: International African Institute.

Gaye, Mamadou (1973–1974). *Les Bois Sacrées dans le Départment de Bignona (le Droit au Seuil des Sanctuaires).* Mémoire, Ecole Nationale d'Administration, Dakar.

Geertz, Clifford (1973). *The Interpretation of Cultures.* New York: Basic Books.

Giddens, Anthony (1984). *The Constitution of Society: Outline of a Theory of Structuration.* Berkeley: University of California Press.

Ginzburg, Carlo (1983). *The Night Battles: Witchcraft and Agrarian Cults in the Sixteenth and Seventeenth Centuries.* Baltimore: Johns Hopkins University Press.

Girard, Jean (1969). *Genèse du Pouvoir Charismatique en Basse Casamance (Sénégal).* Dakar: IFAN.

Golberry, Silvester Meinrad Xavier (1808). *Travels in Africa, Performed by Silvester Meinrad Xavier Golberry.* Vol. 2. London: Jones and Bumford.

Goody, Jack (1977). *The Domestication of the Savage Mind.* Cambridge: Cambridge University Press.

——— (1987). *The Interface between the Written and the Oral.* Cambridge: Cambridge University Press.

——— (1986). *The Logic of Writing and the Organization of Society.* Cambridge: Cambridge University Press.

——— (1971). *Technology, Tradition, and the State in Africa.* London: Oxford University Press.

Gottlieb, Alma (1992). *Under the Kapok Tree: Identity and Difference in Beng Thought.* Bloomington: Indiana University Press.

Goyau, Georges (1937). *La Congrégation du Saint Esprit.* Bernard Grasset.

Gravand, Henri (1961). *Visage Africaine de l'Eglise: Une Expérience au Sénégal.* Paris: Editions de l'Orante.

Gray, J. M. (1966 [1940]). *History of the Gambia.* London: Frank Cass.

Griaule, Marcel. (1970). *Conversations with Ogotemmêli.* London: Oxford University Press.

Hair, P. E. H. (1984). "An Interim and Makeshift Edition of André Alvares de Almada's *Brief Treatise on the Rivers of Guinea.* Unpublished manuscript, University of Liverpool.

——— (1990). "An Interim Translation of Manuel Alvares S. J. *Etiopia Menor e Descripcao Geografica da Provincia de Serra Leoa* [1615], Unpublished manuscript, University of Liverpool.

Handem, Diane Lima (1986). *Nature et Fonctionnement du Pouvoir Chez les Balante Brassa.* Bissau: Institio Nacional de Estudos e Pesquisa.

Hanin, Charles (1946). *Occident Noir.* Paris: Editions Alsatia.

Harms, Robert (1981). *River of Wealth, River of Sorrow: The Central Zaire Basin in the Era of the Slave and Ivory Trade, 1500–1891.* New Haven: Yale University Press.

Haurigot, G. (1887). *Le Sénégal.* Paris: H. Lecène.

Hecquard, Hyacinthe (1853). *Voyages sur la Côte et dans l'intérieur de l'Afrique Occidentale.* Paris: Imprimerie de Benaud.

Hegel, G. W. F. (1956). *The Philosophy of History.* New York: Dover.

Henige, David (1974). *The Chronology of Oral Tradition: Quest for a Chimera.* Oxford: Clarendon.

———— (1982). *Oral Historiography*. London: Longman.

Herbert, Eugenia (1993). *Iron, Gender, and Power: Rituals of Transformation in African Societies*. Bloomington: Indiana University Press.

Hewett, J. F. Napier (1969 [1862]). *European Settlements on the West Coast of Africa with Remarks on the Slave Trade and the Supply of Cotton*. New York: Negro Universities Press.

Hill, Jonathan D., ed. (1988). *Rethinking History and Myth: Indigenous South American Perspectives on the Past*. Urbana: University of Illinois Press.

Hoursiangou, L. (1953). *Français et Portugais en Casamance et en Haute Guinée*. Memoire, Institut International d'Administration Publique, Paris.

Idowu, E. Bolaji (1962). *Olodumare, God in Yoruba Belief*. London: Longman.

Isichei, Elizabeth (1973). *The Ibo People and the Europeans: The Genesis of a Relationship to 1906*. New York: St. Martins.

Jackson, Michael (1989). *Paths toward a Clearing: Radical Empiricism and Ethnographic Inquiry*. Bloomington: Indiana University Press.

Janzen, John (1982). *Lemba, 1650–1930: A Drum of Affliction in Africa and the New World*. New York: Garland.

Jore, Léonce (n.d.). *Histoire Traditionnelle du Sénégal, Etudes Sénégalaises 9*. Saint-Louis du Sénégal: C.R.D.S.

Jules-Rosette, Bennetta (1975). *African Apostles: Ritual and Conversion in the Church of John Maranke*. Ithaca, N.Y.: Cornell University Press.

Kanoute, Dembo (1972). *Tradition Orale: Histoire de l'Afrique Authentique*. Tr. Tidiane Sanogho and Ibrahima Diallo. Dakar: Impricap.

Klein, Martin (1968). *Islam and Imperialism in Senegal, Sine-Saloum, 1847–1914*. Stanford, Calif.: Stanford University Press.

Koren, Henry J. (1958). *The Spiritans: A History of the Congregation of the Holy Ghost*. Pittsburgh: Duquesne University Press.

Kuhn, Thomas (1970). *The Structure of Scientific Revolutions*. Chicago: University of Chicago Press.

Labat, Jean-Baptiste (1728). *Nouvelle Relation de l'Afrique Occidentale*. Vols. 4 and 5. Paris: Théodore le Gras.

Lasnet, Dr., and A. Cligny, Aug. Chevalier, and Pierre Rambaud (1900). *Une Mission au Sénégal*. Paris: Augustine Challamel.

Lauer, Joseph (1969). "Rice in the History of the Lower Gambia-Geba Area." Master's thesis, University of Wisconsin, Madison.

Leary, Frances Anne (1970). "Islam, Politics, and Colonialism: A Political History of Islam in the Casamance Region of Senegal (1850–1919)." Ph. D. diss., Northwestern University, Evanston, Ill.

LeBlanc, Vincent (1649). *Les Voyages Fameux du Sieur Vincent Leblanc*. Paris: Pierre Bergeron.

LeMaire, Jacques Joseph (1695). *Les Voyages du Sieur LeMaire aux Isles Canaries, Cap Verd, Sénégal, et Gambie*. Paris: Chez Jacques Collambat.

Lévi-Strauss, Claude (1968). *The Savage Mind*. Chicago: University of Chicago Press.

Linares, Olga (1992). *Power, Prayer and Production: The Jola of Casamance, Senegal*. Cambridge: Cambridge University Press.

Lincoln, Bruce (1981). *Priests, Warriors, and Cattle: A Study in the Ecology of Religions*. Berkeley: University of California Press.

Long, Charles (1986). *Significations: Signs, Symbols, and Images in the Interpretation of Religion*. Philadelphia: Fortress.

Ly, Abdoulaye (1958). *La Compagnie du Sénégal*. Paris: Présence Africaine.

Machat, J. (1905). "Documents sur les établissements français de l'Afrique Occidentale au XVIIIe siècle." Ph.D. diss., University of Paris.

Maier, D. J. E. (1983). *Priests and Power: The Case of the Dente Shrine in Nineteenth Century Ghana*. Bloomington: Indiana University Press.

Marche, Alfred (1982). *Trois Voyages dans l'Afrique Occidentale: Sénégal-Gambie, Casamance, Gabon, Ogoué.* Paris: Librairie Hachette.

Marcus, George E., and Michael M. J. Fischer (1986). *Anthropology as Cultural Critique: An Experimental Moment in the Social Sciences.* Chicago: University of Chicago Press.

Mark, Peter (1985). *A Cultural, Economic, and Religious History of the Basse Casamance since 1500.* Stuttgart: Franz Steiner Verlag.

—— (1976). "Economic and Religious Change among the Diola of Boulouf (Casamance), 1890–1940; Trade, Cash-Cropping and Islam in Southwestern Senegal." Ph.D. diss., Yale University, New Haven.

Massiot, Michel (1950). *La Pénétration et l'Expansion des Missions Catholiques dans l'Ouest Afrique Françaises.* Mémoire, Institut International d'Administration Publique, Paris.

Mbiti, John (1990). *African Religions and Philosophy.* Oxford: Heinemann.

McNaughton, Patrick (1988). *The Mande Blacksmiths: Knowledge, Power, and Art of West Africa.* Bloomington: Indiana University Press.

Meillassoux, Claude (1991). *The Anthropology of Slavery: The Womb of Iron and Gold.* Chicago: University of Chicago Press.

Merk, Frederick (1963). *Manifest Destiny and Mission in American History.* New York: Random House.

Middleton, John, and David Tait, eds. (1967). *Tribes without Rulers: Studies in African Segmentary Systems.* London: Routledge and Kegan Paul.

Miers, Suzanne, and Igor Kopytoff, eds. (1977). *Slavery in Africa: Historical and Anthropological Perspectives.* Madison: University of Wisconsin Press.

Miller, Joseph C. (1988). *Way of Death: Merchant Capitalism and the Angolan Slave Trade: 1730–1830.* Madison: University of Wisconsin Press.

Miller, Joseph C., ed. (1980). *The African Past Speaks: Essays on Oral Tradition and History.* Folkestone: Wm. Dawson.

Mission Saint Joseph de Ngasobil (1907). *Guide de la Conversation en Quatre Langues: Français, Volof, Diola, Serer.* Saint Joseph de Ngasobil.

Monod, T., A. Teixeira da Mota, and R. Mauny, eds. (1951). *Description de la Côte Occidentale d'Afrique (Sénégal au Cap de Mont Archipels) par Valentim Fernandes (1506–1510).* Bissau: Centro de Estudos da Guiné Portuguesa.

Monteil, Vincent (1971). *L'Islam Noir.* Paris: Editions du Seuil.

Moore, Francis (1738). *Travels into the Inland Parts of Africa.* London: Edward Love.

Morgan, John (1864). *Reminiscences of the Founding of a Christian Mission on the Gambia.* London: Wesleyan Missionary House.

Mudimbe, V. Y. (1988). *The Invention of Africa: Gnosis, Philosophy, and the Order of Knowledge.* Bloomington: Indiana University Press.

N'Dong, Jean (1992). *Memento des Resultats Definitifs du recensement general de la population et de l'habitat du Sénégal/1988.* Dakar: Bureau d'Etudes de Recherches Documentaires sur le Sénégal.

Needham, Rodney (1972). *Belief, Language, and Experience.* Oxford: Basil Blackwell.

Niane, Djibril Tamsir (1989). *Histoire des Mandingues de l'Quest.* Paris: Editions Karthala.

Nicholson, Sharon E. (1972). "A Climatic Chronology for Africa: Synthesis of Geological, Historical, and Meteorological Information and Data." Ph.D. diss., University of Wisconsin, Madison.

Nicolas, Pierre, and Malick Gaye (1988). *Naissance d'une Ville au Sénégal: Evolution d'un groupe de six villages de Casamance vers une agglomeration urbaine.* Paris: Edition Karthala.

Northrup, David (1978). *Trade without Rulers: Pre-Colonial Economic Development in South-Eastern Nigeria.* Oxford: Clarendon Press.

Nwoga, D. I. (1984). *The Supreme God as Stranger in Igbo Religious Thought.* Ekwereazu, Nigeria: Hawk Press.

Ong, Walter (1982). *Orality and Literacy: The Technologizing of the Word.* London: Methuen.

Ortigues, M. C. and Ed. (1973). *Oedipe Africain.* Paris: Union Generales d'Editions.

Ottenberg, Simon (1989). *Boyhood Rituals in an African Society: An Interpretation.* Seattle: University of Washington Press.

Park, Mungo (1960). *Travels of Mungo Park.* Ed. Ronald Miller. London: J. M. Dent.

Parrinder, Geoffrey (1970). *West African Religion.* New York: Barnes and Noble.

P'Bitek, Okot (1970). *African Religions in Western Scholarship.* Kampala: East African Literature Bureau.

Pélissier, Paul (1966). *Les Paysans du Sénégal: Les Civilisations agraires du Cayor à la Casamance.* St. Yrieix: Imprimerie Fabrèque.

Pereira, Duarte Pacheco (1971). *Esmeraldo de Situ Orbis.* Tr. George Kimble. London: Hakluyt Society.

Prickett, Barbara (1970). *Island Base: A History of the Methodist Church in the Gambia.* Bathurst: Methodist Church of the Gambia.

Quinn, Charlotte (1972). *Mandingo Kingdoms of the Senegambia: Traditionalism, Islam, and European Expansion.* Evanston, Ill.: Northwestern University Press.

Rabinow, Paul (1977). *Reflections on Fieldwork in Morocco.* Berkeley: University of California Press.

Ranger, Terence, and I. Kimambo, eds. (1972). *The Historical Study of African Religion.* Berkeley: University of California Press.

Renault, François (1976). *Liberation d'esclaves et nouvelle servitude.* Abidjan: Les Nouvelles Editions Africaines.

Robertson, Claire, and Martin Klein, eds. (1983). *Women and Slavery in Africa.* Madison: University of Wisconsin Press.

Roche, Christian (1976). *Conquête et Résistance des Peuples de Casamance (1850–1920).* Dakar: Les Nouvelles Editions Africaines.

Rodney, Walter (1970). *A History of the Upper Guinea Coast, 1545–1800,* Oxford: Clarendon.

Rudolph, Lloyd I., and Susanne Hoeber Rudolph (1967). *The Modernity of Tradition: Political Development in India.* Chicago: University of Chicago Press.

Sambou, Pierre-Marie (1977). *Phonologie du nom en Diola Kasa Esuulaalu.* Dakar: Centre de Linguistique Appliqué de Dakar.

Sapir, J. David (1965). *A Grammar of Diola-Fogny: A Language Spoken in the Basse Casamance Region of Senegal.* Cambridge: Cambridge University Press.

Schaffer, Matt, and Christine Cooper (1980). *Mandinko: The Ethnography of a West African Holy Land.* New York: Holt, Rinehart, and Winston.

Schefer, Christian (1921). *Instructions Générales Données de 1763 à 1870 aux Gouverneurs et Ordonnateurs des Etablissements Français en Afrique Occidentale.* Paris: Librairie Honoré Champion.

Schloss, Mark (1988). *The Hatchet's Blood: Separation, Power, and Gender in Ehing Social Life.* Tucson: University of Arizona Press.

——— (1976). "The Hatchet's Blood: Spirits and Society among the Ehing of Senegal." Ph.D. diss., University of Virginia, Charlottesville.

Schutz, Alfred (1967). *The Phenomenology of the Social World.* Evanston, Ill.: Northwestern University Press.

Searing, James (1993). *West African Slavery and Atlantic Commerce: The Senegal River Valley, 1700–1860.* Cambridge: Cambridge University Press.

Silveira, Luis (1946). *Edição Nova do Tratado Breve dos Rios de Guiné feito pelo Capitão André Alvares d'Almada.* Lisbon.

Simmons, William S. (1971). *Eyes of the Night: Witchcraft among a Senegalese People*. Boston: Little, Brown.

Skorupski, John (1983). *Symbol and Theory: A Philosophical Study of Theories of Religion in Social Anthropology*. Cambridge: Cambridge University Press.

Smith, Jonathan Z. (1982). *Imagining Religion: From Babylon to Jonestown*. Chicago: University of Chicago Press.

Snyder, Francis (1981). *Capitalism and Legal Change: An African Transformation*. New York: Academic Press.

——— (1973). "L'Evolution du Droit Foncier Diola de Basse Casamance (République du Sénégal)." Ph.D. diss., Sorbonne, Paris.

Stoller, Paul, and Cheryl Olkes (1987). *In Sorcery's Shadow: A Memoir of Apprenticeship among the Songhay of Niger*. Chicago: University of Chicago Press.

Strobel, Margaret (1979). *Muslim Women in Mombasa*. New Haven: Yale University Press.

Tardieu, Amedée (1847). *Sénégambie et Guinée*. Paris: Firmis Didet Frères.

Thomas, Louis Vincent (1968). *Cinq Essais sur la Mort Africaine*. Dakar: University of Dakar.

——— (1959). *Les Diola: Essai d'Analyse fonctionelle sur une population de Basse Casamance*. Mémoires 58–59, IFAN, Dakar.

Thomas, Louis Vincent, Bertrand Luneau, and Jean Doneux (1969). *Les Religions d'Afrique Noire: Textes et Traditions Sacrées*. Paris: Fayard/Deniel.

Thompson, Leonard M. (1986). *The Political Mythology of Apartheid*. New Haven: Yale University Press.

Thornton, John (1993). *Africa and Africans in the Making of the Atlantic World, 1400–1680*. Cambridge: Cambridge University Press.

Touze, R. (1963). *Bignona en Casamance*. Dakar: Editions Sepa.

Trincaz, Jacqueline (1981). *Colonisations et Religions en Afrique Noire: L'Exemple de Ziguinchor*. Paris: Editions L'Harmattan.

Trincaz, Pierre-Xavier (1984). *Colonisation et Régionalism: Ziguinchor en Casamance*. Paris: Éditions de l'ORSTOM.

Turner, Victor (1968). *The Drums of Affliction*. Oxford: Clarendon.

——— (1967). *The Forest of Symbols: Aspects of Ndembu Ritual*. Ithaca, N.Y.: Cornell University Press.

——— (1969). *The Ritual Process: Structure and Anti-Structure*. Chicago: Aldine.

Van Binsbergen, Wim (1981). *Religious change in Zambia: Exploratory Studies*. London: Kegan Paul.

Vansina, Jan (1978). *The Children of Woot: A History of the Kuba Peoples*. Madison: University of Wisconsin Press.

——— (1968). *Kingdoms of the Savanna*. Madison: University of Wisconsin Press.

——— (1973). *Oral Tradition: A Study in Historical Methodology*. Harmondsworth: Penguin.

——— (1985). *Oral Tradition as History*. Madison: University of Wisconsin Press.

Vigne d'Octoi, M. (1890). *Au Pays des Fétiches*. Paris: Alphonse LeMerre.

Waille, Jacques (1946–1947). *La Pénétration et l'Installation Française en Casamance, 1855–1883*. Mémoires 21, Institut International d'Administration Publique, Paris.

Werbner, Richard, ed. (1977). *Regional Cults*. London: Academic Press.

Willis, Roy (1981). *A State in the Making: Myth, History, and Social Transformation in Pre-Colonial Ufipa*. Bloomington: Indiana University Press.

Wintz, Edouard (1909). *Dictionnaire de Dyola-Kasa*. Paris: Pères de Saint Esprit.

Wolf, Eric (1982). *Europe and the People without History*. Berkeley: University of California Press.

The World Almanac and Book of Facts, 1991 (1991). New York: Pharos Books.

Wright, Donald R. (1977). *The Early History of Niumi: Settlement and Foundation of a Mandinka State on the Gambia River.* Athens: Ohio University Center for International Studies.

II. Articles

Adam, M. G. (1899). "Les Productions de la Casamance." *Bulletin de la Société de Géographie Commerciale de Paris*, vol. 21, pp. 338–363.

Bancel, Lieutenant (1906). "La Casamance." *Bulletin de la Société Géographique d'Algerie et de l'Afrique du Nord*, vol 11, pp. 141–152.

Bauer, Dan, and John Hinnant (1987). "Normal and Revolutionary Divination: A Kuhnian Approach to African Traditional Thought." In Ivan Karp and Charles Bird, eds., *Explorations in African Systems of Thought*, Washington, Smithsonian Institution, pp. 213–236.

Baum, Robert M. (1983). "Crimes of the Dream World: French Trials of Diola Witches." Paper presented to the University of Warwick conference on the History of Law, Labor, and Crime," 1983.

——— (1990). "The Emergence of a Diola Christianity." *Africa*, vol. 60, pp. 370–398.

——— (1990). "Graven Images: Scholarly Representations of African Religions." *Religion*, vol. 20, p. 4.

——— (1983). "Incomplete Assimilation: Koonjaen and Diola in Pre-Colonial Senegambia." Paper presented to the ninety-eighth annual meeting of the American Historical Association, San Francisco.

——— (forthcoming). "The Myth of Ahistorical African Traditional Religions."

——— (1993). "Shrines, Medicines, and the Strength of the Head: The Way of the Warrior among the Diola of Senegambia." *Numen: Studies in the History of Religion*, vol. 40, pp. 274–292.

Beidelman, Thomas (1970). "Myth, Legend, and Oral History: A Kaguru Traditional Text." *Anthropos*, vol. 65, pp. 74–97.

Bertrand-Bocandé, Emmanuel (1856). "Carabane et Sedhiou." *Revue Maritime et Coloniale*, deuxième série, vol. 16, pp. 398–418.

Bertrand-Bocandé, Jean, Gabriel Debien, and Yves Saint Martin (1969). "Emmanuel Bertrand-Bocandé (1812–1881), Un Nantais en Casamance," *Bulletin d'IFAN*, vol. 31, series B 1, pp. 278–294.

Boulègue, Jean (1972). "Aux Confins du Monde Malinké: Le Royaume du Kasa Casamance." Paper presented to the Congress of Manding Studies, London.

Braudel, Fernand (1980). "History and the Social Sciences: The Longue Durée." In F. Braudel, *On History*, tr. Sarah Matthews, Chicago: University of Chicago Press, pp. 25–54.

Brenner, Louis (1989). "'Religious Discourses in and about Africa." In K. Barber and P. F. de Moraes Farias, eds., *Discourse and Its Disguises: The Interpretation of African Oral Texts*, Birmingham: Centre of West African Studies, University of Birmingham, pp. 87–105.

Brooks, George (1989). "Ecological Perspectives on Mande Population Movements, Commercial Networks, and Settlement Patterns from the Atlantic Wet Phase (ca. 5500–2500 B.C.) to the Present." *History in Africa*, vol. 16, pp. 23–39.

——— (1983). "A Nhara of the Guinea-Bissau Region: Mae Aurelia Correia." In Claire Robertson and Martin Klein, eds., *Women and Slavery in Africa*, Madison: University of Wisconsin Press, pp. 295–319.

——— (1984). "The Observance of All Souls' Day in the Guinea-Bissau Region: A Christian Holy Day, an African Harvest Festival, or an African New Year's Celebration?" *History in Africa*, vol. 7, pp. 1–34.

——— (1978). "Perspectives on Luso-African Commerce and Settlement in the Gambia and Guinea-Bissau Region, 16th–19th Centuries." Paper presented at the fourth international Congress of Africanists, Kinshasa.

Brosselard-Faidherbe, Captain (1889). "La Guinée Portugaise et les Possessions Françaises Voisines." *Société de Géographie de Lille.*

Carreira, Antonio (1969). "As Companhias Pombalinas de navegação comércio e trafico de escravos entre a costa africane e o nordeste brasiliero." *Boletim Cultural da Guiné Portuguese,* vol. 24, pp. 59–188, 285–475.

Carvalho, Gabriel (1967). "Contribution à l'histoire de la Casamance." *Afrique Documents,* vol. 91, pp. 133–146.

Catåo, Monseigneur Cónego Francisco Xavier Gomes (1966). "A diocese de Cabo Verde et o clero de Goa." *Studia Revista Quadrimestral,* vol. 19, December, pp. 98–100.

Clark, Stuart (1987). "The *Annales* Historians." In Quentin Skinner, ed., *The Return of Grand Theory in the Human Sciences,* Cambridge: Cambridge University Press, pp. 177–198.

Cooper, Frederick (1979). "The Problem of Slavery in African Studies." *Journal of African History,* vol. 20, pp. 103–125.

Curtin, Philip, and Jan Vansina (1964). "Sources of the Nineteenth Century Atlantic Slave Trade." *Journal of African History,* vol. 2, pp. 185–208.

Dinis, A. Dias (1946). "As Tribos da Guiné Portuguesa na História." In *Portugal Am Africa,* second series, vol. 2, pp. 206–215.

Fage, John (1969). "Slavery and the Slave Trade in the Context of West African History." *Journal of African History,* vol. 10, pp. 393–404.

Fisher, Humphrey (1973). "Conversion Reconsidered: Some Historical Aspects of Religious Conversion in Black Africa." *Africa,* vol. 43, pp. 27–40.

Girard, Jean (1963). "De la Communauté Traditionnelle à la Collectivité Moderne en Casamance." *Annales Africaines,* pp. 137–165.

Goody, Jack, and Ian Watt (1968). "The Consequences of Literacy." In Jack Goody, ed., *Literacy in Traditional Societies,* Cambridge: Cambridge University Press, pp. 27–68.

Gravard, Henri (1975). "'Naq' et Sorcellerie dans les Conceptions Serères." *Psychopathologie Africaines,* vol. 11, pp. 179–216.

Hanin, Charles (1933). "Une Association Nécrophagique de la Basse Casamance." *Revue Général de Colonisation.*

Harms, Robert (1979). "Oral Tradition and Ethnicity," *Journal of Interdisciplinary History.* vol. 10, pp. 61–85.

Horton, Robin (1971). "African Conversion." *Africa,* vol. 41, pp. 85–107.

——— (1967). "African Traditional Thought and Western Science. *Africa,* vol. 37, pp. 50–71.

——— (1970). "A Hundred Years of Change in Kalabari Religion." In John Middleton, ed., *Black Africa: Its Peoples and Their Cultures Today,* New York: Macmillan, pp. 192–211.

——— (1975). "On the Rationality of Conversion." *Africa,* vol. 65, pp. 219–235, 373–399.

——— (1971). "Stateless Societies in the History of West Africa." In J. Ajayi and M. Crowder, eds., *History of West Africa,* vol. 1, London: Longman.

Janneh, Mbalefele (1970). "Jola History." Oral History, Cultural Archives, Banjul, The Gambia.

Joffroy, Henri (1920). "Les Coutumes des Diola du Fogny (Casamance)." *Bulletin du Comité d'Etudes Historiques et Scientifique de l'AOF,* vol. 2, pp. 181–193.

Journet, Odile (1985). "Les Hyper-Mères n'ont plus d'enfants: Maternité et ordre social chez les Joola de Basse-Casamance." In Nicole-Claude Mattieu, ed., *L'Arraisonnement des Femmes: Essais en Anthropologies des Sexes,* Paris: Editions de l'Ecole des Hautes Etudes in Science Sociales, pp. 17–36.

King, Winston (1987). "Religion." In Mircea Eliade, ed., *The Encyclopedia of Religion*, vol. 12, New York: Macmillan, pp. 282–293.

Leyrat, M. R. E. (1936). "Etude sur la Casamance." *Bulletin de la Société Française des Ingénieurs Coloniaux*, vol. 119, pp. 84–114, 167–208.

Linares, Olga (1987). "Deferring to Trade in Slaves: The Jola of Casamance, Senegal in Historical Perspective." *History in Africa*, vol. 14, pp. 113–139.

—— (1981). "From Tidal Swamp to Inland Valley: On the Organization of Wet Rice Cultivation among the Diola of Senegal." *Africa*, vol. 51, pp. 557–595.

—— (1979). "Intensive Agriculture and Diffuse Authority among the Diola of West Africa." Unpublished manuscript.

Linares de Sapir, Olga (1970). "Agriculture and Diola Society." In F. M. McLoughlin, ed., *African Food Production Systems: Cases and Theory*, Baltimore: Johns Hopkins University Press, pp. 195–227.

—— (1971). "Shell Middens of the Lower Casamance and Problems of Diola Protohistory." *West African Journal of Archeology*, vol. 1, pp. 23–54.

Ly, Abdoulaye (1964). "Une Navire de Commerce sur la Côte Sénégambienne en 1685." *IFAN, Catalogues et Documents*, vol. 27.

MacGaffey, Wyatt (1978). "African History, Anthropology and the Rationality of Natives." *History in Africa*, vol. 5, pp. 101–120.

—— (1975). "Oral Tradition in Central Africa," *Journal of African Historical Studies*, vol. 7, pp. 417–426.

Maclaud, C. (1907). "La Basse Casamance et ses Habitants." *Bulletin de la Société de Géographie Commerciale de Paris*, pp. 176–202.

Mark, Peter (1988). "Ejumba: The Iconography of the Diola Initiation Mask." *Art Journal*, vol. 47, pp. 277–283.

—— (1978). "Urban Migration, Cash-Cropping, and Calamity: The Spread of Islam among the Diola of Boulouf (Senegal), 1900–1940." *The African Studies Review*, vol. 21, pp. 1–12.

Marzouk-Schmitz, Yasmine (1984)."Instruments Aratoires, Systèmes de Culture et Différenciation Intra-Ethnique." *Cahiers Orstrom, ser. Sciences Humaines*, vol. 20, pp. 399–425.

Meillassoux, Claude (1978). "Correspondence." *Economy and Society*, vol. 7, pp. 321–331.

Mettas, Jean (1975). "La Traite Portugaise en Haute Guinée, 1758–1797: Problèmes et Methodes." *Journal of African History*, vol. 16, pp. 343–365.

Miller, Joseph, C. (1978). "The Dynamics of Oral Tradition in Africa." In B. Bernardi, C. Poni, and A. Triulzi, eds., *Fonti Orali—Oral Sources—Sources Orales. Anthropologia e Storia—Anthropology and history—Anthropologie et Histoire*, Milan: F. Angeli, pp. 89–90.

Nicholson, Sharon E. (1979). "Historical Climate Reconstruction." *Journal of African History*, vol. 20, pp. 31–49.

Ottenburg, Simon (1958). "Ibo Oracles and Intergroup Relations." *Southwestern Journal of Anthropology*, vol. 14, pp. 295–317.

Packard, Randall M. (1980). "The Study of Historical Process in African Traditions of Genesis: The Bashu Myth of Muhiyi." In Joseph Miller, ed., *The African Past Speaks: Essays on Oral Traditions and History*, Folkestone: Wm Dawson.

Pélissier, Paul (1958). "Les Diola: Etude sur l'habitat des riz cultures de Basse Casamance." Travaux du Département de Géographie 6, University of Dakar.

Portères, Roland (1962). "Berceaux Agricoles primaires sur le Continent Africain." *Journal of African History*, vol. 3, pp. 195–211.

Portères, Roland, and J. Barrau (1981). "Origins, Development and Expansion of Agricultural Techniques." In J. Ki-Zerbo, ed., *UNESCO General History of Africa*, vol. 1, *Methodology and African Prehistory*. Paris: UNESCO, pp. 687–705.

Quinn, Charlotte (1972). "Relations between Mandingo Rulers and Stranger Groups along the Gambia River during the Nineteenth Century." Paper presented to the Conference on Manding Studies, School of Oriental and African Studies, London.

Roche, Christian (1973). "Ziguinchor et son passé (1645–1920)." *Boletim Cultural da Guiné Portuguesa*, vol. 28, pp. 35–61.

Rodney, Walter (1966). "African Slavery and Other Forms of Social Oppression on the Upper Guinea Coast in the Context of the Atlantic Slave Trade." *Journal of African History*, vol. 7, pp. 431–443.

——— (1965). "Portuguese Attempts at Monopoly on the Upper Guinea Coast, 1580–1650." *Journal of African History*, vol. 6, pp. 307–322.

Sagnia, B. K. (1984). "A Concise Account of the History and Traditions of Origin of Major Gambian Ethnic Groups." *Occasional Publications of the Gambia National Museum*, vol. 4, Banjul: Gambia National Museum.

——— (1984). "Social and Religious Significance of Traditional Jola Male Initiation." *Occasional Publications of the Gambia National Museum*, vol. 6, Banjul: Gambia National Museum.

Sambou, Earnest (1978). Extract of Master's thesis on parallels between Christianity and Diola Religion, title unavailable, University of Toulouse.

Sapir, J. David (1977). "The Fabricated Child." In J. D. Sapir and J. C. Crocker, eds., *The Social Use of Metaphor: Essays on the Anthropology of Rhetoric*, Philadelphia: University of Pennsylvania Press, pp. 193–223.

——— (1977). "Fecal Animals: An Example of Complementary Totemism." *Man*, vol. 12, pp. 1–21.

——— (n.d.). "Fragments for a Paper on Kujaamat and Kasa Siwuum." Unpublished manuscript.

——— (1970). "Kujaama: Symbolic Separation among the Diola-Fogny." *American Anthropologist*, vol. 72, pp. 1330–1348.

——— (1981). "Leper, Hyena, and Blacksmith in Kujammat Diola Thought." *American Ethnologist*, vol. 30, pp. 526–543.

——— (1971). "West Atlantic: An Inventory of the Languages, Their Noun Class Systems, and Consonant Alteration." In Thomas Sebeok, ed., *Current Trends in Linguistics*, vol. 7, *Linguistics in Sub-Saharan Africa*, The Hague: Mouton, pp. 45–112.

Schoffeleers, J. M. (1972). "The History and Political role of the M'Bona Cult among the Mang'anja." In Terence Ranger and I. Kimambo, eds., *The Historical Study of African Religion*, Berkeley: University of California Press, pp. 73–94.

Shaw, Rosalind (1990). "The Invention of African Traditional Religion." *Religion*, vol. 20, pp. 339–353.

Sidibe, B. K. (1972). "The Story of Kaabu: Its Extent." Paper presented at the Conference on Manding Studies, School of Oriental and African Studies, London.

Snyder, Francis (1978). "Legal Innovation and Social Disorganization in a Peasant Community: A Senegalese Village Police." *Africa*, vol. 48, pp. 231–247.

Tastevin, C. (1934). "Vocabulaires Inédits de Sept Dialectes Sénégalais dont six de la Casamance." *Journal de la Société des Africanistes*, vol. 4, pp. 1–33.

Thomas, Louis Vincent (1959). "Animisme et Christianisme." *Présence Africaine*, vol. 26, pp. 5–21.

——— (1966). "Brève Esquisse sur la Pensée Cosmologique du Diola." In M. Fortes and G. Dieterlen, *African Systems of Thought*, London: Oxford University Press, pp. 366–382.

——— (1963). "Economie et Ostentation chez les Diola." *Notes Africaines*, vol. 98, pp. 33–39.

——— (1960). "Esquisse sur les Mouvements de Populations et les contacts socio-culturels en pays Diola (Basse Casamance)." *Bulletin d'IFAN*, vol. 22, série B, pp. 486–508.

———— (1962). "Etude sur la vie pulsionnelle du Diola." *Bulletin d'IFAN*, vol. 24, série B, pp. 105–154.

———— (1970). "Mort Symbolique et Naissance Initiatique (Bukut chez les Diola-Niomoun)." *Cahiers des Religions Africaines*, pp. 41–71.

———— (1963). "Notes sur l'enfant et l'adolescent Diola." *Bulletin d'IFAN*, vol. 25, série B, pp. 66–79.

———— (1970). "Nouvel Exemple d'oralité négro-africaine: Récits Narang-Djiragon, Diola-Karabane et Dyiwat, (Basse Casamance)." *Bulletin d'IFAN*, vol. 32, série B, pp. 230–305.

———— (1967). "A Propos des religions négro-africaines traditionelles." *Afrique Documents*, vol. 93.

———— (1969). "De Quelques Attitudes Africaines en matière d'histoire locale (Introduction à une psycho-sociologie de la connaissance historique." In Jan Vansina, R. Mauny, and L. V. Thomas, eds., *The Historian in Tropical Africa*, London: Oxford University Press, pp. 358–370.

———— (1964). "Responsabilités, sanctions et organisation judicaire chez les Diola traditionnels de Basse Casamance." *Notes Africaines*, vol. 104, pp. 106–113.

———— (1960). "Un système philosophique sénégalais: La cosmologie des Diola." *Présence Africaine*, vol. 32–33, pp. 64–76.

Vallon, Lieutenant (1862). "La Casamance, Dépendance du Sénégal." *Revue Maritime et Coloniale*, vol. 6, pp. 463–465.

Van Binsbergen, Wim (1986). "The Land as Body: An Essay on the Interpretation of Ritual among the Manjak of Guinea-Bissau." Paper presented at the Satterthwaite Colloquium on African Religion and Ritual, Satterthwaite, England.

Vansina, Jan (1974). "Comment: Traditions of Genesis." *Journal of African History*, vol. 15, pp. 317–322.

———— (1962). "A Comparison of African Kingdoms." *Africa*, vol. 3, pp. 324–335.

———— (1983). "The History of God among the Kuba." *Africa: Rivista Trimestrale di Studi e documentazione dell' l'Instituto Italo-Africano*, vol. 28, pp. 3–39.

———— (1981). "Oral History and Its Methodology." In J. Ki-Zerbo, ed., *Unesco General History of Africa*, vol. 1, *Methodology and Prehistory*, Berkeley: University of California Press, pp. 142–165.

Waldman, Marilyn R. (1990). "Unity and Diversity in a Religious Tradition." In Carole Elchert, ed., *The White Lotus*, Ithaca, N.Y.: Snow Lion, pp 1–5.

Waldman, Marilyn R., with Robert M. Baum (1992). "Innovation as Renovation: The Prophet as an Agent of Change." In Michael A. Williams and Martin S. Jaffee, eds., *Innovation in Religious Traditions*, Berlin: Mouton de Guyter, pp. 241–284.

Weiss, Henri (1939). "Grammaire et lexique diola du Fogny (Casamance)." *Bulletin d'IFAN*, vol. 1, pp. 412–578.

III. Archives

A. Senegal

Archives de Sous-Préfecture de Loudia-Ouloff, Casamance (ASPLO)

"Recensement, 1977."

"Calendrier Historique: Arrondissement de Loudia Ouoloff."

"Evénements Historiques des Villages—Dossier Rouge, Sous-Préfecture de Loudia-Ouloff," no date, nos. 1–24.

Oussouye Mission Archives (OMA)

"Registre des Baptêmes, Mission de Carabane, 1875–1937."

"Registre des Baptêmes, Mission d'Oussouye, 1928–1950."

Personal Papers of Augustin Badiane, Oussouye (APAB)

Letters, catechism books, and photographs.

Personal Papers of Teté Diadhiou, Ziguinchor (APTD)

Dossier Alinesitoué (mostly closed).

"Colonie du Sénégal, Cercle de Ziguinchor, #1.526/C," 11/21/1942.

Archives de la Préfecture d'Oussouye (APO)

"Journal d'Almamy Sambou, chef de canton, canton de Pointe Saint-Georges."
"Liste des préfets du Département d'Oussouye."

Archives Nationales du Sénégal, Dakar (ANS).

1D 16. "Expédition de la Basse Casamance par Pinet Laprade, 1860."
1D 50. "Affaires de Casamance, 1886."
1D 170. "Opérations au Sénégal, 1901–1912."
2D5 3. "Casamance: Administrateur Supérieur, Correspondence Départ addressé au Gouverneur et divers, 1918."
2D5 7. "Casamance: Commerce, Impôts, 1857–1914."
2D5 8. "Casamance: Justice, Libérations Conditionnelles, Affaires Jugées, 1917–1934.
2D5 10. "Casamance: Dossier Divers, 1914–1924."
4D 71. "Recruitement Divers, 1914–1924."
4D 77. "Recruitements, 1918."
1G 14. "Mission Dagorne en Casamance, Mission Lachevié dans le Fleuve, 1838."
1G 23. "Rapport de M. Bertrand-Bocandé, Résident de Carabane, sur un voyage au pays de Kiou, 1850."
1G 34. "Explorations Haute Casamance et de ses Rivières, 1860–1866."
1G 328. "Casamance par Labretaigne du Mazel, 1906."
1G 343. "Casamance, 1911: Envoi de la Monographie du Cercle."
2G1 47. Sénégal: Cercle de Carabane: "Rapports Mensuels d'Ensemble, 1895."
2G1 52. Sénégal: Cercle de Carabane: "Rapports Politiques, Commerciaux, et Agricoles, Mensuels, 1896."
2G1 55. Sénégal: District de Casamance: "Rapport d'Ensemble semestriels, 1896."
2G1 56. Sénégal: Résidence de Bignona (Fogny): "Rapports Politiques, Agricoles, et Commerciaux Mensuels, 1897."
2G1 57. Sénégal: Cercle de Carabane (Basse Casamance): "Rapports Politiques, Agricoles, et Commerciaux Mensuels, 1897."
2G1 64. Sénégal: Cercle de Carabane: "Rapports Politiques Mensuels, 1899."
2G1 72. Sénégal: District de la Casamance: "Rapports Politiques Mensuels, 1899."
2G1 86. Sénégal: Cercle de Ziguinchor: "Rapports Politiques, Agricoles, et Commerciaux Mensuels, 1901."
2G1 87. Sénégal: Cercle de Ziguinchor (Basse Casamance): "Rapports Politiques, Agricoles, et Commerciaux Trimestriels, 1901."
2G2 21. Sénégal: Résidence de Carabane (Basse Casamance): "Rapports Politiques, Agricoles, et Commerciaux Mensuels, 1902."
2G2 27. Sénégal: Cercle de Ziguinchor: "Rapport Trimestriel d'Ensemble, 1902."
2G2 28. Sénégal: Cercle de Ziguinchor: "Rapports Politiques, Agricoles, et Commerciaux Mensuels, 1902."
2G3 50. Sénégal: Résidence d'Oussouye (Basse Casamance): "Rapports Politiques Mensuels, 1903."
2G3 56. Sénégal: Cercle de Ziguinchor (Basse Casamance): "Rapports Politiques Mensuels, 1903."

2G4 31. Sénégal: Post d'Oussouye: "Rapports Mensuels d'Ensemble, 1904."

2G4 43. Sénégal: Résidence d'Oussouye (Basse Casamance): "Rapports Politiques Mensuels, 1904."

2G6 32. Sénégal: Cercle de Casamance: Résidence de Ziguinchor: "Rapports Mensuels d'Ensemble, 1906."

2G8 39. Sénégal: Casamance, Administrateur Supérieur: "Rapports Mensuels d'Ensemble, 1908."

2G11 47. Sénégal: Casamance, Administrateur Supérieur: "Rapports Mensuels d'Ensemble, 1911.

2G12 65. Sénégal: Casamance, Résidence d'Oussouye: "Rapports Mensuels d'Ensemble, 1912."

2G13 56. Sénégal: Territoires Casamance, Administrateur Supérieur: "Rapports Mensuels d'Ensemble, 1913."

2G14 51. Sénégal: Casamance, Administrateur Supérieur: "Rapports Mensuels d'Ensemble, 1914."

2G17 36. Sénégal: Cercle de Ziguinchor: "Rapports Mensuels d'Ensemble, 1917."

2G18 32. Sénégal: Cercle de Kamobeul (Casamance): "Rapports Mensuels d'Ensembles, 1918."

2G19 26. Sénégal: Casamance, Administrateur Supérieur: "Rapports Mensuels d'Ensembles, 1919."

2G23 70. Sénégal: Territoire de la Casamance, Administrateur Supérieur: "Rapports d'Ensembles Semestriels, 1923."

2G26 66. Sénégal: Territoire de la Casamance: "Rapport Politique Général Annuel, 1926."

2G27 82. Sénégal: Territoire de la Casamance: "Rapport Général Annuel, 1927."

2G28 59. Sénégal: Territoire de la Casamance: "Rapport Général Annuel, 1928."

2G 29. Sénégal: Cercle de Ziguinchor: "Rapport Général Annuel, 1929."

2G43 73. Sénégal: Cercle de Ziguinchor et d'Oussouye: "Rapport Politique Annuel d'Ensemble, 1943."

2G44 100. Sénégal: Cercle de Ziguinchor: Subdivision d'Oussouye: "Rapports Mensuel d'Ensemble, 1943."

13G 2. "Copies des Traités Contenus dans le registre no. 1 de 1 à 109 inclus."

13G 4bis. "Traité de Paix entre le village d'Itou et le village de Kion, par la mediation du résident français de Carabane."

13G 6. "Traités Conclus Avec les Chefs Indigènes, 1845–1886."

13G 13. Versement 17 Ziguinchor, 1926–1943: "Association secret d'Anthrophagie en Casamance."

13G 22. "Situation Générale du Sénégal: Instructions Ministerielles, 1785–1845."

13G 67. "Politique Musulmane, Activité des Marabouts, 1905–1917."

13G 300. "Papiers de Pinet-Laprade, 1889."

13G 360. "Casamance: Politique Générale du Gouvernement, 1820–1842."

13G 361. "Casamance: Situation Générale, 1845–1859."

13G 363. "Sedhiou: Compte Rendus de Personnel, de Materiel, de la Situation Commercial de nos Relations avec les Peuplades Indigènes, 1854–1859."

13G 365. "Postes de Sedhiou et Carabane, Travaux et Etat des Lieux, 1858–1895."

13G 366. Casamance: "Correspondances du Résident de Sedhiou et Carabane, 1861–1862."

13G 367. Casamance: "Correspondance des Commandants de Sedhiou et Carabane, 1863–1865."

13G 368. Casamance: "Correspondance du Résident, 1866–1867."

13G 369. Casamance: "Correspondance du Résident, 1868–1872."

13G 370. Casamance: "Correspondance du Commandant, 1872–1879."

13G 371. Casamance: "Correspondance des Commandant de poste 1887–1891."

13G 372. Casamance: "Correspondance du Résident, 1892–1894."

13G 373. Casamance: "Correspondance du Résident, 1895–1898."

13G 374. "Correspondance du Résident, Casamance, 1899–1900."
13G 375. Casamance: "Documents Provenant divers des Archives de Ziguinchor, 1892–1914."
13G 378. Casamance: "Reorganisation de la Casamance, Arrête de 12 juin, 1907."
13G 380. Casamance: "Affaires Politiques, 1907–1909."
13G 383. Casamance: "Affaires Politiques: Rapport sur la situation politique-agitation chez les Bayottes, 1916."
13G 384. Casamance: "Affaires Politiques: Rapport sur la situation politique de la Casamance—occupation militaire de la Basse Casamance (Bayottes), 1917."
13G 399. "Registre servant à la correspondance de l'Administration Supérieur, ouvert le 14 février, #1 Sedhiou, le 14 février, 1896."
13G 440. Casamance, 1862–1864.
13G 442. Casamance, 1877–1889.
13G 443. Carabane: "Administrateur Carabance, Basse Casamance, 1897–1898."
13G 444. Carabane, 1898–1899.
13G 455. "Correspondances échangés entre le Commandant de Carabane et le Commmandant Particulier de Gorée, 1839–1859, 1861–1864."
13G 464. Casamance: "Affaires Politiques, 1889."
13G 465. Casamance, 1890.
13G 466. Casamance: "Affaires Politiques, 1891."
13G 485. District of Casamance, 1896–1897.
13G 492. Casamance, 1899.
13G 502:4. "Operation de police contre les Floups de la region d'Oussouye, 1903."
13G 507. Casamance (Basse): "Journaux de Poste."
13G 510. Casamance, 1904.
13G 542. District of Casamance: "Correspondance, 1915."
13G 547. District de la Casamance, 1918.
17G 33. "Missions Catholiques, 1896–1920."
17G 381. "Tournée de Madame Savineau, Rapports, 1937."
22G 39. "Recensement Général, 1876 à 1877."
22G 40. 'Correspondance Diverse, Statistique et Recensement, 1870–1886."
22G 42. "Recensement de la Population des Cercles du Sénégal, Casamance, 1891–1892."
K18. "Rapports sur l'Esclavage dans les Zones de l'Administration Directe du Sénégal, 1903."
Ziguinchor (Tribunaux), 60 Folio 1913–1928.

B. France

Archives Nationales (ANF)

Archives Privés Noirot. Papiers du Gouverneur V. Ballot, 185 Mi 2.
Colonies C6 Dossier 1–6.

Archives Nationales d'Outre Mer (ANOM)

Affaires Politiques, 597: 1 "Rapports Politiques, 1914–1917."
Dépôt des Fortifications, Portefeuille 26, 1771–1844.
Gorée de Dépendences, IV, Dossier 2, 1856–1859.
Sénégal I Dossier 19, Malavois, 1836.
Sénégal I Dossier 37, "Gouverneur du Sénégal et Dépendences à Monsieur le Ministre de la Marine et des Colonies, 8 janvier, 1851."
Sénégal I Dossier 80, 1879–1895.

Sénégal I Dossier 97bis, "Rapports Politiques, 1907–1909."
Sénégal III Dossier 3, "Mission Dangles, 1828."
Sénégal III Dossier 8, "Hecquard, 1851."
Sénégal IV Dossier 25, "Expansion Français, Casamance, 1829–1854."
Sénégal IV Dossier 51, "Expansion Territoriale Casamance, 1859–1873."
Sénégal IV Dossier 107, "Pointe St. Georges, Séleki, 1886–1891."
Sénégal IV Dossier 108, 1890.
Sénégal IV Dossier 131, "Expansion Territoriale, 1903, Basse Casamance."
Sénégal VI Dossier 1, "Affaires Diplomatiques, Angleterre, 1816–1840."
Sénégal VI Dossier 4, "Affaires Diplomatiques, Angleterre, 1840–1860."
Sénégal VI Dossier 5, "Affaires Diplomatiques, Portugal, 1840–1860."
Sénégal VI Dossier 14, "Affaires Diplomatiques, Portugal, 1881–1885, Conflits en
    Casamance."
Sénégal VIII Dossier 33, "Affaires Politiques, Epreuve du Tali Chez les Balantes
    (Casamance), 1912."
Sénégal XIII Dossier 8, "Compagnie de Galam et Casamance, 1836–1843."
Sénégal XIII Dossier 37, "Coton."
Sénégal XV Dossier 23, "Entreprise, 1889–1890, Cousin Concession, Casamance,
    1889–1890."
Sénégal et Dépendences I Dossier 95, "Correspondance générale: Cercle de Basse
    Casamance et Lt. Nouri, 1901."
Série Géographique Afrique VI Dossier 2, "Affaires Diplomatiques, Angleterre,
    1839–1852, Casamance."
Série Géographique Afrique VI Dossier 4, "Affaires Diplomatiques, Portugal,
    1836–1858, Casamance."
Série Géographique Afrique VI Dossier 31, "Affaires Diplomatiques, Portugal, 1882,
    Conflit en Casamance."
Série Géographique Afrique VI Dossier 35, "Affaires Diplomatiques, Portugal, 1183,
    Conflits en Casamance."
Série Géographique Afrique VI Dossier 39, "Affaires Diplomatiques, Portugal, 1884."
Série Géographique Afrique VI Dossier 53, "Casamance Delimitation."
Traité, Carton II, 251–253.

Bibliothèque Nationale, Service des Cartes *(BN)*

Collection du Service Hydrographique de la Marine, Portefeuille 111–112.
Fonds Courant Res. G.B. 1964, "Carte de la Concession de la Compagnie du
    Sénégal, 1690."
Fonds Courant Ge D 10631, "Carte Idéale d'une partie de la concession de la
    Compagnie Royale du Sénégal depuis le Cap-Blanc jusqu'au Bissaux, 1719."
    Sr. Brue à M. de St. Robert.
Fonds Courant Ge D 16315 "Carte de l'Afrique Française, 1726."

Bibliothèque Nationale, Manuscrits (BN)

Fonds Français, Nouvelle Acquisition 9453 Côtes d'Afrique—La Vigie, "Campagne
    sur les Côtes Occidentales de l'Afrique, cannonier brig., la Vigie," 1842.
Fonds Français, Nouvelle Acquisition 9459, "Traités faits dans la rivière
    Casamance, Côte Occidentale d'Afrique."
Fonds Français, Nouvelle Acquisition 9463, "Mélanges," 1837.
Manuscrits Français 12080, "Détails historiques et politiques sur la religion, les
    moeurs et le commerce des peuples qui habitent la côte occidentale d'Afrique
    depuis l'Empire de Maroc jusqu'à la rivière de Casamance et de Gambie,"
    M. Le Brasseur, Juin 1778.

Fonds Français 24.196, "Oratoire." Folio 25 (Approximately 1480).
Mémoires de la Société Ethnologique, Tome 2 G 26639, "Vocabulaires Guiolof, Mandingue, Foule, Saracolé, Séraire, Bagnon et Floup, Recueillis à la Côte d'Afrique pour le Service de l'Ancienne Compagnie Royale du Sénégal."
Fonds Orientaux, Fonds Africain #4, "Dictionnaire des Langues Française et nègres dont on se sert dans la concession de la Compagnie Royale du Sénégal Saavoir Guilof, Foule, Mandingues, Saracolé, Séraire, Bagnon, Floupe, Papel, Bissagots, Nalous et Sapi."

Institut de France (IDF)

Fonds Terrier Ms 5926, "Papiers de Brière de l'Isle, Ballot, Dodds."
Fonds Terrier Ms 5927, "Papiers de Brière de l'Isle, Ballot, Dodds."
Mss 5904 Correspondance of Dr. MacClaud.

Archives du Ministère des Affaires Etrangères (MAE)

Correspondance Politique, 1889, Portugal "Délimitation Cabinda-Guinée, 1889–1900."
Mémoire et Documents, Afrique et Colonies Françaises, 1574–1779.
Mémoire et Documents, Afrique et Colonies Françaises #12 Sénégal et Côtes Occidentales, 1670–1790.
Mémoire et Documents, Afrique: Sénégal, Tome 40, 1836–1839.
Mémoire et Documents, Afrique: Sénégal et Dépendances, Tome 41, 1841.
Mémoire et Documents, Sénégal: Tome 50, 1879–1882.
Mémoire et Documents, Sénégal et Dépendances, Tome 84, 1883–1884.

Société des Mission Evangeliques de Paris (SMEP)

Jean Faure, "Histoire de la Mission Evangelique de Paris au Sénégal, 1862–1914."
Lettres du Missions Evangeliques de Paris au Sénégal, 1863–1866.

Archives des Pères du Saint Esprit (PSE)

Annales Apostoliques de la Congregation du Saint Esprit, 1887–1922.

Archives, "Carabane et Sedhiou, 1880 à 1892, Journal de Père Kieffer."
Archives, "Carabane et Sedhiou, Journal de Père Girod, 1884."
Archives, "Carabane, Journal de la Communauté, 1898–1920."
Archives, Dossier A Sénégal, 1900–1911.
Archives 146, "Missions des Deux Guinées. Notes sur la Mission de Deux," R. P. du Patquet, 1848.
Archives 147, Travaux Divers, "Notes du R. P. Abiven pour une Histoire Religieuse du Sénégal."
Archives 153, "Voyages de P. Aragon à Sedhiou," April 1848.
Archives 154, 1850–1927.
Archives 164 B, "Sénégambie-Casamance," "Annales Religieuses de la Casamance (Groupement Diola)," "Lettres Sénégambie, 1911–1918."
Archives 261, "Sénégambie, 1919–1938."
Archives 262, "Sénégambie Correspondance, 1927–1935."
Archives 295, "Précit Civil Diola."
Archives 295, IV "Le paganisme des Diolas du Fogny," par P. Jacquin, Supérieur de la Mission de Bignona.
Bulletin de la Congregation du Saint Esprit, 1879–1956.

Wesleyan Mission Archives, University of London (WMA)
Boxes 286–288, 294–295, 298. Correspondence Sierra Leone and Gambia, 1843–1898.

IV. Interviews

Interviews were conducted during eight periods: August 1974–August 1975, May–August 1976, September 1977–February 1979, July–August 1987, March–April 1988, May–July, 1994, May–September 1996, and June–July 1997. Approximately nine hundred people were interviewed. Because of the large number of people interviewed, I list only the major informants. Informants are listed by place of birth or place of permanent residence. Section A is for Esulalu, section B for non-Esulalu Diola, and section C for non-Diola.

A. Informants from Esulalu

Djeromait

Coly, Jean, Christian elder of Djeromait; interviews on village history.
Lopy, Jacques, of Manjaco descent; interviews on Manjaco and Diola shrines and the history of Djeromait.

Efissao

Bassin, Constance, interviews on the history of Efissao.
Diedhiou, Hyacinthe, originally of Kadjinol; interviews on the history of Efissao.

Elinkine

Chiam, Jean Baptiste, interviews on the history of Elinkine.
Faye, Dyaye Babu, interviews on the founding of Elinkine, its spirit shrines, and the spirit shrines of Carabane.

Eloudia

Diatta, Aliou, shrine elder; interviews on Eloudia's shrines and history.
Diatta, Sikarwen, shrine elder; interviews on shrines associated with priest-king, early history of Eloudia, Atta-Essou, and theology.
Diatta, Thomas, shrine elder; interviews on nineteenth-century history and spirit shrines.
Diedhiou, Kemehow, interviews on Diola agriculture, early history, and migration.
Diedhiou, Lome, shrine elder; interviews on Eloudia's spirit shrines.
Kila, Badjaya, Gent lineage and shrine elder; interviews on founding of Eloudia by Atta-Essou and the shrines of the priest-king.

Kadjinol

Kadjinol-Ebankine
Bassin, Amokabaw, shrine elder; interviews about slave trade and shrines associated with the slave trade.
Bassin, Djalli, shrine elder; interviews about male circumcision and Ebankine's spirit shrines.
Bassin, Hélène, interviews about Christian-awasena relations, witchcraft accusations, and marriage customs.
Bassin, Moolaye, shrine elder; interviews about spirit shrines, especially Hupila and the early history of Esulalu.

Bassin, Nuhli, shrine elder; interviews about the slave trade and spirit shrines associated with it as well as the early history of Esulalu.

Manga, Anto, shrine elder; interviews about the nature of the spirit shrines, especially Houle and Bukut, as well as some historical materials.

Sambou, Danaye, shrine elder; interviews about the spirit shrines and nineteenth-century Kadjinol.

Sambou, Djiremo, shrine elder; interviews about the creation of Bukut, the early history of Esulalu, and the slave trade.

Sambou, Kebeh, shrine elder; interviews about shrines and war.

Sambou, Terence Galandiou Diouf; interviews about the early history of Esulalu, spirit shrines, witchcraft, Christian-awasena relations, and the importance of dreams in Diola religion.

Hassouka

Badji, Sihumucel, shrine elder, Coeyi; interviews about the nature of the spirit shrines, the origin of the priest-king shrines, ritual restrictions on the priest-king, and the Koonjaen.

Diatta, LeBois, shrine elder; interviews on the priest-king and the early history of Kadjinol.

Sambou, Djadja, interviews on the spirit shrines of Kadjinol.

Sambou, Djilehl, shrine elder; interviews on blacksmiths and their shrines, the nature of the spirit shrines, and the history of Kadjinol.

Sambou, Ehleterre, interviews on the early history of Kadjinol, the nature of the spirit shrines, and their initial establishment in Kadjinol.

Senghor, André Bankuul, church deacon; interviews on Christian-awasena relations, witchcraft accusations, funeral customs, and the early history of Esulalu.

Senghor, Samouli, shrine elder; interviews on the history of various spirit shrines, especially those associated with kingship.

Senghor, Terence, interviews about Diola land law.

Kafone

Diatta, Edouard Kadjinga, interviews about early Esulalu history and spirit shrines, especially associated with the Gent lineage and Coeyi.

Diatta, François Buloti, interviews about spirit shrines, sexual mores, and structures of language.

Diatta, Gnimai, interviews about social etiquette, the role of women in Esulalu society, and social customs.

Diatta, Kuadadge, shrine elder; interviews about the nature of the spirit shrines, the office of priest-king, the Koonjaen, and the early history of Esulalu.

Diatta, Sidionbaw, interviews about the nature of the spirit shrines, their history, and the early history of Esulalu.

Diatta, Sikakucele, priest-king of Kafone; interviews on ritual practices, especially on the Gent lineages and Egol.

Diedhiou, Adiabaloung, interviews about techniques of prayer and the blacksmith shrines.

Diedhiou, Ameliké, interviews about the early history of Esulalu, especially in relation to the slave trade and Ehugna.

Diedhiou, Antoine Houmandrissah, detailed interviews about the history of Esulalu, including genealogies of the major lineages of Kafone.

Diedhiou, Asenkahan, interviews about the nature of the spirit shrines and social mores.

Diedhiou, Bruno Gitao, interviews about social customs, economic organization, and Christian-awasena relations.

Diedhiou, Diongany, interviews about social customs and the nature of the spirit shrines.
Diedhiou, Dionsal, interviews about social customs, the nature of the spirit shrines, and the history of Kadjinol.
Diedhiou, Djisambouway, interviews about the early history of Kadjinol, especially as it relates to the slave trade and the growth of Kafone's spirit shrines.
Diedhiou, Edula, shrine elder; interviews about Bruinkaw and Ehugna.
Diedhiou, Ekusumben, interviews about the early history of Esulalu, the Koonjean wars, witchcraft, and the nature of the spirit shrines.
Diedhiou, Elizabeth, interviews about the early history of Esulalu.
Diedhiou, Emehow, shrine elder; interviews about the early history of Esulalu.
Diedhiou, Gilippe, shrine elder of Gilaite; interviews about Gilaite and about blacksmiths.
Diedhiou, Gnapoli, interviews about structures of prayer, blacksmiths, and social customs.
Diedhiou, Henri, shrine elder; interviews about blacksmiths, spirit shrines, and the early history of Esulalu.
Diedhiou, Indrissa, interviews about the early history of Kadjinol, especially shrine histories and social customs of the precolonial period.
Diedhiou, Joseph Salinjahn, interviews about the early history of Kadjinol.
Diedhiou, Kapooeh, shrine elder Hoohaney and Gilaite; detailed instruction about the role of priests and elders in various cults, as well as ὶιe early history of Esulalu.
Diedhiou, Landing, interviews about the history of Kadjinol and about fishing.
Diedhiou, Marie Augustine, interviews about the early history of Esulalu and about the Diola community of Dakar.
Diedhiou, Musasenkor, interviews about the early history of Esulalu, Ehugna, and Gilaite.
Diedhiou, Ompa Kumbegeny, inteviews about the history of Kadjinol and the nature of the spirit shrines.
Diedhiou, Ramon Bapatchaboo, interviews about the history of Kadjinol, especially as it relates to Cabai.
Diedhiou, Samedymolly, interviews about the nature of spirit shrines and about Diola architecture.
Diedhiou, Samuel, shrine elder of Gilaite and Silapoom; instruction about blacksmiths and blacksmith shrines.
Diedhiou, Siliya, shrine elder of Silapoom; interviews about blacksmiths and blacksmith shrines.
Diedhiou, Simeon, interviews about the nature of spirit shrines and about social customs
Diedhiou, Sinyendikaw, interviews about the early history of Esulalu.
Diedhiou, Siopama, shrine elder and healer; interviews about the nature of the spirit shrines and of spiritual experience, the importance of dreams, witchcraft, healing, and the history of spirit shrines.
Manga, Elizabeth, interviews about the history of the Kolobone Manga lineage and about social customs.
Manga, Matolia, shrine elder of Ehugna; interviews about Ehugna and about relations between the sexes.
Manga, Michel Anjou, interviews about Esulalu history, witchcraft accusations, the Koonjaen, and Christian-awasena relations.
Manga, Sihendoo, interviews about early Esulalu history and the nature of the spirit shrines.
Sambou, Assinway, shrine elder of Hutendookai; interviews about the nature of the spirit shrines, the afterlife, visionary experience, and early history.
Sambou, Diashwah, shrine elder of Djimamo and Cayinte; interviews about pre-

colonial wars and the involvement of spirit shrines, especially the history of Cabai.

Sambou, Elizabeth, interviews about the nature of the spirit shrines, witches, evil, and social customs.

Sambou, Etienne Abbisenkor, instruction about the various spirit shrines.

Sambou, Hubert Econdo, instruction about the nature of the spirit shrines, social mores, wrestling, and Christian-awasena relations.

Sambou, Mungo, interviews about the history of the spirit shrines and Diola views of creation.

Kagnao

Djikune, Grégoire, interviews about the early history of Kadjinol and Djeromait, the nature of the spirit shrines, the slave trade, and Christianity in Esulalu.

Djikune, Henri, interviews about social mores and Christian-awasena relations.

Manga, Djalice, interviews about the spirit shrines of Kagnao.

Sambou, Acanediake, interviews about the early history of Esulalu and the nature of the spirit shrines.

Sambou, Alappa, interviews about relations between Bandial and Esulalu, and about Esulalu religious practices.

Sambou, Antoine Djemelene, shrine elder; interviews about the nature of the spirit shrines, witches, concepts of God, systems of morality, the slave trade, the institution of the priest-king, and the Koonjaen.

Sambou, Badiat, interviews about the nature of the spirit shrines and the early history of Esulalu.

Sambou, Abbé Earnest, a Catholic priest; interviews about the parallels between Christianity and awasena religion.

Sambou, François Djatockoé, interviews about religious practice, witchcraft accusations, and nineteenth-century history of Esulalu.

Sambou, Isador, interviews about Christian-awasena relations and about the recent history of Esulalu.

Sambou, Ompa, interviews about the early history of Kadjinol.

Senghor, Suzanne, interviews about the nature of the spirit shrines, especially Ehugna.

Kandianka

Diatta, Kubaytow, interviews about the early history of Esulalu, especially shrine histories.

Diatta, Mandiaye, interviews about contemporary religious practice and political disputes.

Diatta, Michel Amancha, interviews about the early history of Esulalu, the office of priest-king, reincarnation, ethics, marriage customs, the Koonjaen, and the early history of Esulalu.

Diedhiou, Kadi, interviews about marriage customs and social mores.

Manga, Etienne, catechist; interviews about the early history of Esulalu and about Christian-awasena relations.

Sambou, Basayo, interviews about precolonial social mores and the nature of the spirit shrines.

Sambou, Silokolai, interviews about marriage customs and religious practices.

Senghor, Badjassaw, shrine elder of Hupila; interviews about the history of various spirit shrines, especially Hupila, and the rituals that are central to their worship.

Senghor, Michel Djigoon, interviews about the priest-kingship and the early history of Esulalu.

Sergerh

Diatta, Attabadionti, shrine elder of Elenkine-Sergerh; interviews on various spirit shrines, the nature of the ammahl, and the early history of Esulalu.

Diatta, Djangi, interviews on the history of the Gent lineage and the early history of Esulalu.

Diedhiou, Beatrice, interviews on social customs and Christian-awasena relations.

Manga, Andre Kebroohaw, interviews on the history of the Kolobone-Manga lineage and general religious and political issues.

Sambou, Sedu Benoit, interviews on nineteenth-century Esulalu history.

Senghor, Abbas Ciparan, interviews on the early history of Esulalu.

Senghor, Asambou, shrine elder of Bukut; interviews on male circumcision and Diola religion in general.

Senghor, Boolai, interviews on the nature of the spirit shrines, concepts of afterlife, and Christian-awasena relations.

Senghor, Leo, interviews on land disputes and nineteenth-century Esulalu.

Senghor, Pierre Marie, Catholic priest; interviews on early penetration of Christianity in the region.

Kagnout (Bruhinban, Ebrouwaye, and Eyehow)

Assin, Sambouway, interviews about early Esulalu history, the nature of spirit shrines, and religious practice.

Bassin, Pakum, interviews about the history of Kagnout's spirit shrines, early Esulalu history, and Christianity in Esulalu.

Djibune, Hilaire, catechist; interviews about the history of Kagnout, the history of spirit shrines, the visionary tradition in Esulalu, and the growth of Christianity.

Sambou, Antoine, interviews about the history of Kagnout.

Sambou, Bernard Ellibah, interviews about the history of Kagnout and political issues in Esulalu.

Sambou, Djikankoulan, interviews about the early history of Esulalu and the nature of the spirit shrines.

Sambou, Eina, interviews about the early history of Esulalu and the nature of the spirit shrines.

Sarr, Kasaygilette, interviews about Kagnout's spirit shrines.

Loudia-Ouloff

Cissoko, Bakary Dembo, interviews on Islam and on blacksmiths in Muslim communities, as well as the history of Loudia-Ouloff.

Cissoko, Boolai, interviews on the history of Loudia-Ouloff and Islam.

Manga, Bubackar, originally from Eloudia; interviews on the founding of Loudia-Ouloff, its relationship with Eloudia, early Esulalu history, and his conversion to Islam.

Mlomp (Kadjifolong, Djibetene, Djicomole, Etebemaye, Haer)

Diatta, Abdoulaye Gaitch, interviews about Mlomp's spirit shrines.

Diatta, Djamonde, interviews about the history of Elou Mlomp and its spirit shrines, as well as Esulalu communities in Dakar.

Diatta, Edouard Hounakaw, interviews about the history of Mlomp's spirit shrines.

Diatta, Grégoire, catechist; interviews about the early history of Esulalu, the Koonjean, land disputes, Cayinte, social mores of the precolonial period, and the history of Christianity in Esulalu.

Diatta, Paponah, shrine elder of Bukut, Bruinkaw, and Hupila; interviews on the history and nature of various spirit shrines, about Diola concepts of God, ethics, and history, about precolonial Esulalu history, and about Elou Mlomp.

Diatta, Songant Ebeh, interviews about witches, spirit shrines, and land disputes.

Diatta, Tidjane, interviews about witches and spirit shrines.

Diop, Hadi, interviews about Islam in Esulalu.

Manga, Alouise, interviews about the precolonial history of Esulalu and about the priest-king.

Manga, Robert, interviews about Elou Mlomp and the growth of Christianity.

Manga, Sebeoloute, elder of Coeyi; interviews about the origin and the development of Mlomp's priest-king and about the precolonial history of Esulalu.

Manga, Yerness, elder of Coeyi; interviews about the origin and the development of Mlomp's priest-king.

N'Diaye, Ibu, interviews about the growth of Islam in the region and regional politics.

Sambou, Assalabaw, interviews about Mlomp's spirit shrines.

Sambou, Djatti, shrine elder; interviews about the spirit shrines of Haer.

Sambou, Emmanuel Djikune, interviews about the priest-king of Mlomp.

Sambou, Julien Mien, interviews about the spirit shrines of Mlomp.

Sambou, Lampolly, interviews about Esulalu's early history.

Sambou, Malanbaye, interviews about Esulalu's early history and the nature of the spirit shrines.

Sambou, Patrice, interviews about nineteenth-century Esulalu and early Christianity.

Sambou, Ramon, interviews about spirit shrines associated with hunting and palm wine tapping.

Sambou, Sebikuan, priest-king of Mlomp; interviews about the priest-king and about Diola ethics and cosmology.

Sambou, Signondac, interviews about precolonial Esulalu.

Senghor, Thierno, interviews about the spirit shrines of Cadjifolong and the nature of the spirits themselves.

Senghor, Tomis, interviews about precolonial Esulalu and the spirit shrines.

Pointe Saint-Georges (Punta)

Diatta, Paul, interviews on the history and shrines of Pointe Saint-Georges.

Diatta, Ramon, interviews on the history of Pointe Saint-Georges.

Sagna, Edouard, interviews on the history of Pointe Saint-Georges.

Samatit

Assin, Alougoulor Marie-Thérèse, shrine elder of Ehugna; interviews about the history of Samatit and of the Ehugna shrine.

Assin, Cyriaque, interviews about the nature of Samatit's spirit shrines, the slave trade, and the early history of Samatit.

Assin, Cyriaque, interviews about the early history of Samatit.

Assin, Wuuli, priest-king of Samatit; interviews about the spirit shrines of Samatit and the early history of that community.

Baben, Agnak, interviews about reincarnation, visionary experience, the nature of the spirit shrines, and the history of Samatit.

Diatta, Sooti, village chief; interviews about the history of Samatit and its spirit shrines.

Djibune, Sophie, interviews about the spirit shrines of Samatit, especially Ehugna.

Sam Sam

Sakho, Alfa, interviews on the founding of Sam Sam, its relations with Samatit, Islam, and al Hadji Umar Tall.

Santiaba

Abutch, Mark, interviews on the histoy of Santiaba and the office of priest-king at Kagnout. He is a member of the priest-king lineage for Kagnout-Eyehow who settled at Santiaba.

B. Diola from outside Esulalu

Badiane, Augustin (Oussouye), interviews about Huluf Diola religion and the growth of Christianity there.

Badiane, Kafiba (Oussouye), interviews about Huluf Diola religion, the importance of dreams, and the growth of Christianity there.

Badji, Marie Joseph (Balandine), interviews about Christian-awasena relations, witchcraft, gender relations, and Catholicism. She is a sister of Saint Joseph.

Bassin, Georges (Essil), interviews about the Bandial-Essil region, economic issues, and about the origins of Bukut.

Baye, Sheriff (Diembering), interviews about the slave trade.

Diadhiou, Têtê (Ziguinchor), interpreter and local official during the colonial period. Interviews about Diola religion, the slave trade, and the prophetess Alinesitoué.

Diatta, Goolai (Kabrousse), interviews about Alinesitoué and slavery.

Diedhiou, Alouise (Kabrousse), interviews about Alinesitoué.

Diedhiou, Father Nestor (Mangangoulak), interviews about Djougoutes, its wars with Esulalu, and the growth of Christianity.

Ehemba, Mère Victoire (Edioungou), interviews about Diola history, dance, and the growth of Christianity in the region.

Lambal, Ampercé (Ousseye), interviews about the Huluf priest-king.

Manga, Amymoh (Enampore), interviews about Enampore's royal rain shrines and the origins of Bukut.

Manga, Fidel (Kolobone), interviews about Djiguemah, the Koonjaen, and Gent.

N'Diaye, Amath (Diembering and Ziguinchor), a Protestant schoolteacher; interviews about Diola religion, Islam, and Christianity, as well as slavery at Diembering.

Senghor, L'Abbé Diamacoune (Senghalene), interviews about Diola history, Alinesitoué, and Diola Christianity.

Tendeng, Moositaye (Bandial), interviews about Bandial religion and Bandial-Esulalu relations.

C. Non-Diola

Most of these interviews with twenty-two informants focused on the colonial and independence eras. The one major exception is cited here.

Salla, Father Antonio, a Spanish missionary; interviews on the nature of Diola religion, the structures of Diola languages, and the growth of Christianity in the region.

D. Other Researcher's Interview Notes

Linares, Olga, excerpts from her notes of interviews she conducted in Samatit. These interviews focused on the Ehugna shrines and on the village of Sandiannah, which was conquered by Samatit in the nineteenth century.

Index

283

CPSIA information can be obtained at www.ICGtesting.com
Printed in the USA
BVOW04*2031031215

427655BV00011B/5/P